The Royal Shopping Guide

Nina Grunfeld was born in London in 1954 and attended St Paul's Girls' School and Reading University. In 1976 she moved to California where she worked as a graphic designer for various record companies. Since returning to London she has written *The Complete Book of Household Lists* (Pan Books, 1984) and is now a full-time author.

Nina first became aware of the Royal family as she passed Kensington Palace daily in her pram on the way to the Peter Pan statue. Having missed the Queen's Jubilee she returned to London in time for the Royal Wedding, and one day over breakfast, staring at her porridge packet, she thought she would like to know what else the Royal family bought. This book is the result.

Also by Nina Grunfeld
in Pan Books
The Complete Book of Household Lists

The Royal Shopping Guide

Nina Grunfeld

Pan Original
Pan Books London and Sydney

First published 1984 by Pan Books Ltd,
Cavaye Place, London SW10 9PG
9 8 7 6 5 4 3 2 1
© Nina Grunfeld 1984
Designed by Peter Holroyd
Illustrations by Julia Whatley
Additional photographs by Godfrey New
ISBN 0 330 28475 4
Photoset by Parker Typesetting Service, Leicester
Printed and bound in Great Britain
R. J. Acford, Chichester, Sussex

To Nicholas

Acknowledgements I would like to thank Catriona Luke and Sue Maloney, my two assistants, who worked so hard and enthusiastically while the book was being researched and written. Thanks also to Drew Smith, Victoria Huxley, William Underhill, Sarah Chalmers, Janie Joel (for her telephone calls), *Majesty* magazine, and to two people who were involved throughout the duration of the book but who wish to remain nameless. Of course, many thanks to Pan, my publishers, for realizing the book, and to all the warrant holders and non-warrant holders without whose help this book would have been impossible to write.

While writing this book I was lucky enough to meet many of the Royal Warrant holders themselves. They were charming and courteous. But they were also very discreet. I thank them for telling me about their shops or companies, about themselves and about what they think makes their product or service unique and worthy of Royal patronage. Anything you read in this book about why the Royal family shop in these shops, why they buy what they do and what their likes and dislikes are was found out by the author by other means. No personal information about the Royal family has come from a Royal Warrant holder.

I am especially grateful to the following companies for their support and help:

Army & Navy Stores, Bridger & Kay, British American Cosmetics, John Broadwood & Sons, Cadbury Schweppes, Chubb & Sons Lock and Safe Co., Cole & Son (Wallpapers), Ede & Ravenscroft, C. Farlow & Co., J. Floris, G. C. Francis, Stanley Gibbons, W. & H. Gidden, Thomas Goode & Co., Andrew Grima, L. G. Harris & Co., Hawes & Curtis (Tailors), House of Fraser, Ind Coope, Cornelia James, C. John (Rare Rugs), G. B. Kent & Sons, Kirkness & Gorie, Lever Brothers, John Lobb, S. Lock, Maggs Bros., Joseph Mason, A. R. Mowbray & Co., Paperchase, Parker Pen Co., Henry Poole & Co., Presents (although they no longer sell Royal coat-hangers), Ridgways, The Royal British Legion Poppy Factory, Royal Doulton Group, Z. V. Rudolf, The Ship's Wheel, Simpsons of Piccadilly, Sleepeezee, Frank Smythson, Spink & Son, Spratt's Patent, Steinway & Sons, Swaine, Adeney, Brigg & Sons, Temple & Crook , Truefitt & Hill, United Biscuits, Wartski and all the companies who so very kindly supplied the items used on the cover.

All photographs and illustrations, except where mentioned below, have been supplied by the companies who appear in this book. I am most grateful to them for their help.

The photographs and illustrations listed below are reproduced with the kind permission of the following companies:

Page ii Camera Press; pages viii, ix, x and xiii The Mansell Collection; page xv London Express News and Feature Services; page 25 Tim Graham; page 27 The Photo Source/ Central Press; page 35 The Mansell Collection; page 45 The Photo Source/Fox; pages 49 and 53 Camera Press; page 61 The Mansell Collection; page 68 Camera Press; page 71 The Photo Source/Keystone; page 76 Camera Press; page 78 The Photo Source/Fox; pages 80 and 84 Camera Press; page 87 The Mansell Collection; page 94 Camera Press; page 100 The Photo Source/Central Press; pages 106 and 108 Camera Press; page 125 The Mansell Collection; page 130 The Photo Source/Fox; page 132 Camera Press; page 136 BBC Hulton Picture Library/The Mansell Collection; page 138 Courtauld Institute of Art; page 140 The Mansell Collection; page 157 London Express News and Feature Services; page 164 The National Portrait Gallery; page 171 The Mansell Collection; page 178 Camera Press; pages 181 and 184/5 London Express News and Feature Services; pages 195, 198, 202 and 205 Camera Press; page 216 The Photo Source/ Keystone; page 224 Camera Press; pages 234 and 238 The Mansell Collection.

Contents

Introduction *ix*

Regal requirements
Carriages *1*
Jewels, medals, etc. *4*
Maundy Thursday *6*
Outfitters *7*

Interiors
Carpets *10*
Cleaning *13*
Crockery and cutlery *20*
Decorating *25*
Flower arranging *36*
Furnishings *36*
Household *38*
Kitchen and bathroom *41*

Parks and gardens
Dogs *43*
Garden parties *44*
Nurseries *48*
Signs *52*
Tennis courts *52*
Thatchers *53*

Keeping up appearances
Chemists *55*
Hairdressing *56*
Healer *59*
Manicurists *60*
Perfumes, soaps and make-up *60*

The Royal wardrobes
Accessories *67*
Coats and casuals *69*
Designers *77*
Embroiderers *86*
Fabrics *87*
Hats *88*
Jewellers *92*
Maternity wear *98*
Shoes *99*
Suits and shirts *103*
Under it all *110*

And so to bed
Beds *112*
Bedding *114*
Nightwear *117*

The Royal nursery
Clothes *119*
Dancing *120*
Furnishing *121*
Toys *123*

The Royal larder
Breakfast *124*
Butchers *130*
Cheese *133*
Confectioners *134*
Drinks and tobacco *137*
Fishmongers *150*
Groceries *152*
Tea and coffee *162*

Time off
Collecting *167*
Fishing *172*
Games *173*
Music *175*
Photography *179*
Picnics *180*
Reading and writing *182*
Relax with the television *189*
Riding *190*
Shooting *196*
Sportswear *197*
Tennis *201*
Theatre *201*

Travel
Luggage *203*
Motor cars and mopeds *207*
Vehicle hire *210*

In Her Majesty's Service
Banking *212*
Carpet cleaners *212*
Cleaners *215*
Furniture and clock repairers *217*
Launderers *218*
Miscellaneous *219*
Photographers *221*
Piano tuner *226*
Printers *226*
Protection *228*

Christmas
Better presents *231*
Cards and wrappings *232*
Crackers and games *233*
Festive food *235*

Index *239*

ANNO · ÆTATIS ·   · SVÆ · XLI

Introduction

The Royal Warrant

The Royal Warrant is a mark of recognition that an individual is a supplier of goods or services to the Royal household. It allows the grantee of the Royal Warrant to use the term 'By Appointment' and to display the Royal coat of arms on their company's products as well as in their premises and on their stationery and other printed material such as shopping bags and advertisements.

Royal Warrants have been in existence in one form or another since the Middle Ages, when suppliers of goods and services to the Sovereign would receive the honour of formal recognition. In the reign of Henry VIII, a Mr Thomas Hewytt was appointed to 'Serve the Court with Swannes and Cranes and all kindes of Wildfoule'. Anne Harris was appointed as 'the King's Laundresse' to wash 'the napery which shall serve the King's Own Table'.

Henry VIII, fond of 'Swannes and Cranes and all kindes of Wildfoule', as portrayed by Hans Holbein

When Elizabeth I was Queen, her household book listed the Yeoman Purveyors of 'Veales, Beeves & Muttons; Sea & Fresh Water Fish'. In 1684 goods and services to the palace included a 'Haberdasher of Hats', a 'Watchmaker in Reversion', an 'Operator for the Teeth' and a 'Goffe-club Maker'.

During the 18th and 19th centuries, the names of tradesmen supplying the Royal household were recorded in the *Royal Kalendar*, a yearly almanac. In the edition of 1789, a 'Pin Maker', a 'Mole Taker', a 'Card Maker' and a 'Rat Catcher' are among other tradesmen appointed to the court. A notable omission was the 'Bug Taker' – at that time one of the busiest functionaries about the court, though possibly not one to be recorded in a *Royal Kalendar*. A Mr Savage Bear was a purveyor of fruits and garden things and Mr William Giblet supplied meat to the King's table.

There is no clear evidence when tradesmen first displayed the Royal coat of arms outside their shop or premises. At first it was probably done out of enthusiasm rather than by authority. But a record of two official grants to use the Royal coat of arms appears during the reign of William IV (1830–37) and in the reign of his successor, Victoria, the practice became established of granting

William IV was the first monarch to grant the use of the Royal coat of arms to his tradesmen

Royal Warrants in their present form – that is, a formal document appointing a tradesman as a supplier of goods or services to the Royal household and authorising him to display the Royal arms. Queen Victoria granted an enormous amount of warrants over her long reign, including many to women. By 1860 there were about a dozen women grantees, including a 'Worker of Bookmarkers', a 'Modeller of Wax Flowers' and Mrs Anna Ede, a 'Robe Maker' (see page 7).

Throughout the ages the favour or recognition from the Sovereign has been regarded as the ultimate honour and in the 20th century it still remains a much-sought-after accolade.

At present a Royal Warrant can be granted by only four members of the Royal family: The Queen, The Queen Mother, The Duke of Edinburgh and The Prince of Wales, who first became eligible to grant a Royal Warrant on 1 January 1980. A business may hold warrants from more than one member of the Royal family, and a handful of companies hold all four. As yet there are no plans for The Princess of Wales to grant her own warrants.

To become eligible for a Royal Warrant a business must have supplied goods or services to the Royal household for at least three consecutive years. It may then apply to the Lord Chamberlain's Office (which supervises the system) and the application will be considered by the Royal Household Tradesmen's Warrants Committee. Even if the applicant is a company or firm, the grantee will always be one of the directors or partners as an individual.

Grantees are sent a strict set of rules to stick to if they are to retain their warrant. The rules are designed to preserve the dignity of the warrant and prevent commercialisation. Warrant holders may not, for example, 'accept invitations to associate themselves with special press features on the Royal family where the proximity of the feature and their advertisement will have a particular significance to the public'. Only one set of the Royal arms must be visible at any one time, whether on the warrant holder's stationery or packaging or vehicles or in his premises. It must also not be a component of a building, in case a warrant holder stripped of the honour had to have the building demolished in order to remove the insignia. The Royal coat of arms must only be displayed on the products for which the warrant was granted and not on the rest of the manufacturer's range. And, most importantly, a grantee is not allowed to make any verbal or written reference to The Queen or any member of the Royal family regarding the goods or services which are supplied to them.

A Royal Warrant is initially granted for ten years after which time it comes up for review. However, it may be cancelled at any time, and the reasons for doing so are not necessarily given. The Royal Warrant is also reviewed if the grantee dies or leaves the business, whether the initial ten-year period has expired or not, or if the firm goes bankrupt, winds up or stops making the product for which the warrant was granted. After the initial ten years, if the Royal Warrant is granted again, it will usually be for a further ten years, though it could be for five or less depending on the discretion of the member of the Royal family granting the warrant.

There are about 800 Royal Warrant holders today, mainly in Britain. Every year between 20 and 30 new companies become warrant holders and about the same number lose their Royal Warrant.

The Royal Warrant Holders' Association

The Royal Warrant holders have their own association, founded in 1840. It originally consisted of no more than a gathering of 'Her Majesty's Tradesmen' who met every year on 25 May in honour of Queen Victoria's birthday. It became known by its present title, the Royal Warrant Holders' Association, in 1907. Today its head office is in Buckingham Gate, facing the side entrance of Buckingham Palace. The association make sure there is no imitation or infringement of the use of the Royal coat of arms and that the warrant-holding members of the association abide by the rules which govern them. Although membership of the association is not obligatory, its aim is to promote the interest of Royal Warrant holding firms generally and to act as an authorised channel of communication between Royal Warrant holding firms and the Royal Household on all matters relating to the Royal Warrant. It also takes the necessary steps to protect the use of the Royal arms under the Trade Marks Act and the Trade Descriptions Act.

The Royal Household

Royal Warrants of Appointment are granted direct to the households of The Queen Mother, The Duke of Edinburgh and The Prince of Wales. Tradesmen who hold Royal Warrants to The Queen, however, will be granted them for one of four separate 'departments' – the Department of Her Majesty's Privy Purse, the Department of the Master of the Household, the Lord Chamberlain's Office or the Royal Mews.

Department of Her Majesty's Privy Purse

The Department of Her Majesty's Privy Purse is run by the Keeper of the Privy Purse and Treasurer to The Queen. It is financed from the tax-free revenues of the Duchy of Lancaster (comprising some 52,000 acres of mostly farmland and moorland), which in 1982 was £1,075,000. The Privy Purse deals with the private expenditure arising from The Queen's responsibilities as head of state, and covers the cost of such items as clothes, robes and uniforms. It also provides a pension fund for past and present employees who are not otherwise provided for. The Privy Purse is responsible for maintaining The Queen's private residences at Sandringham in Norfolk and Balmoral in Scotland and for further assistance to members of the Royal family in meeting their official expenses. It is also responsible for charitable subscriptions and donations and staff welfare and amenities. Warrant holders allocated to this department can be found in **The Wardrobes**. They include the Royal dressmakers, milliners and shoemakers (such as Hardy Amies, Simone Mirman and H. & M. Rayne) and tailors (such as Kinloch Anderson and S. Redmayne). Robin Callander, drystane dyker at Balmoral, and Suttons Seeds (see **Parks and Gardens**) also come under the Privy Purse. So do jewellers, except Garrard & Co., who are allocated to the Lord Chamberlain's Office.

Department of the Master of the Household

The Department of the Master of the Household was formerly the responsibility of the Lord Steward and was known as the Lord Steward's Department. Its business was to take the accounts of the daily expenditure, to make the necessary provisions and payments for the household, and to see to the good government of the Sovereign's household servants. The Lord Steward was in charge of the Royal household below stairs, and appointed those

Opposite:
Queen Victoria granted
many Royal Warrants
during her long reign

tradesmen who supplied the palace as distinct from the Sovereign. In the reign of Edward VI, the Lord Steward's role was defined thus:

He may lodge readily the King's wines; and make provisions for wool, coal, hay, oats for that season; and if policy will it, for wheat, ale, beef, mutton and such other as the country may bear.

Today the Lord Steward of the Household functions only as a great officer of state on ceremonial occasions. His former administrative and executive duties are now undertaken by the Master of the Household, who has his office in Buckingham Palace.

The Department of the Household is financed by The Queen's Civil List (see below) and includes warrant-holding companies such as provision merchants, wine merchants, caterers and suppliers of cleaning equipment. They can be found in **Interiors, And so to Bed**, **Keeping up Appearances** and **The Royal Larder**.

Lord Chamberlain's Office

The Lord Chamberlain's Office is situated in St James's Palace and is also funded by The Queen's Civil List. The Lord Chamberlain is responsible for all ceremonial duties relating to the household. In 1842 his duties were defined as 'superintendence and control of all officers and servants of the household above stairs'. Today the Lord Chamberlain is the senior officer of the household. He carries a white staff and wears a golden key on ceremonial occasions as symbols of his office.

The Lord Chamberlain's functions include appointing Royal chaplains, Royal physicians and surgeons and other household officers, superintending the Royal collection of works of art, making arrangements for Royal garden parties and supervising aspects of the internal administration of the official Royal residences. Among the Royal Warrant holders serving the Lord Chamberlain's office are Toye, Kenning & Spencer and Wilkinson Sword who can be found under the chapter **Regal Requirements**.

Royal Mews Department

The fourth department which a Royal Warrant holder to The Queen may supply is the Royal Mews. This department is also financed by the Civil List. It is the responsibility of the Master of the Horse, the third-ranking dignitary at court, who is in charge of the sovereign's stables and responsible for providing the horses, carriages and motor cars required for processions and for the daily needs of the Royal family. His day-to-day duties are carried out by the Chief or Crown Equerry. The Royal Warrant holders found in this department are coachbuilders, livery outfitters, saddlers and motor car manufacturers; they are listed in **Regal Requirements**, **Time Off** and **Travel**.

The Civil List

The Civil List is an allocation paid annually to members of the Royal family by the Treasury from the Consolidated Fund – a public fund – under an Act of Parliament. In exchange the Sovereign surrenders to the Exchequer the revenue from the Crown Estate (which comprises properties throughout Great Britain and traditionally belongs to the Sovereign 'in right of the Crown', and is quite separate from his or her personal property) and certain hereditary revenue. In the year 1982–83, The Queen received £3,704,217 from the Civil List, The

Opposite:
The Princess of Wales, buying sweets from the local Tetbury sweet shop near Highgrove, surprises a passer-by

Queen Mother £306,600 and The Duke of Edinburgh £171,100. The figures are updated annually – the last increase, in March 1982, represented an 8% rise.

The Civil List finances the cost to the sovereign of running the three departments of the Royal household and other expenses incurred by Her Majesty in the course of her official duties as head of state. Her Majesty's other costs are met by the Privy Purse – see above – and Her Majesty's own expenditure as a private individual is met by her own personal resources.

The Prince of Wales is not on the Civil List. As Duke of Cornwall he is entitled to the revenues of the estate of the Duchy – about 129,000 acres in south-west England and London. Prince Charles became entitled to these revenues at the age of 21, but voluntarily undertook to surrender half to the Exchequer in lieu of tax. Since his marriage he now surrenders a quarter. In 1982 he kept £600,000 of the £800,000 Duchy profits.

Beyond the Civil List, more than three-quarters of the costs of official duties are met by the taxpayer. This includes the upkeep of the Royal yacht *Britannia*, and the Queen's Flight – both on the defence budget. The Royal train is paid for by British Rail, and the upkeep costs of Buckingham Palace, Windsor Castle, St James's Palace and Kensington Palace are met by the Department of the Environment, which also pays for the fuel and electricity at Balmoral and Sandringham when The Queen is in residence.

The Royal Shopping Guide

The shops and manufacturing companies in this book – not all of them Royal Warrant holders – have been included as being likely to be of interest to the ordinary consumer, and though their products might be available retail, the Royal family are often supplied direct. You are unlikely to bump into any members of the immediate Royal family in shops. The Princess of Wales still goes shopping for clothes, nowadays more for her children than for herself; but increasingly her personal designers are visiting her. The Queen, The Queen Mother, Prince Philip and Prince Charles have not been seen in a shop for several years.

The Royal family may come to use a particular supplier in various ways. Many warrant holders have had family connections for generations and their continuing use is a matter of tradition. The Royal family have on occasion spotted an advertisement in the local paper themselves, but more often than not they get recommendations from their members of staff.

The standard of products provided for the Royal family is, as you might expect, exceptionally high. In the case of manufacturing companies, special items are often made solely for them. Discontinued lines are sometimes kept on, or special colours and styles might be used which the public are unable to buy. The Royal family are often charged differently, too. One warrant holder told me that the prices paid by the Royal family bore little resemblance to the prices in his catalogue. Others left me with the clear impression that working for the Royal family was such an execptional honour that nothing else mattered.

Regal Requirements

Carriages

G. C. FRANCIS MVO, FRSA
2 Walfield Avenue
Whetstone
London N20 9PR

(01) 445 3655

Heraldic artist to HM The Queen.

'I don't know anyone else who, full-time, paints heraldry in oils and gold leaf on motor vehicles,' Mr Francis told me. He is now indeed – like his father, grandfather and great grandfather before him – as he says, 'a one-off'.

Mr Francis served his apprenticeship with his father, a strict taskmaster who used to tell his young son, 'Never let me hear you say "it's good enough": you're the best.' The principle clearly paid off. When Mr Francis started working on his own after the war the work was mainly for coachbuilders painting family heraldry on the sides of carriages. Today his work can be seen on cars and carriages, in churches and even on the occasional private helicopter. Mr Francis thinks there's nothing ostentatious about displaying a crest or coat of arms on a private car. Indeed, he considers a Rolls looks naked without his work on it. The crest, of course, usually appears on the back doors – the chauffeur rides in front – unless the owner drives himself.

Mr Francis's working methods are also unique. He uses sable brushes which he shaves down to a fine point so they look like 'a hair from a mermaid's eyelash', according to an American lady who attended one of his many lectures. And he paints on an easel like any true artist, using a rest-stick for fine detail work. To avoid too much travelling, Mr Francis resorts to a process designed by his grandfather: he paints the crest on to a specially treated piece of paper which is then transferred to another paper so that the crest appears back-to-front. That's how it is sent to you, and it is a simple matter to apply it to the side of your car in accordance with Mr Francis's instructions.

The most famous commission Mr Francis ever refused was to paint John Lennon's white Rolls-Royce with flowers. Most of the royal coaches have been painted by Mr Francis and his forefathers. His own work was recently seen on the sides of the Glass Coach which transported Lady Diana Spencer from Clarence House to St Paul's

The Irish State Coach is normally used by The Queen for the State Opening of Parliament. It was also used recently by Her Majesty to return to Buckingham Palace after the Silver Jubilee firework display. Mr Francis's father and grandfather painted the main heraldry on the coach. Mr Francis has also worked on the coach, including painting the sovereign's personal cipher in the ornament on the quarter rails

Cathedral on her wedding day. Mr Francis has now painted *Honi Soit Qui Mal Y Pense* so often that he knows exactly where to start the lettering so that the '*u*' is always at the top centre. But if it isn't, he'll just add a couple of extra holes in the garter and neither you nor I will ever notice.

If you want a crest on your car, Mr Francis will advise you on the size and positioning, but otherwise he'll only need to know the design of your crest and the colour of your car. The cost will be between £15 and £50. But for a discreet touch of snobbery – it may be worth it.

Although Mr Francis 'retired' eight years ago, he still works most days, sometimes until late into the evening. If you want further information on having a crest painted, write to him at the above address.

HENLYS (LONDON) LIMITED
Capitol Way
Capital Industrial Park
Edgware Road
London NW9 0EQ

Coachbuilders to HM The Queen.

Henlys date back to 1917 when a Mr Henly started selling former War Department vehicles to the public. Today the firm of Henlys are generally known as a motor retailing and distribution business. But their subsidiary company, Henlys (Central London), have been servicing the coaches in the Royal Mews since 1956.

They prepare the coaches which take the Royal family to Royal Ascot every year. The firm collect the coaches from the Royal Mews about 10 weeks before the event and they seconde the skills of two of the finest coachbuilders – no easy task as the trade is rapidly dying out. After a complete overhaul the final job is to oil the wheels so they don't squeak during the procession. 'It's quite a performance,' says Eric Brown, a Henlys director. The company also service other carriages in the Royal Mews, such as those which King George V brought back from India and the carriages used for collecting ambassadors.

RICHARD A. LINGWOOD
Unit B
Braintree Road
Industrial Estate
South Ruislip
Middlesex

(01) 841 7477

Gold leaf manufacturers to HM The Queen.

Although Richard Lingwood only received his Royal Warrant in 1980, gold leaf has been used for many years by several Royal Warrant holding companies. Arnold Wiggins, the Royal picture-frame makers (page 35), Mr Francis, the Royal heraldic artist (see above), A. R. Mowbray, the Royal suppliers of fine bindings (page 186) and Gordon Offord, the Royal coachbuilders (see below) all use gold leaf.

The visit of King George V and Queen Mary to the Joseph Mason stand at the Royal Agricultural Show in Derby in 1933

Richard Lingwood has a team of nine trained staff helping him in the highly complicated and exhausting process of making gold leaf. First, the gold bullion is bought and melted together with either silver or copper, according to the colour required: a whiter or redder gold. The molten gold is then poured into a mould. Once set, it is rolled – a process which Richard Lingwood and his wife used to do at weekends. Today it is done mechanically by two rollers which in one and a half hours produce a gold ribbon, 56 feet long and 1¼ inches wide. The ribbon is cut into squares, placed between sheets of paper and into parchment bands, 150 bags are placed on top of each other and the gold is beaten by hand into four-inch squares. Each square is then divided into quarters and the process is repeated twice more.

The end product is a sheet of gold, four millionths of an inch thick – supposedly thinner than a beam of light. It has to be handled with pincers and treated with extreme care lest it tears or blows away. It is then sold in books of 25 leaves for between £7.50 and £9.50, depending on the quality and, no doubt, the price of gold.

Monday–Friday: 7.30–3. Richard Lingwood's gold leaf is available from the above address.

JOSEPH MASON PLC
Nottingham Road
Derby DE2 6AR

Derby (0332) 31721/7

Manufacturers of coach paints to HM The Queen.

Joseph Mason were started in 1800 by a landscape gardener who decided to train his two sons in the trade of varnish making. In those days there was no such thing as 'ready-to-use' paint. Instead varnish, or a kind of linseed oil, was mixed on site by painters and thinned out to produce either a matt or glossy paint-like substance. Masons were known as 'varnish makers and colourmen' and soon established a reputation amongst builders of coaches and stately carriages. In recognition of their high standards, they were awarded a prize medal for 'excellence of varnishes and colours' at the Paris Universal Exhibition in 1867.

In 1933 Royal interest in the company began when King George V and Queen Mary visited Masons' stand at the Royal

Agricultural Show in Derby and saw a scale model of the Irish State Coach which had been painted entirely in Joseph Mason material. Masons were awarded their first Royal Warrant in 1982.

Today, among the many vehicles coated in their paint are all black Rolls-Royce cars – as were the Rolls-Royce wartime ambulances – all bright yellow Telecommunication vans and recently, all four first-class carriages of the Orient Express, which provide the first leg of the journey from London to Folkestone.

Monday–Friday: 8–4.30. Mason's paints are available from the above address. Give them a ring and they will, if necessary, send one of their team of troubleshooters to assess your requirements. Most of Masons' orders are for small quantities of individually produced cans or drums of paint (decorative, industrial, vehicle refinishing or specialised coatings) matched to a particular specification.

GORDON J. OFFORD
Waynflete
Boyle Farm
Thames Ditton
Surrey KT7 0TU

Coachbuilders to HM The Queen.

The family of Offord were coach and carriagebuilders from 1791 until last year when Mr Offord, having no son to succeed him, retired. But even in the last years of his business, Mr Offord no longer made coaches, but repaired, serviced and maintained them. Mr Offord lamented the decline of coachbuilders. He told me: 'Twenty years ago when the Shah of Persia wanted a coach built for him, nobody in this country could do it.'

At the turn of the century, Offords employed some 40 to 50 people, but in recent years Mr Offord worked on his own. One of the assignments he continued until his

Front and back view of the prize medals for 'Excellence of Varnishes and Colours' awarded to Joseph Mason at the Paris Universal Exhibition in 1867

retirement was the monthly trip to the Museum of London where he would carry out his 'caretaking service' to the Lord Mayor's carriages and coaches, including the sumptuous State Coach which his company looked after for over 100 years. Another regular assignment, since Offords were granted their Royal Warrant in 1935, was ensuring the general well-being of The Queen's Gold State Coach. Although traditionally used only for coronations, this coach was also brought out at the time of The Queen's Jubilee, in 1977. Mr Offord remembers with pleasure how The Queen stopped one sunny day in May and watched him working on the Gold Coach in the Royal Mews.

Jewels, medals, etc.

The Imperial State Crown as worn by The Queen on State occasions is on display in the Tower of London. Garrard's are responsible for the maintenance of the Crown and the other Crown Jewels

GARRARD & COMPANY LIMITED
112 Regent Street
London W1A 2JJ

(01) 734 7020

Goldsmiths and Crown Jewellers to HM The Queen and HM The Queen Mother.

'Basically we're a family jeweller,' William Summers, one of Garrard's directors and Crown Jeweller, told me. Their most important family has 'one of the best collections of jewels in the world'. With this regal connection, Garrard are responsible for preparing the Crown Jewels and regalia for coronations, state occasions and also for maintaining them, which involves an annual fortnight in the Tower, cleaning and checking the Crown Jewels. As goldsmiths their commissions from the Royal family have included such treasures as the engagement ring given to Lady Diana Spencer by The Prince of Wales.

Garrard's connection with the Royal family dates back to their beginnings in 1722, when George Wickes, the founder, opened his first shop just around the corner from the house of Frederick Louis, Prince of Wales, who lived in Leicester Square. Garrard were first appointed Crown Jewellers by Queen Victoria, in 1843. It was a flourishing period for them. In 1842, Garrard made their first Ascot Gold Cup; in 1851, they made the America's Cup for the Royal Yacht Squadron, which is still in use today, and as an engagement present for Queen Victoria, Prince Albert commissioned a sapphire brooch surrounded by diamonds – which is still worn by The Queen.

Although Garrard feel that 'the time we really come into our own is at a coronation', the rest of the time they successfully run an extremely impressive jeweller's. They have a staggering range of items in their shop. The jewellery department sells both modern and antique pieces and they will also design jewellery to your specifications, swap a piece you bought from them 10 years ago, or re-vamp your unworn tiara. Moreover, they estimate that over half a million watches currently worn worldwide today have been supplied by them.

Garrard's Special Commission department is used mainly by governments, companies and clubs. Their designers will create and make any insignia, stars, collars, sashes and badges you require. Among their past commissions have been maces for London Mayors, brooches for every unit in the British Armed Forces, a complete range of medals and decorations for the government of Ghana and a gilt and enamel McDonalds trophy.

When I visited Garrard, their staff were hard at work in the silver department polishing the cutlery and tea and coffee services. The smell of their special anti-tarnish silver polish (£2) permanently hangs in the air.

Monday–Friday: 9–5.30; Saturday: 9.30–12.30. One catalogue a year is produced, costing £3.00. It can be mailed throughout the world. Other special brochures are available too: 'The Garrard Portfolio of Special Commissions', 'Regent Plate by Garrard', 'Watches and Clocks at Garrard', 'Sterling Silver', two cutlery catalogues and others. Contact Garrard for further information.

SPINK & SON LIMITED
5, 6 & 7 King Street
London SW1Y 6QS

(01) 930 7888

Medallists to HM The Queen, HRH The Duke of Edinburgh and HRH The Prince of Wales.

The clients in Spink's medal department range from heads of state to the collector in the street. And the bi-lingual English and Arabic business card of Mr Joslin – an expert in British and foreign awards and medals, and one of Spink's directors – leaves us in no doubt as to Spink's main market. About 95 per cent of their medal-manufacturing business is export.

'We deal in the past, the present and the future,' said Mr Joslin. Spink design and make orders, decorations and medals, re-novate medals, replace lost ones and advise you when, where and how to wear your medals. They also stock the 'most com-prehensive medal collection in the world', enabling one to start one's own collection with anything from a First World War Victory medal for only £2, to a Waterloo medal for rather more.

The walls of the medal department are decorated with an impressive array of the medals that Spink have designed and made.

When a head of state orders decorations from them their expertise is vital, for it is imperative that every detail is right: there are so many pitfalls – diplomatic, social and aesthetic – to be avoided. Thorough study is needed to find out exactly what the medals are for and then to advise what classes of medal to make and how to issue, record and register them. Once the medals have been decided on, they are made in Spink's London factory with its staff of 35, who include diamond setters, engravers and gold- and silversmiths.

Spink have held their Royal Warrant since Queen Victoria's time and have sup-plied insignia including the Orders of the Garter, Bath, St Michael and St George. They are also occasionally engaged by foreign heads of state to supply awards of appreciation for The Queen which are presented at state visits.

Monday–Friday: 9.30–5.30. Spink have a colour brochure, 'Orders, Decorations and Medals', that 'will be dispatched on request from government representatives'. They also have a 'Numismatic Circular' for collectors. 10 issues annually. Ask Spink for details.

TOYE, KENNING & SPENCER LIMITED
Regalia House
19–21 Great Queen Street
London WC2B 5BE

(01) 242 0471

Suppliers of gold and silver laces, insignia and embroidery to HM The Queen.

If you've got something to say, Toye, Ken-ning & Spencer will say it for you. They get the message across, on sweatshirts, ties, badges, shields, spoons, medals and key rings.

Henri Toye was a Huguenot who es-caped from France in 1685 to avoid re-ligious persecution and set up as a goldsmith in Bethnal Green. Mr Toye, the present chairman, is a direct descendant. In 1801, Toye, Kenning & Spencer were founded, merging Toye's firm with a busi-ness from Birmingham. In the past 300 years the business has developed in an astonishing variety of ways.

The original goldsmith's part of the business still flourishes. Toye, Kenning & Spencer make fine silverware, specialising in insignia and commemorative work such as medals and trophies. They have also long

The Omani Order of Al-Said (family order) as made by Spink & Son. The Order was originally awarded in limited numbers at the turn of the 20th century and then lapsed. Sultan Qaboos revived the order for his state visit to Britain in 1982 when one was awarded to Her Majesty The Queen. The insignia is made in 18 carat red-and-white gold and set with diamonds and rubies (detail)

been associated with the skill of enamel work. They make civic and corporate regalia, glowing with heraldic colour. And they tap the old-established Birmingham tradition of fancy items in enamel and precious metals with their range of enamelled miniature boxes which recall the snuffboxes and bonbonnieres of the 18th century. Enamel work has led them into making badges and from badges they have branched out into every kind of mark of identity. They make the sumptuous badges of The Queen's Watermen and car stickers for organisations such as the World Wildlife Fund, of which Prince Philip is President.

The company also make everything for a uniform except the garment itself. Their catalogue evokes a regiment in all its finery with bandsmen wings and bayonet frogs, gorget patches and guidons, swords and sporran tassles alongside the more workaday belts, buttons and buckles.

Monday–Friday: 9–5. Brochures of Toye, Kenning & Spencer's special commissions available.

WILKINSON SWORD LIMITED
11/13 Brunel Road
London W3 7UH

(01) 749 1061

Sword cutlers to HM The Queen and HRH The Duke of Edinburgh.

If ever you are knighted, it will probably be a Wilkinson sword – albeit a very old one – that taps you lightly on the shoulders. For since the reign of Queen Victoria, Wilkinson have been the Royal sword manufacturers.

Wilkinson Sword can trace their history back to 1772, when Henry Nock, a notable gunsmith of the day – who later became gunmaker to King George III – had a shop in Ludgate Street in the City of London. James Wilkinson, the company's namesake, began as an apprentice of Nock's, but went on to become his partner and to inherit the business in 1805. Wilkinson & Son, as they were then known, soon established a reputation for their military and sporting arms and swords. Today, no longer in the gunmaking business, they are the only remaining sword cutlers out of the principal two dozen which supplied military swords in England in the past two centuries, and they are recognised as the leading swordmakers in the world.

Wilkinson Sword still supply ceremonial and collectors' swords. In their archives they have patterns and government specifications that date back 150 years and can still be reproduced. Wilkinson's 30 swordmakers make swords for all of the 40 regiments of the British Army – with different swords for each regiment – and for the armies of the Commonwealth, for the Royal Navy, the Royal Air Force and many overseas governments. They will make you a sword for that special occasion and engrave it if you want. Starting at a price of about £100, you can choose from any one of their many designs – apart from their Household state swords which are only for the use of the Household Cavalry. Or their 'Jubilee Sword', with a limited edition of 100, which Wilkinson struck especially to commemorate The Queen's Silver Jubilee.

Monday–Thursday: 9–5; Friday: 9–4.30. For further information about swords, telephone the above number.

Maundy Thursday

**BARROW HEPBURN
EQUIPMENT LIMITED
Corunna Works
Stewarts Road
London SW8 4UZ**

(01) 622 9900

Manufacturers of Royal Maundy Purses to HM The Queen.

When you see intrepid men scaling the ladders of radio masts or towering industrial chimneys, they are undoubtedly protected from falling by a cunning safety harness manufactured by Barrow Hepburn. But this heavy-duty equipment is a far cry from the gentler cottage industry of producing the Royal Maundy Purses for which the company hold the Royal Warrant. Before they branched into other fields, Barrow Hepburn were the largest tanners in the UK, and in 1963 they acquired S. Clarke & Co., the previous Maundy Purse makers.

Maundy money is specially minted silver coinage ceremonially distributed by The Queen every year to the 'deserving poor'. The ceremony is usually held in Westminister Abbey, and takes place on the day before Good Friday. There are as many recipients as the years of the Sovereign's life, and each receives two of the purses, one containing shillings (as many as the years of the Sovereign's reign) and the other holding pence (as many as the years of the Sovereign's life). One purse is of white sheepskin tied with red leather, the other red sheepskin tied with white leather. They are made in batches every seven years by loyal ladies toiling in Barrow Hepburn's modern factory in Battersea.

Barrow Hepburn have other special commissions. They make the red dispatch boxes in which The Queen is sent her daily government papers. They also manufacture every sort of leather briefcase, holder and accoutrement for man and beast – from a firewoman's shoulder bag to bridles, breastplates and saddles for today's horse. Once their saddles were worn by horses whose riders helped to guard the North West Frontier, but today they are more peacefully used by the Household Cavalry.

Monday–Friday: 9–4.45. Mail order catalogue available.

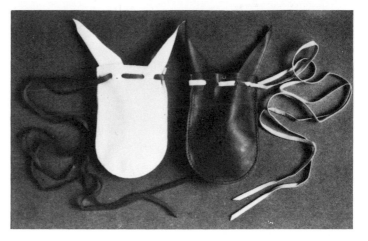

ceremonial distribution of Maundy money. It is her task to construct the 12 to 18 floral mounds carried by Her Majesty, the rest of the Royal family, the bishop and all the other officials taking part in the ancient ceremony.

For each of the nosegays, 103 flowers and herbs are used in a 'recipe' traditionally intended to ward off evil vapours. Daffodils, violets, primroses, white stocks and cheerfulness (a form of narcissus) are used, together with rosemary, thyme and cupressus to form nine-inch nosegays or seven-inch ones for the children who assist at the ceremony. Originally the flowers and herbs would have been taken from the hedgerows and meadows, but today they come from Mrs Bennett-Levy's garden – she was formerly a nursery owner – and those of her friends.

The traditional red and white purses with long strings are made of soft leather and in the same style as those of earlier times

Outfitters

VALERIE BENNETT-LEVY
9 Shepherds Hill
Haslemere
Surrey GU27 2NB

Suppliers of nosegays to HM The Queen.

Valerie Bennett-Levy is not a shopkeeper. She sells neither to The Queen nor to anyone else. But she has held a Royal Warrant for 25 years for providing nosegays to The Queen, a service Mrs Bennett-Levy describes as an 'honorary job'.

What Mrs Bennet-Levy's honorary job entails is, once a year, a sleepless night of frantic work in a hotel kitchen in London or whatever city (it varies) is hosting the

EDE & RAVENSCROFT LIMITED
93 Chancery Lane
London WC2A 1DU

(01) 405 3906

Robe makers to HM The Queen, HM The Queen Mother and HRH The Duke of Edinburgh.

The interior of Ede & Ravenscroft, in the shadow of the Law Courts, breathes pomp and ceremony. The dark wood walls are lined with mementoes of Royalty, such as a swatch of fabric from the investiture robe made by Ede's for Prince Charles, and a robe worn at the coronation of Queen Victoria by William Leaper Newton, later the Mayor of Derby; his robe so outshone The Queen's that, not amused, she forbade him to wear it again.

Ede & Ravenscroft were established in 1689, and they have been robe makers to every English monarch since William and Mary. The robes and court dress which were everyday wear at Court in the 17th century now survive only for ceremonial occasions and in those bastions of conservatism, the Law and the Church. But Ede & Ravenscroft still flourish. Interestingly, a good half of their trade is export: designing and making robes for African chiefs, for new universities, for dignitaries of every kind. The firm consider themselves the experts not only in matters of dress and protocol, but also in the creation of new ceremonial wear.

Staunch upholders of tradition, they still make wigs on their premises for barristers and judges. Each wig is made to fit the individual and takes 'one month and a lot of horses' tails'. In the old days you could tell a novice barrister by the whiteness of his wig, but nowadays there is a judicious mix of darker tones in even new wigs to spare the beginner's blushes. A wig will cost upwards of £165, but it can last three lifetimes.

Ede's 'Bar Room' is worth a visit even though it is now an office. The walls are spectacularly covered with early engravings of judges. At the turn of the century, judges would be taken there before they tried on their new wigs and given a free haircut to make quite sure the wig would fit. Today judges are expected to get their own haircut. But a tradition Ede's *have* held on to is the sewing of their label upside down in a gown. In theory it is so the label can be read the right way up when the gown is hanging on a peg. Unfortunately, if a 20th-century barrister decides to use a hanger instead, the label is upside down.

Monday–Friday: 9–5. Mail order catalogue available. '80-90 per cent of our business is mail order.' Ede & Ravenscroft will mail worldwide.

FIRMIN & SONS PLC
100 Crawford Street
London W1H 1AN

Button makers to HM The Queen and HM The Queen Mother.

Firmin & Sons firmly believe an army is only as good as it looks. 'It is not enough for a defence force to be efficient: it must also look efficient to command respect.' They have been dressing the officers and men of many nations in ceremonial and dress uniforms and accoutrements of all types for the past 300 years. Their buttons were worn by Wellington's men at Waterloo – 'and probably by Napoleon's too'.

Their first Royal Warrant was granted by King George II and they have received a warrant from every succeeding British Sovereign since then. Firmin supply buttons, badges, helmets, breastplates, swords, buckles, belts and other items of dressage for the two regiments of the Household Cavalry (as seen on the uniforms made by Johns & Pegg, see page 107).

The first record of the small button factory from which Firmin & Sons developed dates from 1677 when the business was owned by Thomas Firmin, a noted philanthropist in the City of London. His

Two of Ede & Ravenscroft's team working on a black and gold robe for a university chancellor

address at the time was 'At the sign of the Red Lion over against Norfolk Street in the Strand.' Today a small amount of high-quality handwork is still done in London at their head office in Crawford Street but the bulk of their work is carried out at their Birmingham factory and their smaller branch in Portsmouth.

Today Firmin supply uniform buttons, badges and accessories to police, transport and military services all over the world. Over two-thirds of their business is export. Firmin's buttons are made in solid silver and other precious metals. They can be almost any size or shape required, with raised or indented patterns in any design you choose, and either pierced or shanked.

The company also make caps, hats and helmets, swords and sabres, medals and ribbons, embroidered badges, and a variety of accessories which make up 'an essential part of any uniform', such as pistol holders, sashes, epaulettes, gold lace and trimmings.

Firmin & Sons products are available to the trade only.

18th century advertisement for Sam Firmin, Button-Maker

Interiors

Carpets

BRINTONS LIMITED
PO Box 16
Exchange Street
Kidderminster
Worcestershire DY10 1AG

Carpet manufacturers to HM The Queen.

From the Hotel Pierre in New York and Hilda's Nightclub in Singapore to Windsor Castle, the name on the back of the carpet is Brintons. These Royal Warrant holders have a client list that reads like a *Who's Who* of hotels, government buildings, airports and palaces.

Brintons have been in Worcestershire for more than 200 years. Their ancestors can be traced on the county records back to the 17th century when they were spinners, dyers and weavers. Their first spinning mill was bought by William Brinton in 1783 when weaving carpets was still a cottage industry. By the early 1900s, Brintons had made and patented their own Brinton Jacquard Gripper loom and by 1924 production was at one million square yards a year.

Today almost all the carpets manufactured by Brintons are woven on looms which have been designed and built within the company. Brintons claim these are 'the latest and most efficient machines in the world'. The company still remain a family business run by the sixth generation, Topham Brinton, but the smallholding which began as a quarter acre is now a 14-acre site with sales companies throughout the world.

Brintons carpets are available to the trade from the above address and to the public from carpet retailers and major department stores.

BURY COOPER WHITEHEAD LIMITED
Hudcar Mills
PO Box 14
Bury
Lancashire BL9 6HD

Felt and carpet manufacturers to HM The Queen.

This Lancashire-based company have held the Royal Warrant as felt manufacturers to The Queen for more than 30 years. Their high-quality carpet felt can be found on the floors of Harrods and other top stores. But cast an eye around your home and you might well find Bury Cooper's felt lurking in other places. Your slippers perhaps, or in the piano or even a humble corn plaster in your bathroom. And as Prince William probably knows, Paddington Bear wouldn't be seen in anything else.

Bury Cooper, as one of the world's biggest feltmakers, are experts in finding new uses for felt – probably the oldest fabric made by man. In 1980, when northern textile firms were forecasting gloomy days, Bury Cooper directors Bob Ponting and Peter Walter were pacing up and down their felt carpets thinking of yet another use for their product. They noticed the hat trend stimulated by The Princess of Wales and developed a new range of millinery felt for the home and overseas market, since which they have come right back on top in the hat trade.

Bury Cooper Whitehead products are available to the trade from the above address and to the public from carpet showrooms.

CARPETS INTERNATIONAL
PO Box 15
Mill Street
Kidderminster
Worcestershire DY11 6XE

Manufacturers of carpets to HM The Queen.

Humphries of Kidderminster were originally a family business founded by Benjamin

Humphries in 1790 and run by his family until the beginning of this century. The last Humphries to have control were the third generation who were badly hit in 1895 when the American carpet industry dumped huge quantities of Axminster carpet on the British market; selling it at 1s. 10d. a square yard against the cheapest Humphries Axminster at about five shillings. Many of the leading carpet manufacturers joined forces to produce a competitive 'Imperial' quality carpet, but the three Humphries brothers could not raise the money for the new spool Axminster loom which was needed to go into competition. In 1900 they were finally forced to borrow the capital for the loom but it put the company in dire financial straits.

One of the firm's designers, Herbert Smith – a totally ruthless man – was just starting to work his way up in the firm. By 1906 he had become general manager and the company made a profit for the first time in 13 years. He sacked many of the staff and converted the plant to electricity. Three years later he had become managing director and bought out the Humphries brothers – in monthly instalments.

His success at Humphries was so spectacular that another carpet firm, Charles Harrison & Sons asked him to work his magic for them. He did. Then he bought the company from them. Herbert Smith continued to buy up companies and spinning mills until 1920 when his empire was complete and his own company, Carpet Trades, was born.

After his death in 1945, Carpet Trades continued to flourish. It went public and merged with Crossleys of Halifax. Sir Herbert Smith would have been proud. Today Carpet Trades and its subsidiary companies have become Carpets International – the largest self-contained manufacturing group in Europe. The carpets are made by Gilt Edge – recognised by their distinctive gold selvedge, Crossleys, Kosset and the Carpet Manufacturing Company.

They produce quality Axminster and Wilton, combining the traditional expertise of the Axminster and Wilton weavers with 20th-century skills of tufting and bonding. Their tonal and hard twist carpets in plain and modern and traditional patterns come in varying piles and blends. Carpets International also offer a bespoke service by which designs are created to meet the special requirements of architects, interior designers, hotels and restaurants around the world.

Carpets International carpets are available to the trade from the above address and to the public from carpet retailers and major department stores.

C. JOHN (RARE RUGS) LIMITED
70 South Audley Street
Mayfair
London W1Y 5FE

(01) 493 5288

Suppliers of carpets to HM The Queen.

Since 1947, a particularly elegant corner shop in Mayfair has been the site of C. John. Today, it is filled with rolled-up carpets, most of them extremely large and none of them under 100 years old. C. John sell handmade carpets, rugs, tapestries and textiles from all over the world. But their unique reputation is for French carpets. According to Mr Sassoon, the managing director and nephew of the founder, they have probably the largest selection in Europe.

Mr Sassoon's proudest recent acquisition was a magnificent English handknotted Moorfields carpet, designed by Robert Adam, and woven at the Chiswell Street factory, Moorfields, in 1770. An almost identical carpet can be seen in the

The English handknotted Moorfields carpet recently acquired by C. John

Red Drawing Room at Syon House in London.

C. John received their Royal Warrant in 1966 as suppliers of carpets. You may not be able to buy for investment, as some of C. John's other clients do, at prices between £5,000 and £10,000. But don't be put off: for around £100 you could own a small piece of late 19th-century needlework from C. John.

Monday–Friday: 9.30–5.

NAIRN FLOORS LIMITED
PO Box 1
Kirkcaldy
Fife KY1 2SB
Scotland

Manufacturers of floorcoverings to HM The Queen.

Nairn Floors are the only manufacturers of linoleum in Britain today. They say they have probably been supplying floorcoverings to Royal households since 1847 when the company were founded, but they have only held their warrant since 1972.

Today Nairn Floors are part of the Nairn International Group of Companies, now Britain's leading exporters of floor- and wallcoverings. Nairn were the first company in Europe to manufacture cushioned vinyl floorcoverings – their toughest product.

Nairn linoleum as seen at an exhibition that featured the life and work of Sir Edwin Lutyens

Their designs range from the traditional to the bright and breezy. They say their fashionable designs and colours are one of the many factors which make them unique. 'Our distinctive styling, quality and general technical superiority allow us to build on our reputation as world leaders,' they told me.

They have a classic range of mosaic patterns, an 'Autograph' range with its graphic linear look, several stately marble effects and parquet, quarry tile or cork look-alikes. Nairn vinyl wallcoverings are also available in a variety of designs.

Nairn products are available to the trade from the above address and to the public from carpet and wallpaper retailers and major department stores.

THE WILTON ROYAL CARPET FACTORY LIMITED
Wilton
Salisbury
Wiltshire SP2 0AY

Wilton (0722) 742441

Carpet manufacturers to HM The Queen.

Deep in the heart of the sleepy Wiltshire countryside an army of weavers is busy at work in Britain's oldest carpet factory. Carpets have been made at Wilton Royal for over 300 years. Their customers have included Queen Victoria, the Sultan of Turkey, sundry Maharajahs, the Ritz and millions of ordinary homes.

From the outside the pretty 17th-century building belies the fury of activity which goes on behind the factory doors: for hundreds of yards of carpet pass through the powerful looms every day.

The first part of the Wilton Royal factory was built in 1655 for use as a finishing and assembly centre for the tapestries made by weavers at home. At that time, carpets were more frequently found on walls than floors. It was only after the Earl of Pembroke smuggled two Huguenot master weavers, Antoine Dufosse and Pierre Jemaule, out of France in wine barrels that a revolution in carpet-making took place.

With their knowledge at Wilton's fingertips the weaving process became faster and more people could afford to put carpets on the floor instead of the wall. This was the start of the long heyday of classic Wilton carpets – thick, heavy and glowing with colour. Many are still to be found underfoot in stately homes today. The business soon attracted Royal patronage and was incorporated by a charter of William III in 1699. They have held a Royal Warrant since 1908.

Weaving of the traditional kind is still carried out at Wilton, though now only by machine: the last hand loom went in 1958. Wilton Axminster carpets are made in this way, but Wilton mostly manufacture the newer, tufted carpets.

Wilton's carpets sell at prices from £8 per square yard for the cheapest tufted to £23 per square yard for the Royal Wiltshire Axminster for exceptionally heavy wear – no doubt the kind that lines the corridors of power.

The Wilton Royal Carpet Factory is open to the public. Telephone: Salisbury (0722) 742733 for details. Wilton carpets are available to the trade from the above address and to the public from carpet retailers and major department stores.

marine world and the oil industry. They also make Novafrost, a chewing-gum remover for carpets.

Nova products are available to industrial and commercial users.

Wilton's peaceful factory in Wiltshire

Cleaning

BRITISH NOVA WORKS LIMITED
57–61 Lea Road
Southall
Middlesex UB2 5QB

Manufacturers of floor maintenance products and waxes to HM The Queen.

British Nova's products are used throughout the world. The company have been supplying the Royal palaces since the early 1960s and claim to be one of the UK's largest private manufacturers and suppliers of industrial maintenance chemicals and equipment.

Besides the floor maintenance polishes for which they hold their warrant, British Nova produce a range of materials for carpet care, hygiene and general cleaning of buildings through to sophisticated surface treatments and other chemicals used by the

EASTERN COUNTIES LEATHER COMPANY PLC
Langford Arch
London Road
Sawston
Cambridgeshire CB2 4EG

Manufacturers of chamois leather to HM The Queen.

The Eastern Counties Leather & Parchment Co. as it was then known, was founded in 1879, thanks to the tyranny of one man in the small village of Sawston, Thomas Sutton Evans.

In 1850 Thomas Sutton Evans inherited a tannery business from his father and a few years later started his own chamois leather manufacturing company in Sawston. Mr Evans insisted his employees draw their wages at one of his many public houses where he would force them to buy a beer before he paid them. By the mid 1870s he was ordering his employees not to go to church services.

On 6 February 1879 a motley crowd of local men, including a medical practitioner, a printer, a druggist, a leather dresser and the local Congregational minister met to put a stop to his behaviour. Their plan was to start a company to provide alternative work for the men suffering under Mr Evans. The Eastern Counties Leather & Parchment Company was formed.

At the end of the 19th century the parchment side of the company had ended due to a lack of demand, but Eastern Counties continued to make chamois leather, gloves and leggings (leather gaiters). By 1925 the business was collapsing. The directors put the company into the hands of a London auctioneer to sell it, but no offers were received. In March of the following year the chairman of Eastern Counties received a letter from Charles Moore, a leather dresser, who at the time was renting some of the company's facilities. Charles Moore wrote: 'I feel confident that if appointed works manager I could make a profit for the Eastern Counties.' He was appointed.

Today Eastern Counties is run by Charles Moore's grandson using many of the same processes to make the leather products that have been used since the company started. Apart from their full-oil chamois leather – made of sheepskin, not the skin of the chamois – they also make sheepskin coats and gloves. Eastern Counties were awarded their first Royal Warrant in 1976.

Eastern Counties chamois leather is available from all good specialist motoring stores, ironmongers and department stores.

J. GODDARD & SONS LIMITED
Frimley Green
Camberley
Surrey GU16 5AJ

Manufacturers of silver polishes to HM The Queen and suppliers of Dry Clean to HM The Queen Mother.

Goddard were granted their Royal Warrant to The Queen in 1956 and to The Queen Mother in 1964. Since 1969 the company have been owned by another Royal Warrant holder, Johnson Wax (see page 16), trading from the same Surrey factory.

Joseph Goddard was originally a chemist with a talent for making his own cures and compounds, who in 1829 had bought his own shop in Leicester. One of his famous cures was a 'Halt Remedy' for foot-rot in sheep. At the beginning of the 19th century, most people used steel forks and steel and horn spoons for eating. But in 1833 the first silver-plated forks and spoons were made. Joseph Goddard realised they would never stand up to the rough treatment of the mercurial polishes of that time, designed to work by removing the top layer of silver along with the tarnish. So he invented Goddard's Non-Mercurial Plate Powder – the first proprietory silver polish in the world. The chemist shop was sold.

It was almost 100 years before Goddard were able to improve on the original product. The plate powder had to be mixed into a paste with either water or methylated spirit before it could be applied to the surface of the silver. In 1936, Goddard introduced a silver polish with the plate powder ready mixed. Three years later, they introduced Silver Cloth, a soft cotton cloth impregnated with silver polish to restore the shine to lightly tarnished silver. Their most recent additions to the silver-cleaning market are their Long-Term Silver Foam and Silver Cloth – ideal for Royal silverware.

Goddard also manufacture Dry Clean aerosol, for instant removal of greasy spots – and small enough to fit in your handbag.

Goddard products are available from hardware stores and supermarkets.

JAMES GRAY & SON IRONMONGERS & ELECTRICIANS LIMITED
89 George Street
Edinburgh
Scotland EH2 3EZ

Edinburgh (031) 225 7381

Suppliers of cleaning materials to HM The Queen.

In their handsome listed building in one of Edinburgh's finest Georgian streets, Grays sell almost everything in the hardware and household field. In their basement you can buy basic DIY and gardening tools as well as garden furniture, barbecue sets and lawn mowers. On the second floor Grays have 'one of the biggest ranges of period fireplaces in Scotland' with both original and reproduction fireplaces from £200 to £1,000 which they will install for you. They carry a good selection of electrical equipment and kitchen furniture – from hobs to plugs. Also kitchen hardware, gadgets and novelties. On the ground floor you can buy your alcoholic golfing friend a set of freezer golf balls to cool his drink at the 19th hole.

James Gray received their first Royal Warrant in 1899, when the company were known as Smiths & Co., for supplying lamps and oil to Holyroodhouse, The Queen's official Scottish residence. Today they hold their warrant for supplying cleaning materials. You can find these on the ground floor.

Monday–Friday: 9–5.30. Saturday: 9–1.

HOOVER PLC
Perivale
Greenford
Middlesex

Manufacturers of vacuum cleaners and laundry equipment to HM The Queen and HM The Queen Mother.

The founder of the Hoover organisation – known to his workers as 'Boss' – was inspired to make his first vacuum cleaner in 1908 after a visit from one of his relatives who had brought with him a model of his latest invention – an 'electric suction sweeper'. Boss Hoover regarded the model as a 'crude machine made of tin and wood with a broom handle' but immediately recognised its potential.

Boss Hoover and his son had been looking for other possible enterprises to add to their already successful harness and leather goods manufacturing business in Ohio. It was the end of the horse and carriage era and the beginning of the motor car and they knew their products would not be in demand for much longer. So Boss Hoover started to manufacture and sell vacuum cleaners based on the crude design he had been shown.

The Hoover cleaner grew in popularity and by the end of the First World War the business had been turned over entirely to making domestic appliances. In 1919 Hoover Limited were registered in London and a sales office set up. Success in the British market led to the decision to build the factory at Perivale in Middlesex – an impressive white and green art deco building on the A4, the former main road to Heathrow airport.

After the Second World War there was a renewed demand for Hoover cleaners in both British and overseas markets. The

*The Hoover
headquarters in Perivale,
outside London*

company began to expand their range of products, and encouraged by the government's policy of developing high unemployment areas, Hoover set up a factory in Merthyr Tydfil in Wales manufacturing washing machines. Another was set up in Cambuslang on the outskirts of Glasgow for the production of suction cleaners, since when about 26 million Hoover cleaners have been made in Britain.

Today the word 'Hoover' is synonymous with vacuum cleaners but the company are also known for washing machines and dryers, fridges and freezers, commercial heavy-duty cleaners and burglar alarms. All cleaner production in the UK is now done at Cambuslang but the Perivale factory still remains the headquarters of the British Hoover organisation. The Hoover Worldwide Corporation has its head office in Boss Hoover's home city in Ohio.

Hoover were granted their first Royal Warrant in 1927 for supplying vacuum cleaners to the Royal household, and today the warrant also covers laundry equipment.

Hoover products are available from Hoover dealers and major department stores.

JEYES GROUP LIMITED
Brunel Way
Thetford
Norfolk IP24 1HF

Manufacturers of hygiene products to HM The Queen and HM The Queen Mother.

John Jeyes patented his first disinfectant fluid in 1877, which became the Jeyes Fluid we know today, an effective and powerful cleaning chemical for use in both homes and industry.

At the end of the 19th century the company became the first to introduce flat-pack toilet paper. About 60 years later they added Ibcol (an aromatic disinfectant) and Sanilav (a toilet cleaner) to their range of products. Jeyes bought three companies, Parazone (manufacturers of bleaches), Three Hands (who made washing-up liquid and bactericidal hand soap) and Brobat (another bleach manufacturer), which gave them the much wider range of products which are still on the market today.

The expansion meant that in 1970 Jeyes, originally based in London's East End, moved to their present 17-acre complex in Thetford, and changed their name to Jeyes UK Limited. Today Jeyes make everything from floor-care products to paper towels.

Jeyes products are available from hardware stores and supermarkets.

JOHNSON WAX LIMITED
Frimley Green
Camberley
Surrey GU16 5AJ

Manufacturers of wax polishes, cleaner and hygiene products to HM The Queen and HM The Queen Mother.

A torpedo from an enemy submarine sank the first consignment of Johnson wax to Britain in 1915. The company had started in 1886 when Samuel Curtis Johnson, who had a parquet flooring business in America, began to make wax pastes to keep his floors in good condition. By 1914 his son, Herbert Fisk Johnson, was having more success trading in wax than floors, so he opened his first overseas branch in London's High Holborn. Despite the mishap at sea a consignment of wax finally did arrive in Britain and the company are now the biggest privately owned of their kind in the world.

Their headquarters are still in Wisconsin, USA but their British products are manufactured under the chairmanship of the founder's grandson, Samuel Curtis Johnson, in the heart of Surrey. They received their warrants for supplying polishes, cleaner and hygiene products to The Queen and The Queen Mother in 1970. These include Johnson's furniture and floor polish in lavender or the original with beeswax, Teak Wood Care spray polish and Favor cream spray, Glade air freshener, Glade Shake n' Vac, Sparkle and Pledge polishes and Future wax polish.

Johnson Wax products are available from grocers, hardware stores and supermarkets.

LEVER BROTHERS LIMITED
Lever House
3 St James's Road
Kingston upon Thames
Surrey

Soap and detergent makers to HM The Queen and HM The Queen Mother.

In 1884 a successful wholesale grocer, William Hesketh Lever (later to become Lord Leverhulme) radically changed the face of the soap industry. Until then soap had always been sold in pieces cut off a long bar. Mr Lever presented soap tablets already cut, stamped, wrapped and packed in a carton bearing the brand name Sunlight. As a further new approach, he then created an awareness of the product by advertising.

By the mid 1890s Mr Lever was selling nearly 40,000 tons of soap a year. To the original Sunlight soap he had added Lifebuoy in 1894 which exploited the new public interest in hygiene. This was followed in 1899 by Sunlight (later Lux) soap flakes, a scouring block, Monkey Brand, and later Vim scouring power. In 1908 Mr Lever bought the firm R. S. Hudson and with it a soap powder, Rinso, and by 1909 Lever Brothers' best-known product, Persil, had been introduced. By the time of his death in 1925, William Lever controlled about 60 per cent of the output of soap in Britain.

Lever Brothers are now owned by Unilever. Their principal products are toilet soaps and a range for fabric washing and conditioning as well as household cleaning. They produce over 400,000 tons of products a year and their soaps and detergents, for which they hold their Royal Warrants, account for about 15 per cent of Unilever's worldwide annual turnover.

Today Lever Brothers have 4,000 employees. Many of them still live and work in the Port Sunlight Village created by William Lever as a village community for the employees who worked at the soap factory. William Lever's vision for the 13-acre village on the banks of the Mersey, was for a community with 'houses in which our workpeople will be able to live and be comfortable; houses with gardens back and front, and in which they will be able to know more about the science of life than they can in a back slum, and in which they will learn that there is more enjoyment to life than in the mere going to and returning from work'. The village has its own art gallery, pub, railway station, church and social club . . . not forgetting the soap and detergent factory.

Lever Brothers products are available from grocers, hardware stores and supermarkets.

Lever Brothers advertisement complete with visual pun

The Proctor & Gamble trademark

PROCTOR & GAMBLE LIMITED
PO Box 1EE
Newcastle upon Tyne
Tyne & Wear NE99 1EE

Suppliers of soap and detergents to HM The Queen. Manufacturers of soaps, detergents and shortening to HM The Queen Mother.

In 1930 during the Great Depression in America, the Proctor & Gamble Company of Cincinnati in Ohio decided to venture across the Atlantic to invest some money in Britain. They bought Thomas Hedley & Co., a Newcastle-based soapmaking company which had been producing only one brand, Fairy Soap. Five years later Proctor & Gamble crossed the Pacific to buy a small business in the Philippines but it was not until after the Second World War that they really started building a major international business.

Today Proctor & Gamble operate in 23 countries around the world and their products sell in over 160. They were granted their Royal Warrants in the 1960s. The once-solitary Fairy Soap now has a large family of other soaps, detergents and personal care products including Ariel washing powder, Crest toothpaste, Head and Shoulders shampoo and Pampers disposable nappies. They also make a range of industrial products including cleaning detergents, chemicals, shortenings, margarines and edible oils.

Proctor & Gamble products can be identified by their distinctive moon and stars trademark which originated in America in the 1800s, when a wharfhand started painting crosses on the Proctor & Gamble crates. The riverboat stevedores came to depend on the symbol to identify Proctor & Gamble's cargo. After a while the cross became a star and the star was put into a circle. One star became 13 – signifying the 13 colonies of America – and then the stars were joined by a face in a crescent moon.

Proctor & Gamble products are available from grocers, department stores and supermarkets.

RECKITT & COLMAN LIMITED
PO Box 26
1–17 Burlington Lane
London W4 2RW

Manufacturers of air fresheners, polishes and cleaners to HM The Queen (Reckitt Household Products). Manufacturers of antiseptics to HM The Queen (Reckitt & Colman Pharmaceutical Division). Manufacturers of mustards and sauces to HM The Queen (Colmans of Norwich).

J. & J. Colman Ltd had held their first Royal Warrant as suppliers of mustard to Queen Victoria, and Reckitt & Sons theirs as suppliers of metal polish to Edward VII. But as Reckitt & Colman, the company were first granted a Royal Warrant to King George VI for supplying mustard, metal polish, black lead and antiseptics. Now Reckitt & Colman produce everything from OK Fruity Sauce to Tom Caxton's home-made bitter. Few households in Britain could claim not to have at least one Reckitt & Colman product somewhere under their roof.

Colman and Reckitt were originally two firms in fierce competition with each other. In 1913 they took the first steps towards pooling their resources and started exporting to South America as a joint company, Atlantis Limited, instead of as two separate ones. The courtship worked. By 1938 they were trading together as Reckitt & Colman Ltd. Today they employ over 37,000 people, manufacture their products in 40 different countries and sell them in over 100.

Their products fall into six categories: food (from the warrant-holding mustard to Gale's honey); wine (including St Raphael apéritifs and Tequila Sauza); household products (Brasso, Mr Sheen, Mansion Polish and Harpic to name but a few); toiletries (from Nulon handcream to Steradent denture cleaner); pharmaceuticals (including warrant-holding Dettol) and creative and leisure products (from Dryad's craft materials to Windsor & Newton's artist's colours).

Reckitt & Colman products are available at most shops.

STURTEVANT ENGINEERING COMPANY LIMITED
**Westergate Road
Moulsecoomb Way
Brighton
Sussex BN2 4QB**

Manufacturers of vacuum cleaners to HM The Queen.

When Sturtevant bought another company in 1971, they did not just gain an asset, they inherited a Royal Warrant too. The company they bought, New Welbeck, held a warrant for supplying industrial vacuum cleaners to the Royal household, and Sturtevant have carried on the tradition since then.

Although Sturtevant are primarily an engineering company, their vast range of vacuum equipment is used throughout industry for anything from cleaning out coal and ash in boiler houses to sprucing up the horses' stables. They made vacuum cleaners even before they bought New Welbeck, and sold their first – a ⅓ hp turbine cleaner – in 1912, but only started full-scale manufacturing in 1921. During the 20s and 30s, the bulk of their trade was supplying vacuums for cinemas and power stations.

Don't be surprised if they suggest you use a Tiger, a Puma, a Lynx or a Panther to do your heavy-duty cleaning; Sturtevant clearly have a fixation with big cats. Their machines can be found purring their way round the Royal Mews.

Sturtevant industrial vacuum cleaners are available to industry from the above address. Sturtevant offer a consultation and design service and will manufacture and install cleaning systems to suit specific needs. They will also give free demonstrations.

TEMPLE & CROOK LIMITED
**3 & 5 Kinnerton Street
London SW1X 8JY**

(01) 235 2166

Suppliers of brushes and hardware to HM The Queen.

Temple & Crook are the only ironmongers in Belgravia, and their sales ledger reads like *Who's Who*. Although a lot of their trade is to builders working locally, at Temple & Crook you are just as likely to bump into a butler from one of the stucco mansions in Belgrave Square.

The firm opened in 1810 to provide household utensils and equipment for the new town houses of the titled and rich which were going up in Belgravia and Mayfair at the time. Their specially designed cast-iron kitchen ranges were much in demand in the latter half of the 19th century, I was told by their current managing director, Mr Streeter. Temple & Crook received their first Royal Warrant in 1922 and they have held one ever since. Today their orders from Buckingham Palace are for all the bits and pieces they don't want a lorry load of.

Temple & Crook still design and install kitchen ranges, but are more involved in decorating and jobbing building services with a personal touch. They will come and fit any one of their 160 different types of light bulbs and carry out all manner of small electrical repairs. They cut most kinds of keys and also provide the service of collecting your keys, cutting them and returning them to you the next day.

Their strangest modern commission was to design and make a chromium-plated frame to assist Emperor Haile Selassie with getting in and out of his bath.

Monday–Friday: 9–5.30; Saturday: 9–1. Will send goods anywhere in the world and offer a free delivery service in London for orders of £10 and over.

An early kitchen range as fitted by Temple & Crook – they could do the same today

This doll's tea service was produced by Royal Doulton for Queen Mary. It can be seen in the doll's house on display at Windsor Castle

A selection of commemorative items made by Royal Doulton to celebrate royal events

Crockery and cutlery

CAITHNESS GLASS PLC
Harrowhill
Wick
Caithness
Wick (0955) 2286

Glassmakers to HM The Queen Mother.

Caithness Glass was founded in Wick in 1960 to provide employment for Caithnessians, as the traditional fields of work in the area, namely farming and fishing, were rapidly dying out. The company started by producing only hand-blown glassware, but eight years later expanded their range to include engraving. A year later Caithness Glass began to make paperweights – specialising in abstract designs rather than the more traditional styles – a couple of which can usually be seen on the writing desk of The Queen Mother, and most recently they have developed a range of jewellery using intricate 'canes' of moulded, multi-coloured glass.

Since then, Caithness Glass have opened a further two factories, the most recent of which, in Perth, was opened by The Prince of Wales in 1979. The Queen Mother whose residence, the Castle of Mey, is also in the county of Caithness granted Caithness Glass their Royal Warrant in the early 1970s.

Caithness Glass products are available from china and glass shops and department stores. Visitors are welcome to their factories at Oban and Perth. Their factory shops sell mainly Caithness Glass second quality products.

DOULTON FINE CHINA LIMITED
Nile Street
Burslem
Stoke-on-Trent
Staffordshire ST6 2AJ

Manufacturers of china to HM The Queen.

Doulton Fine China might never have started had it not been for a wayward son who ran away to sea. In 1815 the widowed Mrs Jones offered 22-year-old John Doulton the partnership in the Vauxhall Walk Pottery which she had been keeping for her long-lost offspring. The shrewd young

Doulton decided to take up the offer and invested his life savings of £100 in the business.

The firm have been passed down to generations of Doultons since then. John Doulton's second son, Henry, who entered the business aged 15 in 1835, became the driving force behind their new innovations. By 1885 he had been awarded the Albert Medal by Edward VII, then The Prince of Wales, and later became the first potter to be knighted by Queen Victoria for his services to ceramic art and science.

The company were first granted their Royal Warrant in 1901 and they were specifically authorised to use the word 'Royal' to describe their products. Today their most recent development is their English Fine China for which they now hold the warrant to The Queen.

Doulton describe this china as 'delicate in appearance but astonishingly tough, truly translucent and whiter than most foreign chinas'. They also say it is a good base for the use of decorative gold and platinum 'lending itself well to a wide range of coloured decorative treatments'. Choose from their Romance collection in pure ivory bone china, Flirtation in floral pastels, Royal Gold with its regal gold edging or, for those with long-term plans, Eternity in dramatic black and white.

Doulton Fine China merged with two other Royal Warrant holders, Royal Crown Derby and Minton (see pages 23 and 22) to form the Royal Doulton Group. Today the factory at Burslem is the centre of the Royal Doulton Group producing china tableware, figures, Toby jugs and giftware.

Doulton fine china is available from china and glass shops and department stores.

THOMAS GOODE & COMPANY (LONDON) LIMITED
**19 South Audley Street
London W1Y 6BN**

(01) 499 2823

Suppliers of china and glass to HM The Queen, HM The Queen Mother and HRH The Prince of Wales.

Stationed at either side of the entrance to Thomas Goode's shop is a seven-foot pottery elephant standing on a carved wooden plinth. But these magnificent pieces of Minton ceramic, complete with their gilded howdahs and richly coloured ornamental design are not for sale. Not even for the £300,000 they would probably fetch at a public auction today. Nor were they ever for sale to any of Goode's Maharajah customers in the past who were wealthy enough to offer open cheques for them. Thomas Goode have always been astute enough to know the value of a distinctive trademark. Generations of children have begged their parents to take them to see the famous elephants. Many of Goode's customers have also brought along their children to step inside the 'magic doors' installed by ingenious Victorian engineers. They open as soon as you put your foot on the welcome mat.

Thomas Goode was first established in business as a 'chinaman' (selling china) in Mill Street off London's Hanover Square in 1827, then he moved to the now-famous red brick building in South Audley Street. Within a week of opening the new shop in 1845, one of Mr Goode's first customers was His Serene Highness Prince Esterhazy who lived in neighbouring Chandos Street. The Royal families of Europe, the Maharajahs of India and other Eastern potentates soon followed. In 1863 Thomas Goode received his first Royal Warrant from Edward, Prince of Wales. A year later Goode's ledger records an order from The Prince for £1,000 in one day. It was the largest order Goode had ever received. Four months later, in August of the same year, The Prince ordered another £1,000 worth of goods. His Royal Highness had recently married Princess Alexandra of Denmark and was establishing his personal household. Thomas Goode were later granted their warrant by Queen Victoria and have held it in succession since then.

Thomas Goode have become an institution. They have 13 showrooms displaying china, porcelain, crystal and ornamental items. One room – patronised by The Princess of Wales who collects china owls and rabbits – contains a collection of ornamental china birds and animals. The main china showroom houses Thomas Goode's gallery of plates, commissioned and designed by them for many British Sovereigns (including Queen Victoria and the Prince Consort), European Royal Houses, Viceroys, exclusive clubs, distinguished regiments and some of the stateliest homes in England and America.

In the glass showrooms are fine hand-cut crystal and plain glassware from Waterford, elegant Baccarat stemware and gilded opulent Saint Louis glassware. The Sèvres room, decorated in Japanese style, has a selection of antique china and glassware, and the Regency room houses a display of 18th- and 19th-century furniture and ornamental items. Thomas Goode also sell sterling silver and plated wares and a range of table lamps with handmade silk shades. Other departments contain less expensive kitchenware and a range of gifts.

'Whether it's one piece or 100, if something has been made we can get it for you,' Goodes boast. They can also give advice on anything from how to free a stuck decanter stopper to designing a banquet dinner service. And they offer a repair and restoration service which is useful should you drop a plate from one of their personal monogrammed dinner services – the ultimate in status symbols, at over £900 for a 60 piece set.

Monday–Friday: 9–5; Saturday: 9–1. Mail order catalogue free to customers in the UK (approximately £3 to overseas customers).

The glass showroom at Thomas Goode & Co.

HARRODS LIMITED

See page 156.

MINTON LIMITED
China Works
Stoke-on-Trent
Staffordshire

China manufacturers to HM The Queen.

'To set a table with Minton says much about taste, style and a way of life.' Queen Victoria made her first Minton purchase in 1840. After that, both she and Prince Albert were regular customers. News of the relationship between the British Royal family and Minton soon spread and the company subsequently received commissions from many of the Royal and aristocratic houses of Europe.

Today Minton's dinner services are still to be found in palaces, embassies and stately homes all over the world. You will recognise some of them by their 22-carat gold or platinum trims. Their Buckingham collection in ivory and gold is produced by using an acid etching process for the gold piping – a method developed and patented by Herbert Minton the founder, in 1863.

For Queen Elizabeth's coronation in 1953, Minton's art director, John Wadsworth, was chosen to design the vase which was given as a gift from the British pottery industry to Her Majesty. The Queen now owns the first copy and the others were given to each of the member countries of the Commonwealth. In 1968 Minton became part of the Royal Doulton Group.

Minton china is available from china and glass shops and department stores. The Minton Museum in Stoke is open to visitors; contact the above address for further details.

PARAGON CHINA LIMITED
Atlas Works
Beech Street
Longton
Stoke-on-Trent
Staffordshire

China potters to HM The Queen and HM The Queen Mother.

Paragon make 'dainty' teacups which force little fingers into aristocratic curls. They have been making china for the Royal households since they were granted their first warrant by Queen Mary in 1933. Later their Two for Joy design which depicted a legend about magpies led them to another Royal encounter. The then Duchess of York, the present Queen Mother, was delighted by the design. Magpies had been seen at the christening of Princess Elizabeth. So The Duchess of York consented to a photograph of the baby Princess being used by Paragon on their china. And in 1936, their commemorative cup – made for the coronation of King Edward VIII – which Paragon described as 'one of the most ambitious conceptions of the industry', rapidly became a collector's item after the abdication. Paragon adapted the design for the coronations of King George VI and The Queen.

Paragon breakfast and dessert services were first made in 1903 by the Star China Company which had been founded in 1899 by Herbert James Aynsley and William Illingworth to produce tea services. By

Right:
Paragon have a tradition of making loving cups to celebrate Royal events. This one marks The Queen's Silver Jubilee in 1977

Samples from a Minton service first commissioned by Queen Victoria in 1893, the 'Balmoral Tartan' service. The hand-painted border features the Balmoral Tartan and the service was for use at Balmoral Castle

1919 the Paragon range had become so popular the name of the company was changed to the Paragon China Company and 11 years later, following Herbert Aynsley's retirement it became known as Paragon China Limited. Today Paragon are part of the Royal Doulton Group.

Paragon china is available from china and glass shops and department stores.

THE ROYAL CROWN DERBY PORCELAIN COMPANY LIMITED
Osmaston Road
Derby
Derby DE3 8JZ

Manufacturers of fine bone china to HM The Queen Mother.

George III first gave this company the right to mark its fine china with a crown and in 1890 Queen Victoria demanded that the title of 'Royal' be added to Crown Derby. Today they hold the warrant to The Queen Mother and are part of the Royal Doulton Group.

The first fine china was made in Derby in the 1750s. Many of the early patterns of the 18th and 19th centuries like the Imari 1128, with its magnificent shades of mazarine blue, red and burnished gold are still carried on in the Royal Crown Derby collection. Their shapes range from traditional to modern, from the scalloped-edged design known as Clarence with its embossed motifs, elegantly footed cups and deep, fluted saucers and plates to the new bone china shape Queen's Gadroon commissioned by The Queen Mother when she visited their factory in 1971.

Skilled painters continue the Derby tradition of quality and style. Special recent pieces include the Connoisseur range of hand-painted Derbyshire scenes by Michael Crawley and coffee cups painted with birds in their natural habitat by John McLaughlin. Princess Anne, following in her grandmother's footsteps, chose Royal

Crown Derby as her wedding present from the British Pottery industry.

Royal Crown Derby china is available from china and glass shops and department stores.

SPODE
Spode Works
Stoke-on-Trent
Staffordshire ST4 1BX

Manufacturers of china to HM The Queen.

Josiah Spode started his own factory in 1770. His first great success was in 1784 with the introduction of the Willow Pattern and other oriental designs by a new and inexpensive method of underglaze transfer printing. In 1797 Mr Spode died and was succeeded by his son, also named Josiah Spode, who started producing porcelain as well. In the early 19th century he perfected a formula for using bone ash to create what is today known as 'bone china'.

In 1833, after Josiah Spode had died William Taylor Copeland bought the company which continued to prosper. In the early 1840s, Mr Battam, an employee, invented a clay composition called Parian Ware. The new paste, made in imitation of white marble, was fashioned into statuettes and small groups of figures. Mr Copeland foolishly forgot to patent the discovery and it was soon copied by other factories.

Today Spode, part of the Royal Worcester Group, continue to produce many of their traditional patterns including their oriental designs. They also make bone

A replica of a Royal Crown Derby inkstand made for Queen Victoria at the end of the 19th century. A similar one was later presented to Princess Mary, the Princess Royal, on the occasion of her marriage in 1922

The Derby China Works in 1785

china dinner services with fleur-de-lys borders and the elegant Green Embassy service, with its green and gold border, 'ideal for the application of a family crest or monogram'.

Spode china is available from china and glass shops and department stores.

STEVENS & WILLIAMS LIMITED
Royal Brierley Crystal
North Street
Brierley Hill
West Midlands DY5 3SJ

Brierley Hill (0384) 70161

Suppliers of table glassware to HM The Queen.

There are three ways to recognise a piece of Royal Brierley crystal: firstly from the 'ring' you'll hear when you tap it gently, secondly by the minute imperfections and the way each piece differs from the next: proof that you've bought a hand-made product, and finally by the 'Brierley' signature – but that's cheating.

Royal Brierley's tradition dates back to 1610, when the Huguenots first settled in the West Midlands where good supplies of wood, coal and fireclay were available, and established the area as a glassmaking centre. In 1740 John Pidcock, one of the last of the Huguenot descendants, married the daughter of Mr Honeyborne a well-known glassmaker of 'Brier Lea Hill', a marriage which eventually led to the formation of Royal Brierley Crystal.

Early in the 19th century, Joseph Silvers leased the Honeyborne glasshouse at Brier Lea Hill. One of his daughters married William Stevens and the other Samuel Cox Williams who both took control of Silvers' business in 1847, changing the name to its present title, Stevens & Williams. Today the owners, the sixth generation of the Stevens and Williams families, consider themselves 'one of the world's oldest yet most progressive crystal glassmakers'.

The difference between ordinary cut glass and lead crystal is the addition of approximately 24 per cent lead oxide to the silica and silver sand – the basic ingredients of glass. But Royal Brierley Crystal produce only 'Full Lead Crystal' which contains a minimum of 30 per cent lead oxide. They claim that the extra quantity of lead added is what makes the 'world of difference between full lead crystal and ordinary lead crystal'. Royal Brierley don't leave it at that. To each 'mix' is added a tiny sachet of black powder – but they'll never tell you what that is.

Royal Brierley received their first Royal Warrant from George V in 1919 and it has been renewed by each successive monarch since. All of their stemwear patterns, which have graced many Royal tables throughout the world, include at least 15 sizes of glass from liqueur glasses to goblets and Royal Brierley will gladly advise you on all aspects of crystal etiquette – if ever you have to host a state banquet. They'll also tell you how to look after your crystal.

Royal Brierley is available from glass and china shops and department stores. Royal Brierley also invite you to come and look round their factory and promise you 'the same Royal welcome' they gave The Queen.

THE TOKEN HOUSE

See page 232.

THE WORCESTER ROYAL PORCELAIN COMPANY LIMITED
Severn Street
Worcester
WR1 2NE

Manufacturers of china and porcelain to HM The Queen.

The Worcester Royal Porcelain Company was founded in 1751 by Dr John Wall. From the beginning the company's products were influenced by their studies of old Chinese blue and white porcelain. Early on they made a name for themselves by being the first in ceramic history to apply printed transfers from copper engravings to the surface of glazed porcelain. By 1770 they were introducing ornamental vases and services decorated in brilliant enamels with exotic birds, floral panels, scenic views and fable subjects, against gilded ground colours. In 1788 King George III and Queen Charlotte visited the factory and gave their permission for the company to call themselves china manufacturers to Their Majesties. From that time the factory has been known as the Royal Porcelain Works.

Today Royal Worcester are best known for their limited edition bone china models, which include bird, military and equestrian sculptures as well as historical figures such as Elizabeth I and Edward VI.

Royal Worcester china is available from china and glass shops and department stores.

Decorating

ALLAN & DAVIDSON
**142 Queen's Road
Aberdeen AB1 8BR
Scotland**

Aberdeen (0224) 33706

Interior decorators and painting contractors to HM The Queen.

'Decorating is a bit of a compromise,' Mr Davidson told me. 'When you are young you start off with lots of innovative decorating ideas, but then you realise you can only use them if you are asked to and most of our customers are very conservative.'

Mr Davidson is neither very old nor very cynical. He always wanted to be a painter and decorator and he has more than achieved his ambition. 1983 was not only his 30th year in business, but also the year he was awarded his first Royal Warrant. Today he has an interior decorating business in Aberdeen's elegant suburbs, painters and workshops in Culter, a nearby town, a retail shop and four painters in Ballater – close to Balmoral – and painters and another shop in Banchory where Mr Davidson gives advice to his customers every Saturday morning.

Most of the firm's work is private residential work and comes through recommendation, but Allan & Davidson also act as commercial and maintenance contractors for oil companies and estates – Royal and other. Mr Davidson will come round to your home, if asked, bring his many sample books and offer advice on interior decoration, wallpapers and fabrics.

Telephone Mr Davidson during the week at the above number or visit him at his shop in Banchory on Saturday mornings.

LAURA ASHLEY LIMITED
**9 Harriet Street
London SW1X 9JS
(and branches)**

(01) 235 9796

Laura Ashley's designs conjure up cottages in the country, croquet on the lawn and cucumber sandwiches for tea. It is the instant English look, with a strong emphasis

At home with The Prince and Princess of Wales in Kensington Palace. Spot the Laura Ashley cushions on the right of the sofa, the Clare House lampshade, the General Trading Company vases and, more difficult, the bottle of Malvern mineral water behind Prince Charles's shoulder

on floral prints and soft pastel colours. The style is totally coordinated: from matching wallpapers, curtains and upholstery, including lampshades, tiles and paint – right through to clothes.

The company was started by Laura Ashley's husband, Bernard, in 1953 when he began printing textiles on a hand-powered silk screen printing machine which he had made himself. The couple began designing their own furnishing prints and household linens and selling them to the major London stores. By 1962 their products were being sold to about 500 wholesale customers around the world. A year later they moved to their present head office in the Ashley hometown, Powys in Wales. At the same time they bought their first retail shop in Machynlleth, an old Welsh town on the Dovey River, and started to develop a more sophisticated finishing process for the fabrics.

The company continued expanding. They were soon able to open their first London shop, in South Kensington, followed shortly by another in the Fulham Road in 1968. Laura Ashley shops began to open in almost every country in the world. Today there are over 100 and another 50 planned for America.

Recently the Ashleys – including the second generation of the family – decided to add a range of more formal, sophisticated fabrics to their present designs. Many of the new prints are characteristic of specific periods of history. There is a print version of a silk woven in Lyons in the late 18th century – full of rococo swags and bows – and a reproduction flamestitch embroidery which was first seen in Florence in the 14th century. The prints contrast boldly with their former, more timid pastel designs.

Not everyone opts for the completely coordinated look. Laura Ashley is sometimes found discreetly hiding in the home. Two small, round cushions were seen on the pink sofa in the otherwise classical room at Kensington Palace when The Prince and Princess of Wales held a photo-call for the then nine-month-old Prince William on the eve of their Australian tour. The two cushions were covered in a plum-coloured Wild Cherry Laura Ashley print and piped in plum with a ruffled edge.

The Princess of Wales was also believed to have favoured Laura Ashley's clothes before her engagement to Prince Charles. Their feminine dresses with romantic swirling skirts, frilled collars and puffed sleeves are very much in the style of dress The Princess of Wales used to wear.

Monday–Friday: 10–5.30; Wednesday: 10–7; Saturday: 9–6 (Harriet Street branch). Laura Ashley products are available from Laura Ashley shops and leading department stores around the world. Mail order catalogues for clothes, furniture or contract furnishings are available from: Customer Services, Laura Ashley Limited, Carno, Powys, Mid Wales SY17 5LQ.

G. P. & J. BAKER LIMITED
PO Box 30
West End Road
High Wycombe
Buckinghamshire HP11 2QD
High Wycombe (0494) 22301

Suppliers of furnishing fabrics and wall-coverings to HM The Queen.

In 1948 George Baker was sent by the government to Turkey to lay out two Embassy gardens in Constantinople. In his diary he recorded that he took with him, 'a collection of plants for the Embassy, also a collection of fruit trees for the Sultan'. Once the Embassy gardens were completed, Mr Baker set up a nursery in Turkey and sold cuttings. His brother James, back in England, sent him a parcel of linens to sell – and a trading venture was started.

In the late 1850s George Baker had two sons, George Percival and James. George Percival worked for his father as a gardener's apprentice. At the age of 21 he took a three-month holiday in Persia where he picked up his first Persian textile prints and realised the potential for exporting carpets to England. On his return to England he began to sell carpets sent by his father from Turkey, while the Persian prints he brought back were adapted and printed by Swaisland Company at Crayford. In 1884, together with his younger brother James, they formed G. P. & J. Baker. Nine years later they bought the print works at Crayford and began producing the designs on which the present-day collections are based.

Today Baker's archives of old textiles – including Peruvian burial cloths – and prints provide the inspiration for their designs. Of their range of printed fabrics, some are imported but most are specially made in this country. There is a very distinct propensity of floral and oriental designs, influenced by their family's life in the Far East and their father's career as a gardener. G. P. & J. Baker received their first Royal Warrant in 1982.

Monday–Friday: 8.30–5 (High Wycombe showroom) and Monday–Friday: 9–5. (London showroom at 17–18 Berners Street, London WP1 4JA). Both showrooms are open to the public, though only the trade can buy. Baker's fabrics are available to the public from interior decorators or department stores.

CASSON CONDER PARTNERSHIP
35 Thurloe Place
London SW7 2HJ

(01) 584 4581

The Casson Conder Partnership, founded by Sir Hugh Casson KCVO and Neville Conder, is one of the leading architectural practices in Britain today. Their 'list of principal works', to be seen in their glossy brochure, is wide-ranging and their clients as impressive as the National Westminster Bank, the Crown Estate Commissioners and the Royal family.

In over 30 years of practice, the Casson Conder Partnership have been responsible for such diverse works as the footbridge over Regent's Canal in London Zoo, the decorations in Whitehall seen at the coronation of Queen Elizabeth II, the museums at South Kensington in London. Interiors which the Partnership have designed include the Royal Albert Hall, for which Casson Conder worked out the colour scheme for the redecoration of the auditorium and foyer, and Windsor Castle and Buckingham Palace – both state and Royal apartments – for which both alterations and redecorations have been carried out.

Sir Hugh Casson also designed the apartments on the Royal yacht *Britannia*, which was launched in 1954 at a cost of two million pounds. Sir Hugh described the decor as 'a restrained English country-house style'.

Sir Hugh Casson was born in 1910 and studied at St John's College in Cambridge. He has been in private practice as an architect since 1937. He received his knighthood in 1952 and was made Knight Commander of the Royal Victorian Order in 1978. Today he spends most of his time at the Royal Academy of which he has been President since 1976.

Monday–Friday: 9.30–5.30. Telephone Casson Conder Partnership for their brochure. Note that they mainly carry out large commissions.

The sun room on board the Royal Yacht Britannia. Sir Hugh Casson once described the décor as 'a restrained English country-house style'

CLARE HOUSE LIMITED
35 Elizabeth Street
London SW1W 9RP

(01) 273 8480

Suppliers of lampshades and fittings to HM The Queen.

'It keeps me young,' said Elizabeth Clare Hanley as she tiptoed between the lamps and shades piled high in her small shop in Belgravia.

Ms Hanley, an American, came to London in 1949 and started her business in interior design, after studying design at Parsons in New York. 'I wanted to specialise in lighting,' she told me. Today interior designers come to her for advice: 'they're scared of lighting'. Clare House sell stock lampshades in fine silks and chintzes, stretched or pleated, plain or ruffled. They also sell lamps and bases, but most of their customers bring vases to be converted to lamps. Ms Hanley's craftsman carries out the conversion and, if necessary, need not drill a hole in your valuable vase. Ms Hanley says, 'We're the top of the market, we can do everything.' They have already matched an ageing rust-coloured lampshade for John Cleese, converted an umbrella stand into a lamp with a brolly-shaped shade, and rushed through several new lamps for Buckingham Palace and Holyroodhouse.

Clare House also carry out work for the National Trust, often matching old fittings and shades. The shop was awarded its Royal Warrant in 1977. Today they make mainly table lamps which 'aren't terribly cheap'.

Monday–Thursday: 9.30–6; Friday: 9.30–5.

COLE & SON (WALLPAPERS) LIMITED
18 Mortimer Street
London W1A 4BU

(01) 580 2288

Suppliers of wallpaper to HM The Queen.

Luckily the Cole family are collectors. Albert Percival Cole – who founded Coles in 1910 – began to collect historic wood blocks in the 1930s. Today Coles have a unique collection of over 3,000 wood blocks (90 per cent of which are original), some of which date back to the late 18th century. Among the collection are the blocks used for printing original wallpapers in Kensington Palace, the Brighton Pavilion and Hampton Court. They also own the Pugin-designed wood blocks used for printing the wallpaper for the Houses of Parliament both in the 1840s and in its recent restoration in 1983.

Today Coles are one of the only two British companies who still hand-print wallpapers with wood blocks, using techniques almost identical to those used 250

years ago. You can buy ready-printed hand-blocked wallpaper from £15 a roll, order an existing design in a different colour scheme for slightly more, ask Coles to design a new wallpaper for you, or send them a fragment of your existing wallpaper to reproduce. But a new design could be expensive. For a four-colour printing you would need four blocks specially made (at approximately £400 each) and then the printing of the wallpaper would cost you £50 a roll with a minimum of 10 rolls.

In Coles' elegant little shop they have thousands of wallpapers, both hand- and machine-printed, from vinyls to hessians with an average price range of £8–20 a roll. In addition to the fine Cole collection of wood blocks, Christopher Cole (one of their directors) now collects old wallpaper fragments from as far back as the 16th and 17th centuries. So when you start stripping old wallpaper from the walls of that cottage or castle you've just bought, please send a fragment to him.

Monday–Friday: 9–5. Mail order available; just send Coles your enquiries or a swatch of existing wallpaper that you are looking for and they'll do their best to help you. Their pattern department will send free samples of wallpapers and fabrics on request – usually the same day.

GEORGE DONALD & SONS LIMITED
6–24 Netherkirkgate
Aberdeen
Scotland

Aberdeen (0224) 645388

Suppliers of paint, wallpapers and glass to HM The Queen.

January is George Donald's quietest month, 'but before the war', Mr Anderson, their managing director, told me, 'there were no DIY sales at all. Painters from Aberdeen would only be employed from March to July – or possibly until September on outside work – then they would take the boat to London to work on houses where the owners were grouse shooting in Scotland. The decorators would then return to Aberdeen for Christmas.' One tradition Mr Anderson is sad no longer exists, is the pre-Christmas decorating rush. 'In Glasgow and the Lancashire area,' he said, 'people used to want newly decorated homes for the New Year. That was good business.'

George Donald & Sons sell mainly to the

One of Cole & Son's craftsmen hand-printing wallpaper in the traditional way using one of their collection of wood blocks

Two of Coles' wallpapers: Missenden (left) and Louis Quinze

trade. They supply wholesale to an area as far north as the Shetlands and as far south as Dundee and Perth, and they also have a delivery service in that area for glass. In Aberdeen they continue the contracting side of their business of decorating and glazing. To the public who walk into their old-fashioned building they sell glass and DIY and decorating materials. Donalds also stock paints from eight different manufacturers and wallpaper books which they change every two years.

The firm was established in 1820 as a glazier's and moved to their building in Netherkirkgate– tucked away in the centre of Aberdeen – 52 years later. From 1920 to 1961, George Donald & Sons held their Royal Warrant as decorators, but it ended with the death of Mr Anderson Senior. His son, the current managing director, reapplied in 1980 for his present warrant to The Queen.

Monday–Friday: 8–12.45 then 2–5.

CHARLES FARRIS LIMITED
Bishopsgate Works
527 Staines Road
Hounslow
Middlesex TW4 5DN

(01) 570 1161

Chandlers to HM The Queen.

Charles Farris's other main customers are the Church and the BBC. For churches they supply a wide range of 'consumable' goods, mainly altar candles, but also sanctuary lights, wine, wafers, charcoal and incense. And, as for their other client, 'hardly a week goes by without an order for candles for films or television'. Most of

the candles you see on the small screen are provided by Charles Farris, who also made the thousands of candles used in Jean Seberg's *Joan of Arc*. Farris are now experts in the art of film lighting, and make their film-star candles with extra thick wicks to give off a greater light.

Today, they stock over 100 different types of candles for church use, including many beeswax candles. But their 32 staff will also make you any candle you want to your specification, as they do for the Royal family. And, for when you want to be in the dark, you can buy a candle extinguisher, too.

Farris's candles are available from agents all round the country – mainly SPCK bookshops. They also supply many churches and the BBC on a direct basis – and may well supply you too.

FRASERS
145 Princes Street
Edinburgh EH2 4YZ
Scotland

Edinburgh (031) 225 2472

House furnishers to HM The Queen.

Frasers' seven-floor department store in the shadow of Edinburgh Castle at the end of Edinburgh's busy Princes Street was originally the brainchild of Robert Maule. In 1856 he first opened a retail draper's at Kincardine-on-Forth and began by selling woollen shawls and tartans which were manufactured at his own factory. Later he moved the business to Leith and took his son Robert into partnership. Father and son moved the shop to its present site in

1894 and extended the range of stock to include china, glass, household, linens, furnishings and children's wear as well as fashion fabrics and costumes.

By the early 1900s when the store received their first Royal Warrant, Robert Maule, junior, had become sole partner. He was knighted in 1913 but died 18 years later leaving the store in the hands of trustees. In 1934 it was taken over by H. Binns, one of the most enterprising store groups in the north of England. In 1953 Binns was in turn taken over by the House of Fraser which controls the group today. Other shops in the group include Harrods (see page 156), the Army and Navy Stores (see page 138), Bairds of Scotland and Switzer of Ireland.

Monday–Friday: 9–5.30; Thursday: 9–8; Saturday: 9–6.

L. G. HARRIS & COMPANY LIMITED
**Stoke Prior
Bromsgrove
Worcestershire B60 4AE**

Manufacturers of painting and decorating brushes to HM The Queen.

The firm of L. G. Harris were started in 1928 when the present chairman of the company, Leslie George Harris, set up an

agency in Birmingham to sell other manufacturers' products on commission. In 1936 they moved out of the city into the small village of Stoke Prior in Worcestershire where they are based today. The major components for brushes are bristle and wood, and Harris pride themselves on being the only brush factory in the country to process the Chinese pigs' hair into bristles. Since 1948 they have been acquiring and planting up devastated areas with hardwoods and now have 2,000 acres of woodland which provides them with the timber for the handles, keeping their imports to a minimum.

Harris are clearly the intellectuals of the brush world. Their witty advertising slogans: 'Before you start think of the finish' and 'Why Harris split hairs', and their excellent brushes have gained them recognition as leading British brush manufacturers. They have held the Royal Warrant since 1961 and today produce a range of products from the smallest ¼-inch paintbrushes to their 24-inch yard brooms. All their products are guaranteed with the promise that 'the bristles won't fall out'.

Harris products are available from DIY shops and hardware and department stores.

In 1951 Harris began to advertise their brushes with a duke and duchess who were depicted in a variety of situations involving Harris brushes

R. R. BEATON.

J. & W. HENDERSON LIMITED
Millbank House
Berryden Road
Aberdeen AB9 2JW
Scotland

Aberdeen (0224) 631617

Suppliers of paint and wallpaper to HM The Queen.

J. & W. Henderson are Scotland's largest builder's merchants. Their Royal Warrant, granted in 1975, is only for their paint and wallpaper division in Berryden Road – though with three acres of selling space that can't be described as small.

The company began as a wholesale business in 1919, and only started retailing in 1967. They now sell to both the trade and the public. In Henderson's vast showroom, they stock thousands of rolls of wallpaper and claim to be able to offer 'any pattern of any manufacturer', though they specialise in Crown wallcoverings. Mr Fraser, Henderson's director, told me their paint department could also cope with any request, from the non-specific 'I want a middle green for my garden shed' to the demanding 'a shade of sandalwood, but not Dulux'.

Last year Henderson started selling ceramics, bathrooms and flat-pack kitchens. There are eight bathrooms on display in front of their showrooms and as many kitchen settings. There's only one drawback – you have to fit them yourself.

Monday–Saturday: 8–5. Thursday: 8–8.
Bring your car – there's room for 485 cars in Henderson's car park.

JENNERS
48 Princes Street
Edinburgh EH2 2YJ
Scotland

Edinburgh (031) 225 2442

Suppliers of furnishing materials to HM The Queen.

Jenners is the crème de la crème of Edinburgh's main shopping street. With its mixture of Jacobean and French architecture it is as much a tourist attraction as the nearby Holyroodhouse. Outside on the parapets, cupids and caryatids look down on the hustle and bustle of Princes Street. Through the solid teak swing doors, along the marble mosaic floor and past counters of Spanish mahogany there is the Grand Hall with its tiered galleries and open roofs – the centre of Jenners.

The original store of Kennington & Jenner opened in 1838 as a result of the two young men being sacked from their jobs when they took a day off to go to the races. Today Jenners is the oldest independent department store in the world and the only one of its kind left in Britain. They earned their reputation as a 'top shop for top people' and to some extent that myth still clings, though Jenners are very keen that they become known as the top shop for everyone.

Jenners hold the Royal Warrant for supplying furnishing fabrics to The Queen, no doubt to be found in the rooms of her Scottish residences, Balmoral and Holyroodhouse. But it is their fashion department that puts them at the top of the league. They carry a wide selection of French, German and Italian labels and stage two fashion shows a year in their Assembly Rooms. Their china and glass shop is the largest anywhere north of London where they sell everything from

Jenners of Princes Street

*Jenners' toy department
in 1895*

limited edition paperweights to handmade perfume flasks. While in the food department, wedding cakes, Christmas puddings, pâté, mustards and marmalade are among Jenners' own specialities.

It is the sort of shop where you would expect to find a silver swizzle stick for £7.70 for your cocktail party or a gold razor at £16.95. It could be said that Jenners have thought of everything: even a chauffeur to park your car and a porter to carry your heavy bags.

Monday–Saturday: 9–5.30. Christmas catalogue available from the above address.

PETER KNIGHT (BEACONSFIELD) LIMITED
45 London End
Beaconsfield
Buckinghamshire HP9 2HP

Beaconsfield (049 46) 5561

and

PETER KNIGHT (ESHER) LIMITED
5 High Street
Esher
Surrey KT10 9QL

Esher (78) 64122

Suppliers of interior furnishings to HM The Queen (Beaconsfield branch) and suppliers of fancy goods and lighting to HM The Queen (Esher branch).

Peter Knight MVO claims his service to The Queen is of 'a highly personal nature'.

Mr Knight started his business in Esher in 1960 offering 'accessories for the home', including cookware, specialised lighting and occasional furniture plus a free interior advisory service. The shop was awarded its first Royal Warrant to The Queen three years after it opened. Mr Knight later opened another shop in a Victorian five-bedroomed house in Beaconsfield. Taking advantage of the rooms, Mr Knight displayed his wares in room sets with styles varying from reproduction to colonial bergère-style chairs, French provincial bureaux and a few modern pieces. In them he put his up-market toys, porcelain, glass and silk flowers – accessories designed to bring 'character' into your room. The shop contains other departments as well, such as lighting, oriental rugs, fabrics, cookware and gifts – where you can buy wine thermometers, inflatable lips (to use as a backrest in the bath) and asparagus cookers. Mr Knight still offers an interior design service, though now the advice is only free if the work is over £250. Otherwise the cost is between £30 and £50. Mr Knight has since opened another shop devoted mainly to cookware, in East Molesley, Surrey.

'Everything for the home from the cellar to the dome' is the slogan of the three shops. Mr Knight ensures their excellent publicity which so impressed Harrods they sent one of their staff along to find out his techniques.

Monday–Saturday: 9–5.30; Wednesday: closed (Beaconsfield branch). Monday–Saturday: 9–5.30; Wednesday: 9–1 (Esher branch).

HENRY NEWBERY & COMPANY LIMITED
51/55 Mortimer Street
London W1N 8AU

Suppliers of furnishing trimmings to HM The Queen.

When you open your castle to the public, Henry Newbery can supply all the furnishing trimmings on either side of the barrier rope, indeed even the rope itself.

Although their showroom is only open to the trade, you can look at Newbery's pattern book – containing over 2,000 stock trimmings: fringes, braids, borders, edgings, tassels and tassel tie-backs – at better-quality furnishing shops. Or send your interior decorator to see them with the curtain fabric of your choice and Henry Newbery can make special two- or three-colour tassel tie-backs to match. But unless you ask for it especially they won't make them in silk – it's just too expensive. At a starting price of £100 for two six-inch tassels you can believe it.

Henry Newbery's standard stock consists mainly of British trimmings, but their team of outworkers can match existing trimmings for you, create new ones or reproduce old ideas from their early brochures. Most trimmings today are in pale pastel shades, 'though we do occasionally supply black', says Mrs Johnson, the sixth generation of her family in the company since their founding in 1782.

Although most of Newbery's records were lost in the war, you can see their trimmings in the most prestigious of places: from the state bed at Althorp House to the interiors of the coaches at the Royal Mews.

Henry Newbery is open to the trade only.

ARTHUR SANDERSON AND SONS LIMITED
52 Berners Street
London W1P 3AD

(01) 636 7800

Suppliers of wallpapers, paints and fabrics to HM The Queen.

When Arthur Sanderson founded the company in 1860, it was to import French wallhangings. It soon became evident that imported wallpapers were inadequate to meet the rising demand and changing tastes of the public. Mr Sanderson felt the quality

of design of British wallpaper at the time was not high enough so he opened his own factory in 1879 and began to print papers by hand-block. He died three years later and was succeeded by his three sons who rapidly installed eight printing machines and increased the number of staff from 40 to 300.

In 1930 Sanderson took over a wallpaper manufacturer, Messrs Jeffrey & Co. of Islington, who were already in charge of the production of Morris & Co. Wallpapers, a company which had been founded by William Morris and contained his collection of pearwood printing blocks. Sanderson took over the printing of Morris wallpapers and when the firm went into liquidation in 1940, Sanderson acquired their stock of wood blocks. Today Sanderson are still making money from their shrewd purchase and are the envy of many wallpaper manufacturers. In 1983 they reprinted 75 wallpapers from the Morris blocks in a collection entitled Morris & Co. They cost from £25 to £120 per roll and should be hung by a professional decorator since they require hand-trimming and are not washable.

In 1965 Sanderson became part of the Decorative Products Division of Reed International. Today they employ 2,200 people weaving textiles for curtains, upholstery fabrics and bedlinen, manufacturing wallcoverings and hand-block printing. Sanderson will also carry out special printings of their designs providing the printing blocks are in good condition – a service they perform for the National Trust.

Monday–Friday: 9.30–5.30; Thursday: 9.30–7; Saturday: 9.30–2.

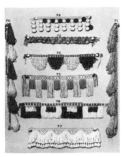

A typical example of special trimmings made by Henry Newbery in their customer's choice of colours as shown in a 1930 catalogue. Newbery's can still make all the trimmings shown

'Celandine' was designed by J. H. Dearle and originally produced in 1869 by Morris & Company. Today it is one of the papers in Sanderson's 'Morris & Co.' range

TISSUNIQUE LIMITED
10 Princes Street
Hanover Square
London W1R 7RD

(01) 491 3386

*Suppliers of furnishing fabrics to HM
The Queen.*

When the company were founded in 1967,
Tissunique's name was cunningly devised
from the words 'tissue', the French for
fabric, and 'unique'.

Tissunique was started to import and
wholesale high-class fabrics of French
origin into this country. Since then they
have specialised in distributing to interior
designers the 'best ranges' of continental
fabrics and wallpapers from 10 different
manufacturers worldwide. They not only
import exceedingly beautiful materials –
from plain chintz, starting at £10 a metre,
to hand-woven damask by Prelle et Cie,
starting at £120 a metre – but have also
begun to commission special ranges of
their own. Their most recent is The
National Trust Collection, a range of six
chintzes specially recreated by Tissunique
and Prelle et Cie from original late 18th-
and early 19th-century chintzes and
printed cottons, still surviving in British
houses.

*Tissunique's elegant showroom is open to
the trade only, but their fabrics are
available through interior designers or
large department stores.*

WARNER & SONS LIMITED
7–11 Noel Street
London W1V 4AL

(01) 439 2411

*Suppliers of silks and furnishing fabrics
to HM the Queen and HM the Queen
Mother.*

From a Distant Land, The Coromandel
Pearl, The Isles of Java, Moongate and
White Crysanthemum; the names of some
of Warner's fabrics could be titles of romantic novels.

Warner & Sons, who have been
supplying the Royal households since
1886, know their fabrics are desirable.
'Silk,' they say, 'will always be in demand
by people who require the look of luxury
and elegance.' Edward V demanded silk
and received it for his coronation. Warner
wove 'the finest of silks, velvets and cloth
of gold' for him, and again for the coronations in 1911, 1937 and 1953.

Today, in conjunction with Greef Fabrics of America, Warner furnish cottages,
offices, stately homes and palaces throughout the world. On display at their Noel
Street showroom – where the receptionist
ensures you are either from the furnishing
trade or a very important customer before
permitting you to enter – they have their
own current selection of several thousand
fabrics and wallcoverings to which they
add new collections every year in spring,
summer and autumn.

Warner are also proud of their extensive
archives containing 30,000 textile samples
which document their woven and printed
furnishing fabrics dating back to 1870. For
each sample the archives indicate the designer (including fabrics by Edward Baw-
den and Arthur Mackmurdo) and year of
production, and if a cloth was produced for
a specific occasion or location this too is
noted. The archives also contain over 2,500
hand-woven samples from the 1820s all of
which are in perfect condition. Warner will
weave or print any of the designs in their
archives to special orders of 120 metres
minimum per colourway. And if none of
their 30,000 samples appeal to you, Warner
will design a fabric for your exclusive use.

Many of Warner's fabrics are still woven
on the same jacquard hand looms which
were bought by Benjamin Warner when he
founded the then silk weaving firm in 1870.
The looms are now the only hand looms
weaving wide silk furnishings commercially in the UK. A cotton chintz fabric

*Above:
'Stamford Borders' from
the National Trust
Collection for Tissunique*

*Right:
'Dauphine' from
Warner's Saint Germain
collection*

from Warner's Personal Choice collection will cost about £25 a metre.

Warner's are open to the trade only. The public can buy their fabrics from department stores, furnishing shops or through their interior designer.

WHYTOCK & REID LIMITED
Belford Mews
Edinburgh EH4 5DN
Scotland

Edinburgh (031) 226 4911

Once Whytock & Reid have renovated your furniture you won't recognise it. One of their 20 cabinet makers will put it together again, one of their polishers will make it sparkle, one of their upholsterers will add the cover and finally one of their sewers will stitch it up. If you wonder why the sofas and chairs in any of the Scottish National Trust houses look so pristine, it is because Whytock & Reid have re-upholstered them.

In pre-war times Whytock & Reid used to 'close' houses when their occupants left Edinburgh for the summer, cleaning the carpets and curtains ready for their return. Today the company will design alterations to your home, decorate your entire house and build the furniture. A custom-built open bookcase starts at £500. Their enormous double storey showroom – designed 10 years ago by an architect from the Lorimar school – is filled with antique and modern furniture ('not pine'). And their five floors of workshops provide space for 30 craftsmen working by traditional methods, as well as designers willing to help you with your special needs.

In 1807 Richard Whycock established his textile manufacturing business in Edinburgh and began pioneering new techniques in the weaving of carpets and damasks. His Brussels carpets have recently been reproduced by Whytock & Reid. In 1838 he received his first Royal Warrant as carpet manufacturer. Meanwhile in 1829 in Ayr, John Reid had completed his seven-year apprenticeship as an upholsterer and started working as an upholsterer and cabinetmaker. By 1851 his firm in Ayr was employing 15 men and seven boys. In 1876 John Reid's three sons went into partnership with Whytock's son, Alexander, to form Whytock, Reid & Company in George Street in Edinburgh. By 1886 the Whytock family had lost interest in the business, but David Reid, who joined the

company in 1964, is now the fifth generation of Reid in the family firm.

Monday–Friday: 9–5.30; Saturday: 9–12.30. Elegant catalogue available showing Whytock & Reid's wide range of sofas and easychairs.

Framed by Arnold Wiggins & Sons

ARNOLD WIGGINS & SONS LIMITED
30–34 Woodfield Place
Harrow Road
London W9 2BJ

(01) 286 9656

Picture-frame makers to HM The Queen and HM the Queen Mother.

'There isn't a major museum in the entire world that hasn't got a Wiggins frame,' says director Mrs Horsman-Lanz. No doubt that includes The Queen's Gallery too.

Arnold Wiggins stock antique frames collected over the years. Choose from miniatures to ones big enough for the largest gallery pictures from all over Europe. They match frames to the appropriate period and claim they can usually offer a choice of every era. They also alter or repair existing frames to match design, colour and tones of originals, or carve new ones to order.

The Wiggins family were cabinet makers in Bethnal Green in the late 19th century: carving, ebonising, polishing and gilding. Eight craftsmen and women continue their tradition today.

To give a quotation, all Arnold Wiggins need are the measurements of your picture and a description – if you want a period frame – then they can work out the amount of footage, carving and moulding needed. On average they take six weeks to make a frame and can arrange collection and delivery.

Monday–Friday: 9–5.30. Telephone Wiggins first for an appointment. Catalogue available. Wiggins also work for customers abroad. All they need are the measurements of the canvas and, if possible, a photograph.

C. H. BRANNAM LIMITED
Litchdon Potteries
Barnstaple
Devon EX32 8NE

Pottery makers to HM The Queen Mother.

These Devonshire potters can make anything from a floral toothbrush holder to a clay bird table. Pottery has been a traditional art in Barnstaple for several hundred years. C. H. Brannam make Royal Barum Ware pottery. They hold the warrant for supplying The Queen Mother's household with items like their Goldenmoments flower pot and saucer – a white traditional shaped pot with a rose design – and their clay flower pots, ranging from 1½ inches to 18 inches in height, which can be found in many of the Royal Estates.

Brannam also make flower vases and a range of kitchen ware in Royal blue and oatmeal glazes, including coffee pots, storage jars, cups, saucers and wine coolers.

Royal Barum Ware is available to the trade from the above address and to the public from garden centres, gift shops and department stores.

Flower arranging

MOYSES STEVENS LIMITED
Berkeley Square
London W1X 5DH

(01) 493 8171

Florists to HM The Queen Mother.

Since 1934 Moyses Stevens have inhabited an extremely impressive, almost intimidating, five-window corner shop in Berkeley Square. Their main line of work is supplying flowers for the chairmen and directors of neighbouring W1 offices. 'We have very few ladies with shopping bags,' said Monica Simmonds, the granddaughter of the founder. 'Our main clients can all be found in Burke's Peerage.'

Moyses Stevens supplied the bouquet for Princess Anne to carry at her wedding and used to sell flowers to the former Prince of Wales, later Edward VIII, before his abdication. They hold a Royal Warrant to The Queen Mother and supply several foreign Royal families. They also deliver abroad. A recent assignment was sending lavish toys and flowers to Saudi Arabia for a children's party.

Since they were founded 110 years ago, Moyses Stevens have boasted of being able to do anything with flowers. They are 'not just flower arrangers' and their displays often include dried flowers or artificial ones (an everlasting single orchid will cost £2) supplied especially from Hong Kong. It means they can provide any flowers in any configuration you want – even out of season.

Monday–Friday: 8.30–5.30; Saturday: 8–1.

Furnishings

JAMES L. ARCHIBALD & SONS LIMITED
6–14 Great Western Road
Aberdeen
Scotland

Aberdeen (0224) 56181

Cabinetmakers and upholsterers to HM The Queen.

In 1901, James L. Archibald, a master cabinet-maker, opened a small shop in Aberdeen. With the outbreak of the Great War, interest in home furnishings declined, so Mr Archibald turned his skill to the manufacture of aircraft parts. Luckily, by 1925 the furnishing business had recovered. Mr Archibald continued with his planned extension of the showroom in the Great Western Road and since then the Archibald family have never looked back.

Today Archibalds turn their hands to many things from selling duvet covers to designing and manufacturing all types of ecclesiastical furniture. In their large corner shop on the Great Western Road they sell furniture, including a large bed selection, aimed at the 'young couple setting up their first home' and carpets, curtains, pillows and other soft furnishings. Archibald Interiors ('our show-house') is only a few doors away, where complete room settings, from traditional to Scandinavian – all slightly predictable – are displayed. Archibalds will offer help on interior design and will bring furniture to your home so you can admire it 'in situ' on a 'no strings attached' scheme.

In 1956 Archibalds were granted their Royal Warrant as cabinetmakers and upholsterers to The Queen. Most of that work is carried out in their contract department and workshops, around the corner in Albury Road. From here they provide a complete furnishing service for offices, executive suites, hotels, reception areas, churches and palaces. Together with your architect, their two interior designers will plan your entire decoration scheme – colour, furnishings and lighting. And, if necessary, their team of 60 specialists including cabinetmakers, french polishers and upholsterers, will make and install whatever furniture is required. Archibalds also deliver free of charge to anywhere in the north-east of Scotland – that includes Balmoral.

Monday–Friday: 8.45–5.30; Saturday: 9.30–4.30 (showroom hours). For contract department telephone: Aberdeen (0224) 56181.

GORDON RUSSELL LIMITED
Broadway
Worcestershire WR12 7AD

Broadway (0386) 853345

Manufacturers of furniture to HM The Queen, suppliers of furniture and furnishings to HM The Queen Mother.

Gordon Russell's desks, cabinets and dining room tables are made from Rio rosewood or American black walnut. They come in sleek functional designs with matching chairs often edged in chrome with contrasting PVC seat coverings. All are made by their craftsmen in Broadway. 'Our products convey prestige in a way that quietly demonstrates executive seniority. Our furniture has a sense of presence.'

Gordon Russell are at home in the boardroom. Their executive furniture is designed with the boss in mind. But they will custom-build items for any purpose, such as the furniture they made for the apartments in Windsor Castle for which they received the Guild Mark of the Worshipful Company of Furniture Makers. Other work made for the Royal family includes a lecture desk and lectern presented by the Duke of Edinburgh, as its President, to the Royal Society of Arts. Gordon Russell hold their warrants for supplying furniture and furnishings to the Royal households, but as a child The Queen first saw an example of their work when they made her a set of wooden building blocks – all of different woods.

Gordon Russell furniture is available from the above address or from Gordon Russell retailers.

THE SHIP'S WHEEL
Traill Street
Thurso
Caithness
Scotland

Thurso (0847) 62485

Furniture and picture restorer to HM The Queen Mother.

You can spot this little antique shop in winter by the huge ship's wheel hanging over the front door, and in summer by the crowd of tourists hovering outside the door, hoping for a glimpse of The Queen Mother.

The wheel was bought by the father of Mrs Munro, the proprietor of the shop, in 1922 for one shilling from a timber yard.

The Queen Mother and her lady-in-waiting, Lady Fermoy, leaving The Ship's Wheel

A selection of stock from The Ship's Wheel, a local haunt of The Queen Mother while staying at Castle of Mey

When the Munro children decided to open their little antique shop in 1952, they thought it might be a good omen. Clearly it was.

The Ship's Wheel is a small but fascinating shop, which as well as selling antiques, also repairs them, from furniture to china. It received its Royal Warrant from The Queen Mother in 1976.

Monday–Saturday: 9–12, then 2–5; Thursday: 9–12. The Ship's Wheel will export antiques anywhere in the world.

D. & R. TAYLOR
107 Norfolk Street
King's Lynn
Norfolk

King's Lynn (0553) 3378

Upholsterers to HM The Queen.

Mr Taylor is a modest man. Although he has worked at Sandringham since 1948, it was only in 1967 that he realised he was eligible to apply for a Royal Warrant.

He started his shop in 1946 and today, at 65, he is still very much involved in the business. He sells everything for the DIY curtain maker, from a wide range of furnishing fabrics, including the warrant-holding Sanderson, Baker and Warner (see pages 33, 26 and 34), to curtain hooks. And 'in a modest way' conducts an interior design service, assisting customers in their decisions about curtains, carpets and furniture. On the same site he also has The Workbox, a haberdashery department. But the warrant-holding side of his business is

his furniture restoration. Mr Taylor is a member of the Association of Master Upholsterers and in his workshop he restores and polishes cabinet furniture and will upholster anything from a chaise longue to an upright chair.

Monday–Saturday: 8.30–5.30.
Wednesday: 9.30–12.30.

Household

ARMY & NAVY STORES LIMITED
101–5 Victoria Street
London SW1E 6QX
(and branches, including their sister store, Barkers of Kensington)

(01) 834 1234

Suppliers of household and fancy goods to HM The Queen and HM The Queen Mother.

The store was established in Victoria Street in 1871 as the Army & Navy Cooperative Society by a group of army and navy officers with a capital of £15,000. The object was to supply its members (shareholders, subscribers and their friends) with articles for domestic use and general consumption at the lowest prices. With a subscription of five shillings a year it was more of a club than a department store.

The Stores could supply members with everything from cradle to grave. For London members they would even decant the port and deliver it before dinner. They would wind their members' clocks once a week and could provide them with theatre tickets, motor cars and a carrying chair in order that they could be borne by natives through tropical jungles.

In 1874 the Stores started manufacturing to keep their prices down. Within 13 years they employed a total of 1,221 specialists.

As the Stores had been established by naval and military personnel, in 1891 the company felt compelled to establish bases

ON ARRIVAL IN THE EAST

ON disembarking at Bombay, Members will find the Society's representative there to meet them, ready to make arrangements for travellers and do everything possible to assist with their baggage, railway tickets, and accommodation. This is the first service that the Society is able to render its members on arrival in India, but one that is of immense assistance to all new-comers to the East.

in India to maintain contact with its many members stationed there. The first one was opened in Bombay, followed by stores in Karachi, Calcutta and others throughout India. They flourished, members were well looked after and trade was developed with government officials, the Indian Civil Service and ruling Princes. One Maharajah gave an order for 12 gross of brassières. Another bought a large store showcase full of watches, silver and other items and installed it in his palace. The branches were all closed after India's Independence in 1947.

In 1897 the company decided that champagne should be withdrawn from the list of free refreshments for staff working overtime. Later, at the beginning of the First World War trade fell. A Canadian member of staff invented the form of tin hat used during the war for which the Stores received a quarter penny royalty from the government for each helmet. With the return of peace, the Store found itself handicapped by its traditions. Although it now opened its doors to everyone, the public did not buy and the technical continuation of membership precluded advertising.

After the Second World War a night telephone system was installed so customers could telephone their orders outside opening hours. Today the job is still done – by an answering machine. In 1953 Army & Navy began to buy department stores, among them Harveys of Guildford, Clarks at Wolverhampton and Harrison Gibson's two stores at Bromley.

In 1973 they started to modernise and rebuild the original Victoria store completely, which took four years. It reopened under the name of the Army & Navy Victoria with four sales floors and a total of 148 departments. Since 1975 they have been part of The House of Fraser.

Mondays, Wednesday and Thursdays: 9–5.30; Tuesdays: 9.30–5.30; Friday and Saturday: 9–6. Army & Navy no longer have a mail order catalogue though they do sell reprints of their 1907 catalogue, 'Yesterday's Shopping'.

*Opposite:
Bellamy's chair and litter, as used in Africa and India, for sale in the Army & Navy catalogue, 1907*

BRYANT & MAY LIMITED
Totteridge Road
High Wycombe
Buckinghamshire HP13 6EJ

Match manufacturers to HM The Queen.

Matches replaced tinder boxes as a more effective method of lighting candles as a result of a happy accident which occurred in Stockton-on-Tees in 1827. A chemist by the name of John Walker was mixing antimony sulphide and potassium chlorate in his pharmacy. On finishing he bent down to scrape the mixing stick on the floor to clean it, and to his utmost surprise the action produced flares.

In 1841, 15 years later, William Bryant and Francis May decided to build an empire on matchsticks. In 1861 they introduced the first safety match called Brymay. It was launched with the slogan 'protection from fire' and with the words 'non-poisonous' in small print. Other brands of matches they produced were called Swan Vestas, Puck, Club Matches and Wax Vestas.

Bryant & May were granted their first Royal Warrant by George V, although he probably never used them quite as much as his cigar-smoking father Edward VII might have done.

Bryant & May matches are available from tobacconists, off-licences and supermarkets.

CALEYS (COLE BROTHERS) LIMITED
High Street
Windsor
Berkshire SL4 1LL

Windsor (95) 63241

Suppliers of household and fancy goods to HM The Queen and suppliers of household and fancy goods and millinery to HM The Queen Mother.

Caleys' small three-floored department store is situated opposite the main gates of Windsor Castle. The history of the store is uncertain, but the first mention of Caley appears in the local press in 1813 when M. Caley, dressmaker and milliner, announced the removal of an established business from Thames Street in Windsor to Castle Street – roughly where the statue of Queen Victoria stands today.

By 1820 Mr Caley was milliner to Queen Victoria as well as The Princesses and The Duchess of Gloucester. In 1824 he set up shop at the present premises in High Street with his brother, John William Caley, haberdasher, silk mercer and lacemaker. By 1853 the shop was known as Caley Brothers, drapers and haberdashers, milliners and dressmakers. Nearly 50 years later they had opened a branch in Piccadilly as well as employing 172 people in the Windsor shop.

In 1940 Caleys became part of the John Lewis Partnership which includes Peter

Jones of Sloane Square in London, where it is rumoured The Prince and Princess of Wales kept one of their wedding lists. The Princess has also been seen shopping at the Peter Jones lingerie department on several occasions.

Caleys carry most of the John Lewis lines. Tuesday–Friday: 9–5.30; Thursday: 9–6.30; Saturday: 9–6. Caleys is closed on Mondays.

CROMPTON PARKINSON LIMITED
Guiseley
Leeds LS20 9NZ

Manufacturers of electric lamps to HM The Queen.

Crompton Parkinson make tungsten 'lamps' in every colour of the rainbow and fluorescent tubes in eight shades of white, from Northlight (which closely matches the northern sky light) to their De Luxe Natural (particularly good for restaurants or food displays). They also manufacture a range of special 'lamps' – ones that simulate candle flames for use in Royal dining room chandeliers, low light bulbs for Prince William's nursery, floodlight lamps for deterring intruders and Charmlight, 'to flatter complexions'. They have lit up the Royal family since 1949.

Crompton Parkinson lamps are available to the trade from the above address and to the public from all electrical, hardware and department stores.

SHIRRAS, LAING & COMPANY LIMITED
46/52 Schoolhill
Aberdeen
Scotland

Aberdeen (0224) 645242

Ironmongers to HM The Queen.

On both sides of the corner shop, in large gold Victorian capital letters are the words 'Shirras, Laing & Co. Ltd, Purveyors to the Queen'. The building was designed and built for Shirras Laing in 1890, and the lettering refers to Queen Victoria.

The beginnings of one half of the company date back to 1829 when James Laing set up in business as an ironmonger, later expanding the sphere of his work to include bell-hanging as well. In 1841, the other half of the firm began when William

Shirres (later Shirras) started his business as a tinsmith. The two companies amalgamated in 1885 to form Shirras, Laing & Co. operating as tinsmiths and electrical engineers. In 1889 they were awarded their first Royal Warrant by Queen Victoria as purveyors of braziery (iron baskets which contained lit charcoal or coke and acted as portable heaters, presumably in those days vital in Balmoral). Most of Shirras Laing's business was, however, in making the street lanterns for Aberdeen and ranges of railway and domestic oil lamps. They are also believed to have been the first electrical contractor in the city, wiring such buildings as the Town House and Marischal College. In 1902 their electric light department was declared 'still unremunerative' and closed.

Shirras Laing today hold their Royal Warrant as ironmongers, even though their shop has become a household store, selling mainly high-quality cookware, china and glass.

Monday–Friday: 9–5.30. Saturday: 9–1.

Kitchen and bathroom

GLYNWED CONSUMER & BUILDING PRODUCTS LIMITED
Batman's Hill
Bilston
West Midlands WV14 8UP

Manufacturers of kitchen and bathroom equipment to HM The Queen.

The Glynwed Group are the parent company of Vogue Bathrooms (formerly Allied Ironfounders) and Leisure Kitchens, both of whom supply equipment for these very important places in the Royal palaces.

You can choose from Vogue's Florida, Caribbean or Bermuda designs. Whichever you decide on, Vogue say that as soon as you fit one of their baths in your bathroom it will become 'your favourite resort'. Vogue are Britain's largest manufacturers of porcelain enamelled cast iron baths. They have been making them for over 100 years and there are now about 12 million in use in the UK. Look out for their Elysian Lacro Spa whirlpool too.

Leisure Kitchens were bought by Glynwed in 1970. They claim to be the first manufacturers of both the modern stainless steel sink and the combined sink and drainer coated in vitreous enamel and pioneers of the 'continental style' inset sink which became popular in the UK in the 1950s. They say their latest sinks have a 'shade more style'. They come in a choice of eight colours and with either a shiny or ceramic-effect surface. Leisure also make showers, cubicles and vanity basins.

Glynwed kitchen and bathroom products are available from all major department stores and specialist kitchen and bathroom shops.

HUBBARD REFRIGERATION LIMITED
**The Street
Martlesham
Woodbridge
Suffolk IP12 4RE**

Woodbridge (039 43) 4181

Suppliers of automatic ice-making machines to HM The Queen Mother.

In 1965, Hubbard imported their first Scotsman ice-making machine from America and started trading. Now after only a relatively short time in business, they can already boast a Royal Warrant from The Queen Mother and a Scotsman back-up service of engineers, maintenance and technical staff in almost every country from Honduras to the Ivory Coast.

The Scotsman machines make three sizes of ice cubes, from delicate gin and tonic size to the large variety handy for filling up the champagne buckets. An additional

flaker fitted to the machine can provide even, regular grains – pretty enough to make a nice bed for the lobsters or a firm foundation for cocktails. Hubbard's smallest model produces 35 pounds of ice a day and their largest, the Continuous Flow Cuber, up to 1,232 pounds.

Hubbard have rapidly built up their share of the ice-machine market to about 70 per cent of the trade. They claim their machines are unique as they 'spray water vertically upwards into inverted cups where the ice is formed' while most ice machines produce ice on a cutter grid system. And in true unabashed American style, the Scotsman brochure states: 'We are not afraid to say that the ice made with our machines is the most pure, hygienic, crystal clear ice that one could ask for.'

Scotsman ice machines are available from the above address.

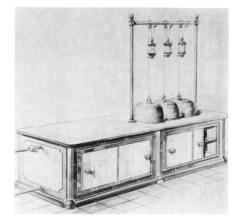

Parks and Gardens

Dogs

A. NEAVERSON & SONS LIMITED
Peakirk
Near Peterborough
Cambridge PE6 7NN

Peterborough (0733) 252225

Dog kennel manufacturers to HM The Queen.

Although The Queen's corgis have never visited Neaverson's workshops, Royal gundogs have been sleeping in Neaverson's kennels for years: 40 of their quorn (gundog) kennels have been sold to Balmoral and Sandringham. The kennels are a foot larger than the standard size, but no special Royal fittings were requested.

The kennels are made of Russian timber, 'the best quality', according to Arthur Neaverson, the founder's grandson, and they claim to make everything they sell. The cheapest kennel costs £52.

Her Majesty The Queen first heard about Neaverson through the Royal grapevine, when one of her former land agents on the Sandringham estate bought some kennels from them in the 1960s. Neaversons were granted their Royal Warrant in 1970.

Monday–Friday: 9–5.30; Saturday: 9–12.30 (ring first). Mail order catalogue available.

SPRATT'S PATENT LIMITED
New Malden House
1 Blagdon Road
New Malden
Surrey KT3 4TB

Suppliers of dog foods to HM The Queen.

Before the middle of the 18th century no one had thought about what pets should eat. In 1860 James Spratt, noticing this gap in the market, set about developing a special biscuit for dogs designed to provide a nourishing, balanced diet. He prepared

Single quorn kennel from Neaversons – home of Royal gundogs

his new dog cake from 'the gelatinous parts of the finest Beef-Cattle from the Prairies' together with biscuit, flour, oats and barley malt meal. He tested the cakes on his own dogs and patented the recipe in 1862. James Spratt then opened a shop at 28 High Holborn, London, and became his own publicity agent, so successfully that four years later he employed his first assistant, a 14-year-old called Charles Cruft who later founded Crufts Dog Show.

One of Charles Cruft's main duties at the shop was book-keeping. He kept careful records of both private and trade buyers, distinguishing the latter by placing an 'X' beside their names in the ledger. From then on it became Spratt's trademark and every biscuit was stamped with an 'X' to distinguish it from any rival biscuits. Charles Cruft became the company's first travelling salesman, placing so many orders that in 1870 the company had to buy a factory in Bermondsey. Mr Spratt died 10 years later and shortly afterwards Mr Cruft retired to develop the Crufts Dog Show, but the company had already established itself. In 1904 a further factory was built at Poplar.

During the First World War Spratt's efforts were diverted into the manufacture of biscuits for humans. Over 70,000 tons were produced and Spratt's continued supplying biscuits during the Second World War. The company were also involved in supplying biscuits for the crews and husky dogs of various Polar expeditions. A misunderstanding occurred on the Anglo-American expedition to Greenland when a larger quantity of dog biscuits were delivered than had been ordered. When the

The outside of a Blackpool shop in 1949 covered with Spratt's advertisements. Note the different Spratt's logotypes for birds, dogs and cats

team returned in 1933, the commander wrote to Spratt's: 'May I take this opportunity of telling you how excellent the biscuits were, not only for our dogs but for ourselves. We ran out of flour and for the last three months of the expedition your biscuits took the place of bread.'

In 1960 Spillers, a major food company, acquired overall control of Spratt's. Spratt's Patent Ltd still manufacture a wide range of products such as Big Value tinned dog food, Flavoured Bones dog biscuits and Weetmeet – favoured by the Royal dogs. They have recently started manufacturing a range of rabbit, guinea pig and gerbil foods. Spratt's also run an animal travel service, most notably used when they shipped the first dog back to the Falklands. They will transport any animal anywhere in the world and deal with legal and medical problems.

Spratt's pet foods are available from most pet shops and supermarkets throughout the country.

Garden parties

BLACK & EDGINGTON PLC
29 Queen Elizabeth Street
Tower Bridge
London SE1 2LU

(01) 407 3734

Tent and Flag makers to HM The Queen and HM The Queen Mother.

Black & Edgington are so popular that if you wanted them to arrange a marquee for your party this summer you would have had to book them by Christmas last year. Although Black & Edgington have thousands of tents for hire, during the summer they are often in use at Royal garden parties, Henley Regatta, Wimbledon or the Farnborough Air Show – for which they supply all the tents.

Black & Edgington have held their Royal Warrant since they were first granted it by Queen Victoria. Today they work mainly for industrial clients installing marquees for exhibitions. But they also stock tents which can be adjusted to fit your garden. Blacks will visit the garden and design you a marquee that fits both your home and your purse with a range of different finishes for both inside and out. They can even make a marquee that will look just like the inside of your house. They will then deliver, erect, dismantle and remove it. For a 15-by-30-foot garden, the price will start at £450. From Blacks you could also buy the flag to put on top.

Monday–Friday: 9–4.30. Telephone Black & Edgington to come and look at your garden and give you a quotation.

CRAWFORDS CATERING
Easter Dalry House
Distillery Lane
Edinburgh EH11 2BD
Scotland

Edinburgh (031) 337 7978

Caterers to HM The Queen.

Crawfords suggested menus include such delicacies as quails' eggs in aspic jelly, suprème of chicken chaud froid and fresh pears poached in port. With over 50 years of experience, Crawfords have an excellent reputation for catering for every type of event from state banquets, sports tournaments and exhibitions to the annual Royal garden party at Holyroodhouse.

Crawfords supply four standard menus ranging from finger buffets to banquets – all with dishes to make your mouth water. Their chefs enjoy creating special dishes to suit the occasion. Crawfords can also provide waitress service and will decorate and fully furnish marquees. As they say: 'Just give us a venue, a guest list and a budget and we will take care of the rest. No event is too large or too small for Crawfords.' They usually cater for 10,000 people at the Royal garden party.

Telephone Crawfords for a quotation and their brochure.

KIMBOLTON FIREWORKS
7 High Street
Kimbolton
Huntingdon
Cambridgeshire PE18 0HB

Huntingdon (0480) 860498

'Royal ladies are not so wild about fireworks, but Lord Mountbatten loved them and so do The Duke of Kent and Prince Charles.' Kimbolton Fireworks have been in charge of the fireworks displays for many Royal occasions including the anniversary of The Queen's coronation celebrations in 1978 and at her Silver Jubilee display. They also arranged the displays for The Queen Mother's 80th birthday in 1980. Kimbolton displays are seen regularly at events like the Henley Regatta, the Cambridge Festival, the Aldeburgh Carnival and the Eurovision Song Contest.

The idea of the vicar owning a fireworks factory might sound odd but The Reverend Mr Lancaster who started Kimbolton Fireworks in 1964 is quick to point out the relationship between fireworks and the Church. 'All over the world fireworks are used for religious festivals. There's a church in Malta which has fireworks made especially for Saint's Day, so there's no real incompatibility.' Reverend Lancaster grew up in Huddersfield, one of the main areas

Spot The Queen. One of the June 1983 garden parties at Buckingham Palace with marquees provided by Black & Edgington

of firework production in England. Fireworks were always one of his great hobbies. Today he runs the factory alongside his work for the Church and his job as the village schoolmaster.

Reverend Lancaster and his team like to have total control over their displays. 'Making fireworks is very creative. It's a mixture of aesthetics and chemistry,' he said. 'Sometimes there are people at the event who have artistic interests and want the fireworks to do things that the fireworks won't do.' Kimbolton Fireworks know exactly what to do. They have the capability to manufacture every type of firework and make most of their own, including the classic Roman candles, Caprice ('horizontal wheels, gold changing to silver') and the Rocket ('without which no display is complete').

Reverend Lancaster has four teams of operators who travel all over the country and the continent to carry out their displays. The minimum price for such a display is between £800 and £1,000. The 'whole works' from the Kimbolton team could cost between £15,000 and £20,000 and will need between six and eight people to stage. For that price Reverend Lancaster says 'the sky really is the limit'.

In school term, telephone the above number before 8.45 a.m. or after 4.00 p.m. Kimbolton Fireworks also make home-packs from £50, for you to set up your own display and they run a free 'teach-in' course once every two years to show you how to use fireworks properly. Products and details of the course available by mail from the above address.

JOE LOSS LIMITED
Morley House
Regent Street
London W1

(01) 580 1212

'Whether I am playing at Buckingham Palace, Windsor Castle, aboard the *QE2* or in any establishment anywhere in the world, every night is a première for me,' Joe Loss

said. Since 1930 when he became Britain's youngest bandleader, his thousands of 'premières' have established him as a household name. Today his music is literally played round the world on the *QE2*, where he has been resident bandman for the past 10 years.

Joe Loss, who was born in the East End of London, began his 'love affair' with music at the age of six. His parents wanted him to become a classical violinist, but Mr Loss loved dance music. Today he still loves it and his work has been honoured by many different people. His personal life was filmed twice for *This is Your Life*. The

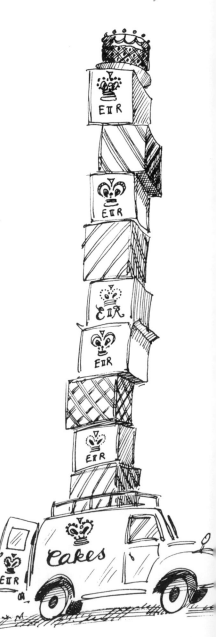

Joe Loss Orchestra was the first Western dance band ever to appear in China at the invitation of the Chinese authorities. In 1978 he was awarded the Order of the British Empire (OBE) and appointed a Member of the Royal Victorian Order (MVO) by The Queen in 1984. Mr Loss performs annually for the Royal family. He played at the pre-wedding balls of Princess Anne, Princess Margaret and Princess Alexandra; at the 70th birthday party of The Queen Mother, and was flown halfway round the world from the *QE2* to provide the music for the 50th birthday party of Her Majesty The Queen.

Today The Joe Loss Orchestra still plays for private parties and charity functions. There are 14 members of the band, some of whom have been playing with him for 20 years. The cost of hiring a five-piece band starts at £700 and the entire band, including Mr Loss himself, from £2,000. The music varies from standards, big-band music to chart music and of course, the famous 'In The Mood', Joe Loss's signature tune.

The Joe Loss Orchestra can be contacted at the above address.

ANDREW WILSON & SONS LIMITED
St Ann's Mount
39 Spring Gardens
Abbeyhill
Edinburgh
Scotland

Edinburgh (031) 661 2485

Catering equipment hirers to HM The Queen.

Andrew Wilson & Sons are situated opposite Holyroodhouse The Queen's official residence in Edinburgh which Her Majesty lives in for one week of the year. This is usually at the beginning of July when she is visiting Edinburgh for official functions. The company have held their Royal Warrant since 1946 for supplying catering equipment for the Royal garden parties held in the grounds there, and which approximately 10,000 people attend.

Andrew Wilson & Sons started in 1880 when Mrs Margaret Wilson, the grandmother of the present managing director, Robert Wilson, opened a small shop at Norton Park in Edinburgh where she sold crockery. Frequently asked by customers if they could hire equipment, she decided to expand that side of her business. Her main clients then were small church groups, working men's clubs and later, during the First World War, the Services. By 1937 Mrs Wilson's daughter-in-law, Sarah, had joined the business and she shrewdly bought all the catering equipment which was being sold off at a local country mansion. This proved to be invaluable when the Wilsons occasionally helped out the NAAFI services in catering for Second World War troops.

Today, although 90 per cent of the Wilsons' business is to hotels and outside caterers, they also cater for parties of 10 or more. The 150-year-old house used to have a lawn in front of it where parties could be held, but it is now used as a warehouse to hold the Wilsons' many pieces of silver – measured in tons rather than by numbers – and other priceless items. The firm can supply anything from a mustard spoon to a portable dance floor, and recreate a gothic scene, with silver goblets and wooden turrets, or the inside of the Café Royal – which they did for the film *Chariots of Fire*.

Monday–Friday: 8–12.30; 1.30–5. Andrew Wilson & Sons have a 'Hire price list' available. They deliver throughout Scotland.

A wedding reception held in the 1930s in Andrew Wilson & Sons' front lawn

Below:
The silver plated plates and salvers are often hired from Andrew Wilson & Sons for medieval banquets

Nurseries

ABBEY ROSE GARDENS
Nashdom Lane
Burnham
Buckinghamshire

Burnham (062 86) 3000

Rose growers and nurserymen to HM The Queen.

Abbey Rose Gardens are the only rose growers in England to hold a Royal Warrant which they have done since 1977. From their two nurseries in Buckinghamshire they supply the Royal gardens with rose bushes, climbers, standards, miniatures, shrubs, conifers and fruit trees.

The firm is a small business which has been run by the Newman family since they founded Abbey Rose in 1951. The Queen's Superintendent of Gardens inspects their rose field each summer and selects specific varieties for the private gardens at Windsor Castle less than 20 miles away. Abbey Rose also supply plants to the Crown Estates for Windsor Park.

Their catalogue contains over 150 different roses, from £1.40 for a bush hybrid tea rose to £12.50 for a weeping standard rose. Abbey Rose helpfully include a chapter on planting and pruning roses as well as general garden tips.

Monday–Friday: 9–1, 2–5; Saturday: 9–1, 2.30–4.30; Sunday: 10–1. Saturdays and Sundays only from October to December, and March to May (Nashdown Lane nursery). Abbey Rose gift vouchers are also available from £5.00. Contact them at the above address for their mail order catalogue.

CARTERS TESTED SEEDS LIMITED
Upper Dee Mills
Llangollen
Clwyd LL20 8SD
Wales

Seedsmen to HM The Queen and HM The Queen Mother.

In Carters' memorandum book for 4 January 1886, in neat copperplate writing, one can read: 'Messrs Cater & Co. appointed Seedsmen by Royal Warrant to Her Majesty the Queen.' Presumably the writer was so overwhelmed by the Royal favour that he misspelt the name of his own firm.

The first published reference to Carters appeared in the London Directory of 1804, when James Carter practised as an apothecary and herbalist in London's Drury Lane. On one of his visits to the continent he bought a small quantity of Aster seed to give to his customers as a spring gift. He received so many flattering letters in thanks that he decided to sell seed on a commercial basis. Before long herbalism was taking second place.

During the 19th century, Britain was developing as a horticultural nation and Carters quickly became seedsmen of international repute. They supplied seeds to Delhi for the Viceroy's garden and in 1906 were summoned to the Cannes golf links by the Grand Duke Michael of Russia, uncle of Czar Nicholas II. As a result, two of the Cannes golf courses were resown with Carters seeds. Carters also laid the Wimbledon tennis courts and continue to supply seeds for the All England Lawn Tennis and Croquet Club. Today the lawn seed mixture is constantly adjusted to cope with the rigorous demands made on the turf now the pace of the game has increased.

Carters have held their Royal Warrant continuously since that first warrant awarded by Queen Victoria. Today they supply seeds to Sandringham for the gardens which are open to the public in the summer, and to Windsor Castle. In the past Carters have also held many foreign Royal Warrants, including those for the Kings of Belgium, Italy, Portugal and Siam.

Carters Tested Seeds are available from gardening shops and department stores.

DOBBIE & COMPANY LIMITED
Melville Nursery
Lasswade
Midlothian EH18 1AZ
Scotland

Edinburgh (031) 663 1941

Seedsmen and nurserymen to HM The Queen.

Dobbie have held their Royal Warrant since the early 1960s when they became 'The Scottish Royal Seed Establishment'. Since then their business has changed. They now concentrate on producing a wide range of trees and shrubs, specialising in Ericaceous stock such as rhododendrons. Their rhododendrons have some fairly aristocratic names: Lord Roberts,

Opposite:
This Royal portrait was taken to commemorate The Queen Mother's 70th birthday in 1970. Cecil Beaton took the photograph in amongst the azaleas at Royal Lodge, Windsor

Lady C. Mitford and the Marchioness of Landsdowne – described as 'a lilac rose with a black eye'.

Dobbie were founded in Rothesay in 1965 by James Dobbie, a retired chief constable of Renfrewshire. Today the company produce about £500,000 of stock a year. They sell wholesale to public authorities and landscape contractors and hold the Royal Warrant for supplying all types of hardy nursery stock to the Royal households – mainly trees, shrubs and roses for their Scottish Estates, Balmoral and Holyroodhouse.

Monday–Saturday: 8–5; Sunday: 10–5 (Melville Nursery). For opening hours of the three other Scotstock nurseries – of which Dobbie are one – telephone the above number. Mail order catalogue available.

HILLIER NURSERIES (WINCHESTER) LIMITED
Ampfield House
Ampfield
Romsey
Hampshire SO5 9PA
(and garden centres)
Braishfield (0794) 68733

Nurserymen and seedsmen to HM The Queen and HM The Queen Mother.

Hillier Nurseries describe Prince Charles as 'smooth, vigorous and fairly fragrant'. His Royal Highness might be flattered but at Hillier they are talking about roses. The Prince Charles Rose is one of 8,000 plants and shrubs listed in Hillier's catalogue, designed to turn the most naive gardener into an expert horticulturalist.

The company was started in 1864 by Edwin Hillier, the grandfather of Sir

Opposite:
The cover of Suttons' catalogue in 1887 printed in high imperial style to commemorate Queen Victoria's Golden Jubilee

Harold Hillier, the current President, who bought a small nurseryman's and florist's business in Winchester. When Harold Hillier took over the family firm in 1953, the total land holding was about 70 acres. Today they have over 500 acres of land which includes the 115-acre Arboretum founded by Sir Harold, itself stocked with some 14,000 different specimens of trees and shrubs.

In 1953 Sir Harold received the highest award of the Royal Horticultural Society, the Victorian Medal of Honour – instituted to commemorate the reign of Queen Victoria – and limited to only 63 holders, all of whom must be British horticulturists, resident in the UK. Although insistent that he is a plant-collector, 'I'm not a gardener really', Sir Harold's knowledge of gardening was possibly most strangely put to the test a few years ago, when the producer of *Mastermind* asked him to set the questions. A contestant had selected 'trees of temperate lands' as her special subject and as the producer later remarked: 'that really stumped us until we lighted on Harold Hillier, Horticulturist to The Queen Mother'.

Hillier's relationship with the Royal family can be traced back to 1936, when The Duke and Duchess of York visited the Winchester nursery at West Hill, with only a quarter of an hour's notice of their intention to call. The Queen Mother returned 42 years later, this time to open the Hillier Aboretum. Now Hillier supply several Royal households.

Hillier's five garden centres are open Monday–Saturday: 8.30–5; Sunday: 8.30–4. Hillier's Trees and Shrubs manual costs £5.95 (paperback) or £10.95 (hardback). It contains 'practical advice and botanical expertise relating to some 8,000 trees, shrubs and climbing plants hardy in the northern hemisphere'.

BEN REID & COMPANY LIMITED
Pinewood Park Nurseries
Countesswells Road
Aberdeen AB9 2QL
Scotland
Aberdeen (0224) 38744

Nurserymen and seedsmen to HM The Queen.

At the turn of the century, Benjamin Reid enjoyed blowing their trumpet. In the halcyon year of the Diamond Jubilee they published in their catalogue a list of over 90 British aristocrats who bought from them, headed by Queen Victoria, whom they had 'had the honour of supplying with seeds and plants for the past forty-eight years'. This Scottish firm of nurserymen and seedsmen still supply the seeds for the Royal Estates, plus a full range of forest trees and shrubs.

So today when you wander among the landscaped grounds of a stately home, many of the tall trees you see now may have come from a Ben Reid sapling. And if you've grand acres to fill you can still buy from them seedlings of forest trees – both conifer and deciduous – from £30 a thousand. The nursery also sells high-quality shrubs, alpines, fruit trees, roses, bulbs and bedding plants.

Monday–Friday: 9–12 then 1–4.30. Mail order catalogue available. Ben Reid gift tokens for any amount from 50p upwards.

SUTTONS SEEDS LIMITED
Hele Road
Torquay
Devon TQ2 7QJ

Torquay (0803) 62011

Seedsmen to HM The Queen and HM The Queen Mother.

John Sutton founded the House of Sutton in Reading in 1806 during the reign of

'Farmer' George III. The House of Sutton was a small corn merchant's dealing in agricultural seeds, corn and grasses for pastures. Later his son, Martin, a botanist, joined him in the business and they began to take advantage of the penny post and the new railway network for mailing their seeds to customers all over the country. Suttons soon became the pioneers of the mail order seed business.

Inevitably mail order brought the first illustrated catalogues and Suttons were soon producing their own annual seed catalogue. In 1885 they were granted their first Royal Warrant by Queen Victoria which prompted them to start producing special edition covers to commemorate Her Majesty's jubilee anniversaries. Their 1897 catalogue with its gold embossed design on a dark green background containing nearly 200 pages of text has since become a collector's item.

Suttons also named their latest vegetables in honour of the occasion. For Queen Victoria's Golden Jubilee they introduced the Royal Jubilee Pea, 'the largest and most distinct ever produced'. And for her third jubilee they brought out a giant-sized 12-inch runner bean, Suttons Best of All, which can still be bought today.

Despite the bitter blows of the First World War, Suttons continued to flourish under Royal patronage. By 1935 they had grown to such an extent they were able to list 18 new sweet peas in their catalogue as well as a new late potato called The Duke of Kent – a bargain at £1 for 14 pounds. In the 1960s a key innovation was the development of their own moisture vapour transmission proof laminates, Sutton's Harvest Fresh foil seed packets, which they say allow them to offer seeds in 'harvest fresh' condition.

In 1976 the company moved from Reading to Torquay. Although some seed crops are home grown, most of Suttons' seeds are grown in the sunnier climates of France, Italy and California and then transported to Torquay for packing. As in the early days much of their business is still done through mail order. As soon as their catalogue is sent out around the country, orders start pouring in – at about 3,000 a day.

Suttons mail order catalogue is available from the above address. Their products can also be bought over the counter at over 7,000 shops, garden centres and department stores in the UK, or from Suttons Trial Grounds at Stoke Gabriel in Devon.

WILLIAM WOOD & SON LIMITED
Bishop House
Bath Road
Taplow
Berkshire SL4 0NY

Burnham (062 86) 4321

Garden contractors and horticultural builders to HM The Queen and HM The Queen Mother.

William Wood & Son design landscapes which 'bring back the lost countryside to the very heart of our towns and villages'. It was William Wood who planted the 12 30-foot high plane trees at the north and south entrances of the US Embassy in London, constructed both the outside and inside landscapes at Brent Cross Shopping Centre and hid many new motorways by replanting trees and shrubs on the adjacent verges and embankments.

William Wood's business was very different 30 years ago. Their 1950 catalogue shows photographs of rose gardens in Buckinghamshire, lawns in Wiltshire and York-stone fountains in London all viewed through gothic windows and brick arches. But although the company have changed, they still design and make anything from an artificial lake to a roof garden; even if it means carrying all the materials over the rooftops.

William Wood were started in 1850 to sell coal and building materials, but since the 1890s they have been making horticultural fantasies come true. Their first Royal Warrant was granted in 1901 by Edward VII as horticultural specialists, another in 1934 to The Prince of Wales (later Edward VIII) as hard court constructors, and since 1938 as garden constructors and horticultural builders both to George VI and today to The Queen and The Queen Mother. William Wood have been through a lot of changes – presumably the grass is always greener on the other side.

For quotations and current catalogue telephone William Wood at the above number. 'The price of a town garden could vary enormously from £1,000 to £50,000 depending on what is required.'

Signs

IRS LIMITED
Lion Works
Castleacre Road
Swaffham
Norfolk PE37 7HS

Swaffham (0760) 21399

Sign and notice makers to HM The Queen.

IRS make signs as small as those 'press', 'on' and 'off' buttons on control panels to signs as large as a house used on motorways. They also make signs as prestigious as the heraldic emblems at the entrances to cities and towns, and for insurance companies and banks.

IRS started in 1930 to make traffic signs in line with the Road Traffic Act and now make all the Ministry of Transport signs. A road sign lasts 10 to 15 years. They were awarded a Royal Warrant in 1981 for the car park and nature walk signs at the Royal parks. They will make private signs for any purpose and always have in stock signs mandatory under the Health and Safety regulations.

Monday–Friday: 8–5.30. Contact IRS at the above address to discuss your sign ideas.

Tennis courts

EN–TOUT–CAS PLC
Syston
Leicester
Leicestershire LE7 8NP

Leicester (0533) 696471

Tennis court manufacturers to HM The Queen.

En-tout-cas have been making sports surfaces since 1910. Their first tennis court, Red Championship, a red shale court with a surface of loose shale dressing to allow slide, was sold all over the world. Soon both their tennis courts and athletics tracks were commissioned by governments, clubs, individuals and Royalty. In the First World War nearly 300 tennis courts were made at various naval depots, military camps and aerodromes so as to provide open-air exercise and recreation for the officers. The company became established as the builders of courts to the All England

Club at Wimbledon, a position they still hold today. In 1948, En-tout-cas built a track for the Olympic games and in 1954 Roger Bannister ran the first four-minute mile on one of their tracks.

En-tout-cas were awarded their first Royal Warrant by George V in 1919 and they still hold one today as tennis court manufacturers, although The Queen is not very interested in tennis, leaving the bestowing of the Royal blessing on Wimbledon to The Duke and Duchess of Kent. En-tout-cas build every type of sports and athletic surface, either purpose-designed for a specific sport or adapted for multi-sports use. They formulate surfaces specifically for the climate in which they are to be located and make tennis courts with 13 different types of surface. At the top end of the market is their Savanna court (approximately £20,000 plus VAT) which promises 'the excitement of playing on grass – all year round'. The bladed granular surface not only looks as good as real grass but works more efficiently, draining quickly after heavy rains and requiring minimal maintenance. All En-tout-cas need to lay one of their courts is to be shown the site and given the go-ahead. Six weeks later the court will be ready. But if you want En-tout-cas to make you a tennis court you have to plan ahead. They are very busy, especially in the spring.

En-tout-cas have branches throughout the UK and will make tennis courts around the world. Contact them at their above address and they will put you in touch with one of their sales administrators.

Thatchers

ROBIN FRASER CALLANDER
Haughend
Finzean
Aberdeenshire
Scotland

Feughside (033 045) 264

Drystane dyker to HM The Queen.

Robin Fraser Callander took a university degree in geology, but today he works as a self-employed drystane dyker, building and repairing traditional dry-stone walls.

Balmoral Castle, near Ballater in Aberdeenshire, is one of The Queen's private residences. 'Balmoral' is Gaelic for 'the majestic dwelling'. The castle is built of granite in the Scots baronial style

Although dry-stone walls look like a random arrangement of stones, the skill lies in balancing the stones so that the wall is solid, as no materials are used to cement the stones together. The job involves moving one ton of stone an hour – when weather and daylight permit. Mr Callander taught himself by maintaining and repairing his own stone walls and then learnt more from an old craftsman. Nine years ago he bought a derelict croft at Finzean near the Balmoral Estates and discovered the last Royal drystane dyker had died 50 years earlier so there was a considerable amount of work to be done in repairing the old stone walls on the Balmoral Estates, including Birkhall (The Queen Mother's Balmoral Estate).

Mr Callander is also a skilled heather thatcher. He taught himself from books as the craft had died out entirely in Scotland. Heather thatching is considered superior to reed and straw thatching since heather thatched roofs last between 60 and 100 years. The heather blanket which is placed on the roof is up to 15 inches thick with much of the bulk composed of the woody stems. Since learning the skills, Mr Callander has published books on heather thatching and drystane dyking which 'have had surprisingly high sales in north-east Scotland'.

For further details about Mr Callander's drystane dyking and heather thatching services, or his books, contact him at the above address.

FARMAN & SON
Station Road
Salhouse
Norwich
Norfolk NOR 5SZ
Norwich (0603) 720294
Reed thatchers to HM The Queen.

'Thatching is dying out,' Mr Farman told me. 'Well, the work isn't, but the thatchers are.'

Mr Farman is the fourth generation of Farman in the business and today he works with his son. The company used to venture into the neighbouring counties but Mr and Master Farman will only work in Norfolk where there are enough roofs to keep them busy. They were awarded their Royal Warrant over 20 years ago for work done on the roofs of the stables and summerhouses on the Sandringham Estate.

The Farmans use only the best Norfolk reeds for their roofs and work in much the same way as their forefathers did, using pins rather than ropes and making roofs 12 inches thick to provide superb insulation. Mr Farman told me that one of his thatched roofs is unlikely to need much repair attention for 60 odd years, but to re-thatch will cost between £3,000 and £5,000.

If you live in Norfolk and would like your roof thatched, contact Farman & Son at the above address.

Keeping up Appearances

Chemists

ALLEN & NEALE (CHEMISTS) LIMITED
55 High Street
King's Lynn
Norfolk

King's Lynn (0553) 2459

Chemists to HM The Queen.

Allen & Neale are situated right 'on the doorstep of Sandringham'. Since 1822 there has been a chemist's shop on the site that Allen & Neale now occupy, but it was first in 1890 that the company were established.

Although Allen & Neale have held their Royal Warrant since 1950 it is only as chemists. They are also small manufacturers specialising in toiletries and can make up combination oils to your requirements from pot pourri, rosemary, cinnamon, lemon, lavender and bergamot oils. They also sell their own Melamond hair lotion 'which adds lustre to grey hair'.

Monday–Saturday: 9–5.30; Wednesday: 9–5.

D. R. HARRIS & COMPANY LIMITED
29 St James's Street
London SW1A 1HB

(01) 930 8753

Chemists to HM The Queen Mother.

In the tiny laboratory behind the chemist's shop, piled high with glass jars and cardboard boxes, Trevor Harris and his small team of assistants still make many of the toiletries found in the shop. The crushed rose petals are there ready to be transferred into White Rose perfume and the pots of honey to be added to the Florimel hair tonic. But the one secret kept by Mr Harris is the essential part of his Milk of Cucumber and Roses. The cucumber mixture is made by Mr Harris at home and brought into the shop in buckets when it is ready to be added to the rest of the ingredients.

Since 1790 this family business has served the gentry and the court of St James's. In 1938 they were granted their first Royal Warrant as chemists to Her Majesty The Queen, now the Queen Mother. A Victorian decor is the setting for their wonderful concoctions. Their bath oils are apparently the silkiest, their shaving creams the most adventurous – in almond, cologne, rose and lavender – and their Pick-Me-Up (at £1.85 for 100 ml) still as effective a cure for hangovers as it has been for over 100 years.

Monday–Friday: 8.30–6; Saturday: 9.30–5. Mail order catalogue available from D. R. Harris & Co.

J. & D. MURRAY
10 Bridge Street
Ballater
Aberdeenshire AB3 5QP
Scotland

Ballater (0338) 55425

Chemists to HM The Queen and HM The Queen Mother.

'The world passes this little street,' said Mr Murray as he showed me the letters he has received from all over the world. One of them read: 'I have seen the remarkable result of your cream on Mary and would like to order some.' Mary's friend had written from Canada and was referring to Ironside's Emollient Skin Cream which has been made in Ballater for over 50 years. The cream has been deemed 'matchless for the complexion' and costs 75 pence for 120 ml and 98 pence for 170 ml. It is J. & D. Murray's most popular product. Mr Mur-

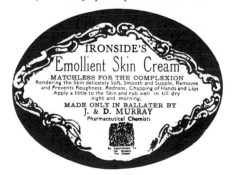

ray has also 'invented' an aftershave (Highland Fern) and several perfumes (Balmoral Mist and Dee Heather) which he sells in his little chemist's shop.

Originally from Elgin, some 30 miles south of Ballater, Mr and Mrs Murray, both pharmacists, bought the shop in Ballater in 1970. In 1973 they were awarded their first Royal Warrant from The Queen Mother, and three years later they received another from The Queen. Mr Murray tries to cater for all his clients, from the local farming community to the passing tourists.

Monday–Saturday: 8.45–5.30, sometimes open Sundays during the tourist season. The Emollient Skin Cream is available mail order from J. & D. Murray.

WOOD'S PHARMACY
50 High Street
Windsor
Berkshire SL4 1LR

Windsor (95) 61666

Pharmaceutical chemists to HM The Queen.

Wood's was founded in 1770 (when it was known as Pickerings) and for the next 40 years supplied the Royal household of George III. Their Royal Warrant was first granted by Queen Victoria – although it seems they had no medicine for a broken heart. Apart from a brief period in the 1960s, Wood's has held a Royal Warrant ever since.

Wood's Pharmacy is a pretty Regency building beside the gates of Windsor Castle. The front is painted powder blue with 'Wood's Pharmacy' in proud Victorian gold lettering over the entrance. Mr Patel, the owner, has more sense than to modernise it: he's planning to leave it as it is, bare boards and all.

Monday–Saturday: 9–5.30. Wood's will deliver in Windsor.

Hairdressing

HEAD LINES HAIR AND BEAUTY LIMITED
33 Thurloe Street
London SW7 2LQ

(01) 584 9900

When the press first made it known that it was Kevin Shanley at Head Lines who cut The Princess of Wales's hair, Mr Shanley was swamped. 'There were lots of people coming in for the 'Lady Di' hair cut. Today you only get one or two,' he said.

Kevin Shanley has been cutting and highlighting The Princess of Wales's hair since she first came to live in London. She has had her eyelashes dyed at Head Lines too. At first, after all the publicity, The Princess of Wales would visit Head Lines very early in the morning to avoid other clients, but today Mr Shanley visits the Palace and accompanies The Prince and Princess of Wales on many of their tours. For the past couple of years he has been cutting Prince Charles's hair as well.

Head Lines is situated in a large Georgian house with blinds in the window opposite South Kensington underground station. Inside it is decorated in white with details picked out in peppermint. Kevin Shanley believes in creating a 'calm friendly atmosphere'. Most of his clients are conventional and live in the area. 'We don't attract the King's Road type,' Kevin Shanley says. 'You can learn to cut hair in the same way that you can learn to fix a plug. The difference between a good hairdresser and an average one is that the good hairdresser has an eye for it.' A cut and blow-dry at Head Lines costs from £17 and highlights from £30 for half a head to £45 for the whole head.

Kevin Shanley is 28 and was born in London. 'Being one of seven children there were always plenty of heads to practise on.' At 16 he decided to become a professional hairdresser and four years later started working at Head Lines. Three years ago he bought the other partners out. Today there are 10 hairdressers at Head Lines, but Claire Shanley, Kevin's wife, cuts his dark curly hair for him.

Monday–Friday: 9–6; Saturday: 9.30–4.

G. B. KENT & SONS LIMITED
London Road
Apsley
Hemel Hempstead
Hertfordshire HP3 9SA

Brush-makers to HM The Queen.

Kent are the oldest brush manufacturers in the world. They have held their Royal Warrant throughout nine reigning monarchs since George III. The company were founded by William Kent, a Yorkshire man from the West Riding, who set up a brush-making firm in St James's in Mayfair in 1777. By the 1820s they were also making toothbrushes and held the warrant for this service to George IV, and later to William IV. The toothbrushes were all stamped with the Royal coat of arms. By the middle of the 19th century Kent were producing over 9,000 toothbrushes a week. Most of the handles at that time were made from the leg bones of bullocks and their rate of production meant they got through about 600 head of cattle a week.

After King William the firm held their Royal Warrant as brushmakers to Queen Victoria. By this time they were also making ivory-handled mirrors ornamented with elaborate hand carvings. The ivory leftovers were used to make shoe horns, paper knives and the handles of

moustache and whisker brushes. In 1932 Arthur Kent, the last in the family line died leaving no descendants. The firm of Kent were taken over by Cosby Brushes. One of the most innovative brushes at the time was the Cosby Hygenic refillable hairbrush now known as the Kent-Cosby Allure, which has a detachable bristle base. Another unusual line in production were hairbrushes which had the backs made from the foundations of old Waterloo Bridge and Lord Nelson's flagship, *Victory*.

Kent hairbrushes are today made for men, women and babies. They also make a range of nail brushes, bath and shower brushes and styling brushes specifically for hair salons. Some of their brushes – including the ones purchased by the Royal family – are still handmade. Although the firm no longer produce ivory- or silver-backed brushes they will carry out repairs for those still in existence. Kent brushes are well known for their durability – they have been known to outlive their owners.

Kent brushes are available from chemists and department stores.

75 Farringdon Road in East London. Headquarters of Kent Brushes from 1897 to 1940

NEVILLE DANIEL LIMITED
175 Sloane Street
London SW1X 9Q9
(and branches)

(01) 235 2534

Hairdressers to HM The Queen.

Neville Daniel were awarded their Royal Warrant shortly after The Queen's hairdresser, Charles Martyn, joined their Sloane Street branch five years ago. Mr Martyn still accompanies the Royal party on foreign tours.

Daniel and Neville opened their first salon in New Cavendish Street in 1974. Today they have three hairdressing salons all 'positively blue'. Their Sloane Street branch is pale blue with three floors to cater for everything to do with beauty and hairdressing. The ground floor and mezzanine are the hairdressing sections. They specialise in colour, especially in highlighting and low-lighting (colour tints from £16 and a full head of highlights from £55). In their basement there are six 'beauty rooms' where clients are offered facials, waxing, massage and make-up services. Neville Daniel employ 60 staff in their Sloane Street salon for their clients of 'all ages, catered for in our own definite way'. A cut and blow-dry starts from £16.

Monday–Saturday: 9–5.

TRUEFITT & HILL
(PRODUCTS) LIMITED
23 Old Bond Street
London W1X 3DA

(01) 493 2961

Hairdressers to HRH
The Duke of Edinburgh.

The atmosphere of Truefitt's is like an old film set, with cream-jacketed barbers, many of them white-haired and moustached, snipping away at the heads of their distinguished clients sitting on the polished barbers' chairs lined up in a row of 12 on the left side of the salon. The staff at Truefitts check the obituary, births and wedding columns every morning so they know whether to express their condolences or congratulations to their customers. But you won't see their most distinguished client there. The Duke of Edinburgh has his hair cut at Buckingham Palace.

For 15 years Truefitt & Hill cut Prince Charles's hair, but since his wedding, His Royal Highness has been using Kevin Shanley (see page 56). The manager, Mr Beard, was pleased Prince Charles kept his Truefitt's style for the front and sides, but adds, 'We used to give him a gentleman's trim. I suppose nowadays a lot of the ladies like to see really long hair.' Mr Beard recommends his clients have a haircut 'as often as possible. The average client only comes here once a month – disgusting really.'

In 1805, Francis Truefitt took premises at 40 Old Bond Street and established himself as 'Court Hair Cutter' and 'Court Hair Dresser'. But even with only one employee, Francis was soon appointed Wigmaker to George IV. The company still make wigs today. In the late 1800s, Truefitts became the first ladies' hairdressers, operating on the first and second floors of their present address. They claim to have produced the first-ever lipstick as well – but they don't sell that today. They still produce shampoos and colognes sold in distinctive beige and green wrapping.

Monday–Friday: 9–5.30; Saturday 9–12.30.

GEO. F. TRUMPER
9 Curzon Street
London W1Y 7FL

(01) 499 1850

Hairdresser to HM The Queen.

Along one side of each of Trumpers' two floors are rows of individual cubicles, each with grey marble work surfaces and the essential mirror surrounded by Trumpers' products perched elegantly on little mahogany shelves – privacy for the discerning gentleman customer.

Outside the shop, etched in gold capitals in the large glass window are the words: 'Court Hairdresser and Perfumer to the late King George V from 1919–1936'. But Mr Trumper was awarded his first Royal Warrant by Queen Victoria and the firm have held it ever since. Their latest Royal tribute is Royal Cologne, to commemorate the wedding of The Prince of Wales to Lady Diana Spencer.

Geo. F. Trumper established his barber shop in Curzon Street in 1875. In the vaults underneath the shop he created exclusive perfumes, toilet waters and pomades, using bergamot from France, violets from Ajaccio, limes from the West Indies and roses from Damascus. His oils and essences for gentlemen were popular with the Royal Court. Fragrances including Wellington cologne and Marlborough aftershave were specially concocted.

Today Trumpers still blend the same formulae by hand in the traditional manner used over 100 years ago, allowing their colognes and lotions to mature for many months before being filtered into bottles.

Try Astor aftershave ('for the man of affairs, a fragrance for an active life in the public eye') or Coronis hair dressing – unchanged since it was brought out to mark the coronation of King George VI in 1937. Haircuts at Trumpers start at £8.50.

Monday–Friday: 9–5.30; Saturday: 9–1. If requested, Trumpers will cut your hair at 8.30 a.m. Book first for appointments.

Healer

KAY KIERNAN
Bluestone Clinic
16 Harley House
Marylebone Road
London NW1

(01) 935 7933

Kay Kiernan describes herself as a 'pain therapist'. She has been treating Royal aches and pains since she set up her practice in 1972. A signed photograph from Princess Margaret adorns one of the walls in her clinic and reads: 'For Kay – Margaret'. But when Kay Kiernan heard she was to be visited by The Queen for the first time she coyly remembers thinking: 'Queen of what? It suddenly dawned on me it was THE Queen.' Ms Kiernan was asked to treat The Queen's shoulder which had been severely strained by chopping logs at Balmoral. Normally the injury would have been dealt with by a member of the Royal Medical Household, a group of experts responsible for The Queen's health. But Her Majesty was recommended to try Ms Kiernan by Princess Margaret who is not only a patient at the Bluestone Clinic but a longstanding friend.

Ms Kiernan treated The Queen's injury with two 90-minute sessions on a Pulsed Electro Magnetic Energy machine known as PEME. The PEME machine is a neat little box with a movable arm at the end of which is a flat plate, approximately seven inches in diameter and two inches thick, which is pressed against the injury. It works by warming the damaged tissues and pulsing energy into them thereby speeding up the healing process for torn muscles, sprains and strains. Ms Kiernan discovered the machine while on a trip to America. She had originally trained as a nurse and after working with doctors in the States, learning how to use PEME machines, she decided to bring one back to this country. For the first 18 months Ms Kiernan worked in a room in a doctor's surgery. Then she opened the Bluestone Clinic (called after a North American Indian who predicted that one day she would enter the business). She now owns five of the £3,500 machines.

Because of the fast healing qualities of PEME it is used widely by many people from the world of sport, dance and live entertainment who need to be in peak condition all the time; Ms Kiernan looks after the torn muscles of the dancers from the Festival Ballet. Princess Alexandra, the late Douglas Bader and former Olympic ice-skating champion Robin Cousins. It is ideal, too, for patients both before and after plastic surgery. 'I can get people facing the world in about half the normal time,' she told me. Although the treatment is largely used by invalids or clients with injuries Ms Kiernan says it can be of help even if you are healthy to 'perk up your system'.

Ms Kiernan's clinic is situated in the basement of the building. One room is devoted entirely to PEME. In another, Ms Kiernan offers laser treatments to firm sagging necks and tighten and smooth eye, mouth and forehead lines. She will also carry out acupuncture with lasers. A second cubicle is set aside for massage. Ms Kiernan offers Swedish massage ('we know how to cope with the dirty phone calls') which is a form of remedial massage to relax the muscles before manipulative therapy – the more vigorous form of massage, also carried out at the clinic.

Ms Kiernan, a sprightly, young-looking middle-aged lady, clad in pale blue tracksuit, regularly takes treatment herself at the clinic, often fitting in an hour session before she opens to her clients. 'Massage is the best thing in the world. It is suitable for everyone from tiny babies to 95-year-olds. It is no good putting extra years on your life if you don't increase the quality,' Kay Kiernan said, producing a cheeky post-card: 'To Kay, the lady who reaches places other ladies don't reach.'

Monday–Thursday: 9–5.30 (last PEME appointment is 4 p.m.); Friday: 9–1.30 (last PEME appointment is midday). Ms Kiernan also works Saturdays in an emergency. PEME treatments £10 for an hour. Massage is £8 for half an hour and laser treatments are from £20 per treatment.

Manicurists

RICHÉ OF HAY HILL LIMITED
14 Hay Hill
Berkeley Square
London W1X 7LJ

(01) 493 3368

Manicurists to HM The Queen Mother.

Mr Riché, who has studied both biology and physiology, regards complaints of dandruff, hair loss and allied problems as being due as much to nervous tension as to physical problems. Customers may be sent to what he privately calls his 'psychological department' where their complaint is diagnosed and receives the appropriate treatment. Mr Riché proudly told me that many of his clients have been recommended to visit him by the best Harley Street doctors.

From a hairdressing family, Mr Riché started his own salon in 1939 and moved in 1942 to Hay Hill. He considers his peak period 1952 ('the time of the coronation') but 'I was extremely renowned all through the fifties and sixties as a hair fashion leader.' Although Vidal Sassoon succeeded in changing the image of hairdressing, Riché still caters 'for nearly everyone you can find in *Debretts*' and their children and grandchildren. Riché's staff of 15 include both male and female hairdressers, and although their customers are still predominantly women, they do cater for men who don't want a short back and sides – among them Sir Laurence Olivier.

Behind their discreet screened window they also offer facials, pedicures and the famed manicure which will cost you approximately £4.50. But if you like washing your own hair try their decadent-sounding Brandy and Egg or Champagne shampoos. And to stop your hair flying away, experiment with their Invisible Hair Net.

Monday–Friday: 9–6; Saturday: 9–1. Telephone first for an appointment, well worth it according to Mr Riché: 'If ever you get into the hands of a really skilled hairdresser you realise what you've had to put up with in the past.'

Perfumes, soaps and make-up

ELIZABETH ARDEN LIMITED
13 Hanover Square
London W1R 0PA

Manufacturers of cosmetics to HM The Queen and HM The Queen Mother.

The founder of the Elizabeth Arden company was named Florence Nightingale Graham at birth, which probably had some bearing on her original career as a nurse. The young Canadian soon gave up her arduous medical training and went to New York to seek her fortune. She found work in a modest beauty salon where she showed such aptitude she was soon offered a partnership. The ambitious Ms Graham had already decided to branch out on her own. In 1910 she opened her first salon on Fifth Avenue, New York's most elegant street. The name for the company was taken from a book she was reading: *Elizabeth and her German Garden*, and a poem called 'Enoch Arden'. From then on Ms Graham was known as Elizabeth Arden. By the time she opened her first salon in London's Bond Street in 1932 her famous Red Door salons were to be found in nearly every city in the States. Although in the early days make-up was relatively unsophisticated Ms Arden made a name for herself with her theory that cosmetics should tone with clothes rather than with personal colouring. In 1971 the Elizabeth Arden company were bought by the American pharmaceutical firm, Eli Lilly.

Today Elizabeth Arden are best known for their Visible Difference and Millenium skin care creams and for their classic Blue Grass perfume. They also bring out new cosmetic colours every season.

Elizabeth Arden products are available from chemists and department stores.

H. BRONNLEY & COMPANY LIMITED
10 Conduit Street
London W1R 0BR

Toilet soap makers to HM The Queen and HM The Queen Mother.

In 1209 King John (known as an exceptionally clean king) was recorded as having had only nine baths in a period of five months. Elizabeth I had a bath once a year 'whether she needed to or no' and in 1837 when Queen Victoria acceded to the throne there was no bathroom in Buckingham Palace.

Since 1883, when 19-year-old James Bronnley founded the firm of H. Bronnley & Co., Bronnley feel their 'contribution to civilisation has been to produce luxury fragrant bathing products'. Today at their factory in Brackley, Bronnley manufacture bath lotions and soaps, including their warrant-holding toilet soaps. 'Making soap,' they say 'demands skill, fantastically expensive materials and careful attention to detail. It is the art of combining fats, colours and perfumes and mixing, milling (Bronnley soaps go through the mill three times to ensure consistency and long life), extruding, stamping and wrapping the finished tablet'. The fats used are avocado oil, almond oil or beeswax which moisten and protect the skin, as well as essential oils made from plant extracts imported from around the world. Scents can be made from the flowers of pinks, lilies, orange blossom, violets and roses, or distilled from the barks of trees such as cinnamon, sandal- and rosewood or from the roots in the case

of iris, ginger, angelica and spikenard. Bronnley make the wooden boxes for their lemon soaps, hand-trim and wrap each piece and design and print their labels.

James Bronnley was inspired by a year in Paris studying soap making and milling to start his company. He leased a shed in Holborn, borrowed £300 from friends, bought a baker's dough mixer and began selling his soaps through London chemists. By 1904 he had his own factory in Acton. When Queen Mary came to Acton in the thirties to open the YWCA centre, Mr Bronnley was invited to welcome her, but declined. He was too shy.

A year earlier, Mr Bronnley had had what he called 'the greatest disappointment of my life'. He and his wife had a baby daughter, Gladys. Mr Bronnley had wanted a son to carry on the business. In 1983 Bronnley celebrated its centenary under the leadership of Gladys Bronnley.

'Elizabeth 1st had only one bath a year whether she needed to or no'

Today together with her husband Hans Rossiter and their daughter Ann, she runs the family firm. Bronnley still cater for distinguished customers for whom they make soaps stamped from the customer's own individual moulds. One such soap was Pomade, commissioned by a West African tribe as a protection against the parching dusty wind.

Bronnley soaps are available from chemists and department stores.

CYCLAX LIMITED
17/18 Old Bond Street
London W1X 4AY

Manufacturers of beauty preparations to HM The Queen.

During the late 19th century women who wanted to visit the exclusive Cyclax beauty salon needed a personal introduction to the salon's owner, Frances Hemming. At that time the salon was situated in London's South Molton Street. Ms Hemming, who was considered an Edwardian beauty, specialised in beauty treatments for the aristocracy. She had studied her beauty techniques in Vienna and with the aid of an English consultant dermatologist, had developed her own cosmetic lotions and creams.

During the 1920s Ms Hemming travelled around the country giving beauty demonstrations in stores. Her products were no longer restricted to the elite and by the 1930s Cyclax companies had been founded in Australia, South Africa and New Zealand. Cyclax received their Royal Warrant in 1961 and today they make up special jars of skin preparation several times a year for Her Majesty and take them to Buckingham Palace.

The company advocate diligent skin care and their products have healthy-sounding names like Pure Milk and Honey cleansers, Flower Fresh Balm skin freshener and the romantic-sounding Milk of Roses moisturiser which 'gives protection to delicate skins throughout the day'. They also make an avocado vitamin cream which helps to reduce redness from sunburn, an All Day Face Firmer which defies wind and dry heat and keeps make-up cool and matt and Neojuvex, a 24-hour skin care cream for dry mature skin because Cyclax think 'you should enjoy your age not look it'.

Cyclax products are available from chemists and department stores.

J. FLORIS LIMITED
89 Jermyn Street
London SW1Y 6JH
(01) 930 2885

Perfumers to HM The Queen and manufacturers of toilet preparations to HRH The Prince of Wales.

When you walk into Floris you feel you're not really grown-up enough to be there – as if you'd sneaked into mother's boudoir to marvel at the treats and spray on some perfume before she comes in and catches you. The interior contains gleaming mahogany showcases acquired from the Great Exhibition of 1851, lined with red satin and filled with toothbrushes, combs, scent bottles and powder puffs from the 18th century to today. The smell of perfume is overpowering. It's almost too perfect.

When Juan Famenia Floris arrived from Minorca in 1730 and settled into 89 Jermyn Street, he opened a barber's shop. Fragrances were made in a room at the back to the order of individual customers. Michael Bodenham, the present managing director, is a seventh generation descendant of Juan Floris and supervises the making of Floris products in their new factory in Sussex. But there is still the odd customer who will come in and ask them to 'have my brilliantine ready after lunch', and one of Floris's staff will run into the basement and prepare the hair oil to their customer's requirements.

Times have changed since Noel Coward sternly rejected the Eau de Vinaigre proffered by Mr Bodenham (then a trembling assistant on his first day of work) declaring, 'My dear boy, you don't expect me to go around smelling of pickles.' In those days, Mr Bodenham told me, 'most men's colognes smelt of carbolic'.

Today gentlemen – both Royal and commoners – can preen themselves with any of a small but exotic selection of Floris fragrances. Their latest masculine smell is Elite, described in their brochure in florid terms as 'elements of Citrus releasing a tangy exhilaration . . . and exotic notes of Sandalwood, Vetyver and Tuberose blending a spicy sensuality with a breath of flowers', and more succinctly by Mr Bodenham as 'for the male chauvinist brigade'. Ladies can turn on the magic with their Malmaison (carnation) scent. It's a 'potent spellbinder'.

Monday–Friday: 9.30–5.30; Saturday: 9.30–4. Floris's mail order catalogue is free of charge and they will mail worldwide.

LENTHERIC LIMITED
Vale Road
Camberley
Surrey

Manufacturers of perfumery products to HM The Queen Mother.

The House of Lentheric were founded in 1885 by Guillaume Lentheric, a hairdresser by trade. He originally opened a hairdressing salon and perfume laboratory on the rue St Honoré in Paris. Guillaume Lentheric had always had an interest in perfume and soon began to create exclusive fragrances for his most honoured patrons who included members of some of the most aristrocratic houses in France. He was quick to see the value his customers placed on the perfumes he made so he started concentrating more on the perfumery side of the business. Within a short time his reputation had increased business to such an extent he had to give up the hairdressing trade and move to a new and larger laboratory and factory at Courbevoie.

Guillaume Lentheric was careful to keep his perfumes exclusive. He began to export his products and soon became known as the master perfumer to almost every court in Europe. Lentheric became a respected name among French society women. The company added a range of skin care and make-up preparations to their perfumes and by the early 1920s, long after the death of the founder, the company records listed 15 princesses of Europe as Lentheric customers. In 1935 Lentheric launched Tweed, one of the great classics of the perfume world.

Today Lentheric is owned by British American Cosmetics which also own Cyclax (see page 62) and Yardley (see page 65).

Lentheric products are available from most chemists and department stores.

A. & F. PEARS LIMITED
Hesketh House
Portman Square
London W1A 1DY

Soap manufacturers to HM The Queen and HM The Queen Mother.

Every year since 1958 over 20,000 mothers have entered their daughters in the Miss Pears Contest in the hope that she will become the next Miss Pears. It is the last of the great Pears advertising gimmicks which were originally started by Thomas J. Barratt who married the great-granddaughter of Andrew, the founder of the Pears company.

Andrew Pears established himself as a hairdresser in London's Soho in 1789. In his shop he manufactured rouges, creams, powders, dentifrice and other beauty aids. He noticed his products were often used to repair the harm caused by the harsh soaps which were then available. Mr Pears decided to produce a soap to treat complexions more delicately. Not only were the harshness and impurities found in other soaps removed from Pears soap but it was delicately perfumed – a novelty in those days – and transparent.

Andrew Pears and his descendants were more concerned about the quality of their products than the quantity sold. For the first 80 years of production a total of £500 had been spent on advertising. Within a few years of joining the firm in 1875, Thomas Barratt was spending no less than £126,000 a year. His first appeal to the public was that Pears soap was safe and healthy and that it made its users beautiful. He obtained a series of testimonials from a number of prominent skin specialists, doctors and chemists. He then turned to 'glamour' advertising, making Lillie Langtry with her Royal associations his first star. Ms Langtry said about Pears: 'Since using Pears soap, I have discarded all others.' Mr Barratt then went on to discard Lillie Langtry. His next campaign was a cartoon borrowed from *Punch* showing a disreputable unwashed tramp laboriously writing his testimonial to Pears: 'Two years ago I used your soap, since when I have used no other.'

In 1880 Mr Barratt initiated one of his

most fantastic schemes. At the time French 10-centime pieces were accepted as valid currency in England. Mr Barratt imported a quarter of a million and, as there was no law forbidding the defacement of foreign currency, he had the name 'Pears' stamped on each one and put them into circulation. This led to an Act of Parliament which declared all foreign coins illegal tender. The coins were withdrawn from circulation and melted down by the Mint. Thomas Barratt then decided to advertise in America. He bought the whole of the front page of the *New York Herald* and published on it a testimonial from Dr Beecher – the United States spiritual leader and brother of Harriet Beecher, author of *Uncle Tom's Cabin*.

News of Pears soap was frequently featured in *Punch*. In 1887 after the firm had moved to New Oxford Street, *Punch* noted that a portrait of Queen Victoria, who now patronised Pears soaps, was hung in front of the new building. It was she who granted Pears their first Royal Warrant and Queen Mary who later favoured the most luxurious version of the transparent soap, perfumed with Attar of Roses.

One of Mr Barratt's most famous advertisements was Sir John Everett Millais' painting of his grandson watching a soap bubble he had just blown through a clay pipe. The painting, entitled 'Bubbles', was first exhibited at the Royal Academy and then sold to the *Illustrated London News* for reproduction. In 1886 Pears bought it for £2,200 to use as an advertisement. It became one of the first posters.

In 1870 the Education Act had paved the way for university and free education. Mr Barratt realised that the dictionaries and encyclopaedias of those days were too expensive. He decided to publish a book which would combine everyday practical information with general knowledge in one inexpensive volume. In 1897 *Pears Shilling Cyclopaedia* was first published. An Irish convict once described it as 'the most popular book in the prison library'. All 600,000 copies were sold and today it is still being printed.

In 1914, shortly after Thomas Barratt's death the firm joined Lever Brothers. Today it takes about three months to make a bar of Pears soap and the basic formula has remained unaltered. The secret of the transparent effect? It's the inclusion and subsequent slow evaporation of alcohol.

Pears soaps can be bought from chemists and at supermarkets.

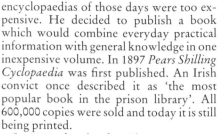

PENHALIGON'S
**41 Wellington Street
London WC2E 7BN
(and branches)**

(01) 836 2150

Manufacturers of toilet requisites to HRH The Duke of Edinburgh.

Penhaligon's relish their past. Their products, shops and catalogue still look as they might have done when William Henry Penhaligon was the Court Barber at the end of Queen Victoria's reign. Slightly precious but very nostalgic.

William Henry Penhaligon was born in 1841 in Penzance and came to London as a young man. His barber's shop soon became established in Jermyn Street. In the back of the shop he made perfumes, toilet waters and pomades. Many of them were

reserved exclusively for his clients including Lord Rothschild and later Sir Winston Churchill. Today Penhaligon's still prepare their fragrances from William Penhaligon's original note books. They use essential oils and natural ingredients imported from all over the world.

Their Bluebell fragrance is described as 'a cool green scent, simple and direct. A memory for the city girl of fresh green leaves and woodland walks' – a bluebell-scented handkerchief costs £8.25. Their gardenia fragrance is 'luscious and heady for hot summer evenings' and Hammam Bouquet, the oldest of their fragrances which is a blend of rose, jasmine and English lavender, is 'only for the most sophisticated of gentlemen'. Hammam Bouquet aftershave is £16 for 100ml.

Monday–Friday: 10–6; Saturday: 10–5. Penhaligon's Pictorial Album (mail order catalogue) costs £2.00. Penhaligon's will mail worldwide.

YARDLEY & COMPANY LIMITED
33 Old Bond Street
London W1X 4AP

(01) 629 9341

Manufacturers of soap to HM The Queen and perfumers and manufacturers of soap to HM The Queen Mother.

The first mention of a Yardley in the beauty business was during the reign of Charles I when a young man of that name paid the monarch a large sum of money to gain a concession to manufacture soap for the whole of London. The details of his success were lost in the Great Fire of London, but it was known that Charles I used lavender to perfume his soap, a fragrance for which the House of Yardley are famous today.

Records of the Yardley family appeared in early Plantaganet scrolls as owners of land in Essex, but it was Hermina Yardley, daughter of William – sword, spur and buckle maker in the late 18th century – who played the most important part in the founding of the House of Yardley. In 1801 she married William Cleaver, heir to a soap and perfumery business founded by his father in the City of London. At that time a revolution in dress was already underway. Perukes for men were going out of fashion. Men were preferring to display their own hair which called for the lavish use of oils and dressings such as bear grease. It was now socially acceptable to be sweet smelling, and cosmetics such as face powders and lip salves were becoming increasingly popular. The new trends were a great boost to the House of Cleaver and business flourished.

When the company exhibited at the Great Exhibition in Hyde Park in 1851 the name of Yardley was already being used. Among their wares was a sample cake of Old Brown Windsor Soap embossed with a picture of Windsor Castle. During Queen Victoria's reign fashions changed considerably. Yardley were by now exporting 22 varieties of soap to the States including the Old Brown Windsor and the cheaper Coal Tar Carbolic and Oatmeal. By 1910 Yardley had bought a shop in New Bond Street where Mr John Seager, a chemist for the firm, remembers one of his first jobs was to 'grind by hand a quarter-inch-long greenish-red cantharides fly with a pestle

and mortar to make hair tonics for men and women'. They were also making dog soaps and mini soaps for children as well as herbal hair washes and shampoo salts. All Yardley's creams were sold in genuine Royal Worcester or Wedgwood pots and their perfumes were bottled in Baccarat glass.

In 1921 Yardley received their first Royal Warrant from The Prince of Wales. Queen Mary granted hers in 1932 and King George V followed in 1949 'particularly on account of the lavender soap', which was a great favourite of his.

This century has been one of expansion for Yardley and they are still looking ahead. They predict that by the year 2000 women will no longer be wearing clothes as we know them for the streets will be heated. Enter Yardley with a brand new range in all-over body make-up.

Monday–Friday: 9–5.30 (Old Bond Street showroom). Make an appointment first for waxing or facial treatments. Yardley's products are available from chemists and department stores.

The Wardrobes

Accessories

CORNELIA JAMES LIMITED
123 Havelock Road
Brighton
Sussex BN1 6GS

Glove manufacturers to HM The Queen.

The Queen was once acknowledged in the *Guinness Book of Records* as having shaken the most number of hands in one day. Since 1945 her hands have been protected by Cornelia James gloves, who are grateful to Her Majesty for having made fabric gloves respectable. At one time, Peter James, Cornelia James's son and sales director told me, ladies wore leather gloves but put to thorough use they 'would rapidly become uncomfortable to the wearer, and would quickly look "tired". Fabric gloves are ideal,' he said, 'because they absorb all the perspiration, yet still remain soft and delicate, and still look smart. What's more, they can go in the washing machine.'

Cornelia James trained at art college in Vienna. After the war she employed a small staff, and began making hand-sewn gloves for the major couture houses, such as Hartnell and Hardy Amies. In the late 1940s and early 1950s it was difficult to buy bright fabrics for clothes, so Mrs James used to dye and make bright coloured gloves in over 100 different colours. In 1956 she was christened 'the Colour Queen of England' by the fashion accessories industry.

Today the company sell over 250 styles of glove, from over-the-elbow gloves starting at £6.50 to lace ones. They have also made gloves for Wurzel Gummidge, the television scarecrow, and all the shiny galaxy gloves used in *Star Wars*, as well as the gloves they make for the Royal family. Cornelia James keep the hand patterns of all their regular customers.

In addition to manufacturing gloves, Cornelia James make fashion scarves. In 1981, each of their six different-coloured scarves to commemorate the Royal wedding were selected by the Design Council. They have recently branched out into company ties and scarves carrying company logos.

Cornelia James gloves are available from boutiques and major department stores. To find out about their company ties and scarves contact the above address.

S. LAUNER & COMPANY (LONDON) LIMITED
86 Clarendon Road
West Croydon
Surrey CR0 3SG

Manufacturers of handbags to HM The Queen.

It was through the Royal shoemakers, H. & M. Rayne (see page 102), that Launer found themselves supplying the Royal family. Bags that match shoes that match costumes have added the finishing touch to many Royal ensembles. The Queen and The Queen Mother still buy many of Launer's bags from Rayne in fabrics that match their new shoes – The Queen Mother favours larger bags with wider pouches at the side to carry the many leaflets she collects on official tours. Launer also make bags to match shoes for Russell & Bromley.

Launer's bags range in price from £50 to £430 for a crocodile bag. Their range of 50 standard handbags in handpicked leathers from Germany, France, England and Italy, with locks from Florence are made by their 20 skilled craftsmen, each of whom can make up to 10 bags a week, in their two factories in London. The rest of their employees produce small leather goods, such as purses, wallets, notecases and jewel rolls to match the handbags.

S. Launer & Co. were founded in 1939 by Freddie Launer. On his death the company were bought by the Simon Martin Group.

Launer bags are available from Harrods, Fortnum and Mason, Asprey, Rayne, Russell & Bromley and other leading stores in the UK, France and Japan.

A selection of S. Launer's handbags

The Princess of Wales
watching polo at
Cowdray Park clutching
one of her rose-patterned
Souleiado bags

SOULEIADO LIMITED
171 Fulham Road
London SW3 5PG

(01) 589 6180

When Charles Demerys took over the 18th-century family fabric printing firm in Provence he discovered 40,000 old hand-carved wooden printing blocks which had been unused for years. He started printing scarves and fabrics in colours associated with Cézanne Provençale landscapes; soft terracottas, poppy reds, cornflower blues, bright greens and pale yellows.

The fabrics were amazingly successful; Pablo Picasso had several shirts made from them, Jackie Kennedy decorated a room at the White House in Souleiado material, Pierre Cardin bought 800 metres of fabric for his villa at Cannes and Candice Bergen, Lauren Bacall and Woody Allen are all regular customers.

Two years ago Souleiado – the name is an old Provençale word describing the way the sun's rays burst through the clouds after it has been raining – opened their first shop in London. They sell a range of rich, intricate paisley and floral fabrics which can be bought by the metre or as bags, sewing cases, tea cosies, cushions, duvet covers, bikinis and umbrellas. An umbrella costs £39. The Princess of Wales has bought five of their 'sacs magaridos' – quilted bags – all in different designs at £30 each, which she often takes with her when she goes to watch Prince Charles playing polo. 'She likes roses', they told me.

Souleiado used to sell clothes as well but found their English clientele were not buying them. 'The English play much safer with colours. They like the chintzy look rather than the bolder colours.' Souleiado's fabrics start at £10 a metre for their traditional collection.

Tuesday–Saturday: 10–1, 2–6.

SWAINE ADENEY BRIGG & SONS LIMITED
See page 201.

Coats and casuals

AQUASCUTUM LIMITED
100 Regent Street
London W1A 2AO

(01) 734 6090

Makers of weatherproof garments to HM The Queen Mother.

The name Aquascutum was inspired by the English weather. The name is Latin for water protection. Their early coats were also weather inspired, 'pure, new wool, soft and comforting to the touch; efficiently proofed to withstand the heaviest downpour'. In 1922, Aquascutum advertised 'an unequalled selection of sporting, motoring and travelling coats, always in stock for immediate wear'. Perhaps that's why on rainy days bedraggled shoppers in Regent Street stare wistfully into their windows.

Aquascutum were granted their warrants as waterproofers to Edward, Prince of Wales in 1897 and as waterproofs(!) to George V in 1911. Today they hold their Royal Warrants to The Queen Mother for their weatherproof garments. Men and women can now buy the classic Aquascutum coat in London and in their outlets around the country. In recent years there have been forays into the world of separates and leisurewear for winter and summer.

Monday–Saturday: 9–5.30; Thursday: 9–7.

LAURA ASHLEY
See page 25.

BENETTON
23 Brompton Road
London SW3 1ED
(and branches)

(01) 589 6503

'We have never offered crazy fashions, just something a little more personal.' Benetton is ideal for the colour coordinated customer, both male and female. Benetton stores are arranged according to colour, not garment. Lining the walls of their shops are layers of brilliant reds, greens and blues and a variety of pastel shades. In each of their colours of the season you can buy an entire coordinated wardrobe, from gloves and shirts to jackets and trousers, with a price range of £12 to £60.

Benetton's speciality is knitwear, but The Princess of Wales likes their cropped trousers, of which she has bought several pairs together with their matching T-shirts. The Princess has also bought bikinis from Benetton. 'She pops in when it pleases her, but she buys with great discrimination,' the manageress of the Brompton Road branch told me, who is used to other less imaginative customers ordering everything in their window at about £400 a time.

Benetton is one of the most striking success stories in Italian industry. It has grown from a one sewing-machine business near Venice to a worldwide clothing empire. Started in 1966 by Giuliana Benetton who persuaded her three brothers to go into business with her selling her knitwear designs, their clothes are now available in more than 2,500 franchised Benetton shops throughout the world.

Monday–Saturday: 10–6.30; Wednesday: 10–7 (Brompton Road branch).

BURBERRYS LIMITED
18 The Haymarket
London SW1Y 4DQ
(and branches)

(01) 930 3343

Weatherproofers to HM The Queen and HM The Queen Mother.

Born in 1835 in a Surrey village, Thomas Burberry, the founder of Burberrys, was first apprenticed to a draper. In 1856 he started a little draper's shop of his own in Basingstoke. He quickly realised that there were no weatherproof clothes on the market and developed a cloth that was untearable, almost impenetrable by rain and yet cool and comfortable to wear. He called it Gaberdine, a name changed only by King Edward VII who on rainy days used to call for his 'Burberry'.

Burberry went on to devise a specialised garment for every pursuit in which a man or woman might get caught in the rain. Burberry clothing became standard equipment for explorers, empire builders and big

Amundsen's Burberry gaberdine tent at the South Pole

game shots. It also became essential for polar travel. Scott, Shackleton and Amundsen all used windproof suits and tents specially designed and made by Burberrys. So did Captain John Alcock, who wore a Burberry outfit on his historic flight across the Atlantic. And Lord Kitchener was wearing a military Burberry when he drowned in the North Sea.

Today Burberrys are worn round the world. Not only have the company grown, but so has their range of products: from cashmere scarves to golf bags. But they still produce some of the finest coats available. The Queen was rarely out of her Burberry on her recent rain-soaked trip to California.

A Burberry raincoat does not come cheap – at over £110 for the classic trenchcoat style – but if you don't mind being a walking advertisement you can sport a 'Burbrolly', in the all-too-distinctive Burberry check, for a mere £48.

Monday–Saturday: 9–5.30; Thursday: 9–7. Free mail order catalogue available upon request. Burberrys will mail worldwide.

CALMAN LINKS (TRADING) LIMITED
241 Brompton Road
London SW3 1LX

(01) 581 1927

Furriers to HM The Queen and HM The Queen Mother.

You may not have seen The Queen or The Queen Mother sporting their fur coats in recent years. But the Royal connection with Calman Links is not only through fur coats (though they are the only furriers with a Royal Warrant). The proprietors have a sister company which supply Ede & Ravenscroft (see page 7) with ermine borders for the state robes which they make. Traditionally, only the Sovereign is permitted to wear the black tails of an ermine on his or her white ermine fur. Peers have black fur spots instead, with their rank denoted by the pattern and density of the spots according to a complex hierachy.

Calman Links do more than just sell fur coats. 'We work with our furs,' Mr and Mrs Winterson told me. Their business starts with buying the raw furs – including mink, sable, chinchilla and ermine – at auctions around the world. The furs are then cured or dressed and arrive at Calman Links 'lovely and pliable', where they are

stored in refrigerated conditions until they are used. The making of a fur coat is astonishingly complex, especially if a herringbone pattern or similar is to be incorporated.

But even for a 'straightforward' mink coat, every detail has to be carefully considered, from the choosing of the 60 or more skins needed to make the coat, where the colour and hue of the minks have to be matched exactly, to the selection of the lining – brown of course, but it must have a golden rather than a pink tone in order to complement the fur. No wonder the cheapest item to be found at Calman Links is an off-the-peg fur jacket for £560.

A large part of Calman Links' business are their made-to-measure furs. As Mrs Winterson said, 'If you're spending between £5,000 and £30,000 on a fur coat you want it to fit you.' The first stage in the fitting is for you to try on one of the ready-made coats in their showroom. Every single coat and jacket in the Calman

The Queen arriving at Liverpool Street Station in February 1968, refreshed after a six-week holiday at Sandringham, accompanied by Heather, Buzz, Foxy and Tiny. Her Majesty is wearing a Calman Links coat

Links showroom is known to the staff by a name, ('Mary' is one) which denotes both its style and its size: sizes are not marked in any way. So by this means the vanity of their treasured customers need never be upset.

Monday–Friday: 9–5. Calman Links will look after your fur coat from 'the cradle to the grave', and will clean and store your furs for you.

HARRODS LIMITED
See page 156.

HAYTHORNTHWAITE & SONS LIMITED
Grenfell House
Rylands Street
Burnley
Lancashire BB10 1RQ

Manufacturers of Grenfell garments to HM The Queen.

In 1922 Sir Wilfred Grenfell, a mission doctor, was invited to Burnley in Lancashire to talk about his work in the bleak outpost of Labrador in Newfoundland. His tales of his heroic service and epic journeys through the arctic wastes kept his audience captivated, but it was a casual remark about clothing that fired the imagination of Walter Haythornthwaite, a Burnley mill owner, who was listening to the tale.

Sir Wilfred had said that the right cloth for Labrador mission workers should be light because travel was always on foot following dog teams, but it should also be strong and weatherproof, for the wearer's life might depend on it. After a year of experiments, Walter Haythornthwaite had produced a cloth which Sir Wilfred described as 'ideal'. When it was decided to give the cloth a name, Sir Wilfred, with a surprising lack of modesty, suggested it be called Grenfell.

Since then Grenfell cloth has been worn by explorers and adventurers all around the world. It was worn by the climbers who went to Everest and by explorers in search of the Abominable Snowman. In 1933 a Grenfell tent formed the highest habitation ever made by man. A mountaineer by the name of Smythe had been forced to his knees in a blizzard at 27,000 feet. Scientists had predicted that any man sleeping at that altitude would never wake. Smythe slept for 13 hours through a wind which forced

The Grenfell trademark as seen in the back of all Haythornthwaite's garments

microscopic snow-crystals through other tents 500 feet below and woke refreshed.

Grenfell cloth was also used extensively for flying suits both by the Royal Air Force and by the Royal Canadian Air Force. It proved to be the ideal cloth for aerial sport and was chosen by the British Olympic Gliding team of 1960. The late Donald Campbell MBE – the world's fastest man on land and water – also wore it, as did his father, Sir Malcolm Campbell, during his water speed races. Grenfell cloth is still supplied to the International Grenfell Association who carry on the work of Sir Wilfred, although the dogs have since been replaced by aeroplanes. The cloth used today on all Grenfell garments, however, is exactly the same cloth which was used then. It is made from the finest cotton and has an exceptionally close weave with no less than 600 single threads to every square inch.

Haythornthwaite & Sons have held their Royal Warrant since 1958 as manufacturers of Grenfell garments to The Queen. They make raincoats for women and trenchcoats for men in both modern and traditional styles. Their shorter modern field coat goes by the name of 'Diana', while their ladies' blouson jacket is known as a 'Sloane'. Haythornthwaite & Sons say they also make 'specials' for special customers.

Grenfell garments are available from leading department stores and clothes shops.

HENDERSON'S
Bridge Street
Ballater
Aberdeenshire
Scotland

Ballater (03382) 432

Outfitters to HM The Queen.

Hendersons is one of those unique shops that in a tiny space somehow manages to sell a complete country wardrobe. But in the depths of winter the shop is so cold you have to be brave to try anything on. If you are hardy enough, you will find everything from kilts to hats, with tweed skirts, jumpers, jackets and trousers in between. There's also a large selection of lengths of tweed and skeins of wool, pyjama cases in the guise of Scottish outfits for £8.50, and bars of soap with a picture of Balmoral that won't wash off.

In season, Monday–Saturday: 9–6; Sunday: 'afternoons only'.

INCA
45 Elizabeth Street
London SW1W 9PP

(01) 730 7941

The Peruvian Indians who made The Princess of Wales's brightly coloured V-neck sweater were 'absolutely delighted' when they were shown photographs of her wearing it. So were Luisa Porras and Isabel Norman, the owners of Inca. Within three days of the photograph appearing in the paper they had had over 400 orders for the sweater. 'People would ring up and say, "Can I have a Lady Di Sweater", or fudge the issue and ask for the sweater with lamas and rows of girls on it.'

Ms Porras and Ms Norman met in Peru in the early seventies and decided to open a shop in London. Their first shop was in Pimlico Road. 'We opened at the right time, just when the ethnic look started in Paris.' At first the shop sold mainly craft items but when in 1974 they moved to Elizabeth Street, they shifted their emphasis to knitwear. The colours used have also changed: they used to be bright, but now the Indians – descendants of the Incas – have been asked to dye the yarn with vegetable dyes, such as lichen, moss and cochineal to achieve subtler effects. The Indians can't understand this at all. 'They like bright, violent colours all mixed together. It gives them a festive feeling,' Ms Porras told me. 'They also love orange, but we can't sell orange in England.' So Inca dictate which colours are to be used. The two ladies give work to thousands of Peruvians, both those living in the mountains and in the slums of Lima. Ms Porras's mother, who lives in Peru, oversees the knitting and the designing and checks that the jumpers don't become too long and thin. 'The one thing that any Peruvian man or woman can do is knit,' said Ms Porras. 'But what they are bad at is finishing off and getting the shape.'

Inca's two floors are filled with the sound of Peruvian music. The first floor holds their sweaters, for children and adults – including the 'Lady Di style' now costing £12.95, their hats ('hats are very important to a Peruvian, they denote not only his status in town, but also whether he is single or married'), waistcoats and Peruvian jewellery. All sizes of brightly coloured straw baskets line the stairs. The Inca craft section is on the first floor.

Monday–Friday: 10–6; Saturday: 10–2.
Mail order catalogue available.

PRINGLE OF SCOTLAND LIMITED
Victoria Mill
Hawick
Roxburgh TD9 7AL
Scotland

Manufacturers of knitted garments to HM The Queen and HM The Queen Mother.

Robert Pringle, the founder of Pringle of Scotland, believed in starting at the bottom and working his way up. In 1815 he began his business by making socks. Later he progressed to underwear and by the late 1920s he had branched out into knitted outerwear.

The Pringle of Scotland factory in the late 19th century

Today Pringle of Scotland, a subsidiary of Dawson International – the largest processors of raw cashmere in the world – export to over 50 countries. All their factories are in the Scottish Border counties, employing over 1,200 workers many of whom come from families who have worked with the company for generations. Pringle make pullovers and cardigans, in pure cashmere, lambswool, shetland and pure wool, in classic shapes and colours. The company handle everything themselves from the raw materials (animal fibres only) through to the spinning, dyeing and manufacturing.

Pringle have held their Royal Warrant to The Queen since 1956 and to The Queen Mother since 1948. They also supply pure cashmere knitwear to Princess Anne and other members of the Royal family.

Pringle garments are available from Pringle stockists and from leading department stores and good clothes shops.

REMPLOY LIMITED
Remploy House
415 Edgware Road
London NW2 6LR

Manufacturers of knitwear to HM The Queen.

This highly versatile company make everything from furniture to surgical footwear. But it is for their range of knitwear that Remploy hold their Royal Warrant to The Queen.

The company's products can be found in homes, offices, department stores and government buildings all over the country, though you'll rarely find anything under their brand name. Remploy work mainly under contract for many of the leading names in British industry. The company employ 11,000 people nationwide and have specialised divisions, streamlined into three groups: furniture, leather and textile products.

Remploy knitwear is available from department and chain stores throughout the country, under individual trade names. Their other products are available from leading British manufacturers.

SIMPSON (PICCADILLY) LIMITED
Piccadilly
London W1A 2AS

(01) 734 2002

Outfitters to HM The Queen, HRH The Duke of Edinburgh and HRH The Prince of Wales.

Simpson were established as bespoke tailors in 1894 by Simeon Simpson. But it was his younger son, Alexander, who gave the business its identity when he took over as managing director after the death of his father in 1932. Although it was a time of great industrial unrest, financial depression and high unemployment, Alexander wanted to create a men's store in the centre of London which could serve as a window for the clothing produced by his own manufacturing company. He wanted the Simpson name to be associated in men's minds with the most up-to-date clothes.

In 1935 he bought the site of the old geological museum in Piccadilly which had moved to South Kensington and instructed Joseph Emberton, an architect, to design the shop he had in his mind. It opened a year later. The shop's non-reflecting windows on either side of the Piccadilly entrance were at the time the largest curved glass windows in the world but the vibrations from London's buses soon cracked them – and their next replacements. Inside, its outstanding feature was the Travertine staircase serving all floors and lit by a continuous window. Today it is a statutory listed building of special architectural and historic interest.

At the time the press called the store 'crazy and magnificent'. Simpson's clothes, which Alexander Simpson had registered under the brand name DAKS (the origin

being a blend of 'Dad' and 'Slacks'), revolutionised people's idea of fashion. They replaced the traditional three-piece suit and braces with a DAKS two-piece and their own patented self-supporting trousers. Their shirts buttoned all the way down the front and had collars already attached by the manufacturer, unlike the tunic style of the time which had to be slipped over the head and the collar fastened separately. Simpson had made the ready-to-wear suit respectable.

In 1937 just five years after he had inherited the business, Alexander Simpson died, age 35. His elder brother, Dr Simpson, was called upon to combine his medical and scientific work with looking after the firm. At the start of the Second World War, Dr Simpson founded the Simpson Services Club on the fifth floor of the store which was used as a meeting place for the officers of the Allied Forces. Lord Mountbatten said of it later: 'undoubtedly many a point was settled in the Simpson Service Club which might not have been settled outside.'

Although it used to be predominantly a man's shop, Simpson have since evolved into a store for men and women. It has always been closely associated with all fields of sport. It has supported and equipped competitors for the Olympic Games, the British Empire Games, Commonwealth Cricket Test matches and International Golfing Tournaments. Over the years Simpson have become a terribly British shop. DAKS town and country casuals are as much a part of the British gentry as Range-Rovers and labradors.

Dr Simpson's daughter, Georgina, joined the board of directors in 1976. Her husband is Anthony Andrews of *Brideshead Revisited* fame who recently won the annual Best Dressed Man award and who, when asked which clothes he likes to wear, invariably says, 'Simpson's'. But as the young and glamorous set have never before had a foothold in the door of Simpson, Ms Simpson has been revamping it. She has opened two new shops within the building for the 'sophisticated young-at-heart', featuring clothing from top British, European and American designers.

Monday–Saturday: 9–5.30; Thursday: 9–7.
One mail order catalogue at Christmas.
Free for British residents.

TOMLINSON & TOMLINSON
8 Hornton Street
London W8 4NW
(01) 937 5173

One spring day The Princess of Wales and her private detective visited Tomlinson & Tomlinson, the spacious corner shop off Kensington High Street. The Princess immediately chose what she wanted and a few minutes later walked out with a 'weather' jumper in dark blue wool showing a picture of large clouds, lots of rain and a lightning flash. It was later worn with a pair of jeans to a polo match in the summer of 1983. To commemorate the Royal visit, Tomlinson display a newspaper cutting of her wearing it in their shop window.

The wood-floored shop is bright and open. It is filled with multi-coloured, multi-patterned handmade and individually designed knitwear all cleverly displayed on hangers. Not a plain jumper in sight.

Monday–Friday: 10–6; Saturday: 10–5.30.

Sheep and horses don't mix. Lady Diana Spencer about to leave her first polo match at Windsor Great Park in her Ford Escort

WARM & WONDERFUL
191 St Johns Hill
London SW11 1TH

(01) 228 8724

The black sheep jumper, contrary to public opinion, was not deliberately chosen by The Princess of Wales as a statement about how she felt her new family saw her. It was given to her by a friend who bought the bright red jumper covered with white sheep – and one black one – from Warm & Wonderful.

Warm & Wonderful is a little all-pink shop which was opened four years ago in South London by Jo Osborne and Sally Muir. They started by knitting everything themselves. Today they have over 200 out-workers, and export to America and Japan. Warm & Wonderful sell machine- and hand-knitted jumpers. The black sheep jumper was machine-knitted then hand-finished with all the little sheeps' eyes added manually. A Sheep Jumper costs £50. Their hand-knitted jumpers can take up to two weeks to make and are often covered with abstract rather than figurative designs with woollen bobbles and bumps incorporated into the texture. Many of their jumpers feature sheep, their trade-mark. There are sheep in their Farmyard jumper and sheep in their Wolf in Sheep's Clothing jumper. There are no sheep in their Pig jumper.

Monday–Friday: 10.30–6.30. Open on Saturday prior to Christmas. Christmas mail order catalogue available and Warm & Wonderful jumpers can be bought at Saks Fifth Avenue, Maceys and other department stores in the States and in Japan.

Designers

HARDY AMIES LIMITED
14 Savile Row
London W1X 1JN

(01) 734 2436

Dressmakers to HM The Queen.

Hardy Amies says his style is 'sporting, expensive-looking and ladylike. Put the initials together and that's what they do: sell.' As one of Britain's foremost couturiers Mr Amies first dressed The Queen – then Princess Elizabeth – for the Royal tour of Canada in 1948, when she was expecting her first baby. In 1977 Mr Amies was made Commander of the Royal Victorian Order, and he continues to make clothes for Her Majesty today.

The House of Hardy Amies is at 14 Savile Row, a fine Georgian building and the house in which Sheridan died. Mr Amies sees his clothes as an investment. When you buy them, he declares, 'You are paying for superb fabric, the time of skilled cutters, seamstresses and fitters – not to mention the time of the designer, the rates and fuel bills.' He admits, however, that you also pay for 'the snob appeal of the address', and for his name on the label. The starting price of a simple wool dress is £750, though it will be altered and delivered free of charge and will last 'five years of hard wear'.

In his 50 years as a designer of couture clothes, Mr Amies has also designed ready-to-wear clothes for women, lingerie, menswear, uniforms for British Airways, accessories for both men and women and household fitments – designs which have resulted in almost 50 licensing agreements all over the world.

Monday–Friday: 9.30–5.30. If you don't see anything you like in the showrooms, tell one of the designers what you're looking for.

MURRAY ARBEID
169 Sloane Square
London SW1X 9QF

(01) 235 5618

Murray Arbeid's clothes are made for occasions. It is probably why Mr Arbeid considers that he is more successful in the

14 Savile Row, London. The House of Hardy Amies

States than in England. 'They have the right social life.'

Mr Arbeid has always been fascinated by the stage, and originally wanted to be a theatre costume designer. Today the atmosphere he has created in his studios in New Bond Street resembles backstage at the Royal Opera House, with rails of brightly coloured and sequined dresses crowded into a tiny room. When Mr Arbeid started designing in the early 1950s he worked for Michael Sherard as an apprentice and learnt to sew. Starting on his own he worked only for private clients but found the work too 'soul destroying'. Today he has only four private clients, among them Dame Janet Baker for whom he makes recital clothes. He satisfies his theatrical tastes in the dramatic clothes he makes for his customers, from the enormous taffeta polka dot boa designed to be flung round bare shoulders to the striking ballgown worn by The Princess of Wales for dinner at Government House. The ballgown was in apricot taffeta with a low V-neck, a hip-length pintucked bodice and leg-of-mutton sleeves.

Monday–Saturday: 10–6. Murray Arbeid clothes start from £250 for a cocktail dress to £2,000 for a couture outfit.

BELLVILLE SASSOON
73 Pavilion Road
London SW1X 0ET

(01) 235 3087

Bellville Sassoon's clothes appeal to 'the young marrieds' – Lady Litchfield, The Duchess of Westminster and The Princess of Wales, all of whom might come to Bellville Sassoon to buy clothes for Ascot and the next ball or wedding. David Sassoon designed The Princess of Wales's going-away outfit, a canteloupe silk dress and jacket with a wide frilly organza white

collar. He also designed the dress – bright pink crêpe de chine with white daisies and a matching battledress jacket – she wore for Prince William's christening and again for her visit to Parliament House in Sydney. Today, although most of The Princess of Wales's clothes are especially designed for her, she does buy some off-the-peg as most of Mr Sassoon's other customers do.

When David Sassoon left the Royal College of Art where he had been studying fashion, he teamed up with Belinda Bellville whose grandmother had been a famous couturier in the 1920s. Ms Bellville has since retired.

The shop with its cream and beige interior is open for customers to buy off-the-peg clothes so there is no need to make an appointment. Most of Mr Sassoon's customers come in to buy his 'little black dresses' which start at £150. For £100 you get 'not a lot', and for £500 you can buy a Bellville Sassoon ballgown. And if the prices are putting you off, his patterns are for sale in the Vogue Designer Collection series.

Monday–Friday: 9.30–5.30. Bellville Sassoon clothes are also available from Harrods and good clothes shops.

DONALD CAMPBELL
8 William Street
London SW1X 9HL

(01) 235 3332

At the age of eight Donald Campbell was given two paper cut-out dolls of the American comic-strip characters, Li'l Abner and his girlfriend Daisy Mae who, alas, had only one dress. Mr Campbell's solution was to cut more clothes and 'from that age on it became a mini-obsession'. Today Mr Campbell no longer cuts any of the clothes he designs although he still makes the patterns.

Mr Campbell was born in Canada and has lived in England since the 1950s when he first worked for couturier John Kavanagh. In 1973 he opened the small two-floored boutique in William Street, with its cane furniture and wooden floors, where his clothes can be found today. He was introduced to The Princess of Wales, then Lady Spencer, by her sister and began making clothes for The Princess when she first came into the public eye.

The most popular dresses in Donald Campbell's collection of ready-to-wear clothes are his afternoon dresses, often silk, waisted and with a set-in sleeve and scooped neckline. 'The English don't like to look too smart,' he says; 'they like blues, greens and pinks which flatter their English skin.'

Many of the dresses The Princess of Wales has bought from Mr Campbell are classic shapes, belted, silk and often in Royal blue, green or pink. His clothes are easy to spot as Mr Campbell frequently uses complementary patterns in the dresses, such as two floral prints or spots and stripes. An exception was the suit The Princess of Wales wore in 1981 to Caernarvon Castle. The pleated dark green skirt was worn with a bright red contrasting jacket with a green collar and belt – true Welsh colours.

Monday–Friday: 9.30–5.30; Saturday: 11–5.30.

CAROLINE CHARLES
11 Beauchamp Place
London SW3 1NQ

(01) 589 5850

Number 11 Beauchamp Place is decorated in soft pink and beige with frescoes of carnations on the walls. There is a large mirror across the end of the shop and a glass dome in the ceiling. It houses Caroline Charles' twice-yearly collection of 'easy, sensuous and amusing' off-the-peg day and evening clothes.

Caroline Charles trained at Swindon College of Art. She first worked for Michael Sherard and then with Mary Quant until she launched her own label in 1963. The Princess of Wales was one of her customers before her engagement to Prince Charles. Her interest in Caroline Charles clothes was later reinforced by the editors of *Vogue* magazine who were consulted about The Princess of Wales's wardrobe. Caroline Charles cites her fashion inspiration as coming from national costumes and old cinema, both of which can be seen in outfits bought off-the-peg by The Princess. Her dress for the Braemar Games in September 1982 was made from a Scottish-influenced plaid fabric with an Edwardian, governess-style bodice complete with starched white collar and cuffs. It was featured in *Vogue* earlier that year at £240.

Monday–Saturday: 10–5.30; Wednesday: 10–6. Caroline Charles clothes can also be bought from major department stores and chic boutiques.

JASPER CONRAN
49-50 Great Marlborough Street
London W1V 1DB

Joan Collins, Selina Scott, Paula Yates and The Princess of Wales all wear Jasper Conran's clothes. And Mummy, Shirley Conran of *Superwoman* and *Lace* fame, does too. At 24 Mr Conran is already one of Britain's most highly rated designers.

Jasper Conran says he finds frills irrelevant and hates prints, flowery or swirly, though a Conran suit worn by The Princess of Wales to the Trooping of the Colour ceremony in 1982 was made from an elegant grey and white floral print. His clothes are cool, chic, classic and beautifully cut by one of the two men who work with him. The rest of his 15 staff are women.

Although Jasper Conran had his first collection in 1978, when he was 18, his most successful was in 1980. It was held upstairs at Langan's Brasserie off Piccadilly and Marie Helvin modelled in return for clothes. Despite the fact it was held at nine in the morning, it was packed.

From his start in a small room at the top

Opposite:
Prince William's christening took place on The Queen Mother's 82nd birthday, 4 August 1982. The young Prince was wearing the lace christening shawl made in 1841 for Edward VII. The Princess of Wales was wearing a Bellville Sassoon outfit and a John Boyd hat. The Queen's hat was made for her by Frederick Fox and her dress and jacket came from Hardy Amies. The Queen Mother's hat was her favourite style from Z. V. Rudolph, and her dress was from Norman Hartnell

of his parents' house in Regent's Park, where he did everything apart from the typing, Jasper Conran now has his own studio where he designs his collections of clothes, shoes and stockings (for Wolfords). He is about to design a range of maternity clothes for Mothercare (see page 121).

Jasper Conran's clothes are available from major department stores and boutiques. Prices start from £80 for a T-shirt top.

VICTOR EDELSTEIN
9 Stanhope Mews West
London SW7 5RB

(01) 373 5462

The Victor Edelstein evening dress worn by The Princess of Wales made its début on the pages of *Vogue* in December 1982. Described as 'strapless gold gauze' with a 'dropped waist and deeply tucked bodice

The Princess of Wales wearing a Gina Fratini ballgown attended The Night of Knights *show at the Barbican Centre early in 1982*

and hem', it cost £550. The Princess bought it in pink, asked Mr Edelstein to add a strap to the bodice on each shoulder – for practical reasons – and dressed it up for the private reception given for her and Prince Charles by Pierre Trudeau in Ottowa in June 1983 and again for a Barry Manilow concert in October of the same year. Since then she bought two of his outfits for her tour of Australia in 1983.

Victor Edelstein is English with Russian parents. He is extremely tall and looks endearingly like an overgrown schoolboy. He remembers first drawing dresses at the age of 10 and being fascinated by historical costume. Although as a boy Mr Edelstein entertained hopes of becoming an actor, on leaving school he worked for Biba, cutting patterns, and later spent two years with Christian Dior-London as an assistant designer. In 1977 he set up on his own in Long Acre in Covent Garden aiming for the wholesale market, but soon changing direction and becoming a couturier.

Today Mr Edelstein works to classical music in Stanhope Mews designing evening clothes or outfits for the female 'lead executive'. His look is formal, classic and sophisticated. 'Most girls don't want frills and ruffles, they want to look sexy. It's their mothers who want them to look romantic and sweet.'

Monday–Friday: 9.30–5.30. By appointment only. Victor Edelstein does not sell off-the-peg outfits, instead you try on samples on which your dress will be based.

GINA FRATINI LIMITED
2 Burlington Place
London W1X 1FB

Gina Fratini was asked to design a dress that was 'formal' for The Princess of Wales to wear at the Royal couple's farewell banquet at the Sheraton Hotel in Auckland at the end of the New Zealand tour. She created a cream-coloured ballgown in organza with a lace trim and matching underskirts to give it a full shape. The pin-tucked bodice was topped by a scooped neckline with a tiny frilled trim and the sheer elbow-length sleeves were trimmed with fine baby ribbon and bows. The dress was typical of Gina Fratini's love of detail. She once used over 70 yards of lace and trimmings for a design for one of her clients. The Princess of Wales had previously worn another of Gina Fratini's designs to the 25th London

Film Festival in November 1981. It was a glamorous dark blue velvet dress with a large puritan white collar. Later, when The Princess of Wales was pregnant with Prince William, Gina Fratini designed several of her outfits.

Gina Fratini studied at the Royal College of Art in the 1960s and, age 20, joined the Katherine Dunham dance company in California as an assistant designer of scenery and costumes. She created her first collection in London in 1966, and in 1971 two of her dresses were chosen by Princess Anne for her official 21st birthday photographs taken by Norman Parkinson (see page 224). Other clients include Princess Alexandra and the Duchess of Kent.

Gina Fratini's ready-to-wear day wear starts at £100 and her evening wear at £200. Her clothes are available in London from Lucienne Phillips and Rich Bitch and from boutiques around the country.

NORMAN HARTNELL LIMITED
26 Bruton Street
London W1X 8DD

(01) 629 0992

Dressmakers to HM The Queen and HM The Queen Mother.

In Norman Hartnell's heyday before a Royal overseas tour the fashion press would be requested to join him at dawn at his Bruton Street showrooms. With the Palace's approval, members of the press would be shown sketches of the outfits to be worn by the female members of the Royal family. Times have changed, and there is now a stricter control on designers talking to the press about their Royal clients.

The House of Hartnell in Bruton Street has an air of past splendour, but it is still breathtaking. A graceful stairway panelled with mirrors and carpeted in deep green leads up to the great Salon – an enormous L-shaped room. The walls are painted celandon green, a green/grey colour invented by Sir Norman, the floor is pale green and the art-deco mirrored columns, the perfect arum lilies and the two giant crystal chandeliers create an atmosphere of tranquillity and luxury rarely to be seen today. On display is the latest Hartnell selection of day, cocktail and evening wear, with ready-to-wear (Hartnell's call it 'boutique') prices starting at £250 and couture prices from £450.

Sir Norman Hartnell began his career while still an undergraduate at Cambridge, when his costume designs for a student play were seen and praised by a Fleet Street journalist. Once in London, he had initial difficulties in overcoming the prejudices of fashion-conscious women who had always looked to Paris; but his first wedding dress, for the bride of The Marquis of Bath, was described as 'the eighth wonder of the world' and from then on Sir Norman was established. His relationship with the Royal family began a few years later, in 1935, when he designed the wedding dress – in palest pink rather than traditional white – worn by Lady Alice Montague Douglas-Scott for her marriage to the Duke of Gloucester. Amongst the bridesmaids were two child attendants, The Princesses Elizabeth and Margaret. The following year, Hartnell was summoned to 145 Piccadilly to make clothes for The Duchess of York, about to become The Queen. Until his death in 1979, at the age of

An illustration by Norman Hartnell of HM Queen Elizabeth II dressed in the robe designed by him for her Coronation in 1953. The gown was in white satin and embroidered with the emblems of Great Britain (the Tudor Rose of England; the Leek of Wales; the Shamrock of Ireland and the Thistle of Scotland) and the Commonwealth (the Maple Leaf of Canada; the Wattle Flower of Australia; the Fern of New Zealand; the Protea flower of South Africa; the Lotus flowers of India and Ceylon and the Wheat, Cotton and Jute of Pakistan)

77, Sir Norman was The Queen Mother's couturier. Today the House of Hartnell continues to serve the Royal family under George Mitchison, their managing director.

'Appointments are made for clients but the salon is always open from Monday to Friday, 10–5 to welcome clients.'

MARGARET HOWELL
24/26 St Christopher's Place London W1M 5HD

(01) 935 8588

The Margaret Howell look is 'classic with a twist'. You can buy a traditional tweed coat, but it will be longer or bigger or have velvet lapels. A two-piece woman's linen suit will have a longer skirt and a shorter jacket than normal and their corduroy trousers – as seen on The Princess of Wales before her marriage, at an informal photo session in Balmoral – will have pleats round the waist. Traditional country English, very solid-looking clothes.

Margaret Howell also designs evening wear. The white tuxedo, black trousers, white silk shirt and bow tie that The Princess of Wales wore to a Genesis concert in March 1984 was one of her designs. The Princess bought the whole outfit for £200.

After studying fine art at Goldsmiths' College, where her only forays into fashion were papier-mâché jewellery and knitting, Ms Howell started designing her finely striped and often collarless shirts for men. This led to trousers and jackets and in 1981 she opened a shop in St Christopher's Place and started designing clothes for women too. Today there are Margaret Howell shops in New York and Tokyo and the original shop in St Christopher's Place is three times bigger. In her shops Ms Howell sells her total English look, from shoes and socks to hats and handkerchiefs. All her clothes are in natural fibres and a speciality is Irish linen.

Monday–Friday: 10–6; Thursday: 10–7; Saturday: 10–5.

Lady Diana Spencer and Prince Charles relaxing during a walk at Balmoral. The Princess of Wales is wearing an Inca sweater with Margaret Howell corduroy trousers and Uniroyal green wellingtons

DAVID NEIL
38 South Molton Street
London W1Y 1HA

(01) 408 1021

David Neil works with Julia Fortescue in a tiny third-floor showroom in South Molton Street. The duo design clothes in strong, vibrant colours under the David Neil label. Their outfits are popular with The Princess of Wales. She wore one of their designs, a bright red and blue crêpe de chine two-piece to the wedding of Nicholas Soames in 1981. The same year one of the suits in their spring collection caught The Princess's eye and they made it up for her in another fabric lest she coincide with someone else who might have bought it. The outfit was a three-piece; camisole top, a blouse with a soft frilled collar and a matching pleated skirt. The Princess of Wales wore it in bright banana yellow, fuschia and Royal blue stripes and it seems to be among her favourites. She wore it to Ascot in 1981 and later in Australia.

David Neil gave up his architectural training to attend a fashion course at St Martin's School of Art. After a spell with Yves St Laurent in Paris he returned to London to work for 'O' in South Molton Street. It was there he met Ms Fortescue. They set up in business on their own in 1981 and were introduced to The Princess of Wales by one of The Queen's goddaughters.

The couple try to work on their designs together but Mr Neil's forte is suits, coats and daywear while Ms Fortescue prefers to design dresses and evening wear. One of the walls of their beige and cream studio is covered with photographs of society weddings for which they made the wedding dresses. A wedding dress starts at £1,000, and a day dress at £200.

Monday–Friday: 9.30–5.30.

BRUCE OLDFIELD LIMITED
41 Beauchamp Place
London SW3 1NX

(01) 584 1363

Bruce Oldfield learnt his basic skills in dressmaking after Dr Barnardo's found him a foster mother in Yorkshire who was a talented dressmaker. 'I was determined to become a designer rather than go down the pits. I don't believe I would have made a great miner,' he says. Mr Oldfield won a

scholarship to study fashion at Ravensbourne Art College in Kent.

He has been described as the 'golden boy' of British fashion. The Princess of Wales has been wearing his clothes since her engagement. 'It was largely a piece of luck,' says Oldfield modestly. 'I just happened to be one of the designers The Princess picked out of the collection of clothes *Vogue* magazine had assembled for her to choose from.' He designed many pieces for The Princess's Canadian and Australian tours. The dazzling bright blue chiffon evening gown which she wore for the Charity Ball at the Wentworth Hotel in Sydney was one of his. Its short-sleeved style laced through with silver threads and offset with a silver cummerbund incorporated The Princess's favourite frilled trim although Oldfield achieved a highly original effect by positioning the frill over the shoulders and down both sides of the dress.

Unlike some of The Princess of Wales's designers, Mr Oldfield is keen to keep his comments on the clothes he makes for The Princess to a minimum. 'We're not really supposed to talk about it. I think the protocol is never deny but never elaborate.'

Monday–Friday: 9.30–5.30. By appointment only.

BENNY ONG
3 Bentinck Mews
London W1M N5FL

As you enter Benny Ong's all-white workshop and studio in Bentinck Mews there is a huge photograph of Mr Ong standing on one foot and smiling. He deserves to be happy. At the age of 34 his clothes are worn everywhere from Brazil to Belgium and by everyone from the Prime Minister of Iceland to The Princess of Wales.

Benny Ong was born in Singapore. In 1968 he came to England to study fashion at St Martin's School of Art. In 1974 he showed his first collection with an emphasis on hand-painted silk evening dresses. Today his look has changed. His clothes are understated, stylish and simple. The Princess of Wales wore two of his ready-to-wear outfits on her trip to Australia in 1983. The first – a white cotton jacquard button-through dress and white leather belt – was worn amidst the heat of Ayers rock and the other, a soft ivory blouse and pale mint green skirt, was worn on a visit to the Karguru School. Benny

Ong clearly knows how to design clothes for hot climates.

Mr Ong has three collections. At the top end of the market is his Designer range, with prices from £150 to £500. The International collection, from which The Princess chose her blouse and skirt, contains clothes for cocktail parties and other special occasions, with prices from £100 to £150, and his third collection, Sunday, consists of leisure wear with an emphasis on young, sporty, casual clothes. The Princess's white dress came from the Sunday collection.

Benny Ong's clothes can be bought from over 60 clothes shops, department stores and boutiques in the UK and from stockists worldwide. 'Nobody visits Bentinck Mews.'

ARABELLA POLLEN
Unit 28
Avon Trading Estate
Avonmore Road
London W14 8TS

(01) 602 3751

'I don't think having a (Royal) crest on the window really helps sales,' said Arabella

The Princess of Wales greets the crowds in Adelaide dressed in an Arabella Pollen banana-coloured striped silk suit, and John Boyd hat

Pollen, the youngest of The Princess of Wales's designers. Yet since Ms Pollen started to work for The Princess she has been described as one of the fashion trades 'hottest properties'. And she admitted that, 'obviously it helps if people know that I design for her.'

The same age as The Princess of Wales, Ms Pollen works from the fourth floor of a warehouse complex in West Kensington as does Zandra Rhodes – one of the few British designers The Princess has not patronised. The daughter of Peregrine Pollen, a former president of Sotheby Parke Bernet in New York who now lives in Royal Gloucestershire, Arabella Pollen claims to have hated clothes until she was 16 when suddenly she became very fashion conscious and made herself a blue suit. Ms Pollen giggled, 'I thought it was very easy.'

A few years later, after a failed attempt to write a film script, she began making clothes for friends to support herself. While on holiday in the Hebrides Ms Pollen started designing a collection of clothes. During her return trip to London she discovered a spinning mill on the Isle of Skye – formerly used by Schiaparelli – which was weaving large window-pane checks in tweed. 'It was an absolute fluke and absolutely vital.' She decided to base her designs on hunting styles of the early 1900s and approached Naim Attallah, a director of Asprey (see page 92) for financial backing. At 19 Arabella Pollen held her first collection at Mr Attallah's offices in Knightsbridge. The clothes had been sewn on her kitchen table from materials paid for by Mr Attallah. Not only did the first collection raise about £20,000, but it was also bought for the shop Taylor and Hadow in Beauchamp Place and seen by Anna Harvey of *Vogue* who advises The Princess of Wales on her clothes.

The first two Pollen outfits worn by The Princess of Wales were identical apart from the colour. They were coat dresses, both almost floor-length, with double-breasted fitted bodices with two rows of buttons down the front and soft gathered skirts. The first, worn in Wales in November 1982, was camel-coloured with a dark brown check and a dark brown leather collar and cuffs. The other, worn in Liverpool in December of the same year, was grey with black collar, cuffs and buttons.

The Princess has since reflected Ms Pollen's ever-changing but always fashionable taste with a banana-coloured striped silk suit worn in Adelaide in 1983 and a blue cotton sailor dress with a white collar and a pale pink bow, again for Australia. Both of these could have been bought off-the-peg from a selection of clothes ranging from £50 to £150. Arabella Pollen has since designed a collection of pyjamas, dressing gowns, ties and bow ties in marble-patterned silk. Available from the Italian Paper Shop at 11 Brompton Arcade.

Arabella Pollen is 'by appointment only' at the above address, but her clothes are available from Taylor and Hadow in Beauchamp Place, Harvey Nichols (see page 115) and other clothes shops around the country.

TATTERS
74 Fulham Road
London SW3 5PF

(01) 584 1532

The Princess of Wales has bought several dresses from Tatters, including a maternity dress and the coral pink silk ball gown which she wore on one of her first public appearances with Prince Charles. The gown had a full two-tiered skirt and a bodice adorned with fine lace – the Tatters trademark.

Tatters was started by Missie Crockett and Graham Hughes 10 years ago. They began by selling antique jewellery, textiles and laces on a small stall but soon moved to premises on the Fulham Road from where they sold original antique clothing. They found it difficult to get stock which led them to copy an antique dress they had bought at a Christie's textile sale. They enlarged it from a size six to a size ten for a friend's wedding dress. Then they started to make modern replicas of original clothing – a complicated task as neither Missie Crockett nor Mr Hughes had ever had any training in cutting or sewing. Today they design their own dresses which are made by 12 seamstresses. The work involved is intricate and the dresses are exquisitely romantic with silk flounces, bows, tucks and plenty of the Tatters lace. Dresses cost between £300 and £1,000.

Monday–Friday: 10–6; Saturday: 10–5.

JAN VANVELDEN
36 Lexington Street
London W1R 3HR

(01) 437 1683

'I often wonder about what happens to my clothes,' Jan Vanvelden said in his faintly Dutch accent. 'What are all these people doing with them?' But Mr Vanvelden knows what The Princess of Wales has done with his outfits. She has worn his dresses and suits with their large white jagged 'Van Dyke' collars on numerous occasions, including at what Prince Charles calls a 'crawlabout' – a photo session for Prince William – in the gardens of the Governor-General's house in Australia near the end of the 1983 tour. Jan Vanvelden's white blouse with its black brushstroke pattern has been worn by The Princess dressed up with a black skirt to Adelaide University where The Princess and Prince Charles showed the crowd how to jive, and dressed down with a white straight skirt to watch her husband play polo. Vanvelden's bright red satin ballgown with a matching lace top, worn by The Princess of Wales for a farewell banquet at Government House in Edmonton in Canada, has been immortalised in a portrait of The Princess by June Mendoza (the only female member of the Royal Society of Portrait Painters) which was unveiled at Grocer's Hall in January 1984.

As a teenager Jan Vanvelden always wanted to be a milliner. He used to make hats for his mother and friends of his parents. After studying fashion in Amsterdam in the 1960s, he tried to get a job with one of the large fashion houses, but failed. He came to England and worked at Simpsons (see page 74) selling DAKS menswear for six months. Later he formed a partnership with Eric Hall, designing for the Salvador label. In 1981 he started his own collection which was an instant success. Today he designs his sophisticated clothes for 'the kind of people who go to New York for the weekend'. Mr Vanvelden's blouses start at £110 and his silk dresses at £300.

Jan Vanvelden's clothes are available from Harrods, Fortnum & Mason, Simpson and boutiques throughout London and the UK, and from boutiques and department stores worldwide. Lexington Street is Mr Vanvelden's workshop and office only.

Embroiderers

S. LOCK LIMITED
County House
33/34 Rathbone Place
London W1P 1AD

(01) 636 0574

Embroiderers to HM The Queen.

Lock embroidered the train for Princess Anne's wedding dress. The nine-foot net took 200 hours to embroider. The approved design was first sewn in white silk and silver thread and then mirror jewels and pearls were applied. In order to preserve secrecy, Lock 'invented' a Greek bride who was being married in Athens in early November. One of the girls working on the train was heard to remark, 'What a pity it isn't for Princess Anne.' The same secrecy was used by 'Miss Peggy', one of

Below right:
A detail of the embroidery by Lock's on Princess Anne's wedding train

Princess Anne's wedding dress (worn here by a model) was designed by Maureen Baker of Susan Small. The train was embroidered by Lock's

Lock's directors, who was 'on holiday' when she sewed the 14-foot-long wedding veil for The Princess of Wales with what she describes as a 'Milky Way' effect using over 10,000 sequins. Miss Peggy was actually working at home in her sitting room.

Lock work for the 'big fashion houses', Hardy Amies, Hartnell and Murray Arbeid (see pages 77, 81 and 77). 'I suppose they know,' said Mr Lock, with a modest cough, 'that we're the best.' Their work has been worn by Cilla Black, Petula Clark, Eartha Kitt and Barbara Cartland as well as by the Royal family. Lock received their Royal Warrant from The Queen in 1972.

The Hardy Amies poppy dress that The Queen wore in 1983 to the 20th Century-Fox Studios in Los Angeles was embroidered by Lock, as was The Queen Mother's 80th-birthday gown, which was covered with orchids sewn in gold and silver thread, studded with diamonds and picked out with clusters of fine pearls. The full-length dress with its crossover neck and three-quarter-length scalloped sleeves was designed by Hartnell. Another Royal commission was new sleeves for a cerise dress which The Queen had decided to bring up to date. The sleeves were snaking columns of intertwining red sequins, edged with gold thread.

Lock's 20 embroiderers work on the fourth floor of the Rathbone Place warehouse. They either embroider by machine or sequin by hand on their tambour frames, following complicated coded patterns drawn on to the reverse side of the fabric. Pearls, diamonds, beads or large sequins are then sewn on by hand from the front to create a three-dimensional effect. To make the bodice of a dress could take 10 hours and it takes at least two years to train as a beader. Their collection of sequins, beads

and pearls dates back to the 1920s. And they still tint sequins to match any colour. Lock work for private customers too; a beaded collar starts from £50.

Monday–Friday: 9–5. Lock have samples of every style and design of embroidery they have ever worked which they can repeat, or they can work out a specific design for your requirements.

Fabrics

P. & J. HAGGART LIMITED
32 Dunkeld Street
Aberfeldy
Perthshire
Scotland

Aberfeldy (088 72) 0306

Tartan and woollen manufacturers to HM The Queen Mother.

In 1801, James Haggart started a woollen and tartan manufacturing business. From the time the wool left the back of a Cheviot sheep until the garment was finished, everything was supervised on site. By the beginning of the 19th century the company had two woollen mills at Aberfeldy equipped with the latest appliances for carding, spinning, weaving, dyeing and finishing. They also possessed extensive warehouses and a high-class tailoring establishment. Haggart were accorded some of the highest awards for excellence of homespuns in both Scotland and England. In 1899 they were awarded a Royal Warrant to Alexandra, Princess of Wales and would bring their goods for Royal perusal to Balmoral, Sandringham and Buckingham Palace.

Today you can buy tartan from £13 a yard or ready-made tartan rugs and scarves. A rug starts at £14.95.

Monday–Friday: 9–1, 2–5; closed Wednesday afternoons. P. & J. Haggart will mail tartans worldwide.

HARVEY NICHOLS LIMITED

See page 115.

LIBERTY
Regent Street
London W1R 6AH

(01) 734 1234

Silk mercers to HM The Queen Mother.

In 1875 the late Sir Arthur Liberty was encouraged by his illustrious friends, Whistler, Rossetti, Burne-Jones and Leighton to open a shop. They were anxious that someone should produce soft-coloured, clinging fabrics in place of the garish and harsh materials of the Victorian age. Sir Arthur knew that to sell these 'alternative' fabrics he would need to provide a homely atmosphere, rather than the lofty marble and gilt aura of other contemporary department stores. When asked by

'The Drawing Room at Balmoral is draped in Balmoral tartan – a quaint warm grey design, arranged by the Late Prince Consort. It is far superior in design to the startling and gaudy Royal Stuart tartan' (1882)

Liberty's Tudor-style building in Great Marlborough Street

the authorities in 1925 to rebuild Liberty's Tudor-style building in Regent Street to fit in with the classical style required for Regent Street, Sir Arthur had no option but to build another part of the store on an adjoining plot of land in Tudor style. The two parts of the store are linked by a three-storeyed bridge and a subway.

Liberty is one of the most delightful places in London to get lost in. In their little rooms within the store Liberty sell oriental carpets, jewellery, pictures, clothes, porcelain, books, perfumes and fabrics. The Queen was often dressed as a child in Liberty print fabrics with the result, it is rumoured, that today she dislikes them. Her mother, The Queen Mother, still honours Liberty with her warrant for their silks, and both The Princess of Wales and Princess Margaret have been known to visit the store on more than one occasion.

Liberty's have an entire floor devoted to fashion fabrics and one room containing nothing but silks. Some are imported from Italy, France and Switzerland but many are Liberty originals, printed by the company on raw silk from China. New designs are added once a year. Their silks can cost between £10 and £50 a metre, but if you can't sew, you can buy their fabrics in ready-made dresses and shirts from the fashion department.

Monday–Saturday: 9.30–6; Thursday: 9.30–7. Liberty's have one mail order catalogue at Christmas, which costs £1. They will deliver all over the country and mail worldwide. Liberty silks can be bought at department stores and specialist fabrics stores around the country.

Hats

JOHN BOYD
91 Walton Street
London SW3 2HP

(01) 589 7601

John Boyd has been making hats for Princess Anne since she was 17, for Margaret Thatcher since she became Prime Minister and for The Princess of Wales since her engagement was announced.

Whether The Princess of Wales likes wearing hats or not – before her engagement she had to borrow a trilby from her sister to attend the races – they have inevitably become part of her overall outfit. John Boyd is thrilled. He makes no secret about being one of The Princess's greatest admirers. When Mr Boyd was in Thailand he spotted some wire combs that he felt would be ideal for keeping The Princess of Wales's hats on her head. He bought the lot – 'She's got really springy hair.'

Mr Boyd has over 100 hats on show in his shop in Walton Street with ready-made hats starting from £35 and model hats from £75. All of his shapes can be ordered specially, in any colour and with or without feathers, veils or pompoms. Mr Boyd designs about 30 shapes for every season and then makes variations on each theme. But he readily admits: 'You always make more hats than you tell people.' For The Princess of Wales he has created unique styles such as her 'Edwardian' hat, tucked into the head at the back, with a large brim at the front, and the coral-coloured 'tricorn' hat first designed to be worn with her going-away outfit by Bellville Sassoon (see page 77). Originally the tricorn was to be included as part of Mr Boyd's collection, but once The Princess had decided she wanted to wear it the shape was reserved for her. Mr Boyd was most relieved that she did not change her mind.

Monday–Friday: 9.30–5.30.

CALEYS (COLE BROTHERS) LIMITED
See page 40.

FREDERICK FOX
169 Sloane Street
London SW1X 9QF

(01) 235 5618

Milliner to HM The Queen.

The first hats Freddie Fox made were for his elder sisters. Born in Urana in New South Wales – a tiny hamlet with a population of 400 in the middle of the plains – Mr Fox, aged 12, would chop up his sisters' hats and remake them. By the time he was 13, Mr Fox was re-making hats for everyone in town, picking them up from customer's on his bicycle one week and taking them back the next. He then started buying material from Sydney and making hats from scratch using his mother's mixing bowls and saucepans to block the crowns. At 17 Freddie Fox left home and got a job in a big hat factory in Sydney. 'The boss there, Valda, was one of the chic-est women I have ever known. The first day she appeared in the workroom she came in in this marvellous Dior dress with a hat which was a little brim twisted into a spiral about a foot high. I had never seen anything like it and my mouth dropped open and I stared. When she spoke to me I went crimson. I was very, very shy.'

Today Mr Fox can no longer be described as shy and his hats are as original, though possibly more practical than those Valda wore. In 1957 Freddie Fox came to England and six years later took over the old-established millinery firm of Langée. Since 1969 he has been making hats for The Queen – to be worn with her Hardy Amies clothes. He also makes hats for other members of the Royal family, including The Princess of Wales, and countless politicians' and diplomats' wives.

Mr Fox has two collections a year and makes hats for shows for several couturiers, such as Hardy Amies and Jasper Conran. Initially Mr Fox does a drawing of the new hat design and then either has a block made at his workshop in New Bond Street or in Paris – 'If I send the design to an English block maker, he'll copy the style.' His hats can be bought either from his 'boutique' range which retail from £20 to £60 or his designer range which start at £60. But no matter what you pay, Mr Fox wants his customers 'to feel as if they've been to me'.

Monday–Saturday: 10–6.

HERBERT JOHNSON
13 Old Burlington Street
London W1X 1LA

(01) 437 7397

Hatters to HM The Queen and HRH The Prince of Wales.

You are unlikely to brush brims with any members of the British Royal family at Herbert Johnson, but David Bradburn, the director, assured me that he has all their head measurements on record and that one of his staff frequently visits Buckingham Palace for fittings.

Herbert Johnson specialise in sporting and country hats, with an off-the-peg tweed cap starting at £18 and a felt hat from £40, but they will make any hat you desire. Their catalogue hints at their sense of fun with names like The Off Parade ('a smooth felt hat with a welted edge to the brim' for £40), The Bombay Bowler ('a lightweight protective helmet ideal for tropical conditions' for £45) and The Bond (£19.50).

About a quarter of Herbert Johnson's business is in supplying military caps. They make hats for 60 per cent of the officers in this country. They also made the Royal Navy cap worn by The Prince of Wales for his wedding, and told me, 'The Prince of

Three hats from Herbert Johnson: The Off-Parade, The Bombay Bowler and The Bond

Wales likes a rather small-fitting cap.'

Just in case you enter Herbert Johnson's unaware of their reputation, the walls are lined with previous Royal Warrants – they've been given one by every successive monarch since their shop opened in 1889 – and numerous blocks (head-shapes) of the rich and famous, including one of the late Czar of Russia.

Monday–Friday: 9–5.30; Saturday: 9–12.30. Mail order catalogue available on request, but be prepared for a wait.

JAMES LOCK & COMPANY LIMITED
6 St James's Street
London SW1A 1EF

(01) 930 8874

Hatters to HRH The Duke of Edinburgh.

When Locks were asked to make a 5¾-size bowler hat – which they still call a 'Coke' after its creator, William Coke – they were somewhat bemused. 'Even the head of a small child isn't that small,' Mr Stephenson, their managing director, told me. But the hat was not for a small child. Months later it appeared on the head of a monkey starring in a Brooke Bond tea advertisement.

The hatters were originally established at the south-east end of St James's Street by Robert Davis in 1676. Mr Davis had emigrated from the City in the wake of his fashionable customers. He died 20 years later leaving his business to his son, Charles, who in 1747 signed up James Lock as apprentice. In 1757 James Lock married his master's daughter, Mary, and in 1759 after Mr Davies's death he inherited the business. In 1765 the shop moved to its present site and in 1805, shortly before the Battle of Trafalgar, Locks supplied one of the first of their many noted customers, Nelson, with his cocked hat complete with special eye-shade. One of their most recent customers was Larry Hagman, J.R. of *Dallas* fame – though they did not supply him with his famous stetson.

The interior of Locks has black wood panelled walls, an unusual 'coffin' staircase – thought to date from 1690 – and stacks of elegant white hat boxes. They also still have their conformateur, a mechanical device which looks like a top hat. When applied to the head it maps out exactly the contours of the head in reduced scale on a small card so that hats can be moulded to fit properly and the card filed for future use.

One member of the Royal family who did not buy hats from Locks was Edward VII but he found another use for the shop. As Prince of Wales he would use Locks as an escape route to get from St James's Street to Crown Passage. One evening he was returning to Marlborough House and wanted to avoid the salute of the sentries outside St James's Palace. He was let in to Locks, then shut up for the night, by Amy Lock, an attractive and merry widow. There was talk and he was forbidden to use the shop as a short cut again.

Locks have supplied Prince Philip with the soft felt hats he often carries behind his back. They also devised a fibreglass polo cap for him known as 'polo cap HRH pattern'. Once, before the Trooping of the Guard ceremony, they had to reassure him that possibly the reason why his Guards' bearskin head-dress felt so uncomfortable was that he only had to wear it once a year. According to Locks, Prince Philip replied, 'You're absolutely right. I'll have to put the thing on and practice.' Prince Charles gets his polo caps from Locks at £95 each, and in September 1981 The Princess of Wales came in to buy her first – and probably last – riding hat. The most memorable of Locks' Royal occasions, however, was in 1953, just before the coronation, when Garrards (see page 4) were re-modelling the Imperial State Crown. To make it more comfortable for Her Majesty, Mr Lock was commanded to devise a modern fitment that would sustain the crown as lightly as

possible upon The Queen's head. This he did and together with Mr Mann, from Garrards, he presented the crown to Her Majesty at Buckingham Palace. 'Isn't that funny – it fits!' said The Queen with undisguised surprise. 'Oh dear,' she added, 'I shouldn't have said that, should I?'

Monday–Friday: 9–5; Saturday: 9.30–12.30. Mail order catalogue available. Lock's hats are sold throughout the world.

SIMONE MIRMAN
**11 West Halkin Street
London SW1X 8JL**

(01) 235 2656

Milliner to HM The Queen and HM The Queen Mother.

Madam Mirman pointed at an open copy of *Harpers & Queen* to a group photograph of a society wedding and showed me the seven women – including the bride – who were wearing her hats. Her work involves careful planning if none of the guests are to wear the same hat – especially if the Royal family are involved. Simone Mirman has been making hats for the Royal family since 1952 when Princess Margaret came to see her and ordered several hats. In the early 1960s The Queen Mother ('who always speaks French to me') became a customer and in 1965 The Queen followed.

Simone Parmentier, as she was then called, began making hats at the age of 15. At art school she won every prize she could and then went on to work with Schiaparelli in Paris. In 1947 she eloped with Serge Mirman and the couple came to London with one pound between them. Ms Mirman started her millinery business in a tiny attic in Spring Street in Paddington and in 1947 moved to her elegant Chesham Place salon where she built up her successful couture millinery business. Twice yearly Simone Mirman would have collections of about 150 of her latest hats, which were presented to the press 'to show what I could do'.

The hats were so outrageous that many remained unsold. Madame Mirman kept them stored away and in 1982, when she moved to her present address, she had over 500 hats 'in velvet, leather, wool, straw, organza, silk and cotton in a multitude of styles and colours' for sale. In September 1982, the Simone Mirman Collection was auctioned at Christies. Most of her hats were bought by the Victoria and Albert Museum.

In the 1950s Madame Mirman said: 'Your hat should make you feel like singing. It should always be a tonic to wear – yet be so comfortable, so much a part of you that you are never conscious of it and can forget about it.' Today her shop and office make you feel like singing. They are decorated in the palest of beiges with hats, from sequined cloche caps to navy and white boaters perched on varying heights of hat stands, and exquisite pale wood antique furniture from her family in France. It is elegance only the French know how to achieve and the only incongruity is a hat on display recently designed for the new female Chief Constable of the Merseyside Police. Madame Mirman has created hats for many 'names', including Vivien Leigh (the hat she wore for her wedding to Laurence Olivier), Bianca Jagger and Elizabeth Taylor, for the film *Zee & Co*. She says you can recognise her hats by their 'simple lines' and 'uncluttered feel'. More recently Simone Mirman has introduced a collection of hats for men which have already been worn by Lord Snowdon and Lord Clarke. Today Madame Mirman feels 'a hat should make the taxi driver open the door for you'.

Monday–Saturday: 9–6. If necessary Madame Mirman can 'make a miracle in one day' if you are in a hurry for your hat and don't see anything on display that will suit or fit you. Hats start at £75.

S. PATEY (LONDON) LIMITED
**1 Amelia Street
Walworth Road
London SE17 3PY**

(01) 703 6528

Manufacturers of hats to HM The Queen.

Although S. Patey hold a Royal Warrant to The Queen, it is unlikely that Her Majesty has ever worn one of their hats, as the warrant is held for the Royal Mews department, providing hats for the chauffeurs and coachman who work there. But S. Patey have made top hats for hunting for Prince Philip and Princess Anne.

Mr Patey started the firm on leaving the army. Then there were only three staff, now there are 20. Today they make hats for the Lord Mayor, for Chelsea Pensioners, Household Footmen, Beefeaters, the BBC costume department, Madame Tussauds and mortar boards for university graduates.

At their shop, situated just off the Walworth Road, you can find hunting caps and toppers as well as grey top hats for Ascot. Hunting caps start from £90 and once they have measured your head, the hat should be ready within half an hour. Their top hats take longer to make. For those Pateys may need to make a block. Top hats take eight hours to make and cost from £140. They will also put your hat straight if it has been trodden on by your horse. The refurbishment service costs £60.

Monday–Friday: 8–5. You can also buy S. Patey hats from Ede & Ravenscroft and Herbert Johnson (see pages 7 and 89).

Z. V. RUDOLF LIMITED

Milliner to HM The Queen Mother.

'Rudolf could design anything – rooms, machinery, hats – I used to call him Leonardo.' Mr Rudolf died in 1980 but his partner, Joy Quested-Nowell, continues a small part of their business, geared around The Queen Mother's schedule with a few other regular clients who like a different hat for every occasion. She works full-time from March until July and then from October to Christmas. 'Millinery is very hard work.'

Mr Zdenko Rudolf von Ehrenfeld, a Czech, was the leading Central European milliner when he came to Paris on a buying

trip in 1948. In self-imposed exile he applied to the British Embassy for an entry visa. The official at the desk looked at him and quietly said, 'I knew there couldn't be two of you.' She had been a client of his in Prague.

Mr Rudolf held his first London show in 1950. Ms Quested-Nowell was recommended to go to him when she was looking for a hat to wear for a wedding. She started modelling for him and in 1953 they took their first premises together on Grosvenor Street.

Ms Quested-Nowell ran the business; 'Rudolf created.' Today she carries on the tradition making a great variety of beautiful hats such as those frequently worn by The Queen Mother.

Joy Quested-Nowell makes hats 'by appointment only'.

Jewellers

ASPREY & COMPANY PLC
165/169 New Bond Street
London W1Y 0AR

(01) 493 6767

Goldsmiths, silversmiths and jewellers to HM The Queen and HRH The Prince of Wales and jewellers to HM The Queen Mother.

Asprey's long association with Bond Street belies their more humble origins as ironmongers in Mitcham. The firm was started by William Asprey, a Huguenot, over 200 years ago, but it was his upmarket grandson, Charles, with his eye for luxury, who moved the business to London's most fashionable street in 1847. He began advertising 'articles of exclusive design and high quality for personal adornment or personal accompaniment'. The shop soon became an arena for the chic and the élite.

During the early days, Asprey's forte were their dressing cases for men and women which won them top prizes at the Great Exhibition at Crystal Palace in 1851. The cases were made of wood, sometimes coromandel, and had tortoiseshell and coral settings. These were later replaced with less cumbersome leather bags. A typical gentleman's dressing bag, which he would carry as he travelled in his private coach on the train, would have been made of Russian leather (in brown, only the Royal family used black). It would contain

Joy Quested-Nowell of Z. V. Rudolf with several of The Queen Mother's hats returned to her for new veils

scent bottles, a plated railway key – passengers were always locked into their carriages for safety – a jewel case, silver shaving brush and an ivory-handled strop for cut-throat razors. The bag would have cost between £21 and £94.

In 1862 Queen Victoria granted Asprey their first Royal Warrant. Edward VII, who had granted them a further warrant, was so delighted with the 'ER' monogram which Asprey designed for his cigarette case that he suggested to the Post Master General that it should be used on pillar boxes throughout the country. The idea was rejected. Queen Mary used to visit Asprey to buy her Christmas presents, but the only member of the Royal family who has been seen making a personal visit of late was Princess Margaret who came to have her pearls restrung.

In the early 1920s Asprey enlisted the skills of the father of Sir John Betjeman, the Poet Laureate, to make games cabinets and exquisite ivory inlaid furniture for them. Asprey's biggest customers at the time were American millionaires, like J. Pierpont Morgan, and Indian Maharajahs who ordered suites of Mr Betjeman's furniture. Sir John wrote of his father's work at that time:

> . . . polished wood and stone
> Tortured by Father's craftsmen into shapes
> To shine in Asprey's showrooms under glass,
> A Maharajah's eyeful.

One of the biggest Maharajah commissions came in 1930 from the Maharajah of Patiala who ordered five huge teak trunks for each of his wives. Each trunk was fitted with solid silver washing and bathing utensils, soap boxes, soap dishes, toothbrush holders and silver bottles with tiger's heads for pouring hot water. They were also fitted with what one member of staff referred to at the time as a 'goesunder', as it goes under the bed – in eighth-inch silver.

Asprey has since been described as the 'classiest and most luxurious shop in the world'. Today they run a first-class jewellery repair service and stock a range of gifts from exquisite modern and antique jewellery to the more humorous (?) leatherbound address book in a set of three volumes entitled 'blonde', 'brunette' and '?', presumably for 'don't knows'. The set costs £36. At Christmas Asprey gift-wrap small presents in white crackers. Their advertisements read: 'Asprey for the art of giving.' At some of their prices one might be forgiven for believing it is infinitely better to receive.

Monday–Friday: 9–5.30; Saturday: 9–1. There is a mail order catalogue which is free to visitors to the shop, otherwise it costs £3. Asprey's mail worldwide.

A 19th-century Asprey's travelling bag with sterling silver fittings, containing everything necessary for the traveller, from nail files to notepads

CARTIER LIMITED
175 New Bond Street
London W1Y 2JH

(01) 493 6962

Jewellers and goldsmiths to HM The Queen and HM The Queen Mother.

Millions of imitation Cartier watches are produced every year. The firm recently showed their disapproval of the practice by hiring a bulldozer to flatten as many fakes as they could find. That was after they had taken the trouble to remove all the movements first.

Cartier have always been innovators in the jewellery world. They invented the clip brooch, made the first luxury waterproof watch for the Pasha of Marrakesh and created the first extra-thin wristwatch, the Tank – a tribute to the American Army. They are also astute salesmen. They sold Richard Burton the pear-shaped diamond which he gave to Elizabeth Taylor.

The Cartier tradition started in 1847 when Louis-François set up business in Paris. He specialised in 'fantasy jewellery', embellishing gold with coloured stones which he soon began to supply to the French Royal Palace. His son, Alfred, joined him in the business after the 1870 Revolution. In 1898 Alfred and his eldest son, Louis, moved their business to 13 Rue de la Paix. Their showrooms were frequented by 'all the Royal families' including The Prince of Wales, later Edward VII – a close friend of the Cartiers. He once said about them, 'If they have become the jewellers of kings it is because they are the kings of jewellers.' In 1902 The Prince of

Wales commissioned 27 diadems for his coronation later that year, and two years later awarded Cartier their first British Royal Warrant – they already had one from the House of Portugal.

Louis Cartier was famed for his clocks and watches. He designed the first clocks for the Royal families of Orleans, Greece and England and the first wristwatch in 1904 for the Brazilian aeronautic pioneer, Alberto Santos Dumont. In 1902 Cartier opened a branch in London and six years later founded their third house in New York. The five-storey mansion on Fifth Avenue (recently classed as a historic monument) was later given to them by the owner, Mrs Plante, in exchange for a two-strand necklace of black pearls.

In the late 1920s Louis Cartier organised the 'S' department selling original creations in enamel and silver, leather goods, stationery and engraved cards. He died in 1942 in Switzerland having just perfected a new metal – palladium – derived from platinum.

In 1972, Robert Hocq, the world's largest manufacturer of gas lighters and creator of the luxury lighter, became president of Cartier Paris. He had been given the Car-

tier licence for his lighters earlier in 1968. Robert Hocq opened the 10th branch of Cartier in Tokyo and the 40 Must boutiques around the world, establishing the doctrine of 'Les Must de Cartier', boutique-style shops which would sell the less expensive Cartier. In 1973 he made his 24-year-old daughter, Nathalie, designer of the high fashion jewellery.

The Cartier shop in Bond Street is discreetly elegant, pale wood walls and free-standing glass cases filled with Cartier jewels, cigarette lighters and spectacles. Even the close circuit cameras hanging from the ceiling look like futuristic works of art.

Monday–Friday: 9.30–5.30.

COLLINGWOOD OF CONDUIT STREET LIMITED
46 Conduit Street
London W1R 0HE
(and a branch at Harrods)

(01) 734 2656

Jewellers and silversmiths to HM The Queen and jewellers to HM The Queen Mother.

Collingwood have been involved with Royal weddings for more than 100 years. They made the wedding band for The Princess of Wales in their workshops, from the same Welsh gold nugget that had been used for the wedding rings of The Queen Mother, The Queen and Princess Margaret.

Collingwood's Royal connections go back to the Prince Regent and cockfighting. The Prince used to visit Thomas Gray's pub to see the cock-fights and drink the ale. Gray was a connoisseur of jewellery, and the Prince suggested he open a jeweller's shop in London. He did so, but it was in 1817 that a Joseph Kitching, one of Gray's apprentices in his flourishing business, started his own shop in Dover Street. His 'number one ledger' showed an impressive list of Royal customers, the first being the daughter of George IV, Princess Charlotte, and her husband Prince Leopold who bought each other anniversary presents. In 1834, Kitching moved to 46 Conduit Street, Collingwood's present premises, and three years later received his first Royal Warrant from Queen Victoria. Henry Collingwood himself only came into the firm in 1853, when Mr Kitching retired. 'Number two ledger' is filled with

The Prince and Princess of Wales with their son, Prince William. The Princess is wearing a necklace of cultured pearls set in diamonds made for her by Collingwood's and given to her as a 'thank-you' present from Prince Charles on the birth of their son

purchases made by Queen Victoria including a diamond necklace given to Princess 'May' of Teck, later Queen Mary, as a wedding gift.

Collingwoods also make medals such as the Royal Victorian Order – instituted in 1896 by Queen Victoria as her personal recognition for services to Her Majesty. It is occasionally given to Royal Warrant holders.

Collingwood's two shops do valuations and buy antique jewellery; they will design and make jewellery to order. The shop is worth a visit even if you cannot afford to buy. Admire the 1890s Indian silver gilt camel in the window. Not only is it a work of art – it's also a tea-pot!

Monday–Friday: 9.30–5 (Conduit Street). Harrods branch has the same opening hours as Harrods (see page 156). Catalogue available free of charge. Have a look, it's a visual treat.

STUART DEVLIN LIMITED
90/92 St John Street
London EC1M 4EH

(01) 235 5471

Goldsmiths and jewellers to HM The Queen.

The Worshipful Company of Goldsmiths describe Stuart Devlin as 'the designer with the Midas touch'. This young Australian designer certainly turns nearly everything he touches to gold, from the tiniest paperweight to the most spectacular candelabrum. Stuart Devlin also uses precious stones to add the final touches to his work, like an 18-carat gold Easter egg which opens up to reveal sapphire and diamond flowers growing out of gold leaves. Stuart Devlin says his aim is to 'enrich the way we live'.

Since the age of 13 when he won his first of many scholarships – this one was to the Gordon Institute of Technology in Australia – Stuart Devlin says he knew he wanted to be a designer. He later won an Art Diploma at the Royal Melbourne Institute of Technology with the highest marks ever awarded, after only one year of study instead of the usual three. In 1958 he won three more scholarships which brought him to the Royal College of Art in London where he studied light engineering design and silversmithing. He left as the only student ever to gain an honours diploma in both subjects.

While on honeymoon in Australia in 1962, Stuart Devlin was commissioned to design the country's new decimal coinage, a series of six coins depicting wildlife in Australia. Later, supervising the stages of die-making of the coins at the Royal Mint, he decided to live in London. In 1975 Stuart Devlin showed his first collection of carved and gilt rosewood furniture. Four years later he was commissioned by the Malaysian Bank to undertake the complete interior decoration of two luxury penthouses. It involved not only choosing all the fabrics and furnishings but also designing and making the furniture and silverware. It is work like this which Mr Devlin says 'gives full reign to his fertile imagination'. His own house in Mayfair has been described as 'one of the most exciting interior design ventures in London today'.

In 1980 Stuart Devlin was made a Companion of the Order of St Michael and St George by The Queen and two years later he was granted a Royal Warrant. His work for the Royal family includes commissions from The Duke of Edinburgh to make and design trophies for sporting events. In 1972 Prince Charles asked Mr Devlin to design his gift for The Queen and Prince Philip for their Silver Wedding Anniversary. In 1977 he was awarded the Queen's Silver Jubilee Medal and a year later was asked by Her Majesty to design and make the gifts for her tour of the Middle East.

Monday–Friday: 10–5.

GARRARD & COMPANY LIMITED
See page 4.

ANDREW GRIMA LIMITED
80 Jermyn Street
London SW1Y 6JD

(01) 839 7561

Jewellers to HM The Queen.

'My jewellery is not the sort that robbers go out of their way to steal,' Andrew Grima told me, 'because once the piece is destroyed they will only get about £200 for the material content even though the jewellery itself may have cost between £2,000 and £3,000.' Although Andrew Grima's jewellery is all made from 18-carat gold or platinum, it is his creativity, the elaborate

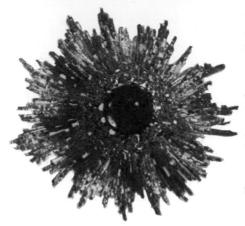

18 carat textured gold wire Sunburst brooch with a central sapphire designed by Andrew Grima

craftsmanship and the originality of the piece that one pays for.

Andrew Grima gave up mechanical engineering for jewellery. His father-in-law had started a 'high-class jewellery workshop' in 1946 and Mr Grima worked with him before starting on his own. He opened his first shop in London in 1966. Andrew Grima knew that to make a name for himself he would have to design modern rather than traditional jewellery. He experimented with casting techniques which had not been used since the Egyptians and tried setting stones in unconventional ways. Mr Grima designed the saddle wire – two wires in the shape of a cross – which held the stone by turning up the edges of the wires. Previously the stone would have been set in a metal rectangle and the setter would have pushed the metal round the stone to hold it in. Mr Grima's method meant that the stone could be shown off to its best advantage with less metal around it. In 1966, he made his famous Wave brooch – containing hundreds of baguette diamonds in the shape of a wave – one of the 15 pieces which won him the Duke of Edinburgh's Prize for Elegant Design. In the same year Mr Grima was given the Queen's Award for Export and four years later he received his Royal Warrant. His first work for Her Majesty was designing a Sunburst brooch – a stone resembling the sun surrounded by gold rays. Since then he has designed and made a brooch that was presented to Madame Pompidou by The Queen in 1972 – Madame Pompidou was so delighted with her gift she immediately pinned the brooch on to her coat.

Andrew Grima's building is a homage to the 1960s. The steel and slate 'sculpture' was designed by Brian Kneale in 1966, with its automatic door and cave-like interior. As well as the Royal family Mr Grima can boast Jackie Onassis, Ursula Andress, the Roux brothers and The Duke and Duchess of Bedford amongst his fans. Pieces start from £300.

Monday–Friday: 9.30–5.30. Andrew Grima has branches in New York, Zurich and Tokyo as well as London. No mail order catalogues as each of the designs is a 'one-off'. Over 14,000 'one-off' pieces have been made by the firm since 1966, all of which began with a sketch by Andrew Grima.

HAMILTON & INCHES LIMITED
87 George Street
Edinburgh EH2 3EY
Scotland

Edinburgh (031) 225 4898

Silversmiths and clock specialists to HM The Queen.

Hamilton & Inches still have silversmiths, watch- and clockmakers and jewellers working for them, though today their watch- and clockmakers mainly carry out repairs. Their silversmiths specialise in traditional Scottish pieces, such as The Quaich – for centuries the favourite drinking cup throughout Scotland (an eight-inch Quaich will cost about £400), kilt pins and 'Luckenbooth jewellery' – brooches used against witchcraft in the late 15th and early 16th centuries (prices for silver Luckenbooth jewellery start at £100 upwards).

'Hamilton & Inches were founded by Gramps in 1866,' the present chairman of the company, Major Inches, told me affectionately. 'Gramps' was Sir Robert Kirk Inches, a formidable character and Lord Provost of Edinburgh from 1912 to 1916. In 1887 Hamilton & Inches acquired their first Royal Warrant when they bought the firm of Robert Bryson & Son, Royal clockmakers. In those days Hamilton & Inches had a wonderful silver workshop where their silversmiths made such treasures as silver wool holders and silver crumb scoops – both of which are on display in the shop today.

Major Inches has run Hamilton & Inches since 1952. The large showroom on George Street is lined with white Corinthian columns, bordered with exquisite mouldings, covered with a vaulted ceiling and slowly being modernised.

Monday–Friday: 9–5; Saturday: 9–12.30. Hamilton & Inches have one mail order catalogue a year.

HANCOCKS & COMPANY LIMITED
1 Burlington Gardens
London W1X 2HP

(01) 493 8904

Goldsmiths and silversmiths to HM The Queen Mother.

If ever you receive an invoice from Hancocks you can rest assured that you are not the first. Over a third of the invoice is taken up with lists of their previous customers, from The Emperor of Russia and The Queen of the Belgians to The Sultan of Turkey and Emperor Napoleon III. Not forgetting Queen Victoria and King George V to whom Hancocks held Royal Warrants. In case you are still unimpressed, Hancocks have displayed their four gold medals at the top – the latest one was awarded in 1873.

Hancocks were established in Bruton Street in 1848 by Mr C. F. Hancock. In 1857, at the end of the Crimean War, he was asked by Prince Albert to make the first Victoria Cross. Hancocks still make the Victoria Cross, the highest British decoration for 'conspicuous bravery or devotion to the country in the presence of the enemy'. It is cast from the metal of Russian cannons taken at Sevastopol and consists of a Maltese cross made of bronze, bearing the Royal crown in the centre surmounted by a lion with the scroll superscribed 'For Valour'.

The small, friendly shop today specialises in exquisite Victorian and early 20th-century jewellery, mainly French, Italian, Japanese and American. The shop also stocks silver spoons, napkin rings (from £30), condiment sets and tea sets. Hancocks supply The Queen Mother with many of the gifts she gives to doctors, nurses and other professionals throughout the year. They also repair, buy, value, part exchange and redesign jewellery. A unique service offered is replacing cutlery. If your antique silver teaspoon vanishes down the waste disposal unit or the steel blades on your knives have rusted away, they will find matching pieces for your set, but only if it is English.

Monday–Friday: 9.30–5. Hancocks deliver and exhibit abroad, but the shop has no mail order catalogue.

PAUL LONGMIRE LIMITED
12 Bury Street
London SW1

(01) 930 8720

Suppliers of jewellery and leather goods to HM The Queen and suppliers of silver and presentation gifts to HM The Queen Mother.

In 1979 an unusual tie-pin in the windows of an old-established jewellery and silver firm at 12 Bury Street in St James's caught Paul Longmire's eye. Within a week he had bought the tie-pin and the entire business. Paul Longmire says, 'We're rather eccentric really.'

Mr Longmire had dealt in antiques for 30 years. Today he specialises in 19th- and early 20th-century jewellery of 'distinctive character'. 'My taste is unique,' he told me. Yet it is shared with his many customers who include The Queen and Queen Mother, whom he supplies with presentation gifts in leather, silver and gold. One such gift is Longmire's silver key ring, from £50. The shop also has a large selection of cufflinks which range from £55 for plain silver up to £3,000.

Paul Longmire's shop has a fake roaring log fire with two leather armchairs on either side which are sumptuously comfortable, if the assistants let you through the remote-controlled door.

Monday–Friday: 9–5.30.

WARTSKI
14 Grafton Street
London W1X 3LA

(01) 493 1141

Jewellers to HM The Queen, HM The Queen Mother and HRH The Prince of Wales.

The sign hanging outside the door of Wartski's elegant little shop in Mayfair, 'Wartski of Llandudno', strikes an incongruous note. But it was in the Welsh resort that Morris Wartski – a Russian Pole and the grandfather of Kenneth Snowman, the present chairman of the firm, founded the business in 1865. Since 1925, Wartski have been renowned for their collection of Fabergé jewellery and objects. Fabergé was the goldsmith to the Imperial Court of Russia in its last glorious years. He created everything from fish-knives to tiaras and his

Front and back view of the Victoria Cross as made by Hancocks

*From left to right: late
18th-century German
mother of pearl box with
gold mounts; Fabergé
enamelled gold clock
with diamond set ribbon
motifs and pearl set
borders; a rare black
enamelled silver gilt
pomander, c. 1600; a
Victorian emerald and
diamond set scrollwork
brooch, and a nephrite
paper knife by Fabergé,
the handle with gold
ropework mount set with
a ruby and a sapphire.
The paper knife was a
present from the Grand
Duchess Xenia to her
cousin the Duchess of
Edinburgh and Wartski's
have the original note
which she sent with it. All
objects are available
from Wartski*

famous gold Easter eggs encrusted with
precious stones. His output was considerable and he had premises in St Petersburg,
Moscow, Kiev, Odessa and London. Kenneth Snowman's father, Emanuel Snowman MVO, was the first person to import
Fabergé's work to the West after the
revolution. The Soviets sold their works of
art in order to obtain the foreign currency
that was so desperately needed.

Wartski's connection with the Royal
family goes back to the time of Edward
VII. Their first Royal Warrant was granted
by Queen Mary who inherited the Sandringham collection of Fabergé assembled
by Edward VII and Queen Alexandra, the
sister of the Czarina Maria Feodorovna.

Queen Mary was a keen collector herself, visiting Wartski frequently. The
present Queen and The Queen Mother are
both interested in Fabergé's work as well.

Wartski also have an interesting collection of antique and 'revivalist' jewellery for
sale. Cases are filled with snuff boxes in
gold and silver and Fabergé pieces starting
at £1,000. Several contemporary jewellers
and silversmiths regularly use Wartski as a
gallery to display their latest pieces. With
friendly and knowledgeable staff, it's a fascinating place to go.

Monday–Friday: 9.20–5.

Maternity wear

ELEGANCE MATERNELLE
198 Sloane Street
London SW1X 9QX

(01) 235 6140

The first entry in the shop's visiting book –
filled with media and aristocratic names – is
a letter from Balmoral. The visiting book
and the shop were started by Mrs Eder in
1959, the year The Queen was expecting
Prince Andrew. Mrs Eder, a French
woman, began making maternity clothes
for herself and later for her daughters.

'People wanted to disguise pregnancy 25
years ago, today they want to flaunt it,'
Mrs Eder told me. The shop sells European
clothes, with a new selection arriving every
two weeks, and caters for everything from
undergarments and trousers to swimwear
and evening dresses for the pregnant
woman from two to nine months. Mrs
Eder showed me a drop-waisted
charleston-style dress for £69 and a cotton
jumpsuit for £32.

*Monday–Friday: 9.30–5.30; Saturday:
9.30–5.*

GREAT EXPECTATIONS
The Conservatory
46 Fulham Road
London SW3 5PE

(01) 584 3468

In 1977 Liz Rees Jones, a consultant for the
magazine *Company*, felt it was 'unfair that
women had to wear different clothes and
fabrics just because they were pregnant.
How could a barrister wear flowery
smocks?' She set out to persuade designers
to use the same material and basic ideas
they had in their collections but to increase
the sizes of their designs.

Until the 1950s, Great Expectations was
a flower shop and the glass conservatory-
style roof is still there. Inside, everything
has been thought of to make shopping
pleasant for pregnant women. The changing rooms are larger than usual, there are
broad-seated chairs scattered throughout
the shop and understanding assistants who
will provide drinks and point out the way
to the loo.

The emphasis is on pregnant rather than
postnatal women. Liz Rees Jones knows
they 'will need all the help they can get. A

lot of people don't look better during pregnancy and are feeling a touch neurotic.' She advises pregnant women to wear matching tights (the shop have their own brand of tights in four colours) and shoes, low-heeled rather than flat. She also advises wearing dark or pure bright colours rather than sludgy tones, 'I was seen in two colours – black and navy – throughout my entire pregnancy.' Great Expectations sells everything from swimwear to floor-length evening dresses. They also stock a range of casual wear – mainly imported from America – from which The Princess of Wales chose several items for her first pregnancy. In this range are jumpsuits from £60, dungarees from £45 and jeans from £30. Great Expectations knit jumpers for adults and children with your name on the front, from £24, and sell tracksuits for £43 each, with their logo positioned directly on your 'bulge'.

Monday–Friday: 9.30–5.30; Saturday: 10–5. Will mail worldwide, but no mail order catalogue available.

Shoes

MANOLO BLAHNIK
49 Church Street
London SW3 5BS

(01) 352 3863

'Feet are the only part of the body that interest me,' Manolo Blahnik pronounced. 'But designing shoes is like designing anything. I could start tomorrow designing screws or baths.' Mr Blahnik has stayed with footwear.

Manolo Blahnik, like his shoes, makes statements. Born in Switzerland of Spanish and Czech parents, Mr Blahnik – today in his early forties – arrived in England 15 years ago. 'I still feel like a foreigner,' he told me, but it suits him. 'The day I feel English I would be bored to tears.' Mr Blahnik lives in Bath, comes to his shop off the King's Road in Chelsea twice a week and travels twice a month to Italy, where his shoes are made by a small manufacturing company outside Milan.

The shop has been in Church Street since 1972. The décor is changed every three years. Until recently it was 'mad Edwardian with drapes and roses and fruits', but when Mr Blahnik overheard a conversation drifting up from the street about how 'pretty' it was, he realised it was time

for a change. 'When people say it is "pretty",' he shuddered, 'I change.' Today it is 'like Naples' with marbled walls and Italianate friezes.

Mr Blahnik designs all styles of shoes, and would like to see everyone who enjoys his shoes wearing them. It's because of this that the rather expensive shoes are put in a sale held once a year. But The Princess of Wales presumably did not go to a sale for the court shoes she wore as part of her going-away outfit.

Manolo Blahnik considers his most successful shoe was a court shoe he made from a 'very simple 18th-century brocade, hand-embroidered by nuns living outside Naples'. It has proved popular in the States – 'the Europeans are too shy'. He wishes his customers had the occasion to wear chiffon or lace shoes, both materials Mr Blahnik loves working with. His work does include crocodile skin shoes – a pair of crocodile court shoes cost £300. 'A few years ago the hunting of crocodile was banned. But now they are reproducing so fast there is a village in the Amazon terrified by them.' Mr Blahnik rolled his eyes in horror. Clearly he feels it's his duty to help the poor natives out.

Monday–Friday: 10–6; Saturday: 10.50–5.30.

HOBBS LIMITED
47 South Molton Street
Lonon W1Y 1HE
(and branches)

(01) 629 0750

Even the Royal family cannot resist a bargain, as The Princess of Wales proved when she made a fleeting visit to Hobbs during their 1982 winter sale. The Princess, then pregnant with Prince William, bought herself three pairs of boots.

Marilyn Anselm, the owner of Hobbs and an ex-sculptor, opened her first shop in Hampstead in 1970. In the beginning she sold French and Italian clothes and shoes. On the 'insistence' of her husband, an economist, she began creating and manufacturing her own clothes designs. In 1979 Ms Anselm, together with a partner, started Bertie, a French-shoe shop, but the partnership failed. Soon afterwards Ms Anselm opened Hobbs. Today she designs all the clothes and shoes sold in the shops.

Monday–Saturday: 10–6; Thursday: 10–8 (South Molton Street branch).

K SHOES LIMITED
PO Box 12
Netherfield
Kendal
Cumbria LA9 7BT

Bootmakers to HM the Queen and HM The Queen Mother.

K Shoes' Royal Warrant was originally held by the firm of H. E. Randall of Piccadilly who had been supplying the Royal household since 1925, but it was transferred when K Shoes bought Randalls in 1967. Today K Shoes supply the footwear for the housemaids resident at Buckingham Palace and Clarence House and the men at the Royal Mews.

K Shoes were founded by Robert Miller Somervell who established a leather business in Kendal in 1842. Six years later he was joined by his brother John and the firm were known as Somervell Brothers. They made completed uppers and leathers for the bespoke shoemakers who were responsible for nearly all the shoes sold in Britain at the time. In 1857 the Somervell Brothers imported their first reliable sewing machine from America and soon made their first completed footwear. Uppers were assembled to soles at the factory and finished by outworkers in the town. But to prevent the unscrupulous craftsmen who 'finished' the work from swopping Somervell's finest quality leather soles for cheap substitutes, they started to brand the soles with the letter 'K' for Kendal. In 1875 the 'K' was registered as a trademark and the company were hence known as K

Shoes. Today K Shoes are part of the C. & J. Clark Group.

K Shoes are available from K Shoe shops and from K Shoes retailers at major department stores.

JOHN LOBB LIMITED
9 St James's Street
London SW1A 1EF

(01) 930 3664

Bootmakers to HM The Queen, HRH The Duke of Edinburgh and HRH The Prince of Wales.

Eric Lobb, the founder's grandson, sat in his office above the shop wearing a 15-year-old pair of shoes, 'the first we made with covered slashed gussets'. Clearly Lobb's shoes last. Mr Lobb is very discreet about Royal feet, although the lasts made for Lord Mountbatten are on display in a glass case by the front door of his shop. Mr Lobb is quite clear about what makes his business different. 'There is no other firm that make only bespoke shoes. We're very different. We're very expensive.'

Lobb are indeed very expensive. A standard man's or woman's pair of shoes starts at £439 plus VAT and a pair of riding boots at £742 plus VAT. But judging from the 20,000 plus lasts that fill their basement in St James's Street it would appear their customers consider the shoes well worth the price.

In the huge glass cases that line the walls of Lobb's there are standard ranges of shoes for you to choose from: full and semi

The Prince of Wales wearing evening pumps to the centenary banquet at the International Press Centre in London, February 1982. A similar pair of shoes are to be seen in Lobb's windows

brogues, Oxfords and casuals ('Norwegian slippers') for men, and court, walking and golf shoes for women plus their five types of boot shapes, but they will make any variation on any theme you care to choose, in any leather from elephant to ostrich, and any heel from a stiletto to a hollowed-out platform.

Ideally Lobb like to measure your feet (in your favourite socks or breeches) before making you a pair of shoes or boots in their little factory in the heart of St James's. But they will make a pair of man's black velvet slippers (£336 plus VAT) to size if you send them a pair of old, comfy shoes. For a crest or zodiac sign embroidered on the front, send them an extra £34.

Monday–Friday: 9–5.30; Saturday: 9–1. Lobb will send shoes anywhere in the world provided they already have your last or you send them extremely detailed measurements.

HENRY MAXWELL & COMPANY LIMITED
11 Savile Row
London W1X 2PS

(01) 734 9714

Bootmakers to HM The Queen.

Maxwell were established in 1750 in Worcester by Henry Maxwell, a spur maker. Persuaded by friends to move to London, in 1756 he took a house in Soho with a forge in the garden on which he made his spurs. Maxwell was granted his first Royal Warrant by George IV 50 years later. By the 1900s, Maxwell's competitors were bootmakers who were also dealing in spurs – so the company decided to make boots. Today they no longer make spurs, but specialise in handmade bespoke footwear, especially men's shoes and boots.

Maxwell are prepared to attempt the 'impossible'. They'll design and make a leather wallet to your requirements, make a shoe tree to the shape of your last and once made a pair of slippers using beaded embroidery a customer brought in. They are also always trying to improve the life of their shoes. Their current record is a pair they made in 1935 that are still in regular use.

Monday–Friday: 9–5.45. Closed daily between 1–2.

JAMES NORTH & SONS LIMITED
PO Box 3
Market Street
Hyde
Cheshire SK14 1RL

Suppliers of safety footwear to HM The Queen.

James North & Sons have been manufacturing safety products since the 18th century. But it was not until 1946 that the company came into the limelight and achieved worldwide fame by producing the first PVC gloves for industry. They began manufacturing a range of protective gloves which could be used in hospitals, the catering business and anywhere where workers came into contact with chemicals. All their gloves have a hygesan protection – a bacteriostat incorporated into the PVC – to break down perspiration and prevent skin infections and unpleasant odours.

Since then they have expanded their products and now make safety footwear for which they were granted the Royal Warrant in 1981 for supplying the Royal households at Buckingham Palace and Windsor Castle. Their safety shoes include all-purpose chukkas and boots with rubber and polyurethene soles, heavier designs – such as Dr Martens (lace-up boots) with air-cushioned soles – heat-resistant shoes and a stylish range for the executive who wants to look smart and play safe. The company offer a six-month guarantee on all their shoes and will replace them if they need to be repaired within that time.

Today James North's clients include the Ministry of Defence, British Nuclear Fuel, ICI and the motor industries, for whom they produce a range of protective clothing, including chemical spray hoods, safety spectacles, face shields and ear plugs.

James North & Sons supply direct to trade and industry. Their safety footwear is available to the public from shoe shops.

H. & M. RAYNE LIMITED
15 Old Bond Street
London W1X 3DB
(and branches)

(01) 493 9077

Shoemakers to HM The Queen and HM The Queen Mother.

Rayne were started in 1889 by Henry and Mary Rayne. Their shoes were then only available to the acting profession. Their customers were Lillie Langtry, George Edwards and other famous actors of the age. In 1920 when their son took over as chairman, he opened a shop in Bond Street to sell to the new fashion-conscious woman shoes previously only available to film and theatre people. In 1959, Oliver Messel, Lord Snowdon's uncle, designed the present shop and gave the rooms such exotic titles as The Vaulted Arcade and The Room of Recessed Alcoves. With the gentle strains of 'Moon River' in the background you could be in the middle of Paramount Studios. In the old days a good pair of women's shoes could take a couple of weeks to make. 'Nowadays we can turn out a pair of shoes in a day, though they're just as long lasting and stylish' – and no

doubt comfortable too. They have to be, for all those Royal walkabouts.

Rayne have branches all over England and the United States. In them you'll find their classic shoes in around 15 to 20 different designs which will vary according to the season, with an average price of £70. For an extra £30 making charge you can have them in any shade of the rainbow you like – or in satin.

Monday–Friday: 9.30–6; Saturday: 9.30–4.30 (Bond Street branch).

UNIROYAL LIMITED
Newbridge
Midlothian
Scotland

Manufacturers of waterproof footwear to HRH The Duke of Edinburgh.

In 1856 Henry Lee Norris founded the North British Rubber Company and started making 'a highly original type of footwear called the Wellington Boot'. In America, at the same time, footwear manufacturers were starting up. In 1892 nine of them joined together to form the United States Rubber Company, known as Uni-

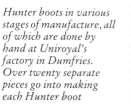

Hunter boots in various stages of manufacture, all of which are done by hand at Uniroyal's factory in Dumfries. Over twenty separate pieces go into making each Hunter boot

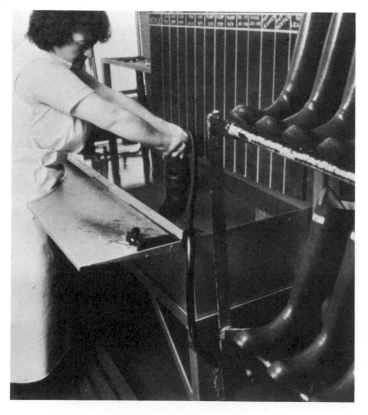

royal. They were joined by the North British Rubber Company in 1954 and together they now make tyres, shoes, hoses, conveyor belts, chemicals and plastics which are sold all over the world.

The footwear division of Uniroyal hold the Royal Warrant to the Duke of Edinburgh. Their distinctive green Hunter boots with the Hunter label prominently displayed at the front are frequently seen on members of the Royal family. The Princess of Wales was wearing her pair of Uniroyal's Huntress boots for an informal photocall held with Prince Charles and his labrador, Harvey, at Balmoral.

Uniroyal's range of Hunter boots are hand-crafted on a last with reinforced support at the ankles and arches. Their four designs include the Huntress (for ladies), the Hunter, their original design which they say is ideal for 'spending all day on the grouse moor', the Royal Hunter with its tough styrene rubber sole and heel covered with hardened studs for extra grip, and their Nu-Hunter boots, made for walking. All come in many fittings.

Uniroyal also make a range of safety footwear under their Argyll label which are used throughout industry and by the Fire Service. The company say their boots are 'built like bulldozers'. They can brand boots with company logos.

Uniroyal footwear is available from gun and tackle shops, country stores and better department stores.

been for hunting boots, 'for a pair of shoes you only need five measurements'.

Recently Paul Wildsmith has taken five measurements of Prince Michael of Kent, Prince Edward and Prince Charles's feet. Prince Charles first came to Wildsmiths on The Princess of Wales's recommendation – friends of hers had shopped there and she liked the shoes. Prince Charles bought several pairs of their Country House Shoe (at £120 for ready-to-wear). When Wildsmith first introduced the casual slip-on Country House shoe in 1945, it was the first slip-on shoe made in London ('before Gucci'), designed to be worn in the country at weekends. Mr Wildsmith told me the shoes would be bought a size bigger than needed so owners wouldn't have to change their socks after a day's hunting. Today it is their most popular shoe.

Wildsmith & Co. were founded in 1847 by Matthew Wildsmith and his wife Rebecca, 'the brains behind the business', Paul Wildsmith told me. Portraits of the six generations of the Wildsmith family peer down from the walls of the staircase. Until 25 years ago the shoes were all made in the shop but today they are made in Northampton to Mr Wildsmith's specifications, as he himself studied shoe and last making. The shoes are made from traditional patterns dating back decades. Ready-made shoes cost from £120 to £150 and made-to-measure from £275. Paul Wildsmith thinks there will be at least 10 years' wear in his shoes, and once they have worn out he offers a total refurbishment service for £30 to £40. Mr Wildsmith will also remember your name.

Monday–Friday: 9–5.30; Saturday: 9–1. Mail order catalogue available and Wildsmith mail worldwide. Refurbishment service offered for all shoes – not just Wildsmith's.

Below left: Wildsmith's Country House Shoe as favoured by The Prince of Wales. Available in black or brown and in suede

WILDSMITH & COMPANY
15 Princes Arcade
Jermyn Street
London SW1

(01) 437 4289

Hanging on the walls of Wildsmith are 'drafts' (drawn outlines of feet) of the feet of Prince Leopold of Belgium, Jerome, Napoleon's brother and Edward Prince of Wales – who had a diminutive size eight foot. Paul Wildsmith, the sixth generation of Wildsmith, thought the 10 measurements surrounding the drafts must have

Suits and shirts

ASHLEY & BLAKE LIMITED
42 Beauchamp Place
London SW3

(01) 584 2682
Shirtmakers to HRH The Duke of Edinburgh.

Ashley & Blake are shirt manufacturers. Their shirts can be bought in shops all over the country, but their showpiece is a charming shop in Beauchamp Place. The cheerful two-floored shop with its white walls and beige carpet sells men's clothes on the first floor and ladies in the basement. They have a large selection of the warrant-holding shirts in two-fold Anderson cotton ('the finest you can get'), from £30. Described as a 'full shirt with a smaller collar', men's shirts range from size 14½ to 17 with a 15¾ inch collar size as well as an average sleeve length of 34 inches which can be shortened if necessary. All the shirts are double-stitched, with two buttons – one on the cuff and one on the lower sleeve. The shop also sells a small but elegant selection of suits, cashmere and wool jumpers for men and jumpers, skirts, dresses and Ashley & Blake shirts for women.

Monday–Saturday: 10–6. Ashley & Blake shirts can be found at other retail stores as well.

WILLIAM BLACKHALL
15 Melgum Road
Tarland
Aberdeenshire AB3 4YL

Tarland (033 981) 359

Tailor and outfitter to HM The Queen.

'I love making kilts, each one is different,' Mr Blackhall told me. And he sews them sitting cross-legged on the table in the small workshop behind his shop. A kilt takes him between 12 and 14 hours to make, requires only one fitting from the customer and costs from £150.

Mr Blackhall's father opened the shop in Tarland – about 15 miles from Balmoral – in 1923 and taught his son the skills of tailoring and kiltmaking. 'I learnt the hard way,' he said. Mr Blackhall now teaches Pam, his young daughter, the same skills, affectionately calling her 'The Boss'. The two of them work together all day, sometimes until late into the night quietly sewing and attending to customers. They also make suits – often four-piece: jacket, waistcoat, trousers and plus fours, but you could have to wait up to nine months for them.

In the shop Mr Blackhall sells 'good, heavy tweeds which my customers like', wools, ties and a selection of Celtic accessories: sporrans, skean-dhu (knives) and waist-belts. Mr Blackhall received his Royal Warrant from The Queen in 1982.

Monday–Saturday: 8.45–5.45.

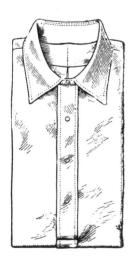

THE BURTON GROUP PLC
(Head Office)
214 Oxford Street
London W1

(01) 636 8040

Tailors to HM The Queen and HM The Queen Mother.

In 1952, at the time of the death of Montague Burton, Burtons' founder, the company were 'the largest men's made-to-measure tailored outerwear business in the world'. In those days Burtons had 600 shops and 14 factories making made-to-measure outfits. One of their factories used to produce 50,000 suits weekly with a staff of 10,000 all of whom could sit down at the canteen at the same time and be served within three minutes.

Today Burtons still made make-to-measure suits but it's a far smaller part of their business. Their made-to-measure suits start from £70 – the same price as their off-the-peg suits – and are made from British fabrics, either all wool or wool mixtures. Their computer helps keep costs down. It works out how to cut the fabric for minimum wastage, then draws the patterns and cuts the fabric. After that, Burtons' 250 staff take over. Among the customers for their made-to-measure suits Burtons can claim teddy boys, chauffeurs, security guards, Royal footmen and the tallest man in Britain, their '7 foot 6 inch mascot'.

The Burton Group operate several chains of retail shops: Peter Robinson, Dorothy Perkins and Evans for women, and Burton Menswear, Top Man and Harry Fenton for men. They also make women's made-to-measure. Burtons have held their Royal warrant to The Queen Mother since 1958 and to The Queen since 1961.

Check with local Burton Group shops for their opening hours.

MESSRS DRISCOLL
21 Ashburnham Gardens
Eastbourne
Sussex

Eastbourne (0323) 25400

Tailors to HM The Queen.

Mr Driscoll was head cutter and fitter at Hartnell (see page 81) before he started his

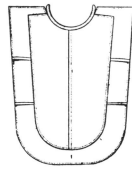

own couturier business with his wife. While at Hartnell, Mr Driscoll made Princess Elizabeth (today The Queen) her first suit. He continued to make many of her informal clothes, such as her skirts and kilts – some of which, Mrs Driscoll tells me, are still in use today. When the Driscolls moved to Eastbourne in 1952 the Royal patronage followed.

Today Mrs Driscoll, now aged 77, still oversees the making of the clothes although her husband died 20 years ago. She is regarded by the Royal family as a 'sewing nanny'. For years Mrs Driscoll has advised, looked after and (occasionally) gently chided the Royal family about their dress sense. Princess Margaret frequently says 'You are always right, Mrs Driscoll', after the caring seamstress has put forward her point of view. The Driscolls made Princess Anne her first tailored suit too, Lady Sarah Armstrong-Jones was confirmed in a dress made by them and they continue to make evening clothes for Princess Margaret. In return the Royal family look after Mrs Driscoll. When she visits London she is invited to lunch and she is often asked to the Royal Enclosure at Ascot.

Another family Messrs Driscoll 'adopted' were the Cartiers (see page 93). Once a year the Cartier sons would come over to England to be clothed by the Driscolls. Today Mrs Driscoll's grandchildren still visit Paris to stay with the Cartier children. Mrs Driscoll works from her home in Eastbourne. Her staff of 35 have shrunk to five although she still has 'Miss May', her 85-year-old fitter working with her. Mrs Driscoll told me never to believe anyone who says it takes a day to make a skirt. According to Mrs Driscoll even someone of 40 years' experience will need a week. Messrs Driscoll charge from £45 to make up a skirt. The material costs extra.

Messrs Driscoll will still take on work, but cannot cope with a lot of orders. You will have to visit Eastbourne; Mrs Driscoll only travels to London for her Royal customers.

HAWES & CURTIS LIMITED
2 Burlington Gardens
London W1X 1LH

(01) 493 2200

Tailors to HRH The Duke of Edinburgh.

John Kent, Royal tailor at Hawes & Curtis, has held a Royal Warrant to The Duke of Edinburgh since 1979. Prince Philip had used Hawes & Curtis as his tailors for many years before then. His previous tailor was Mr Watson who, on his retirement, introduced Mr Kent to Prince Philip as 'Mr Kent, my cutter'.

Mr Kent, a charming man originally from London's East End, studied tailoring at night school and then became an apprentice to a cutter. Today, 15 years after joining Hawes & Curtis, he runs their bespoke tailoring department with a staff of 11, including one tailor who makes only velvet jackets and dresswear – the company's speciality. Prices start at £475 for a three-piece suit or, if like Prince Philip you prefer a two-piece, from £450. 'Everything about Prince Philip is immaculate,' Mr Kent told me. 'He doesn't follow fashion, he's a classic dresser. The cut of his suits has not changed since we first dressed him in 1946.'

Lord Mountbatten was also a customer at Hawes & Curtis as the bespoke tailors were bought by Edward 'Teddy' Watson, Lord Mountbatten's wartime batman. Hawes & Curtis were bought by Turnbull & Asser (see below) about 20 years ago, but the shop still keeps its identity with a selection of classic clothes.

'We can name-drop here with the best,' Donald Amor, their managing director, told me. As well as Prince Charles, who also occasionally buys his suits from them, Frank Sinatra, Prince Andrew and Prince Edward can sometimes be found upstairs at Hawes & Curtis. There they can buy bespoke shirts, made to Hawes & Curtis specifications in Turnbull & Asser's workrooms. Hawes & Curtis make three collar shapes, as opposed to Turnbull's one, and use a firmer lining than the softer look that Turnbull's favour. Hawes & Curtis also sell a vast selection of conservative and stylish ties and the most striking collection of dressing gowns in London, in towelling, cotton, wool and classic silk. A silk dressing gown starts at £125.

Monday–Friday: 9–5.30; Saturday: 9–1. No mail order catalogue, but Hawes & Curtis mail 'parcels of clothes' all over the world for their customers.

JOHNS & PEGG LIMITED
4 Clifford Street
London W1X 1RB

(91) 734 1713

Military tailors to HRH The Duke of Edinburgh and tailors to HRH The Prince of Wales.

Johns & Peggs make the uniforms for the Household Cavalry – who parade daily down through Hyde Park and past Buckingham Palace and provide the mounted guard at the Admiralty in Whitehall.

Many of their customers are ex-army who were first introduced to the shop during their military careers. The styling of their jackets is said to be a closer fit than many Saville Row tailors. Attention to detail is crucial. Customers will come in for three fittings for a suit and they can expect to be cross-examined on such minutiae as how much change they carry in their pockets.

When Johns & Pegg celebrated their centenary in 1958 they discovered they were in fact older than that, but they are still not sure how much older. Mr Johns is the fourth generation of Johns in the business. The last Pegg descendant died about 50 years ago, but the name has been kept on because 'Pegg is so much easier for the French to pronounce than Johns.' In the corner of the shop are two photographs of The Prince of Wales in uniforms made for him by Johns & Pegg; and it was they who made the naval uniform which he wore on his wedding.

The cost of a three-piece Johns & Pegg suit is £500. New customers may have to pay a deposit; but regulars are only asked to pay when they take delivery. 'It used to be that the tailor was the last person you paid,' Mr Johns told me. 'Fortunately it's not like that now.'

Monday–Friday: 9–5.30; Saturday: 9–12.

KINLOCH ANDERSON LIMITED
John Knox House
45 High Street
Edinburgh EH1 1SR
Scotland

Edinburgh (031) 556 6961

Tailors and kiltmakers to HM The Queen, HRH The Duke of Edinburgh and HRH The Prince of Wales.

The Japanese frequently buy kilts from Kinloch Anderson. 'They understand the clan system, although of course they shouldn't be wearing tartan,' Harry Lindley, who joined the company in 1949, told me.

There are tartans that can be bought and worn by Sassenachs or other foreigners, but most tartans are heavily guarded by their clansmen. The Maitland Clan regularly send out mail order lists through Kinloch Anderson to 'Registered Members of the Clan' permitted to wear the officially approved tartan. Beware any weaver who puts the Maitland Clan tartan into their range. Similarly the bright red Royal Stuart tartan with its black checks and yellow, blue and white squares has been the tartan for the Royal House of Scotland for centuries. Today it is the Royal tartan of The Queen. The Balmoral tartan designed by Prince Albert is also reserved for the sole use of the Royal family. This grey/brown tartan with its narrow red and black checks was first used by Queen Victoria when making gifts to her friends and for decorating the Drawing Room at Balmoral. The tartan was described in 1882 as 'a quaint warm grey design, arranged by the late Prince Consort. It is far superior in design and colour to the startling and gaudy Royal Stuart tartan.'

The company were started in 1868, possibly in response to the sudden demand for tartans after Queen Victoria had expressed her liking for Scotland and all things Scottish. In 1888 Kinloch Anderson were military tailors making uniforms for 'all the Scottish regiments – both highlands and lowlands'. Today they describe themselves as 'consultants' as well as kiltmakers. In their small shop situated in John Knox House, they not only know about each of the existing 400 tartans but are often called on to design new ones. But Harry Lindley their tartan adviser will never be seen wearing a kilt in the shop. 'You never wear a kilt to sell a kilt.' If they have your tartan

Opposite:
Kinloch Anderson's kilt is shown to its full advantage as Prince Charles, dressed in Balmoral Tartan, does the Highland Fling with his eight-year-old cousin, Lady Sarah Armstrong-Jones. The photograph was taken at Balmoral by Patrick Lichfield

The Kinloch Anderson shop next door to John Knox's House (see right)

in stock a kilt can be made within a month and fittings are often not necessary. Much of Kinloch Anderson's business is mail order. They also sell a variety of sporrans, kilt stockings, Scottish jewellery, ladies' evening sashes (which they advise on how to wear) and ready-made Argyll jackets (from £92). They will also design and make any jacket you require.

In 1958 Kinloch Anderson decided to become wholesalers and enter the export market. Today they manufacture a wide variety of classic ladies' clothing based on traditional Scottish designs.

Monday–Saturday: 9–5 (winter); 9–5.30 (summer). One mail order catalogue is produced every three years ('the only thing that changes is the jewellery'), which is mailed worldwide. Kinloch Anderson's wholesale garments are available at major department stores throughout the world and at their shop.

HENRY POOLE & COMPANY
15 Savile Row
London W1X 1AE

(01) 734 5985

Livery tailors to HM The Queen.

It is rumoured that when Stanley met Livingstone on the shores of Lake Tanganyika in 1871, they were both dressed in Henry Poole suits.

Henry Poole's history is indeed star-studded, although their beginnings were almost inadvertent. In 1806 James Poole came to London to open a linen draper's business, but nine years later, when Napoleon escaped from Elba, Poole decided to join a Volunteer Corps and had to provide his own uniform. The tunic, which he cut and stitched with the help of his wife Mary, was so admired that by the time of Waterloo he was flooded with enough orders to set up as a military tailor. By the time their son Henry inherited the business in 1846 it was a flourishing concern. Henry, a passionate rider to hounds, met, and had a knack of getting on with, the 'right people'. Soon the premises, by now in Savile Row, were filled with customers being measured for hunting pinks or the new Court dress – which Poole had introduced – in bottle green or mulberry cloth. Poole was also friendly with the future Napoleon III, who in 1853 awarded Henry Poole the title of tailors to the Emperor, the first of their many Royal Warrants. Queen Victoria later granted Poole her Livery Warrant which they have held to this day.

The list of Royalty, dignitaries and celebrities who have honoured Pooles with their custom is impressive. Henry Poole became tailor to Edward, The Prince of Wales, supplying most of his clothing, and Disraeli, clearly a customer, later cast Poole as 'Mr Vigo' in his novel, *Endymion*. More recently, Pooles have dressed Sir

The Warrant of Appointment granted to Henry Poole by Emperor Napoleon III in 1853

Winston Churchill, Emperor Haile Selassie, Yoshida (Japan's postwar Prime Minister) and Charles de Gaulle for whom they made all his wartime uniforms. But although Henry Poole still dress aristocrats and celebrities they will be happy to dress you too: a suit starts at £550. On their premises they have 45 specialists, including three buttonhole-makers, and a choice of over 4,000 different cloths for you to choose from. But Henry Poole will only make clothes for ladies 'if pushed'. Joanna Lumley clearly pushed them successfully – they made a dinner suit for her.

Monday–Friday: 9–5.30. Henry Poole mail order around the world and, if yours is one of their 5 or 6,000 patterns stored in the basement you may not even need a fitting. A special service Henry Poole offer customers living abroad is to store their suitcases for when they come over for Wimbledon or Ascot.

S. REDMAYNE LIMITED
The Old Mill
Warwick Bridge
Carlisle CA4 8RR

Carlisle (0228) 61661

Tailors to HM The Queen.

Redmayne are bespoke tailors by post, ideal for the conservative customer with no time for fittings. The service began with a 'New Suits for Old' advertising campaign launched in the 1930s when Redmayne realised they would have to do something special to attract custom.

Choose from over 1,500 designs in a variety of cloths. Send them your old suit, trousers or jacket and you can expect the replica within eight to 10 weeks. If pushed they do it in 72 hours. The price of a suit will be approximately £325.

Redmayne also work in leather or suede and enjoy unusual requests. Daring customers have already asked for Norfolk jackets with a zip rather than buttons down the front and a waistcoat with fastenings up the side.

The firm were granted the Royal Warrant for the clothes they made for the outdoor staff at Sandringham.

Most of Redmayne's work is mail order, but if you'd rather be measured and fitted those services are available at the Old Mill, or in London, Edinburgh and Exeter. Contact Redmayne for details.

STEPHENS BROTHERS LIMITED
16/21 Sackville Street
London W1S 4EZ

Shirtmaker and hosier to HRH The Duke of Edinburgh.

'I cannot imagine why everybody does not wear them, there is no other sock that I think is half as convenient to wear,' Lord Mountbatten wrote to Stephens Brothers on 5 February 1962. He was referring to their Tenova socks with their elastic grip top and cut-away calves. Stephens Brothers were awarded their Royal Warrant to George VI in 1938 as hosiers and today hold the honour to The Duke of Edinburgh, but unfortunately their socks are not available to the general public.

Since 1919 Stephens Brothers have been making shirts which they sell under their own and other labels including Austin Reed. Stephens Brothers shirts 'have all the distinctions of bespoke clothes', I was told, though their only bespoke customer is The Duke of Edinburgh. Their ready-to-wear shirts are distinguished by subtle details like the number of stitches to the inch (between 14 and 16), the triple-stitched shoulder seaming, two-piece collars, real pearl buttons and the accurate matching of stripes and checks. They also have up to 100 collar shapes to choose from, make extra large sizes and longer than usual sleeves. Their shirts are made from natural fibres, from Egyptian cotton to poplin. Prices range from £20 to £100 for a pleated pure silk herringbone evening shirt. The company also manufacture women's shirts and shirt-waister dresses. The shirts are made in their two factories, one near Blackpool and the other in Ireland, but according to Stephens Brothers their shirts 'are better known in Dusseldorf than in London. The British don't appreciate good clothes.'

Stephens Brothers shirts are available 'in every best store in England bar none'. They are also sold abroad, sometimes under their own label.

THRESHER & GLENNY LIMITED
Lancaster Place
The Strand
London WC2E 7EN
(and a branch in the City)

(01) 836 4608

Shirtmakers to HM The Queen and HM The Queen Mother.

In 1783 Mr Richard Thresher of St Mary's, Strand, was appointed one of the hosiers to George III. In 1834, the firm became Thresher & Glenny. For the first half of the 19th century the firm made it their business to keep Their Majesties warm and then spent the next half trying to keep them cool. When Edward, Prince of Wales went to India in 1877, the company were entrusted with his outfit and that of the whole of his entourage. For many years Thresher & Glenny also held an unbroken record for outfitting successive Indian Viceroys and their Memsahibs. Specialities were sunproof suitings, light ladies' washing frocks, white and khaki drill clothing as well as mosquito nets, tents and sunhats.

Today Thresher & Glenny hold their Royal Warrants to The Queen – for the Royal Mews department – and to The Queen Mother as shirtmakers. The firm make made-to-measure men's shirts from £45 up to £64 for silk. They take four weeks to make but you can buy them in standard sizes from £22. Thresher & Glenny's shirts are made in natural fibres, poplin, cotton, linen and silk, and they feature a soft collar – 'an acquired taste' I was told. The shop no longer has a ladies' department.

Monday–Friday: 9–5.30 (Strand branch).

TURNBULL & ASSER LIMITED
71/72 Jermyn Street
London SW1Y 6PF

(01) 930 0502

Shirt manufacturers to HRH The Prince of Wales.

Prince Charles was introduced to Turnbull & Asser by Lord Mountbatten on leaving university and now has all his shirts made by them. Paul Cuss, the manager of the bespoke department, told me: 'The Prince has the finest of taste. Our shirts are bolder than other Jermyn Street shirts.' 'Bold' by Jermyn Street standards is not shocking.

Turnbull & Asser joined the list of Royal Warrant holders in 1980. They were already used to the rich and illustrious, having clothed the famous from Winston Churchill to Liberace.

They used to make trunk drawers to match their shirts. Today, for £140 they will make a silk dress shirt with a family crest or monogram hand-embroidered. Another speciality is their wide range of striped silks from their Scottish silk mill (£18 a metre) which can be made into shirts (£90 and up). Made-to-measure shirts take from six to eight weeks.

Monday–Friday: 9–5.30; Saturday: 9–1. No mail order catalogue ('We are very low-key'), but privileged customers will be sent swatches of new fabric designs – cotton only.

Under it all

BRADLEYS (KNIGHTSBRIDGE LIMITED)
See page 117.

RIGBY & PELLER
12 South Molton Street
London W1Y 1DF

(01) 629 6708

Corsetières to HM The Queen.

Rigby & Peller, started in 1946 by Mrs Rigby and Mrs Peller, is changing its image. When I called, the first-floor showroom was being turned into a Victorian bedroom scene – without the bed. The décor was pale grey, picked out with dashes of scarlet, lit by chandeliers and furnished with elegant desks and Victorian chairs. The lingerie was discreetly hidden in the wardrobes. The changing room next door has been turned into a sitting room with the same emphasis on luxury and luscious comfort. But their most important customer will never see the new look. Rigby & Peller attend to fittings at the

Palace as they have been doing since they received their Royal Warrant in 1960.

Rigby & Peller made their name for their made-to-measure corselets, foundation garments and lingerie. But as a made-to-measure brassière costs from £50 upwards and involves three fittings, the market was becoming limited. Mrs June Kenton, who bought Rigby and Peller in 1982, knows what she is doing. A former lecturer on the importance of what you wear under your clothes at the Lucie Clayton Grooming School and Model Agency and the owner of Contour shops, with two branches in Knightsbridge and Croydon, Mrs Kenton has definite ideas about how to turn Rigby & Peller into a glamorous and sophisticated place to buy your undergarments.

Not only is Rigby & Peller's image being revamped. Mrs Kenton is also introducing a ready-to-wear range of corsetry, brassières and lingerie, which you will be able to try on in her exclusive surroundings with her staff helping you determine your correct sizing. The starting price of a brassière will be £15 and the sizes stocked will be from 32 to 52. Their speciality will remain their swimwear collection with an alteration service offered to ensure a perfect fit. Rigby & Peller's staff are also used to helping customers buy mastectomy swimwear and corsetry.

But Mrs Kenton's biggest change will be her 'men only' evenings, already a regular in her Contour shops. These evenings have been enormously successful in tempting men to buy something special for their ladies. Mrs Kenton hopes the experience will go down as well in her new Victorian boudoir.

Monday–Friday: 9–5, make an appointment first if possible. Rigby & Peller will send you goods on approval if you don't mind paying the postage.

JOHN SCOTT-NICHOL LIMITED
Old Station Close
Shepshed
Loughborough
Leicestershire

Hosiery manufacturers to HM The Queen.

You can spot a John Scott-Nichol sock by its reinforced toe and heel, its Scott-Nichol crest and its hand-linked toe. This traditional method of making socks means that the sock will have a flat seam rather than a thick ridge above the toe. When the sock comes off the machine it is open at the top and the toe, which is then sewn by hand. Their socks come in a range of conservative colours – navy, black, green and brown – and are plain or ribbed. They are made from either wool, a wool and nylon mixture or mercerised cotton and can be either full or ankle length.

John Scott-Nichol Ltd have made men's and children's socks since 1937. The company were bought by Mr Fewkes in 1964 and are now a small family business housed in modern premises in Loughborough.

John Scott-Nichol socks are available from 'department stores throughout the country and better men's and boy's outfitters'.

And so to Bed

Beds

HEAL & SON LIMITED
195/198 Tottenham Court Road
London W1P 9LD

(01) 636 1666

Upholsterers and suppliers of bedding to HM The Queen.

In 1810 John Harris Heal set himself up in business by opening a bedding shop in London's Rathbone Place. After his death in 1833, his widow, Fanny, kept the business going until their son, John Harris, took control in 1840. John Harris Junior moved the shop to its present site in Tottenham Court Road and was quick to realise the powers of advertising. When Charles Dickens published his novels in weekly parts throughout the 1840s they displayed advertisements for Heals.

It was John Harris's grandson, Ambrose – dubbed an 'utterly ruthless man' by one of his staff – who changed the face of Heals when he joined the firm in 1893. Heals had always been a bedding company. Ambrose began to design further pieces of simple oak furniture, including bedroom suites, at the lower end of the market for the 'weekend cottage'. He began to weed out the more austere designs of the day which were usually in brown oak and mahogany and Heals' designs were carried out in light-toned weathered oak.

In 1914 Heals started rebuilding their bedding factory and part of their premises in Tottenham Court Road to the designs of Ambrose Heal's cousin, Cecil Brewer. In 1927 they were granted their first Royal Warrant as makers of bedsteads and bedding to George V. But in the next two years sales of wooden bedsteads fell. Ambrose Heal's response to the crisis was to devote all the main sales efforts into the bedding department and Heals created an elaborate stand for the Ideal Home Exhibition in 1931. The stand's centrepiece was a four-poster bed decorated with feather plumes and featuring the Royal coat of arms. The stand was a flop. Heals were getting desperate. Ambrose Heal discovered a catalogue from the firm of Messrs Gooch who were producing furniture of Heals' standard and design, but considerably cheaper. At the time, Greenings of Oxford were supplying Heals with their cheaper furniture and Mr Heal insisted that Greenings should produce furniture which could be sold cheaper than Gooch. Luckily an ad-

Heal's four-poster bed at the Ideal Home Exhibition in 1931

The Sleepeezee bed (shown here as it appeared during the day) was so popular in the 1920s and 1930s that Mr Howard Price named his company after it

vertising campaign proved that their customers preferred Heals' more expensive furniture to their cheaper makes. The company were saved from becoming a discount store.

Ambrose Heal celebrated his knighthood in 1933 by introducing tubular steel bedsteads, chairs and table legs. The modern look attracted a considerable amount of press coverage. By 1941 Heals had started to export pottery and furniture but after the war they concentrated on the production of furnishing fabrics, and quickly earned a reputation for their designs. They were granted the Royal Warrant to The Queen in 1957.

In 1965 the previous chairman of Heals, Anthony S. Heal, the fifth and last generation, was awarded the bi-centenary medal of the Royal Society of Arts for his influence in promoting art and design in British Industry. The medal was presented by The Duke of Edinburgh. In 1983 Heals were bought by Habitat Mothercare (see page 121).

Monday–Saturday: 9–5.30; Thursday: 9.45–5.30. Mail order catalogue at Christmas for UK customers only.

SLEEPEEZEE LIMITED
Morden Road
Merton
London SW19 3XP

Bedding manufacturers to HM The Queen.

W. Howard Price, father of the present chairman of Sleepeezee, founded his company, Howard Price Ltd, shortly after the end of the First World War. In the late 1920s, Mr Price was an innovator among bedding manufacturers: he started making beds which could be used as pieces of everyday furniture when not in use. Among them was a model called The Sleepeezee which during the day was a 'luxurious comfortable divan, readily converted into a bed which is no less attractive'. Covered in exotic, striped ticking, the Sleepeezee also had a box compartment in which the bedclothes could be stored. Clearly the bed was so popular the company decided to re-name themselves after their bestseller.

Today Sleepeezee are still concerned with saving space. As well as more classic beds with headboards ranging from brass to wickerwork, they make a range of beds with space-saving drawers, Hydabeds – two or three-seater sofa beds – and the Twosome range, two single beds with one sliding underneath the other when it is not being used. Sleepeezee received their Royal Warrant in the early 1960s.

Sleepeezee beds are available from bedding retailers and department stores. Brochure available from the above address.

SLUMBERLAND LIMITED
Prince of Wales Mill
Vulcan Street
Oldham
Greater Manchester OL1 4ER

Bedding manufacturers to HM The Queen and HM The Queen Mother.

Slumberland's factory, situated at the Prince of Wales Mill, has a fittingly regal address for bedding manufacturers to the Royal households. In 1969 the company were granted both their Royal Warrants for supplying divans and mattresses.

Slumberland claim their beds are unique because of their patented posture springing. This means the body receives the correct support even when two people of considerably varying weights share the same bed. They offer you 'a gentle word of warning. Once you've seen and tried a Slumberland bed, you'll never be satisfied with anything less.' They produce over 20 types of beds and a range of headboards with special features like buffers to protect the wall.

Slumberland's products are available from bedding retailers and department stores. A small single bed (3 ft by 6 ft 3 in) starts at £135. Catalogue available.

WILLIAM S. TOMS LIMITED
Totteridge Road
High Wycombe
Buckinghamshire HP13 6HX

High Wycombe (0494) 22821

Manufacturers of bedding to HM The Queen and HM The Queen Mother.

William S. Toms make pine beds, bunk beds, divan beds, orthopaedic beds, zip-together beds for couples with individual demands, mattresses, headboards and pillows. They also know that as most of us spend one third of our lives in bed, we ought to spend time and care choosing a good one.

Hypnos beds have been made by William S. Toms since 1903 and the company still use traditional methods, producing 11 different kinds of bed in four standard sizes. They also make beds to order. The Department of the Environment approve Toms beds: they've bought their Penn bed (starting price for a small single bed is £250) for use in British Embassies and Residences throughout the world.

You can visit William S. Toms showrooms at the above address from Monday–Friday: 9–5, or ask for a 'Hypnos Beautiful Beds' brochure to be sent to your home. Toms beds are available from bedding retailers and department stores.

Bedding

EARLY'S OF WITNEY PLC
Witney Mills
Burford Road
Witney
Oxfordshire OX8 5EB

Manufacturers of blankets to HM The Queen.

In 1669, at the age of 14, Thomas Early was apprenticed by his father to learn the skills of blanket-making in the town of Witney in Oxfordshire. The trade had been traditional in Witney for generations, probably because of the abundance of sheep on the Cotswold hills. The Early family's first contact with the Royal family came in 1688 when Thomas, by then a master weaver in the town, was chosen to present a pair of gold-fringed blankets to James II. In 1711

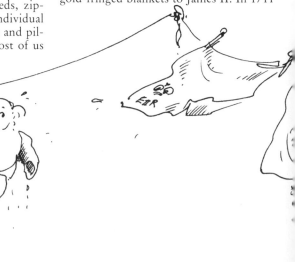

the weavers of the town of Witney received their charter and the Company of Blanket Weavers was formed to prevent substandard goods leaving the town. All blankets made within a 20 mile radius were by law of the Company to be taken to the headquarters in the town, inspected and hallmarked. Queen Anne appointed Mr John White the first Master of the Company of Blanket Weavers, and after his death Thomas Early took over.

Towards the end of the 18th century, mechanisation was gradually being introduced into the blanket-making trade in Witney. Up until that time the master weaver would buy and blend the wool and take it on a pack horse to the farms and cottages around the town and leave it to be carded (combed out) by the men and spun into yarn on spinning wheels by the women and children. The blankets still looked like pieces of sacking even after they had been woven, so they were taken to tuckers who washed, shrank and then stretched them into shape on racks before finally raising the blankets by pulling up the nap to make them fluffy. By 1782 a horse-drawn machine was being used for raising the blankets. It was the start of the Industrial Revolution in Witney.

In 1969 Early's broke the world record for the fastest blanket production. Their blanket was made in 8 hours and 11 minutes, starting at 4 o'clock in the morning when 150 sheep were sheared, and finishing with the first blanket packed in its transparent wrapping later the same day. Other blankets followed. By the evening 50 had been completed. One blanket flew to New York where it was displayed with the notice: 'The wool of which this blanket is made was shorn from sheep in Witney, England this morning.'

Today the company export to over 60 countries. Most of their blankets are now made on the Fiberweaver, which makes blankets direct from the web as it leaves the carding machines. Fiberwoven blankets account for two-thirds of the total production at Early's although they still use the traditional method of blanket manufacturing with ring spinning frames and weaving machines as well. The company make conventional white blankets and a range of colours. Many of their blankets are produced in man-made fibres due to the demand for machine washable fabrics and the upredictable price of wool. The company thrive on the far-sightedness of Thomas Early's father who chose a product for his son which is still in demand over 300 years later.

Early's of Witney blankets are available from bedding retailers and department stores.

HARVEY NICHOLS LIMITED
Knightsbridge
London SW1X 7RJ

(01) 235 5000

Linen drapers to HM The Queen, drapers to HM The Queen Mother and suppliers of household and fancy goods to HRH The Prince of Wales.

In 1813 a small draper's shop was opened by Benjamin Harvey. When he died he left the business to his daughter, Elizabeth, on the condition that she take the shop's silk buyer, Colonel Nichols, into partnership. The union was soon to create one of the most fashionable stores in Victorian London, and indeed today.

The store's plum site in the centre of Knightsbridge was originally chosen to attract trade from passing stage coaches, who would drive past carrying the élite members of London society en route to Bath, in those times the rendezvous of the beautiful and fashionable. After Harvey and Nichols became partners linens and silks remained the sole trade for a short while. Later furnishings were introduced and Harvey

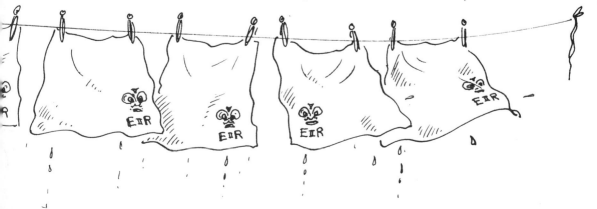

Nichols Indian and Turkish carpets became a speciality.

Today the store has a reputation for the exquisite character of its goods. In all its departments, from household furnishings to jewellery, the very latest exclusive objects can be found. It is also the place to go for that impossible gift. The Princess of Wales reputedly shopped there last Christmas.

Monday–Saturday: 9.30–6; Wednesday: 9.30–7. Mail order catalogue sent at Christmas to account customers worldwide.

McCALLUM & CRAIGIE LIMITED
Whitley Willows Mill
Lepton
Huddersfield
West Yorkshire HD8 0HN

Suppliers of Lan-Air-Cel blankets to HM The Queen Mother.

Being wrapped in a Lan-Air-Cel blanket is 'rather like wearing a sweater as opposed to a tweed jacket – warmth without weight'. Most British mothers would agree. Since the company started 60 years ago there can't be many babies who have not been tucked under one of their satin-bordered cellular blankets.

Today over 600 people are employed in the Huddersfield factory making the Lan-Air-Cel – the original cellular blanket – and the newer Celairic blanket. The Lan-Air-Cel is made from pure wool and comes in several colours – changed according to 'the dictates of fashion' – including their present bestselling rose and pale pink, apple green, camel and topaz. A single blanket costs from £24 and comes with a 10-year guarantee. Their Celairic blanket is pure cotton and often found in hospitals as it can be boil washed. Celairic blankets start from £14 for a single blanket.

Lan-Air-Cel blankets are available from 'such diverse stores as Harrods in London, Nieman Marcus in Dallas and stores in Japan, Australia and across Europe'. They are also available from bedding specialists and most other department stores.

WALPOLE BROTHERS (LONDON) LIMITED
Linen drapers to HM The Queen and linen manufacturers to HM The Queen Mother.

VANTONA INTERNATIONAL LINEN COMPANY LIMITED
20 Brook Street
London W1 2NE

(01) 629 5000

Suppliers of linen to HM The Queen.

These days the only service Walpole Brothers can no longer provide is the hand-embroidering of the family crest on your bedlinen. They still have over 50 styles of intricate monograms for you to choose from, but today they're machine-stitched.

Walpole Brothers, linen manufacturers, were founded by Thomas Simmons in 1766 in Dublin, then a centre of importance in the linen trade. In the 1850s they opened their first shop in London and soon afterwards received their first Royal Warrant from The Prince of Wales, later Edward VII – surely a connoisseur of bed-linen.

Today Walpole Brothers still manufacture a wide range of items which can be found at the shop of their parent company, Vantona International Linen, in Brook Street. There you can buy all the linen you'll need in your kitchen, bathroom and bedroom – for both your home and your yacht. 'We specialise in doing things that are different,' Major Gould, Walpole's managing director, told me. That is no exaggeration. They make extra large sheets, pillows for those allergic to down or feathers, and eiderdowns that won't slip off your bed no matter what you're doing. And if what you're looking for doesn't feature in their standard range, Walpole Brothers will have a good try at making it for you. So don't be put off buying that heart-shaped bed you've always wanted – now you know where to buy the sheets to fit it.

Vantona National Linen Co. Ltd is open Monday–Friday: 9.30–5.30. Two 'sale goods' mail order catalogues are available annually, one in January and one in late June.

Nightwear

BRADLEYS (KNIGHTSBRIDGE) LIMITED
83 Knightsbridge
London SW1X 7RB

(01) 235 2902

Bradleys' customers include The Princess of Wales, Princess Anne and the Saudi and many European Royal families who frequently visit the shop, known as 'the largest specialist lingerie store in England'.

In their bright two-floored shop – one half of it formerly a butcher's – Mrs Scott and her daughter, Mrs Elkan, have a formidable range of lingerie. From your first bra to your last corset, Bradleys staff – all fully trained to measure and fit corsets and other underwear correctly – will help you make the correct choice. Bradleys also sell specialist underwear for women who are breast feeding or who have had a mastectomy, and thermal underwear, leotards and swimwear.

Bradleys also stock nightgowns from £15 to £700 depending on the fabric and the designer label. Before Christmas the shop is filled with men buying exotic little nothings – silk suspenders, stockings and briefs – for their ladies who after Christmas come and exchange them for something more practical. 'We go from the brief and glamorous to more prosaic garments,' I was told.

The service at Bradleys is exceptional. Their staff have been known to visit customers in hospital to discuss their needs after they have had a baby and to sit outside suites in the Ritz until 2 o'clock in the morning waiting with garments for clients flying in to London. No wonder some of their customers are now third generation.

Monday–Friday: 9–5; Wednesday: 9–7; Saturday: 10–5.30. No mail order catalogue available, but Bradleys will send their wares around the world.

NIGHT OWLS
78 Fulham Road
London SW3 5PF

(01) 584 2451

Liz Rees Jones, owner of Great Expectations (see page 98) bought Night Owls in 1981. 'The shop had started off well when it opened in the early 1970s, but it had become a bit mumsy, with requests for floral print nighties. Today, now that people are much more aware of their bodies, night- and underwear have become fashion areas.' Ms Rees Jones must be right. Her satin night dresses at £173 have been featured in *Vogue* as evening dresses.

Night Owls is extremely popular with the Royal family, including The Princess of Wales, and stage celebrities. They still stock the sensible flowery nightgowns and housecoats and the silk Hollywood-style satin pyjamas. They also sell white cotton nightdresses and T-shirt nightshirts for those who neither want to be vampish nor frumpish. Their range of lingerie includes everything from satin 'Teddy' cami-knickers to brassières, and corsets – from £70 – for quickly hiding that unwanted inch from your waist, but you'll need assistance to help you get into them.

Monday–Friday: 10–6; Saturday: 10–4.30. Night Owls will send items by mail to customers anywhere in the UK but you have to know what you want as they have no mail order catalogue.

The Royal Nursery

Clothes

BIMBO
**56 Kendal Street
London W2 2BP**

(01) 402 5317

When Prince William made his first steps in public at Kensington Palace on 14 December 1983, he was snugly dressed in a £45 padded blue snow-suit with an 'ABC' motif. It came from Bimbo and was made by the French firm Colchika.

Bimbo – an affectionate name for a baby in Italian – was the brainchild of Oman Elawadi, an Egyptian, and his ex-wife, an Italian. The shop opened in Kendal Street in 1978. Today they have another branch in the Grosvenor House Hotel. They sell designer wear for children from birth to 16 years old. Much of the merchandise is exclusive to Bimbo and most of the clothes are imported.

The main emphasis is on luxury day- and party-clothes, but there is also a selection of jeans and dungarees and a range of accessories and shoes with bags specially made to match their suits. Girls' day wear outfits are mainly Italian and very much what Mama would wear including elegant white wool suits and silk blouses. Party dresses are priced from £198 to £750. For boys' nightwear, a silk robe and pyjamas start at £165 or wool dressing gowns at £40 and there are silk and velvet romper suits for the evening.
Bimbo say their policy is 'never to allow the customer to walk out without having bought something'. The Princess plumped for the snow-suit for William. It is one of their cheaper items.

Monday–Saturday: 9.30–6.30; Thursday: 9.30–7.30 (Kendal Street shop).

Disappointment reigned when the Palace revealed that the ABC on Prince William's playsuit from Bimbo was nothing more significant than the first three letters of the alphabet

MEENYS (CLOTHES) USA
**197 Kensington High Street
London W8 6BA
(and branches)**

(01) 937 7899

Teddy Craze first opened Meenys as a children's hairdresser. His sister, Annabelle, sold children's clothing from a corner of the room. On a trip to the States Teddy Craze discovered Osh Kosh G'bosh – a factory in Wisconsin which had been making work clothes since the 19th century. Mr Craze brought a supply of children's clothing back with him, including the famous Osh Kosh hickory striped dungarees and the Hotliner dungarees in hard-wearing denim lined with tartan.

The clothes were extremely successful in England, with Meenys as the sole supplier. The hairdressing side of the business was forgotten and Meenys concentrated on clothing. Osh Kosh extended their lines and for the last eight years have been producing baseball jackets for children and adults from £36.50. Meenys now have four shops and sell Osh Kosh clothing for adults as well. They have also extended their range into the total 'American look' with canvas All Star baseball boots for children age five and over, original Penny Loafers from £47.50, sweatshirts, tracksuits and sweaters to match the dungarees.

Meenys say 'you can dress your child completely in Osh Kosh'. The Princess of Wales agrees. She visited the shop in early 1984 and bought several more pairs of Osh Kosh dungarees and some sweaters for Prince William.

Monday–Saturday: 10–6 (Kensington High Street branch).

THE WHITE HOUSE
**51/52 New Bond Street
London W1Y 0BY**

(01) 629 3521

The White House is known as 'the aristocrat of the children's specialists'. White House babies start life in antique Victorian

The children's department at The White House

garters, singlets, lace bloomers 'to wear under jodhpurs' – not forgetting the quilted silk hot water bottle. The showrooms have also expanded to include men's wear with cashmere sweaters, gaberdine suits, gloves, ties, towelling robes and silk underwear. The White House say their shop is a 'place of privilege'. One can only agree.

Monday–Friday: 9–5.30; Saturday: 9–1. Mail order catalogue available, export prices quoted on request. The White House will make anything to order from any of their departments.

cots trimmed with soft muslin and lace. They see the world for the first time from their coach-built prams and drift off to sleep in hand-smocked wool nightgowns wrapped in pure cashmere shawls. Even the font is a less daunting experience for the White House baby dressed in a cascading christening robe of plumetis and handmade lace. For little girls they make sugar and spice organdie frocks threaded with pretty ribbons and for little boys, short velvet trousers and pintucked lace shirts.

The White House say their children's clothes are 'for everybody's little prince and princess'. The Princess of Wales has bought some of their hand-smocked crawler suits for her little Prince. The silk and satin outfits, sometimes known as romper suits, have been a favourite style of The Princess who has dressed Prince William in them for most of his Royal photocalls. When he accompanied his parents on their Australian tour, Prince William's outfits attracted almost as much attention as his mother's usually do.

Since the days of the Belle Epoque in London this Anglo-French shop has been celebrated for exquisite handmade linen, lingerie and children's wear. It was opened in 1906 for the 'more discerning customer'. Today the linen department is renowned for its hand-embroidered organdie and linen table sets (a set for 12 people costs £695), its sheets and pillowcases (sets can cost up to £900) and its embroidered towels and Irish linen. The shop is patronised by Royal families from all over the world coming to furnish their palaces. It is where pampered brides leave their wedding lists.

The White House has a costume showroom which specialises in exclusive collections of ladies' fashions for day and evening wear as well as accessories and swimwear. Their lingerie department is a treasure-trove of silk lace-trimmed lingeries, bridal

Dancing

VACANI SCHOOL OF DANCING
Pineapple Dance Studios
38/40 Harrington Road
London SW7 4LT
(and branches)

(01) 589 6110

As toddlers, The Queen, Princess Margaret, Prince Charles and Princess Anne were all taught the art of graceful movement and curtseying (or bowing) at Vacani's. No doubt the latter skills did not come in exceedingly useful but the former undoubtedly have.

Vacani's was established in 1914 by Marguerite Vacani. 'It started with débutantes learning how to make curtseys, and hold trains and fans,' Elfrida Eden, the present co-director of the school told me. In the 1930s the school was taken over by Betty Vacani, Marguerite Vacani's niece, who first introduced the classes for children for which Vacani's acquired its reputation. It was Betty Vacani who taught the Royal family and who began sending teachers to boarding schools, such as West Heath in Kent, where Lady Diana Spencer was studying, to teach the Vacani dance skills and deportment. Betty Vacani awarded Lady Diana first prize at a dancing competition held at West Heath. Later Lady Diana briefly returned to Vacani's as a student teacher.

In 1982, Madame Vacani retired and the school was taken over by Elfrida Eden, niece of Sir Anthony Eden. Ms Eden is a tall former professional dancer and actress who herself went to Vacani's as a child. She still runs the children's classes in which Gabriella Windsor, daughter of Prince and

Princess Michael of Kent is a pupil. There are 12 a week for children age three and under. With Ms Eden they learn knee bending, tiptoes and ring-a-ring-a-roses, or you can hear Ms Eden, in a voice that she admits sounds 'more and more like the late Joyce Grenfell every minute', saying, 'Come along, try and be exceedingly naughty mice . . .'. From the age of four and a half to five, children are taught ballet – at which point most of the boys leave.

The adult side of Vacani's is being built up by Ms Eden and her partner. They are now holding ballet, tap and ballroom dancing classes for adults, as well as aerobics – all held by qualified teachers. The classes cost £35 for a 10 week term with one lesson a week which if missed can be taken later. What would Madame Vacani think if she saw her débutantes gyrating around the floor instead of curtseying?

Classes are offered every day, except Sunday, at the above address or at Vacani's other branches. Telephone the above number for details.

Furnishing

DRAGONS OF WALTON STREET LIMITED
23 Walton Street
London SW3 2HX
(and a branch in Brighton)

(01) 589 3795

When I visited Dragons, the name 'William' appeared on most of the hand-painted children's furniture on display. It could be coincidence or a shrewd hint at who their most important little customer is. But it is rumoured that the day nursery at Highgrove, the country residence of The Prince and Princess of Wales, is decorated from top to toe with little woodland characters. The sort of service Dragons provide.

The little corner shop looks just like a nursery. The walls and floor are taken up with furniture, toy boxes, rocking horses, mirrors and chests of drawers covered with names and motifs, from Winnie-the-Pooh and 101 Dalmations to flowers and *trompe-l'oeil* effects. Dragons customers are mummies with nanny – 'Nannies generally telling Mums what to buy.' Dragons can make any style and piece of furniture you want. You can buy their standard styles and designs ready painted from the shop or commission one of their 21 illustrators –

Military toy box from Dragons costs £120

each with their own style – to carry out your requests. 'One mother came in with bags and bags of teddies and asked us to copy them on to toy boxes for her child.'

Dragons was started three years ago by Rosie Fisher, an antique dealer with a love of painted furniture. Realising how few pieces of antique painted furniture there were on the market she decided to make her own. Dragons' wooden furniture is made by craftsmen in Sussex and Wiltshire before coming to London to be painted by Dragons' team of artists. Dragons also sell painted roller blinds, personalised cushions and painted furniture for adults.

Monday–Friday: 9.30–5.30; Saturday 10.30–4.30 (Walton Street branch). Mail order catalogue available and Dragons will deliver their furniture worldwide.

MOTHERCARE LIMITED
461 Oxford Street
London W1R 2EB

(01) 629 6621

Although Prince William has worn silk romper suits for some of his more formal occasions, most days he goes out to play in hard-wearing dungarees, cotton shirts, woolly jumpers and – if it's raining – little red plastic wellies: the type of everyday clothes which can be found at Mothercare, the shop for expectant mothers, and children up to the age of 10.

The Mothercare chain was taken over in 1982 by Terence Conran, founder of Habitat. But the company was originally the brainchild of Selim Zelhik in the early 1960s. When he started the business Mr Zelhik, a banker, admitted he had never been inside a retail shop for longer than a few minutes. 'I got out of banking because I didn't enjoy lending money.'

Mothercare was based on the Prénatal shops in France. At that time expectant mothers in England still had to shop between department stores, toyshops and chemists to accumulate the basic equipment for themselves and their babies. With domestic help dying out Mr Zelhik saw that convenience combined with value for money was a winning combination. Another paramount factor was hygiene. He believed that chemist shops had the right connotations so he and his two brothers bought out the Lewis & Burrows chain of chemists and made over a section of each shop to maternity merchandise. But the idea of a boutique within a shop failed and a year later losses totalled £180,000. Mr Zelhik sold the chain in 1961 and instead bought a group of pram and furniture shops from W. J. Harris for £550,000.

Mr Zelhik set about converting the Harris shops and in 1962 the first Mothercare shop was opened in Oxford Street. During the early years there were a fund of horror stories about baby vests disintegrating in the third wash, plastic pants which were inexplicably no longer waterproof and wheels falling off pushchairs because of faulty rivets. Mr Zelhik soldiered on with painstaking attention to detail: when Mothercare decided to extend their age range to 10 in 1975, he had the position of the label changed on the older boys' trousers so it would not show at school for fear the boys might be teased as cissies.

By the time he sold out to Mr Conran, Mr Zelhik thought his middle-class customers had deserted him. He saw rivals emerging in the mothers' and children's clothing field in other department stores. At the time of sale Mothercare was worth £129 million against Habitat's £52 million, but profits had already begun to fall. Mr Conran set about revamping the Mothercare image, declaring it 'still one of the world's most profitable retailers'. Today there are 200 Mothercare shops in the UK and another 200 in the United States. Mothercare's mail order catalogue goes out to 183 different countries with special inserts in nine languages. Apart from clothes the Mothercare shops also provide a range of baby equipment such as prams, cots, baths, potties, playpens and feeding chairs. They also sell safety car-seats like the one for Prince William spotted in the back of the Royal car at Aberdeen Airport in 1984.

Terence Conran is now aiming to bring in clothes for children with 'spirit'. He says that after the age of five children lead their mothers by the hand and tell them what they want. 'We want to make a part of the shop a place where kids will say "Let's go in there" – not ultra trendy but full of life.' He is also concerned about Mothercare's maternity range. 'The missing ingredient here is fashion,' says Mr Conran. 'A girl who has been shopping at boutiques becomes pregnant and is suddenly consigned to clothes that are unflattering. We have to bring in some design names.'

Mothercare products are available from Mothercare shops throughout the UK and the United States. Mothercare catalogue available from: Mothercare Ltd, Cherry Tree Road, Watford, Hertfordshire WD2 5SH. Price 20 pence.

Toys

HAMLEYS OF REGENT STREET LIMITED
188/196 Regent Street
London W1R 5DF

(01) 734 3161

Toy and sports merchants to HM The Queen.

The ground floor of Hamleys is filled with noises of *Star Wars* soundtracks, the clicking of triggers, beating of drums, whirring of electronic games and the puffing sound of the Hamleys train racing round the ground floor 10 feet off the ground. Upstairs the telephonist is coping with a problem customer: 'Toy department, sir? We're all toys.'

The *Guinness Book of Records* states Hamleys is the 'largest' toy shop in the world and Hamleys claim they are the 'finest'. They buy from all over the world and sell to customers of all nationalities. Their team of six buyers travels three months of the year in search of new toys. The Cabbage Dolls imported from the States in 1983 had Americans flying over to queue for them.

Hamleys' busiest periods in the year read like a school timetable and the shop is to be avoided at all half-terms and holidays. It's filled with parents saying, 'Darling,

we've been here all day, don't you think it's time to go home?', and determined children dragging them across the other side of the store. Hamleys can boast over £12 million a year in takings. Their bestselling item is still the teddy bear, as found on their second floor and visited by The Princess of Wales one cold day during the winter of 1982.

The shop was opened by William Hamley, a Cornishman from Bodmin, who came to London in 1760 and started a shop, called Noah's Ark, in London's High Holborn. A century later his descendants had opened a branch in Regent Street, renamed the company Hamley Brothers and were specialising in imported dolls from around the world, chemistry sets and model steam engines. In 1906 Hamley Brothers moved to 200/202 Regent Street where they remained until 1981. In 1938 they were awarded their first Royal Warrant by Queen Mary, and received their present warrant from The Queen in 1955.

Today in Hamleys they sell everything from a hand-held electronic game to a home computer in their A Step Ahead electronic games complex. They also sell a miniature Princess of Wales doll (for £22.95) in their Small World department.

Monday–Saturday: 9–5.30; Thursday: 9–8. Mail order catalogue available every Christmas, free in the shop or 75 pence if mailed. Hamleys will mail worldwide.

The Royal Larder

Breakfast

G. G. BAXTER LIMITED
Sarre
Birchington
Kent CT7 0LD

Suppliers of pork sausages to HM The Queen and HM The Queen Mother.

Baxter were awarded their Royal Warrant for their pork sausages in 1944 by The Queen and a few years ago by The Queen Mother. The sausages are made from all English pork, have a high meat content and very little seasoning. They come in all sizes, from cocktail and chippolata to large four to the pound sizes, and in three brands: Special, Celebrated and Cambridge.

The original Baxter company were founded at the Minories in the City of London in 1836. In 1939, under the threat of war, the firm moved the manufacturing side of the business to a farm in Sarre, one of the Cinque ports of which The Queen Mother is Warden, and converted the buildings for the production of sausages. Today Mr Edwin Baxter, the great-great-grandson of the founder, runs the company and continues making sausages to their 125-year-old recipe.

Baxters also manufacture pies, Cornish pasties and sausage rolls and since 1960 have become one of the largest wholesale butchers in the country, serving hotels, restaurants, schools and such names as Top Rank, Butlins, British Rail ferries and BP.

G. G. Baxter have no retail shops and no connection with a firm of a similar name. Their products are supplied daily direct to the trade and you can only buy their pork sausages from Fortnum & Mason (see page 236) in London and from a few select butchers in neighbouring Kent.

Baxters' pork sausages are available wholesale to the trade from the above address or to the London public at Fortnum & Mason.

FRANK COOPER LIMITED
Claygate House
Esher
Surrey KT10 9PN

Marmalade manufacturers to HM The Queen.

Frank Cooper's Vintage Oxford and Coarse Cut marmalades are robust. They were made for the men who carried the British flag to all corners of the globe. Captain Scott took Frank Cooper's marmalade and canned fruits on his 1907 expedition and some years later some of the same marmalade was found in one of the dumps in excellent condition. Ever since they were first made in 1874, they have reputedly graced breakfast tables from Sandhurst to Everest, from Malaya to the Antarctic. They are made from the biggest and best Seville oranges and cooked no less than five times to render them 'the ultimate in bitter sweet delight'.

Frank Cooper have held their Royal Warrant consecutively since they were first granted one by Queen Alexandra.

Frank Cooper marmalade is available from grocers, delicatessens and food sections of department stores.

JUSTIN DE BLANK (PROVISIONS) LIMITED
46 Walton Street
London SW3 1RB

(01) 589 4734

Bakers to HM The Queen.

Mr de Blank calls himself 'one of the very last bakers in Central London to make bread in the traditional way'. In the basement of his Walton Street shop his 'craftsman' baker works through the night, often producing up to 600 loaves. The flavour of his bread, Mr de Blank says, 'comes from the slow fermentation and the fact that it's cooked on a flat-bottomed oven'. Justin de Blank sell between 30 and 40 different types of bread and a variety of tarts, quiches, cakes, pizzas and sausage rolls.

Opposite:
Three Royal generations at breakfast. Queen Victoria, her youngest daughter Princess Beatrice with her husband, Prince Henry of Battenburg, and their children partaking of breakfast at Windsor Castle in 1896

1895-6

The King of Portugal visits the Queen, November
Birth of the Grand Duchess Olga of Russia, November 15
Birth of Prince Albert of York, December 14
Chitral Expedition
Death of Prince Henry of Battenberg, January 20
Marriage of Princess Maud of Wales to Prince Charles of Denmark, July 22
On September 23 the Queen had reigned longer than any English Sovereign

The Queen at Breakfast

WITH PRINCESS HENRY OF BATTENBERG

THE QUEEN

HER MAJESTY AND THE CHILDREN OF HER YOUNGEST DAUGHTER, PRINCESS HENRY OF BATTENBERG

Mr de Blank, an Englishman brought up in France, was Terence Conran's first marketing director (see page 121) and worked as an architect before venturing into the food business. Mr de Blank opened his first food shop in Elizabeth Street in 1969 and then decided 'bread is the cornerstone of a food shop' so he opened the Walton Street shop with its already existing bakery downstairs. Today Mr de Blank also has a wholesale bakery in South London, which caters for his restaurant at the General Trading Company (see page 231), his shops and Buckingham Palace, and a 'herbs, plants and flowers' shop in Ebury Street. The Ebury Street shop always has a pavement display of plants, herbs and cut flowers outside, and inside stocks over 100 different drying and growing herbs.

Monday–Friday: 7.30–6; Saturday: 7.30–1 (Walton Street branch). Justin de Blank's also do catering.

EXPRESS DAIRY UK LIMITED
Victoria Road
South Ruislip
Middlesex HA4 0HF

Dairy suppliers to HM The Queen.

It has been said that Her Majesty was only convinced she was Queen when in 1952 she first saw her cypher on the Royal milk bottles with their specially printed sides and gold tops showing her monogram. But those bottles contain the milk delivered three times a week from the Royal Dairy farms at Windsor.

Express Dairy milk contains no such embellishments. The company started in 1865 when up to that time all the milk required for London was produced either in London or within a few miles of the city. When foot and mouth disease broke out amongst the herds of cows then in London dairies, Sir George Bartham persuaded farmers in Leicestershire, Buckinghamshire and the Home Counties to provide milk for London. He set up a head office in London's Tavistock Place to ensure quality control, and to prevent the milk souring on its overnight trip to London, Sir George used a refrigeration system to make sure that the milk remained cold. By 1884 they had received three gold medals for their exhibits at the International Health Exhibition.

The company were awarded their first Royal Warrant by Queen Victoria and have held one ever since.

Express Dairy products are obtainable from grocers, supermarkets and Express Dairy vans in and around the London area.

GOLDENLAY EGGS (UK) LIMITED
Carlton House
Sandy Walk
Wakefield
West Yorkshire WF1 2DP

Supplier of eggs to HM The Queen.

Goldenlay Eggs were started in 1970 in a bid to prevent an egg price war between the egg marketing companies. Four egg businesses from around the country decided to join forces because of the pending demise of the British Egg Marketing Board which was expected to create a free market for eggs and the individual companies would be forced into fierce competition with each other.

Since Goldenlay was formed the egg industry has undergone considerable changes. Due to consumer preferences eggs are now virtually all brown-shelled and yolks are golden-coloured. In 1980 Goldenlay became the first egg manufacturing organisation to introduce a standardised golden yolk colour.

Today their farm suppliers use a special fan which enables them to check the colour of the yolk before the eggs are packed. Goldenlay collect supplies from a national network of more than 1,000 farms and distribute them around the country.

Goldenlay eggs are available from grocers and supermarkets.

KIRKNESS & GORIE
The Noust Victoria Road
Kirkwall
Orkney KW15 1DH
Scotland

Supplier of honey to HM The Queen.

In November 1979 Mr Bruce Gorie, Royal supplier of honey, wrote a letter to one of his regular clients in reply to her request for the 'lovely Orkney honey'. He wrote: 'I regret to have to inform you that for the first time I shall be unable to supply you with your full order of six jars. The weather over the past two years has been totally against the poor little bees to the extent that many of the producers have lost most of their bees and my total stock this year is only 24 jars. I will send you four jars and we have to hope for some good weather.'

In 1859 James Kirkness, a cabinetmaker, founded a 'Family Grocers and Spirit Dealers' in Kirkwall. He quickly established a reputation for serving the needs of the local community, exiled Orcadians and visitors alike. But he soon lost his spirit licence when he was caught smuggling. James Kirkness died in 1919, and his daughter and her husband, Mr Gorie, an accountant, both took over running the store. During the wars, Kirkness & Gorie, as the shop had become, helped feed the many servicemen and women based 'overseas' on Orkney. In the 1970s there was another invasion of the community with the development of the North Sea oil industry. Kirkness & Gorie provided the sailors from all over Europe with food and drink to suit their national preferences. The shop closed in 1980 but Mr Gorie continues to supply a few specially selected local products (such as the Highland Park 100° proof malt whisky, the Orkney fudge, Orkney jewellery designed by his sister, Ola, and of course, the Orkney honey) by mail order.

For many years Kirkness & Gorie have been the main suppliers of Orkney honey, renowned for its crystal-clear very light gold colour when it is new and very white colour once aged and its delicious taste. The bees are mainly located in a half-mile patch of land on the rich Orkney farmlands. Their honey, occasionally no more than a few pounds and seldom more than 300 pounds, is extracted in September or October. By January the honey is normally sold out.

Kirkness & Gorie were awarded their Royal Warrant in 1978.

No mail order catalogue available, but write to Kirkness & Gorie between September and January for details of the honey. A jar of honey costs from £2.00 depending on availability.

G. LEITH & SON
Golf Road
Ballater
Aberdeenshire
Scotland

Ballater (0338) 55474

Bakers and confectioners to HM The Queen and HM The Queen Mother.

Mr and Mrs Murdoch moved to Ballater, the closest village to Balmoral (the Royal family's summer home) and Birkhall (The Queen Mother's home at Balmoral), 14 years ago. Today they run a small hotel in the village, own George Leith's the baker's and have a shop in Banchory, about 15 miles away.

Mr Murdoch is a confectioner and makes all the cakes and biscuits on the premises, frequently experimenting with new recipes. His specialities are the local Buttries (unsweetened rolls), Black Buns, Shortbread, Butter Biscuits and the Selkirk Bannoch ('a good big bun') made specially in the summer when the Royal family are in residence. They also sell the most delicious American biscuits laden with butter and bits of chocolate.

The Murdochs' youngest son now runs the bakery with its small team of bakers starting the day at 1.00 a.m. and often baking until midday.

Monday–Saturday: 7–5. G. Leith deliver to neighbouring Tarland, Aboyne, Crathie and the Balmoral Estates.

QUAKER OATS LIMITED
Bridge Road
Southall
Middlesex UB2 4AG

Suppliers of Quaker products to HM The Queen.

Although their name has always been synonymous with oats, Quaker also produce macaroni, minced morsels for dogs and cat foods, canned chicken breasts, pasta, sandwich spreads, pastes and potted meats. They have been established since 1899 and have held the Royal Warrant for supplying all their products since 1950.

During a visit to the firm's Southall factory The Prince of Wales told staff: 'My wife has made me try a Harvest Crunch Bar. I find it a bit hard on the teeth, myself.' His son William on the other hand might cut his teeth on their toys. Quaker also own Fisher Price who make educational playthings which are available at most toy shops, though as yet non-warrant-holding.

Quaker products can be bought at grocers and supermarkets.

J. STOPPS & SONS LIMITED
77 Hummer Road
Egham
Surrey
(and branches)
Egham (87) 32607

Bakers and confectioners to HM The Queen Mother.

The bakery in Egham was built by Mr Stopps and his two sons in 1898. It has been in the hands of the family ever since. Mr and Mrs Stopps still use many of the old recipes and methods, baking bread, cakes and pastry in the same traditional way their forefathers did.

Today the bakery supplies local schools, golf clubs and hotels with their wares as well as their three shops in Egham, Old Windsor and Englefield Green. J. Stopps supply Royal Lodge, The Queen Mother's residence in Windsor, all year round, even when Her Majesty is not in residence. They were awarded their Royal Warrant 10 years ago. Mrs Stopps recommends their crusty bread, and brandy cakes – only available at Christmas.

*Monday, Wednesday and Friday:
8.30–5.30; Thursday and Saturday: 8.30–1
(Egham shop).*

THE WALL'S MEAT COMPANY
Malthouse Walk
Banbury
Oxfordshire OX16 8QL

Suppliers of sausages and meat pies to HM The Queen and HM The Queen Mother.

The story of Wall's begins in 1786 when Edmund Cotterill opened a pork butcher's shop in St James's Market. Four years later he was joined by a young apprentice, Richard Wall, who was later to become the founder of the Wall's dynasty. After a seven-year apprenticeship, Richard Wall was taken into partnership and in 1807 became the sole owner of the business. From his shop he supplied pork to nearby Carlton House, the residence of George, Prince of Wales, who later became Prince

Regent. Richard Wall received his first Royal Warrant from the Prince as purveyor of pork and he continued to serve him after his accession to the throne as George IV.

In 1816 St James's Market was demolished to make way for the construction of Regent Street. Richard Wall moved the business to a new market near the Haymarket. By 1838, when Queen Victoria granted her warrant, Wall's son, Thomas, was running the business. Two years later Queen Victoria's half-brother Prince Karl von Leiningen came over from Bavaria for Her Majesty's marriage to Prince Albert. While staying as a guest at Buckingham Palace the Prince asked Thomas Wall to obtain some typically British pigs for breeding purposes. His Highness was so pleased with the 'fine specimens of pigs which are acquired' that with Queen Victoria's permission he awarded Wall's the Coronation medal.

By 1880 the business was under the management of Thomas's two sons, Thomas and Frederick. By then the shop had been divided into four departments. The Kitchen was for pressed meats, pâtés and soups sold by the bottle. The Smokehouse was for curing the hams. The Bakehouse was for the pies and sausage rolls and the Butcher's department was for preparing orders.

Wall's was a household name by the beginning of the 20th century despite their policy never to advertise. In 1903 when the first production factory was acquired in Battersea, Wall's relented with a 'modest level of advertising'. Three years later the company's turnover had reached £100,000 a year. In the early 1920s they were taken over by MacFisheries. During the next 30 years Wall's experimented with ice-cream, coffee, potato crisps, soya crisps and vacuum-packed cheese biscuits. MacFisheries were taken over by Unilever and in the 1950s Wall's ice-cream became a separate company within Unilever and the other experiments were abandoned to concentrate on the meat side of the business.

Today Wall's manufacture a range of products from traditional thick pork sausages to pies and pastries.

Wall's sausages and meat pies are available from butchers and supermarkets.

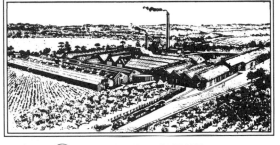

STRAWBERRY PICKING

THE TIPTREE JAM FACTORY

TIPTREE, COLCHESTER, ESSEX.

WEETABIX LIMITED
Weetabix Mills
Burton Latimer
Kettering
Northamptonshire NN15 5JR

Manufacturers of breakfast cereals to HM The Queen and HM The Queen Mother.

Weetabix made their first wheat cereal breakfast biscuits in the early 1930s. At first the cereal was only sold to shops within a limited distance of the Weetabix plant in Kettering. Soon demand for the new kind of food grew and a sales force was recruited to distribute Weetabix all over the country. By 1970 the business had grown from a small company to the largest British-owned breakfast cereal manufacturers in the world. Extra production lines were turning out 52 million biscuits a week but it was still not enough to meet world demand. In 1975 Weetabix built their first factory next to their existing site and have continued to expand ever since.

Today Weetabix also make Alpen, Weetaflakes, Farmhouse Bran and Bran Fare.

Weetabix breakfast cereals are available from grocers and supermarkets.

WILKIN & SONS LIMITED
Tiptree
Colchester
Essex CO5 0RF

Jam and marmalade manufacturers to HM The Queen.

Arthur Wilkin founded Wilkin & Sons as a fruit farm in Tiptree in 1864. He began to make jams 20 years later to prevent the vast quantities of fruit going to waste. A sample of one of his early attempts at strawberry conserve was sent to William Gladstone. The Prime Minister was so impressed by the product that he wrote to Mr Wilkin predicting that 'a considerable trade will grow from these infant undertakings'.

By 1911 the company had over 10,000 individual customers for their conserves. Wilkin & Sons were granted their first Royal Warrant by George V, but British Royalty have been associated with fruit preserves as far back as the reign of Henry VIII who was known among other things as the first English king to eat marmalade.

Wilkin & Sons are still owned by the Wilkin family who describe their preserves as the 'epitome of gracious living'. They now make a range of over 60 products which include the traditional strawberry and damson conserves as well as the more exotic kiwi and green fig preserves. Most of the fruit is grown on their 1,000 acre farmland in Essex – though their Seville oranges are imported frozen from Spain. To this day Arthur Wilkin's descendants still uphold his policy of never using any artificial colouring or preservatives in their products.

Wilkin & Sons jams and marmalades are available from grocers, delicatessens and supermarkets.

Butchers

G. G. BAXTER LIMITED

See page 124.

CAMPBELL BROTHERS (EDINBURGH) LIMITED
60 Queen Street
Edinburgh
Scotland

Edinburgh (031) 225 5471

Purveyors of meat and poultry to HM The Queen.

Thanks to its favourable location opposite the elegant Heriot Row, Campbell Brothers can list among their clients 'several titled families' as well as the Royal family for the one week a year when they are in residence at Holyroodhouse. The large corner shop has held its Royal Warrant to The Queen since 1932.

Campbell Brothers is so spacious it can feel empty, but the shop is always full at lunchtime when many of the nearby office workers come in to buy meat and groceries for their dinner parties. At one stage 68 butchers used to work in the shop, making the haggis, black pudding and sausages which are for sale. Recently Campbell Brothers built a factory in Seafield and today the sausages and haggis are made there. Their haggis costs 64 pence a pound and leading up to Burns night, Campbell Brothers operate a haggis mail order service.

Besides haggis, they also sell more unusual Scottish delights such as circular Ayrshire bacon, for £1.54 a pound.

Most of the meat and poultry sold in the shop is purchased from Smithfield Market in London to obtain a competitive price. Campbell Brothers hang their own steaks for 10 to 14 days and will pluck and dress game for customers. At Christmas they will even prepare and stuff fresh turkeys, ducks and geese.

In the wooden-floored shop not only can customers buy their meat, but also the rest of their meal. There's a large selection of cheeses and delicatessen foods as well as tinned foods, fresh and frozen vegetables and frozen cakes, ice-cream and smoked salmon.

Monday–Friday: 7.30–5.30; Saturday: 7.30–1. Campbell Brothers have one van which will deliver around Edinburgh. The shop will also post haggis for Burns Night or whenever you feel like eating it.

Sandringham is supplied with meat by J. H. Dewhurst and Messrs K. W. Milton

J. H. DEWHURST LIMITED
(Head Office)
23/30 West Smithfield
London EC1A 9DL
(and branches)

Butcher to HM The Queen.

'On average there are 4.275 assistants in a Dewhurst shop,' Dewhurst told me. The 70-year-old firm now have over 1,200 butcher's shops trading under the name Dewhurst throughout the country, including one in Windsor serving Windsor Castle. They also have one in Norfolk, close to Sandringham – reputedly The Queen's favourite home where Her Majesty spends New Year with her family.

Dewhurst shops sell guaranteed British beef, fresh poultry – under the Dewfresh label, and British lamb and pork. Over three-quarters of their meat comes from an associated company, the British Beef Company, who have abattoirs throughout the UK, and only their lamb offal is imported from New Zealand. Worried that the 'romance has gone from butcher's shops due to modern health and hygiene regulations', Dewhurst are attempting to bring it back by selling cooked meats, including ham, and their own pease and black puddings.

Dewhurst have also recently opened the first of their new Meat Markets around the country to cater for the instant shopper. The Meat Markets are partly self-service and partly over-the-counter, stocking a large selection of meats, cheeses, bacons and frozen foods and delicatessen items. Dewhurst staff have already nicknamed them 'protein shops'.

Look in your local telephone directory for your nearest Dewhurst butcher.

EMMETTS STORE
See page 237.

MESSRS JOHN LIDSTONE
12 Lower Belgrave Street
London SW1 0LJ

(01) 730 9373

Butchers to HM The Queen and HM The Queen Mother.

Lidstone's exclusive butcher's shop is housed in an olive green Regency building in the centre of Belgravia. The steps outside are tiled in blue and white marble, an elegant and old-fashioned contrast to the wooden floor covered with sawdust inside. The shop's two Royal Warrants hang from the first-floor balcony.

The butchers in Lidstone's all wear traditional white hats and aprons and chop the tender meat on a well-worn chopping block on the right-hand side of the shop. A cashier at the back deals with the money. Lidstone sell steaks (sirloin, porterhouse and T-bone) – every steak is superbly butchered – calves' liver, game (in season), loin chops and beef (from Aberdeen). This small, upmarket butcher is owned by Dewhurst (see above).

Monday–Friday: 8–4.45; Saturday: 8–12.45. Messrs John Lidstone will deliver 'around Smithfield Market area and in some other parts of London'.

MESSRS K. W. MILTON
38 Manor Road
Dersingham
Kings Lynn
Norfolk

Dersingham (0485) 40270

Purveyors of meat and poultry to HM The Queen.

The Miltons started their butcher's shop in Dersingham in 1954, shortly after Mr Milton was demobbed. Four years later they received their Royal Warrant and until three years ago served Sandringham fully with meat and poultry. Today Dewhurst (see above) have taken over supplying the Royal family with the bulk of their meat. The Miltons still provide some of the bits and pieces, such as their pork sausages – especially when The Queen Mother is staying there. Miltons' other specialities are their home-cooked hams, their tongues and their dressed joints.

Today the modern shop, only one mile away from Sandringham, is run by the Miltons grandson. They are also a general stores, selling vegetables, bread and milk – 'anything anybody wants'.

Tuesday–Friday: 8.30–5; Saturday: 8.30–3.30.

Barbecueing at Balmoral

R. F. & J. SCOLES
1 Chapel Road
Dersingham
Norfolk PE31 6PW

Dersingham (0485) 40309

Butchers to HM The Queen.

Twice a week Ms Scoles travels round Dersingham delivering meat to old-age pensioners unable to leave their homes. She and her husband also make special beefburgers for a young local girl who is allergic to preservatives.

R. F. & J. Scoles' butcher's shop in Norfolk has a faithful clientele. Customers travel for miles to buy meat for their freezers from them. Mr Scoles has been a butcher since he was 11 years old and he and his wife started the traditional shop 15 years ago. Mr Scoles buys meat 'off the hoof'. He chooses it when it is still running around in the fields and then takes it to the abattoir from where it is later delivered to the shop. None of the meat arrives at Scoles either frozen or imported, apart from the kidneys which are sometimes bought in frozen. Much of the meat is local, often coming from the Sandringham Estates.

Scoles' specialities are their pork sausages, which they can make up specially according to your requirements and their brawn (nicknamed 'pork cheese'), made only in the winter and set in jelly in a cheese-like mould. Mr Scoles is a master butcher and will dress joints to your requirements. One of his specialities is stuffing a turkey with a pheasant stuffed with grouse stuffed with partridge stuffed with quail stuffed with teal stuffed with woodcock.

Monday–Friday: 8–1, 2–5; Saturday: 8–1.

H. M. SHERIDAN
**11 Bridge Street
Ballater
Aberdeenshire
Scotland**

Ballater (0338) 55218

*Purveyor of meat and poultry to HM
The Queen Mother.*

H. M. Sheridan is the only butcher in
Ballater, the neighbouring village to Balmoral and Birkhall, The Queen Mother's
Balmoral residence. It is rumoured in the
village that the last time The Queen was
seen in Ballater, a couple of years ago, it
was in Mr Sheridan's butcher's shop. But it
is to The Queen Mother that the shop has
held its warrant for the past couple of
years.

Mr Sheridan started his career 21 years
ago with a mobile butcher's shop. He then
bought a shop in Victoria Road in Ballater,
rebuilt it in four days and moved in. In
1980 he bought his present shop in Bridge
Street. The shop is traditionally large and
airy, dating back to the days before refrigeration when a large cool room was essential for the meat. The high ceiling of the
shop was used for hanging meat, which
today Mr Sheridan still does 'for as long as
possible'.

Sheridan's specialise in sausages, especially venison, Aberdeen Angus beef,
Scotch lamb and pork, poultry and drip-
ping. They also stock 'a wee bit of game, in
season', and fresh fruit and vegetables. Mr
Sheridan does a 'great business in haggis' –
mostly with tourists in the summer.

*Monday–Saturday: 8.30–5.15. 'We close
half-day Thursdays in the winter, open all
day in high season.' H. M. Sheridan deliver
all round the Ballater area.*

Cheese

PAXTON & WHITFIELD LIMITED
**93 Jermyn Street
London SW1Y 6JE**

(01) 930 0250

*Cheesemongers to HM The Queen
Mother.*

Paxton & Whitfield have a secret. It is the
name of the one cheese which, since 1972
when the shop was awarded its warrant,
must always appear on the cheese tray
when it is produced at Clarence House.
The company sell a range of 250 cheeses
from Limburger ('a sticky aromatic cheese
with a strong-smelling rind') to Vulscombe
Devon goat cheese ('bought direct from the
farm, costing £1.84 each for a four-ounce
cheese'). It is their mild cheeses with added
herbs and peppers which are rumoured to
be the favourites on the table at Clarence
House, the London home of The Queen
Mother.

Paxton & Whitfield have been cheesemongers in the small shop in Jermyn Street
since 1797. Today the shop with its dairy
smell, sawdust-covered quarry tiled floor,
blue-coated assistants and glass cases filled
with cheeses is a haven for the 'rather
special' local residents, and the 'country
people shopping for the weekend', as well
as the cheese lover and confused hosts
looking for advice on what cheeses to serve
at their dinner party. Paxton & Whitfield
are cheese experts. Not only will they recommend cheeses, they will also advise on
appropriate wines and ports. They sell over
30 types of sweet and savoury biscuits,
Jackson's of Piccadilly teas, jams and
honeys, and a selection of hams (from
cooked York hams to uncooked Suffolk
and Smoked Phoenix No. 2) – which are
often found hanging from the ceiling.

Paxton & Whitfield are owned by John Adamson & Co., cheese wholesalers, who buy Paxton's French cheeses for them and pot the shop's bestselling Stiltons. Paxton sold over 450 of their five-pound 'baby' blue-veined Stiltons (for £16.50 each) over Christmas. All the cheeses are stored in the cool vaults below the shop, from where during the war, The Queen Mother, as Queen, received her wartime ration of a few ounces of cheese a week. Paxton say a familiar sight around Jermyn Street is their cheese-rolling antics along the pavement when a 180-pound Emmental has to be moved from the warehouse to the shop.

Monday-Friday: 8.30–6; Saturday: 9–4. Since 1981 Paxton & Whitfield have run The Paxton & Whitfield Cheese Club. For £7.50 a month, each month members receive a selection of three cheeses delivered in insulated packages to ensure safe arrival and a newsletter containing information on the cheeses and suggesting suitable wines to drink with them. Christmas mail order catalogue available from Paxtons for their cheeses, hams, teas, hampers and gift packs.

SCOTT'S FISH SHOP
3 Bridge Street
Kirkwall
Orkney
Scotland

Kirkwall (0856) 3170

Cheesemonger to HM The Queen Mother.

Scott's Kirkwall kippers are eaten 'in almost every country in the world'. Their smoked salmon is enjoyed 'from Vienna to Toronto, from Johannesburg to Tonypandy'. Yet it is Scott's Orkney farm cheese which is eaten in Castle of Mey in Caithness-shire, The Queen Mother's Scottish home.

Scott's kippers 'are famous in Orkney – and on the adjacent island of Great Britain', Mrs Helen Watson told me. The shop was started by her husband and today Mrs Watson and her two assistants cure the kippers themselves. They also sell them fresh in the old-fashioned fish shop facing the Kirkwall harbour, overlooking the pier.

'We are famous for our smoked salmon too, right enough,' Mrs Watson said. They sell Scotch salmon in the summer and Canadian salmon during the rest of the year. It took Mr Watson seven years to achieve the

By Appointment to
H.M. Queen Elizabeth,
The Queen Mother
Cheesemonger

For Real Fresh Fish

SCOTT'S FISH SHOP
KIRKWALL ORKNEY

HEAD OFFICE, 3 BRIDGE STREET
Tel. Kirkwall 3170 (STD Code 0856)
FACTORY–ST. CATHERINE'S PLACE

proper cure for the salmon and the recipe remains a family secret, although I was told that one of the ingredients used was proof rum. The salmon costs £8.00 per pound in the piece and £12.00 per pound if sliced.

Their warrant-holding cheeses include Claymore Farm cheese, white, red or smoked, which is only sold in one-pound packs and is also available from Harrods (see page 156). But it is their Orkney farm cheese of which they are most proud. There are only six people on the island who make it and each cheese is different, even if made by the same person. It can vary from a delicious Brie-like cheese which may run off the plate to a crumbly one. It costs £1.40 a pound.

Monday–Saturday: 9–1, then 2–5.30; Wednesday: 9–1. Mail order catalogue available.

Confectioners

ACKERMANS CHOCOLATES LIMITED
9 Goldhurst Terrace
Finchley Road
London NW6 3HX

(01) 624 2742

Confectioners to The Queen Mother.

'My speciality is fresh cream truffles with a lot of alcohol,' Werner Krattinger, the Swiss owner who bought the shop from the Ackermans five years ago, told me. Werner was trained as a chocolate maker in Switzerland and worked for the Ackermans for six years before taking over their business.

Ackermans is so filled with chocolates you hardly notice that the fittings haven't been changed since the 1950s. On the shelves there are 60 different kinds of chocolate, all continental in style and mostly plain. You can also buy nine different types of truffle, from champagne to fresh orange, and if that isn't enough they'll make more to suit your palate.

Ackermans cater for their conservative clients – including The Queen Mother who awarded them their Royal Warrant in 1969 – with style. Their latest creation (for £6.60 a pound) is 'a rather beautiful moulded heart shape filled with a noisette and croquant filling that gives you a crunchy feeling when you eat it', Werner explained as my mouth watered. But if you don't like 'crunchy feelings', why don't you try Ackermans' noisette chocolates which are handmade by roasting hazlenuts with sugar, grinding them into a fine paste and then mixing them with chocolate. Delicious.

Monday–Friday: 9.30–6; Saturday: 9.30–5. Ackermans will mail chocolates – in boxes only – around the world. No catalogue available.

CADBURY LIMITED
Bournville
Birmingham B30 2LU
West Midlands

Cocoa and chocolate manufacturers to HM The Queen and HM The Queen Mother.

The Cadbury's chocolate empire began as a one-man grocery business in 1824 when John Cadbury, a 24-year-old Quaker opened a grocery shop in Birmingham selling tea, coffee, hops, mustard and, as a sideline, cocoa and chocolate. By 1842 he was selling 16 different drinking chocolates and 11 cocoas. A small factory followed and Mr Cadbury took his brother, Benjamin, into partnership. The union lasted

until 1860 but by then competition in the food business was fierce and John Cadbury was glad to hand over the business to his sons, Richard and George.

Cadbury Brothers received their first Royal Warrant from Queen Victoria in 1853 and later from Queen Alexandra and Queen Mary. This Royal hat-trick prompted Cadbury in 1911, the year of the coronation of King George V, to use the theme of the Three Queens on their boxes and tins of chocolates. The design was used as a regular feature for their promotions where a free gift of a box of chocolates was given in exchange for a specified number of coupons from Cadbury's tins or packets of Bournville Cocoa. On one advertisement, Cadbury showed Queen Victoria drinking their cocoa in the Royal train and later they introduced the 'King George V chocolate assortment'.

In 1866, when the brothers decided to introduce pure cocoa essence, the idea of manufacturing chocolate and chocolate confectionery became possible. Richard Cadbury became the first designer of pictorial chocolate boxes. By the beginning of this century a Cadbury's Christmas list of fancy boxes contained at least 70 new designs including caskets covered in plush velvet with bevelled mirrors.

In 1879 the company moved to Bournville, their present site, just outside Birmingham. They employed a continental confectioner known as Frederic the Frenchman who brought with him recipes for nougat, dragées and pâté. Dairy Milk was born in 1905 and the now famous Milk Tray in its deep purple box with gold script

Cadbury's 'Three Queens' design was used on the company's boxes and tins of chocolate in 1911

While watching the National Pony Society's show at the Royal Agricultural Hall in North London, The Princesses Elizabeth and Margaret tucked into a box of Charbonnel et Walker bitter chocolates

Below:
A Charbonnel et Walker boîtes-blanche as seen above

soon followed. In 1919 the company merged with J. S. Fry & Sons and in 1969 they joined Schweppes (see page 148) to form a company with an annual turnover of more than £1,500 million.

Cadbury's chocolate and cocoa can be obtained at grocery shops, supermarkets and department stores.

CHARBONNEL ET WALKER LIMITED
One The Royal Arcade
28 Old Bond Street
London W1X 4BT

(01) 629 4396

Chocolate manufacturers to HM The Queen.

In their tiny shop on the corner of Old Bond Street and the Royal Arcade one can find Charbonnel et Walker's plain dark chocolates. They range from Violette ('crème fondante topped with crystallised petals of violet') to Bittermints ('long dark chocolates filled with our unique blend of mint fondant') to full cream truffles.

Charbonnel et Walker was started by Mademoiselle Charbonnel, a leading Par-

isienne chocolatière, who in 1875, through a 'connection' with the Prince of Wales, later Edward VII, came to London. She opened her shop in Old Bond Street and the company still use many of her recipes today. One of these is for moulded chocolate letters covered with gold foil which can be arranged to spell out anything from a telephone number to an affectionate message. The chocolates come in a round white box with a coloured satin bow. A one-pound Boîte Blanche costs £11.75.

Another Charbonnel speciality is their Theatre Box, a floral box tied with a pink cord to avoid the rustlings of paper wrappings in the theatre. At £2.90 for a quarter-pound box it 'makes the ideal gift for a lady', they say.

Monday–Friday: 9–5.30; Saturday: 10–4. Charbonnel et Walker will mail chocolates anywhere in the world. Each of their chocolates has a number according to the confection of its centre or filling which will help you to order your chocolates by post or telephone.

G. LEITH & SON

See page 127.

PRESTAT LIMITED
40 South Molton Street
London W1Y 1HA

(01) 629 4838

Purveyors of chocolate to HM The Queen.

Prestat is the only shop in the world where you can buy Paddington Bear and eat him. He comes in three sizes in plain or milk chocolate and is only one of the many different figures Prestat make. Another speciality is their chocolate telegrams, messages of up to five sweet words of your choice.

The original proprietors of Prestat were French. They came to London in 1908, and many of their recipes are still used, in particular for their truffles which Prestat consider their speciality. They also still have the fine mahogany showcases from their previous shop. The atmosphere is 'old-fashioned and homely, a high-class chocolate shop', says Joanne Cohen, the owner's niece.

Monday-Friday: 9–6; Saturday: 9.30–5.30. Mail order catalogue available but only chocolates and truffles are posted – figures might break.

JOHN F. RENSHAW & COMPANY LIMITED
Locks Lane
Mitcham
Surrey CR4 2XE

Purveyors of almond products to HM the Queen and HM the Queen Mother.

Just thinking about what Renshaw do with almonds is enough to make you go nuts. They blanch, split, flake, grind, salt and paste them, and as if that wasn't enough they make macaroon and marzipan pastes and a host of other almond-based products.

John F. Renshaw started his business at the end of the 19th century, pushing a barrow round the East End of London supplying almonds to the bakery trade. By 1898 he had formed a company in London and begun trading. In 1923 Renshaws moved to their present site, a converted laundry in Mitcham. Shortly before the Second World War John Renshaw head-hunted a confectioner whose skill with almonds succeeded in spreading the fame of Renshaws throughout London. One of his talents was in the making of petits-fours which so titillated the tastebuds of the late King George VI that he rewarded Renshaws by awarding them their first Royal Warrant in 1950.

Today they import their almonds from California and Europe. You'll probably have bought them unwittingly as own-label brands at most major supermarkets but you can also buy them under the Renshaw label.

Drinks and tobacco

ANGOSTURA BITTERS LIMITED
PO Box 62
Port of Spain
Trinidad
West Indies

Manufacturers of Angostura aromatic bitters to HM The Queen.

Pink-gin drinkers can be forgiven for thinking Angostura bitters were invented expressly for this purpose. The thought, however, could not have been further from the mind of Dr Johann Gottlieb Benjamin Siegert when he invented them. Dr Siegert, a Silesian army surgeon, went to Venezuela to join Simon Bolivar who was fighting to achieve independence. He arrived in Angostura, on the Orinoco River, and was in charge of the hospital. In 1824, after four years of studying the merits of tropical plants, his researches resulted in the making of aromatic, carminative bitters, described as 'a tonic to relieve digestive and similar stomach disorders'. Such was the success of the bitters amongst Dr Siegert's

Manet's 'Bar at the Folies Bergere'. Spot the Bass bottles

patients and friends that he began to manufacture them on a commercial scale. When the family left Venezuela because of the country's unsettled situation and arrived at Port of Spain in Trinidad, the secret of the bitters went with them. The company are still run by Dr Siegert's descendants.

Angostura was at one time used semi-medicinally by the Royal Navy but as the ingredients remain secret it is not possible to determine its true medicinal qualities. Mark Twain encountered the bitters in London and wrote a letter to his wife in 1874 which advised her at great length to have on hand the ingredients for a 'cock-tail' of whisky, lemon, crushed sugar and Angostura bitters for when he returned. It read: 'I love to picture myself ringing the bell, at midnight – then a pause of a second or two, then the turn of a bolt – 'Who is it?' – then ever so many kisses, then you and I in the bathroom, I drinking my cock-tail and undressing and you standing by – then to bed, and everything happy and jolly as it should be.'

Apart from Mark Twain's suggestion that Angostura bitters have aphrodisiac qualities, they have also been known to be used as a pick-me-up and in salt-free recipes. Angostura were granted their first Royal Warrant in 1907 by Alfonso XIII of Spain and five years later by George V of England. They have held their warrant to the British Royal family consecutively since then.

Angostura bitters are available from off-licences, delicatessens, supermarkets and the food halls of department stores.

BASS BREWING LIMITED
The Brewery
High Street
Burton-on-Trent
Staffordshire

Brewers to HM The Queen.

Next time you gaze at Edouard Manet's 'Un Bar aux Folies Bergères' and think wistfully how typically French it all is, take a closer look at the bar. There are two Bass beer bottles bearing red triangles. They contain the world-famous East India Pale Ale, brewed in Burton-on-Trent by the company started by William Bass in 1777.

Burton-on-Trent had attained a reputation for its beers even in Saxon times. It is recorded that Mary Queen of Scots was supplied with beer from the brew-house of Burton Monastery in about 1580. The Trent has a high gypsum content which makes it well suited to the production of pale, sparkling beers in contrast to the heavier beers and stouts of London. The lighter beer (East India Pale Ale) produced for the first time by Bass in 1822, a year after they began exporting to India, proved to be most popular at home and abroad, and particularly in France and Belgium.

Bass merged with Worthington in 1926 and were awarded their first warrant by George V. The two companies later linked with Carringtons. Bass pale ale is now marketed as Worthington's White Shield.

Bass beers are available from off-licences, supermarkets and pubs.

BENSON & HEDGES LIMITED
13 Old Bond Street
London W1X 4QP

(01) 493 1825

Tobacconists to HM The Queen.

Mr Benson and Mr Hedges opened their little tobacconist and gift shop in 13 Old Bond Street in 1820. Today they are the oldest surviving retailers in Bond Street and even though their shop has been refurbished it still retains its Victorian atmosphere, with ornately carved yew-panelled walls.

The Prince of Wales, later Edward VII, used to buy his cigars from Mr Benson and Mr Hedges, but when he was given some blended leaf tobacco by the Egyptian government he took it to the little shop and asked them to make him some cigarettes.

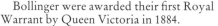

The cigarettes were duly made on the premises and the Cairo No. 1. Egyptian tobacco cigarette was born. Cigarette smoking took off in England and Benson & Hedges with it. Today a packet of 50 Cairo No. 1 cost £4.07, and they are still packaged in the original Victorian style wrapping, though no longer rolled on the premises. Benson & Hedges also stock an extensive range of exotic cigarettes, such as Turkish, Balkan, Russian and their own unique blends including B&H with its sophisticated gold packaging.

Benson & Hedges also sell 'gentlemen's gifts'. From colognes, leather goods and toilet bags to razor sets, wallets and cigar holders. In the back of their shop, Benson & Hedges stock their wide range of cigars. They recommend customers buy cigars in bulk which the shop can store in their basement humidor where the cigars will last for up to 15 years. 'It's a good hedge against inflation,' they told me.

Monday–Friday: 9–5.30. No mail order catalogue but Benson & Hedges will mail items if required.

CHAMPAGNE J. BOLLINGER SA
Ay-Champagne
51 Marne
France

Purveyors of champagne to HM The Queen.

Bollinger describe their most recent introduction, Bollinger Tradition RD (Recently Disgorged) as 'an élite wine in the highest gastonomic traditions'. The Bollinger in question is a champagne from a great vintage, such as 1973, which has been allowed to age slowly, remaining in contact with its natural sediments, for between seven and 10 years. The wine is made 'totally without compromise' and the process is costly. The result: 'the quintessence of quality'.

Jacques Bollinger founded the Bollinger company in 1829 when he married the daughter of Admiral Count de Villermont whose family had been making champagne since the 15th century. As landowners and gentry the Villermonts used to produce a certain amount of wine for themselves and their friends. When Jacques Bollinger married into the family he took on the role of selling the produce from his father-in-law's vineyards under the name Bollinger. The firm was subsequently run by the male members of the Bollinger family until 1899 when Madame Bollinger, wife of Jacques

junior, took over. Madame Bollinger, known as the 'Grande Dame du Champagne', was a familiar sight around the area inspecting her vineyards by bicycle. Having no children of her own she passed the business on to one of her nephews, Christian Bizot, today a director of Bollinger.

Bollinger were awarded their first Royal Warrant by Queen Victoria in 1884.

Bollinger champagne is available from wine merchants.

CARLSBERG BREWERY LIMITED
Bridge Street
Northampton
Northamptonshire NN1 1PZ

Suppliers of lager beer to HM The Queen.

In 1847 J. C. Jacobsen, a Danish brewer, established a brewery on a hill just outside Copenhagen. When it came to choosing a name for the company Mr Jacobsen decided to call it after his newly born son, Carl. Because the brewery was on a hill (*berg* in Danish) it became known as Carlsberg.

Until 1974 the Carlsberg lager sold to Europe was all brewed at the Carlsberg headquarters in Denmark. But today the company have built a £25 million 21st-century-style brewery in Northampton, designed by the award-winning architect, Knud Munk. 'After all, with our Danish background we felt we had a certain design reputation to maintain.' The brewery produces 22 million gallons of lager a year and

Tuxen's painting of the visit of the Prince of Wales, later Edward VII, and Princess Alexandra to the Ny Carlsberg Brewery in 1892

samples of the brew are sent to Denmark periodically to be matched with the original brews.

Carlsberg say theirs is 'probably the best lager in the world'. But the bravado advertising belies their less-talked-about generosity. A proportion of their profits are donated to the Carlsberg Foundation which was created by Mr Jacobsen to encourage the pursuit of scientific knowledge. Over the years the foundation has supported more than 200 expeditions ranging from archeology in the Middle East to exploring the Arctic. They also built the Frederiksborg Museum of Natural History which attracts over a quarter of a million visitors a year. The Glyptoteck Museum, built in the late 19th century by Carl Jacobsen, today houses his private art collection donated by the Foundation after his death.

Carlsberg lager is available from pubs, off-licences and supermarkets.

Christopher & Co. probably supplied the Courts of James I and Charles I, but since the records were destroyed in 1666 in the Great Fire of London they can't be certain. They do, however, claim to be the longest-established wine merchants still trading.

Christopher & Co. import wines from all over the world. They specialise in French wines and sell 65 different clarets of 10 different vintages. They also sell glasses (a tumbler will cost you £1.90) and a Chinese white wine called Great Wall which retails at £3.20 a bottle. Christopher & Co. only stock one English wine however, Langham, a dry white table wine (also £3.20 a bottle). It is rumoured that the Royal ladies favour German wines.

Monday–Friday: 9.30–5.30. Mail order catalogue available, deliveries within the Central London area only.

Queen Victoria was rumoured to enjoy a drink after climbing to the top of a mountain – in this case, Cairn Lochan, which Her Majesty scaled in 1861

CHRISTOPHER & COMPANY LIMITED
4 Ormond Yard
London SW1Y 6JJ

(01) 930 5557

Wine merchants to HM The Queen.

ALFRED DUNHILL LIMITED
30 Duke Street
London SW1Y 6DL

(01) 499 9566

Suppliers of smokers' requisites to HM The Queen.

In 1907 Alfred Dunhill opened a small tobacconist in Duke Street. Today Alfred Dunhill Ltd is a large opulent shop on the corner of Duke and Jermyn Street. Dunhill is a place for serious smokers. Discreet ashtrays are placed strategically around the thick carpeted floors. It's one of the few shops in London where you won't see a 'no smoking' sign. In the showcases items display the familiar Dunhill logo, but no prices. 'If you have to ask the price you can't afford it,' I was told.

The shop contains over 3,500 products. In one corner is their pipe section which King Olaf of Sweden regularly visits on his London trips. Alfred Dunhill's first major success was his 'white spot' pipe, today made from briar grown around the Mediterranean. The pipes start from £34 and are favourites with Americans who have to pay twice the price for a pipe in the States. In 1924 Alfred Dunhill introduced the Unique lighter, the first lighter to in corporate a horizontal flint wheel which enabled the user to hold and operate the lighter with one hand. The same mechanism is used in Dunhill lighters today. Suitably engraved silver-plated Dunhill lighters are sometimes presented by The Queen to visiting dignitaries.

Dunhill also sell their range of watches, fountain pens, jewellery, briefcases and luggage. In 1976 they introduced a range of men's clothing 'designed by Dunhill for Dunhill'. Recently Dunhill have also started selling Dunhill Scotch Whisky, ideal for drinking while smoking one of their many brands of cigarettes.

Monday–Friday: 9.30–5.30; Saturday: 9.30–4.30. Alfred Dunhill usually have a mail order catalogue at Christmas, but also have brochures for each of their ranges. Be prepared for quite a few 'prices on application'.

JOHN DEWAR & SONS LIMITED
Dewar House
Haymarket
London SW1Y 4DF

Scotch whisky distillers to HM The Queen.

In 1846 three Dewar brothers, John, Robert and Tom, began their business of distilling fine malt whiskies. Situated as they were in the Highlands, they could reap the advantages of rich barley and unlimited supplies of soft, pure water – chief ingredients in the production of malt whisky.

By 1886 it was time to show England what whisky was all about. Tom Dewar, or 'Whisky Tom' as he came to be known, ventured out of his Highland retreat with Dewar's White Label and a bagpipe player. All three caused an uproar at the Brewers' show in London's Agricultural Hall. Such was the demand from South of the Border, fired no doubt by the electric sign of a Highlander enjoying his White Label tipple, that Dewars built a new distillery at Aberfeldy on the River Tay in 1896.

In those days Dewar's drinkers included the President of the United States, Theodore Roosevelt, the King of Sweden, the King of Spain and Queen Victoria, who was rumoured to appreciate a wee dram after climbing to the top of a mountain. Queen Victoria granted Dewars their first Royal Warrant.

Today White Label with its blend of 40 whiskies is among the top selling scotches in the United States.

John Dewar & Sons whisky is available from off-licences, supermarkets and pubs.

JOHN HAIG & COMPANY LIMITED
7–10 Hobart Place
London SW1W 0HN

Purveyors of Scotch whisky to HM The Queen.

All Scotland's first whisky enthusiasts needed to make malt whisky was a little barley from the *brae*, a drop of water from the *burn* and some heat from a peat fire.

The name plate of the Haig distillery, hidden in a valley close to Edinburgh, just 25 miles north of the Haig family's ancestral home Bemersyde

Today you also need a good address in Scotland. For it would seem whisky is only whisky when it is scotch. Put that down to the climate or the mist in the glens or the highland spring or the sheer cannyness of families like the Haigs who have been making whisky for generations.

The Haigs can trace their ancestors back 30 generations to the 12th century when Petrus del Haga, a Norman knight whose family came to Britain with William the Conqueror, built himself a castle in Bemersyde on the banks of the River Tweed, where the 30th Laird now lives. And so the roots were laid. For the next few centuries his descendants moved from glen to glen with their distilling secrets until at the beginning of the 19th century they entered the Kingdom of Fife where at Markinch the main business of the John Haig company is carried out today.

Although the first record of whisky being 'exported' from Scotland to London appears about 1750, it was not until the 1800s that vatting and blending was authorised to allow the development of the type of whisky better suited to the Sassenach palate. By the 1920s sales of Haig had grown to such an extent the phrase 'Don't be vague, ask for Haig' was firmly in the language.

John Haig currently produce millions of gallons of whisky a year made up of two basic types, malt and grain. The malt is made only from malted barley and the grain from malted and unmalted barley and maize, and Haig have over 100 distilleries making variations on these types. The standard bottle we can buy in the supermarket today is probably made from as many as 40 of them. This puts the onus on the blender – one of the few people privvy to what Haig like to refer to as the 'mysterious simplicity of making Scotch'.

The three whiskies produced by Haig are the 'standard' Haig blend, the deluxe

Dimple, immediately recognised for its unusual shaped bottle, and the 12-year-old Glenleven. The range should suit the most discerning of tastes and as suppliers of whisky to the Royal household, any of their blends must suffice as a much appreciated wee drop of the hard stuff after a day hunting, shooting and fishing on the Royal estates.

John Haig whisky is available from pubs, off-licences, supermarkets and restaurants.

JOHN HARVEY & SONS LIMITED
12 Denmark Street
Bristol
Avon BS99 7JE
(and branches)
Bristol (0272) 836161

Wine merchants to HM The Queen.

John Harvey's original 13th-century cellars beneath their main Bristol shop were first used to store wines for a monastery. The wines were offered as solace to the sick and needy at the monastery and to their benefactors. In the 18th century William Perry, a merchant, came to live in the house and used the cellars for the wines he imported from the Iberian Peninsula. In 1796 he took a baker's son, Thomas Urch into business with him. Their keenest rivals in the wine trade were two sea captains, a father and son both named Thomas Harvey. The son later married Thomas Urch's sister and it was their son, John Harvey, later an apprentice to his uncle, after whom the business is now named.

John Harvey & Sons no longer blend, bottle and dispatch their sherries and wines in the old cellars – but at their new cellars in Whitchurch Street on the outskirts of Bristol. The company have about 16 sherries under their own label, including

Bristol Cream ('the best sherry in the world') which is drunk by about 16 million people worldwide. The sherry received its name during the early days of John Harvey & Sons when a Frenchwoman was being shown round the cellars. She was asked her opinion of the two sherries, the first being Bristol Milk which had been enjoyed in Bristol since 1634. The woman then tried the second, a finer, older wine and said: 'If the other is Bristol Milk, then this must be the Cream.' The first cream sherry was soon marketed.

The company have been supplying the Royal household since they received their first warrant from Queen Victoria. Their wines today include their Harveys No. 1 Claret ('perfect for entertaining, for celebrating, or for just the sheer pleasure of a good bottle of wine'), their Harveys Specially Selected Moselle ('the classic combination of the Riesling grape and slatey soil producing a light, fresh and crisp wine with a medium dry flavour') and their 1981 Chablis from A. Regnard et Fils 'is among the ultimate in classic Chablis'.

Monday–Friday: 9.30–5.30 (Denmark Street branch). Mail order catalogue available from Harvey House, PO Box 55, Bristol BS99 7JE, or telephone the above number.

PETER F. HEERING A/S
Heering 25
Dalby 4690
Haslev
Denmark

Purveyors of Cherry Heering to HM The Queen.

Peter Frederick Husfuhm Heering first encountered the cherry brandy which was to change his life on the island of Christianshaven in Denmark. It had been made by the wife of the grocer's merchant he worked for and she kindly gave him the recipe. When he started his own business in Copenhagen in 1818, Peter Heering began to sell the cherry brandy which proved so popular with his seafaring customers that he was encouraged to forgo his other trading concerns in butter, cheese and hams to produce more cherry brandy.

Successive Heerings lived on site at the house on Christianshaven's Canal in Copenhagen, which today is a museum housing the presses and the gigantic oak casks in which the drink was matured. The distillery and cherry orchards are at Dalby, about 40 miles south of Copenhagen. Here the process of making cherry brandy is as jealously guarded as in Peter Heering's day.

Heering's cherry liqueur is very dark red in colour and extremely fruity without being cloying. The company were awarded their first Royal Warrant in 1876 by the Prince of Wales, later Edward VII.

Cherry Heering is available from pubs, off-licences, wine merchants and supermarkets.

CHAMPAGNE HEIDSIECK & COMPANY MONOPOLE SA
83 Rue Coquebert
51054 Reims
Marne
France

Purveyors of champagne to HM The Queen.

Champagne Heidsieck was founded in 1785 by Florens-Louis Heidsieck. Soon he

John Harvey & Sons' cellars in Bristol date back to the 13th century

had brought his three nephews into the business with him as he himself was childless and when he died in 1828 he willed the company to them. Within six years two had gone their separate ways but the third, Henri-Louis Walbaum, became head of the firm. In 1846 the company were owned by another Heidsieck, Auguste, who created the company's trade name Monopole.

Heidsieck Monopole own eight vineyards in France and lease another four. Their cellars which cover 12 acres and are 70 feet deep, contain their range of six champagnes, including their Prestige Cuvée Diamant Bleu, all of which are exported to over 132 countries.

Since 1904, the company have owned one of France's historical tourist attractions, the Moulin de Verzenay – the only windmill in Champagne. Built in 1823 to grind the wheat, rye and barley grown on the plains, its sails were stopped in 1901 by its then owner who didn't want the mill to operate after his death. During the First World War it was used as an observation post, visited by King Victor Emmanuel III among others, to observe the enemy lines.

Champagne Heidsieck is available from wine merchants.

IND COOPE LIMITED
The Brewery
High Street
Romford
Essex RM1 1LA

Brewers of ale and lager to HM The Queen.

'The English beer drinker has a pretty good idea of what he expects from a pub. He wants good beer and a place where he immediately feels at home,' Ind Coope, one of Britain's major breweries, told me. That's why in 1980 the company decided to start living in the past and bring back some of the traditions associated with beer drinking into their pubs. 'It wasn't for any sentimental attachment to bygone days, but because the trends of the sixties and seventies towards uniformity in pubs wasn't really working.' The solution was decentralisation. Ind Coope split the company into eight separate operations. The aim was to get back to the 'local' pub with its own individual character and loyal customers. They began refurbishing their public houses and brewing a wide range of traditional cask-conditioned beers.

Today Ind Coope's pubs are instantly

recognisable throughout the country by their distinctive gold and green livery. But each area has its own traditional ale. In the south of England customers can enjoy Friary Meux bitter which was originally established in 1865. In London Taylor Walker, whose headquarters have never moved beyond the sound of the Bow Bells, have now become Ind Coope Taylor Walker. At Romford in Essex the Ind Coope Romford Brewery have introduced John Bull bitter which has achieved double the sales of the bitter it replaced. In the northern Home Counties beer drinkers have welcomed back an old friend in Benskins bitter while the eastern counties have returned to Burton's draught beers.

Ind Coope see themselves as the responsible parents of a large family, with the inevitable rebel child. For Ind Coope it was the Vermont Exchange at Cobham in Surrey. Regulars there were not keen to go back to tradition so the pub now operates as an American-style restaurant cum bar. Ind Coope just want to keep their customers satisfied. The important thing they say is the 'relationship between the English beer drinker, his pint and his pub'.

Ind Coope ales and lagers, including their wonder-working Double Diamond, skolarly Skol and famous Ind Coope Light Ale, can be found at your local off-licence or at Ind Coope pubs around the country.

JUSTERINI & BROOKS LIMITED
61 St James's Street
London SW1A 1LZ
(and a branch in Edinburgh)
(01) 493 8721

Wine merchants to HM The Queen.

Justerini & Brooks are, in their own words, 'a traditional sort of wine merchants'. Established in 1749 they have been holders of the Royal Warrant for nine successive reigns. They sell a wide selection of wines and cigars, specialising in claret and white Rhône wines which can cost from £30 to £400 a case.

Right: Charles Dickens' original cheque payable to Justerini & Brooks in 1860

From left to right: Henri, Remi and Paul Krug tasting their champagne

Below:
Rue Coquebert, Krug's headquarters pictured at the turn of the century

They make a point of giving expert advice to those who wish to invest in wines. Justerini & Brooks offer two alternative investment plans, one 'off-the-peg', the other 'made-to-measure'. For £300 to £1,500 with monthly payments, they will lay down wines for you in one of their four cellars until they're ready for drinking.

Monday–Friday: 9–5.30 (London branch). Mail order catalogue available. Justerini & Brooks will deliver throughout the UK. Special Christmas gift packs available, including a wine (house Moselle) and smoked salmon gift pack.

CHAMPAGNE KRUG
5 Rue Coquebert
51100 Reims
France

Purveyors of champagne to HM The Queen.

A Royal wedding is a very good reason for cracking open a bottle of champagne. Not that an excuse for drinking champagne has ever been needed, but it is nice to have a good reason for popping the cork. The House of Krug were granted their first Royal Warrant by King George VI in 1947. They have been supplying champagne to The Queen since 1952.

The first Krug blends came from the rented cellars of the Rue Saint-Hilair in Reims soon after Johann-Joseph Krug founded the company in 1843 who are now managed by his great-great-grandsons, Henri and Remi. Five generations later they still carry out the first fermentation of the wine in small traditional handmade oak barrels, following the rules laid down by their great-great-grandfather. Most of their competitors stopped using oak barrels long ago because of the expense but the Krug family insist it is the oak which gives the champagne its flavour.

Krug produce less than 500,000 bottles of champagne a year, of which 70 per cent is kept for export. They also have about three million bottles of ageing stock 'sleeping' in their cellars to ensure a slow and natural ripening of the cuvées, which will cover approximately six years of sales. Krug produce three champagnes, Grande Cuvée, Krug Vintage and, most recently, Krug Rose. It is believed that The Queen chose their Krug 1969 (their last great vintage champagne) to toast the wedding of Prince Charles and The Princess of Wales at the official wedding lunch to which only 100 guests were invited. If the Royal couple succeed in their ambition to have a large

family there are many more champagne toasts on the way. Just as well Krug have the odd three million bottles lying around.

Krug champagne can be found in 'the best restaurants and top-class hotels' and at 'expert retailers and specialist wine merchants' throughout the world. A list of main dealers in your country can be obtained from the above address.

CHAMPAGNE MOET & CHANDON
20 Avenue de Champagne
51321 Epernay
France

Purveyors of champagne to HM The Queen.

The art of making champagne was discovered in the 17th century by a former monk and cellarman, Don Perignon. In 1743 Claude Moet founded the house of Moet and put the teachings of Don Perignon into practice. Claude Moet's grandson, Jean Remy Moet, later acquired the Abbey of Hautvillers where Don Perignon had discovered the secrets of champagne. At the turn of the century Jean Remy Moet handed the firm over to his son, Victor, and son-in-law, Pierre-Gabriel Chandon. Since then the company have been known as Moet & Chandon and the historic abbey is still one of their many vineyards.

Moet & Chandon's champagne is made only from the first pressing of the grapes. Their vineyard holding is the largest in Champagne and they export to over 150 countries around the world. Their first Royal Warrant was granted by George V and today is held to The Queen, as well as to the courts of Belgium, Sweden and Spain. Moet & Chandon also hold a warrant for supplying champagne to the Vatican.

Moet & Chandon champagne is available from wine merchants.

H. D. RAWLINGS LIMITED
Winsor Terrace
Beckton
London E6 4LF

Mineral water manufacturers to HM The Queen.

Rawlings were granted their first Royal Warrant by Queen Alexandra at the turn of the century. But the company had been manufacturing non-alcoholic beverages since 1784 and were already long famous for their fruit juices.

In 1980 Rawlings merged with R. Whites, the lemonade manufacturers, and Canada Dry who have been making ginger ale since 1903. Between them the group, known as Canada Dry Rawlings, produce a much wider range of drinks including unsweetened and sweetened fruit juices and their recently introduced Barbican – an alcohol-free lager for those who don't want to be too soft about their drinks. But it is for their mineral water that they currently hold their warrant to The Queen. Rawlings make Buxton spring water, bottled in Buxton in Derbyshire, which comes either still or sparkling.

Rawlings mineral water is available from off-licences and supermarkets.

L. ROSE & COMPANY LIMITED
Grosvenor Road
St Albans
Hertfordshire

Suppliers of lime juice cordial to HM The Queen.

Up until the mid 19th century it was not known that it was lack of vitamin C that was causing scurvy, for centuries a rampant shipboard disease. Then it was discovered that the disease did not occur on ships carrying supplies of lime or lemon juice. As a result in 1867 a Merchant Shipping Act made it compulsory for British ships to carry limes or lemons on board in order to prevent the dreaded scourge. Hence the nickname, common in America, of 'Limeys' for British sailors.

In 1865 Lauchlan Rose, who had abandoned the family shipbuilding company to trade in grain, established L. Rose & Co., a lime and lemon merchant – very much a maritime business – in the Scottish port of Leith. He supplied unsweetened lemon and lime juices, fortified by the addition of 15 per cent of rum which acted as preservative. Limes were easier to supply than lemons as they contain little sugar, whereas the sugar in lemons led to fermentation and therefore spoilage. Mr Rose realised there was a market to be cornered by manufacturing non-alcoholic lime juice. He patented a process for preventing fermentation by adding very small quantities of sulphur dioxide – obtained by passing the gas from burning sulphur through water – to the juice. He sold the lime juice cordial in a tall bottle, heavily embossed with a design of lime leaves and fruit with a trademark of a lime branch which Rose still use today.

Lauchlan Rose's three sons ran the business after his death in 1885, but when his grandson, also named Lauchlan, took over in 1924 the company were facing a decade of difficulties. Bottled lime juice was having to compete with other fruit squashes, modernisation plans were halted by the onset of the depression and Rose's plantation business on the island of Dominica in the West Indies was hit by a disease of the trees and by two hurricanes. As a final blow the Admiralty had switched from lime juice to synthetic ascorbic acid.

But by the mid 1930s, with the introduction of lime marmalade and the popularity of gin and lime as a drink, the company were once again back on their feet. Then limes were discovered to be good for curing not just scurvy but another disease which could also be said to have been rampant for centuries, the common hangover. In 1957 L. Rose & Co. merged with Schweppes.

Rose's lime juice cordial is available at grocers, off-licences and supermarkets.

THE ROYAL BREWERY BRENTFORD LIMITED
The Brewery
Park Street
London SE1 9ES

Brewers to HM The Queen.

The Royal Brewery Brentford is distinguished as the only company to hold a Royal Warrant in perpetuity. The warrant was granted uniquely to The Brewery rather than to a named grantee as is usually the case. They were awarded the honour by William IV when the firm were under the ownership of Sir William Booth. Sir William, who was a Sheriff of London as well as a distiller and brewer was deeply interested in Polar expeditions and financed Captain Ross's Voyage of Discovery in 1828 to explore the Polar Seas. It was on this expedition that the Magnetic Pole was discovered in 1831. In recognition of Sir William's services to king and country, William IV bestowed upon the brewery company the right to perpetually display the Royal coat of arms and to call the company 'Royal'.

The Royal Brewery is today part of the Courage Group which was formed in 1955 by the amalgamation of two major brewery houses, Courage and Barclay Perkins, who had owned The Royal Brewery since 1929. Today the company supply Courage beer to the Navy and British servicemen stationed abroad, such as the British troops in the Falklands. Their beer, often drunk at sea, is also delivered regularly to the Royal Yacht *Britannia*. The company's association with servicemen can be traced back through one of their subsidiary companies, Simmonds, who joined them in 1960. Simmonds' beer was sent to fortify the men on Nelson's ship, HMS *Victory*, at Waterloo and was used later at Sandringham to toast the subsequent victory. Simmonds supplied Queen Victoria's empire-building armies with canteens before the days of NAAFI and in the second half of the 19th century became so closely associated with the services they started following the troops overseas, establishing branches in Malta, Gibraltar, Egypt, South Africa and Cyprus.

Courage have come a long way since John Courage started his brewery in Southwark just across the Thames from the Tower of London in 1787. It was from there that supplies of Courage's porter were sent to the Empress of Russia who asked for 'large quantities for her own drinking and that of her court'. It was also there that the term 'take courage' was first heard.

Courage beer is available from off-licences, supermarkets and Courage pubs.

SACCONE & SPEED LIMITED
17 Cumberland Avenue
London NW10 7RN

(01) 965 8844

Wine merchants to HM The Queen.

In 1839 James Speed set up in business in Gibraltar as a wine and spirit merchant with the Royal Navy and the garrison as his main customers. A year later Jerome Saccone started in the same business, again in Gibraltar. By the turn of the century the two merchants had merged their businesses to form Saccone & Speed. Together they began to expand their trade to the Royal Navy by opening up bases in other countries around the British Empire. Britain soon became the centre for their trade links and by 1932 they had merged with the London firm of wine and spirit merchants, Hankey Bannister. After the Second World War many wine and spirit companies were taken over by breweries and in 1963 Saccone & Speed became part of the Courage Group, later to be taken over by the Imperial Group.

Saccone & Speed are mainly concerned with selecting, shipping, bottling and wholesaling wines and spirits. Their retailing shops trade as Arthur Cooper, wine merchants, and Roberts, wine merchants. The company received their first Royal Warrant to The Queen in 1979.

For opening hours of your local Arthur Cooper & Roberts wine merchant see your telephone directory.

The Don figure trademark was acquired by the Sandemans in 1928. The drawing was bought from the artist, George Massiot Brown, for £50

GEORGE G. SANDEMAN SONS & COMPANY LIMITED
36/37 Albert Embankment
London SE1 7TL

(01) 735 7971

Wine merchants to HM The Queen.

The House of Sandeman were founded as a wine cellar in 1790 by George Sandeman of Perth, London and Oporto. To this day George Sandeman is known for shipping the first true vintage port and for being the last man to go on the floor of the Royal Exchange in breeches and top boots.

In 1913, The House of Sandeman was granted a Royal Warrant by Edward VII, and warrants have been granted by every monarch since. Sandeman doesn't sell direct to the public, but you can buy their port, sherry and brandy from most re-

tailers. Prices for port start at £4 a bottle and can go up to £35 for their 1945 vintage.

Sandeman's wines are available from wine merchants. Customers are welcome to visit the Sandeman lodges in both Portugal (Oporto) and Spain (Jerez).

SCHWEPPES LIMITED
Schweppes House
1/4 Connaught Place
London W2 2EX

Mineral water manufacturers to HM The Queen and HM The Queen Mother.

In 1752, at the tender age of 12, Jacob Schweppes, the founder of what are today the oldest mineral water manufacturers, was put in the charge of a travelling tinker. His parents, who lived in the district of Hesse in West Germany, thought he was too delicate for a life in agriculture so he was sent off with the tinker to mend pots and pans. After a short while the tinker was so impressed by the boy's dexterity he took him back to his parents saying he should be placed with a silversmith where his success and fortune were certain. Jacob Schweppes proceeded to impress the silversmith who in turn suggested he be sent to work in a bijouterie. Eventually Jacob Schweppes was drawn to the city of Geneva, famed as the centre of watchmaking and jewellery, where he settled down to a life in the bijouterie.

He was a keen amateur scientist, interested in the work being carried out on gases and their combination with water. By 1773 he was well versed in the subject of carbonation; he started producing his own mineral waters, giving up all his other work to devote time to the practice, and began to distribute them free of charge to the wealthy inhabitants of Geneva. After a while Mr Schweppes was obliged to place a nominal price on the mineral waters to cover his outgoings, and by 1783 he was running a commercial business selling aerated water. He set up in partnership with two other scientists in Geneva and came to England in 1792 to start a British branch, armed with a letter of recommendation from Geneva's eminent Professor Pictet which he presented to the British government.

The first Schweppes factory was opened in London's Drury Lane the same year, but the business did not have the success he had anticipated. There were a number of apothecaries in London dispensing artificial mineral waters which they made on a machine Jacob Schweppes had long since declared inadequate. His partners in Geneva begged him to return home but he refused. The partnership duly dissolved and Mr Schweppes waited patiently for success. He had the full support of the medical profession and leading physicians who recommended a daily use of his mineral waters. But it was the grandfather of Charles Darwin, Dr Erasmus Darwin, a philosopher, who brought him instant recognition when he wrote in his philosophical work *Zoonomia* in 1796 that a glass of Schweppes water drunk every day was 'the most efficacious internal medicine yet discovered and good for the treatment of stone of the bladder'.

When Schweppes started to produce soda water, the authorities began to regard both the waters as patent medicine and imposed an excise duty on each bottle. In 1798 Jacob Schweppes sold three-quarters of his company to three Jersey men in preparation for his retirement and when he died 23 years later they took over the business. The company received their first Royal Warrant in 1836 from The Duchess of Kent and The Princess Victoria. A year later, just two months after coming to the throne, Queen Victoria granted a new Royal Warrant and the company have been awarded one by every successive monarch since then.

In 1851 Schweppes were appointed the official caterers at the Great Exhibition in Hyde Park, providing refreshments for Queen Victoria and the Royal party. It was here that they first introduced Malvern Water and began their long association with the town of Malvern. The Queen today takes Schweppes Malvern Water with her on her foreign tours and Prince Charles is often spotted cooling down with a bottle of Malvern Water after polo matches.

Schweppes mineral waters are available from grocers, supermarkets and off-licences.

VEUVE CLICQUOT-PONSARDIN
12 Rue due Temple
51054 Reims
France

Purveyors of champagne to HM The Queen

The House of Clicquot were originally established in 1794 as bankers and wine merchants at Reims by François Clicquot and his wife Marie, daughter of Baron Ponsardin. In 1798 the young couple started trading wines from their house at Reims, the heart of champagne country. By 1805, François Clicquot had died and his young widow was left head of the house at the tender age of 28. Madame Clicquot-Ponsardin, who lived to a ripe 89, was a woman with a tenacious grip on life and a wicked sense of humour. She lost little time in making merry her widowhood by adding 'Veuve' to the house name.

The indomitable widow also solved the then topical problem of how to remove the sediment (which resulted from bottle fermentation) from the champagne without removing the bubbles at the same time. She ordered her cellarmen to put the bottles upside down in a specially devised wooden desk. Each day the bottles were given a gentle twist and shake until the sediment had settled on the cork. The cork was removed, a small amount of champagne containing the sediment was taken off, the bottle was topped up and a new cork inserted.

Queen Victoria granted Veuve Clicquot-Ponsardin her Royal Warrant in 1900.

Veuve Clicquot-Ponsardin is available from off-licences and wine merchants.

WHITBREAD & COMPANY PLC
The Brewery
Chiswell Street
London EC1Y 4SD

Brewers to HM The Queen.

Teams of Shire horses still pull the famous Whitbread beer drays around the City of London today. But while the nostalgic reminder of the 18th century is now more a means of advertising than a necessity it is a fitting tribute to Samuel Whitbread, the company's founder, who set the business on the road which has led them to become one of the largest groups in the industry.

Samuel Whitbread was the youngest son of nine children, who in 1736, at the age of 16, was apprenticed by his widowed mother to the Master Brewers' Company in London for the sum of £300. Young Samuel was considered extremely lucky as those who intended to work in brewing at that time usually came from a brewing family. Although ale had been brewed in England for centuries, it was rather an unreliable liquid due to the lack of cooling systems or accurate measurements. It was not unusual for innkeepers to offer 'stale beer' and 'cloudy beer' for the brew would not keep any length of time. A brew known as porter was also made at the time which was brewed from heavily roasted brown malt mashed over and over again, with the result that it was fairly unappetising. When a method was introduced from the continent of boiling hops in the malt before fermentation, the porter became a strong bitter liquid which would keep for longer than a year.

Samuel Whitbread saw a big future ahead for the brewing industry but unlike the principal brewers at the time he neither had a brewery of his own nor any capital. In order to establish himself and raise the capital, Samuel Whitbread put the small sum of money he had inherited into a partnership with the brothers Godfrey and Thomas Shewell in 1742. He worked hard and was always on the lookout for a chance to better himself. The chance came in 1750 when he was able to buy a small brewery in Chiswell Street, the company's present site. He began renting cellars around London but was determined to find a more economical means of storing the vast amounts of porter he was making. He called in Robert Mylne, who had designed Blackfriars Bridge, but his idea was not a success. He then tried John Smeaton, famous for his construction of the Eddystone Lighthouse, but his idea failed too. Samuel Whitbread persisted and eventually he succeeded in devising a system which allowed him to fill his entire vaults with beer.

At about the same time Boulton & Watt had just designed a 10 horsepower steam engine for grinding malt. Mr Whitbread's next task was to acquire such a machine. When King George III, Queen Charlotte and the Princesses visited the brewery in 1787 the machine was one of the first sights which greeted them. Whitbread records: 'His Majesty, with becoming science, explained to the Queen and Princesses the leading movements in the machinery.' In 1796, the year that Samuel Whitbread died, the brewery's output exceeded 200,000 barrels – a record for London.

The brewery was left to Samuel Whitbread's son, Samuel junior, who he had sent off to Cambridge to receive the education he himself had missed. The business continued to be run by Samuel Whitbread and his father's trusted clerks until 1812 when they merged with Martineau & Bland. Today members of the Martineau and Whitbread families are still in control of the business. By the turn of the 19th century there was a growing trade in India Pale Ale in London and so by 1834 Whitbread were also brewing ale. They followed the move by opening a bottling factory in 1868 to cope with the demand for bottled beers. By 1928 the company had bought shares in three other breweries and were able to increase their repertoire of beers, among them Mackeson's Stout which subsequently became one of the brewery's great successes. Today Whitbread's draught, bottled and canned beers are supplied to pubs all around the country. Their hop farm in Beltring in Kent provides them with their own barley, wheat and hops as well as a training ground and holiday home for the Whitbread Shire horses.

Whitbread beers are available from Whitbread pubs, off-licences and supermarkets.

Fishmongers

JAMES BAXTER & SON
Thornton Road
Morecambe
Lancashire LA4 5PB

Purveyors of potted shrimps to HM The Queen and HM The Queen Mother.

Since the early 1960s, James Baxter & Son's potted shrimps have been supplied to the Royal households. But Robert Baxter remains quiet about the recipe, passed down from generation to generation in his family. He would only reveal that the vital ingredients are 'unsalted butter and spices but no preservatives'. The shrimps are caught in Morecambe Bay by fisherman leaving the bay at midnight and returning in the morning with their catch. Years ago Baxters had their own fleet of fishing boats, but today all the work is contracted out. When the shrimps are brought in they are cleaned and their shells are removed by hand before they are potted according to the family recipe. Robert Baxter, one of the descendants of James Baxter who started the company in 1799, suggests the shrimps should be eaten cold with a salad or dressing or heated up on toast.

James Baxter & Son were formerly fishmongers but today they sell their speciality potted shrimps and stock frozen food as well. The shrimps are sold in two-ounce pots for approximately 60 pence and seven-ounce pots at under £2.

Monday–Saturday: 9–5.30. James Baxter & Son will send their potted shrimps by mail but the minimum order is a dozen packs. For further details contact the above address. Shops in London that stock James Baxter's potted shrimps include the Hampshire Hogg in Kensington and Mostly Smoked in Belgravia.

ANDREW DONALDSON LIMITED
126 Norfolk Street
King's Lynn
Norfolk

King's Lynn (0533) 2241

Suppliers of fish and ice to HM The Queen.

In 1888 James Donaldson, the present owner's great-grandfather, started the business (in the days before refrigeration) selling fish and ice. The present Mr Donaldson still sells hundredweight blocks of ice for £2, but today his warrant as suppliers of fish and ice which was first awarded to him by the Prince of Wales, later Edward VII, is somewhat misleading.

Andrew Donaldson Ltd still sell fish but because of their distance from the sea they have no specialities. They stock 'the usual' range of fish bought from Lowestoft, Grimsby and London which is filleted by the shop. But when I called Mr Donaldson was 'up to his eyes in pheasants'. Since he took over the business 15 years ago, the shop has been given a facelift and the stock slowly changed. Although Andrew Donaldson still supply fish to the Royal family during their stay at Balmoral, a large part of the business is now in game. But with her 2,300 acre estates, Mr Donaldson supposed, Her Majesty might not need his game.

Tuesday, Thursday–Saturday: 8–5; Monday and Wednesday: 8–1.

J. W. KNIGHT (FISHERIES) LIMITED
20 Station Parade
Virginia Water
Surrey

Wentworth (099 04) 2634

Fishmonger and poulterer to HM The Queen Mother.

James William Knight opened his wet-fish shop 24 years ago. Today his customers include Elton John and The Queen Mother, as well as a host of showbusiness celebrities. He also has requests from as far afield as New York and Dusseldorf for his wide range of fish, poultry, delicatessen and dairy products.

Mr Knight has worked hard for his success. Every morning at 3 o'clock he drives 20 miles to Billingsgate fish market in London where he picks up his Scottish smoked salmon, his Strasbourg pâté en croûte and his Beluga caviar as well as the rest of his fish produce. The wares are then displayed in his shop and his customers are offered a filleting, deboning and, more unusually, cooking service. Mr Knight also delivers in the local Surrey area and as far north as the Royal Lodge in Windsor, The Queen Mother's residence. He has held his Royal Warrant since 1978.

Tuesday–Friday: 8.30–5.30. Saturday: 8.30–1. No mail order catalogue, but Mr Knight will send goods abroad to customers who know what they want from his shop. J. W. Knight deliver in the area.

E. RUFFELL
13 High Road
Chadwell Heath
Romford
Essex RM6 6PU

(01) 590 7698

Fishmonger to HM The Queen.

The Duke of Kent's household had telephoned Eric Ruffell the night before he spoke to me to order their kippers for breakfast. Mr Ruffell delivers fish in London every morning between 5 a.m. and 7 a.m. after visiting Billingsgate fish market.

E. Ruffell's specialities are home-cured fish, such as herrings, kippers, bloaters and salmon, although he admits he's not too keen on salmon himself, preferring a smoked haddock with a rasher of bacon on top for his own breakfast. 'The problem with fish today is that most people don't know what it is like to eat it fresh. In the old days people would eat fish about three times a week but today when fish is frozen, the cells which contain the moisture fracture because the water expands. Then when you thaw it all the flavour runs out. My father used to say frozen fish tastes like cotton wool.'

The 'old days' that Mr Ruffell remembers so fondly go back to the time when his father, a French polisher and cabi-

netmaker, used to push a barrow around London's East End selling fish in his spare time. He eventually bought his own fish shop in the 1930s and Eric Ruffell started helping him when he was about 10 years old. Eric Ruffell, unlike his father, was determined to start at the top. Dismayed at the state of the fishing industry he wrote to Her Majesty asking to be allowed to supply the Royal households. Eric Ruffell was granted his Royal Warrant to The Queen in 1982.

The fish business may have changed in lots of ways, but Mr Ruffell, who calls himself a Conservative Royalist, is determined to hold on to tradition. With their lack of regard for decimalisation, he and his wife, Doris, who run the shop together, have refused to convert to the 'new' monetary system and still deal in pounds, shillings and pence. Their decision resulted in Mr Ruffell being taken before the Lord Chief Justice in 1973. But after a 25 minute hearing it was decided that the practice was not illegal. 'Nobody dictates to me,' said Mr Ruffell.

Thursday–Saturday: 8–5. E. Ruffell will take orders on the telephone at any time and delivers in London every morning. To contact E. Ruffell from Monday to Wednesday, telephone (01) 599 7169.

Groceries

W. BROOKS & SON (BROOKS-JONES LIMITED)
40/50 Hatcham Road
London SE15 ITX

Purveyors of fruit and quick frosted foods to HM The Queen Mother.

W. Brooks & Son's shop at 184 Regent Street, as illustrated in 'The Day's Doings' of 8 October 1870

The Brooks family shared one thing in common; they all died young. In 1825 the first Brooks, John, opened a fruiterer's shop in Bloomsbury, where the neighbouring squares all housed rich merchants and lawyers. The shop flourished, but Mr Brooks died from rheumatic fever aged 50. In 1846 his eldest son, William, set up his own fruiterer's business in Edgware Road. The location was again ideal. On one side was the aristocratic district of Marylebone, on the other Connaught Square and beyond it Bayswater, in those days an up and coming area. In 1868 he took his son, Edmund, into partnership, changed his company name to William Brooks & Son and took over impressive new premises at 184 Regent Street. The shop became known for its tasteful window displays and exotic fruit and vegetables. But in 1881, aged 59, William Brooks died. His son continued the business. In the elegant Regent Street shop, Edmund Brooks had a private telephone line to Escofier's office at the Savoy Hotel and an 'inner sanctum' where important clients were received. In 1892, William Brooks & Son received their first Royal Warrant as suppliers of vegetables.

Edmund Brooks also served on the Westminster City Council where in 1902 he helped arrange the Royal Progress through London to celebrate King Edward VII's recovery from illness. The following year Mr Brooks died aged 57 and after his death the firm declined. First his brother, Francis Brooks, took over, but he died in 1905. Then their sister Ada Edith Brooks became manager of the business. At this time the company supplied fruit and vegetables to the households of Edward VII at Buckingham Palace, Windsor, Balmoral and Sandringham and the Prince of Wales (later George V) at Marlborough House, York Cottage (Sandringham) and Frogmore House (Windsor). In W. Brooks & Son's ledger, dated December 1907, there is a record of the daily supplies delivered to the King at Sandringham. He clearly enjoyed asparagus, for the household ordered enough quantities of the vegetable for 12 people on 3 December, for five people on the 9th and again for seven on the 10th. The King's bill for fruit and vegetables at Sandringham for that month amounted to £215.10.1.

In 1918, Ada Brooks died aged 52 and a year later a company called Brooks-Jones Ltd were formed to take over the business. By the early twenties the company had lost their Royal Warrants, sold the shop in Regent Street and were only supplying the catering trade.

In 1922 three Mash brothers and a Mr Frederick Henry Harbud bought the company. Mr Harbud became managing director and rebuilt the business, still selling only to the catering trade. In 1933 the company were appointed a warrant by George V. Mr Harbud was fascinated by a new form of food preservation – quick freezing. He began to import quick-frozen products from the United States and with Fropax, Smedleys and Birds Eye (all produced by Messrs Chivers Ltd), his frozen foods were pioneers in the new business. As nobody had freezers at home in those days, the firm continued to supply the catering trade only. In 1956 they became suppliers of fresh fruit and quick-frozen foods to The Queen Mother. Three years later they built their present offices and cold stores where they have the capacity to store over 700 tons of frozen foods.

Today the company are the largest independent suppliers of frozen foods to the catering trade. They supply over 400 lines to hospitals, offices and prisons as well as Clarence House. In 1975 W. Brooks & Son opened Quick Frozen Products, a factory in Weston-super-Mare, to freeze bakery products and pizzas. In 1983 they were taken over by the Distillers' Company.

W. Brooks & Son sell only to the catering trade.

there was usually a feline member of staff on mouse-patrol.

In 1897 the Budgens opened their second grocery shop, in Maidenhead, which soon became their flagship store where they bottled wine and cognac on the premises. Other branches were also opened, but in 1920, the Budgens sold their stores to Alfred Button & Sons, a large established retail and wholesale company. By 1955 Alfred Button could boast a chain of 100 retail stores and nine wholesale depots.

Two years later, Booker McConnell bought the Alfred Button group, renamed all the stores Budgen and started to convert them to self-service. Today the Budgen chain consists of 105 stores throughout London and the Home Counties.

Monday–Wednesday and Saturday: 8.30–7; Thursday: 8.30–7; Friday: 8.30–8 (Ascot branch). Check with your local Budgen store for opening hours.

Above:
The first Alfred Button store at Uxbridge

Alfred Button's delivery fleet including the representatives cars – complete with chauffeurs – 1911

BUDGEN LIMITED
51 High Street
Ascot
Berkshire
(and branches)

Grocers to HM The Queen Mother.

Unless you live in Ascot you probably never knew that Budgen held a Royal Warrant. But the warrant has been held by Budgen's Ascot branch since The Queen Mother granted it in 1969. It wasn't Budgen's first, however. That was granted to their Windsor branch by George V in 1910 for 'oilery and tallow' supplies.

Budgen were started in 1872 by two brothers Budgen, John and Edwin, who opened a shop at Egham in Surrey. Their conditions were very different from those today. Customers were served by shop assistants across wooden counters and many customers had their groceries delivered on credit accounts. Shop hours were extended into the late evening and

JOHN BURGESS & SON LIMITED
Shaftesbury Road
London N18 1SW

Manufacturers of pastes and creamed horseradish to HM The Queen.

The firm of John Burgess & Son have always had an impressive list of customers. Lord Nelson took a supply of Burgess's delicacies to the Battle of the Nile in 1798. They also sent a consignment of their products to his ship HMS *Victory* in 1805 for the Battle of Trafalgar. Burgess were praised by Lord Byron in *Beppo* and by Sir Walter Scott in his *St Ronan's Well*. They also sent supplies to Lord Raglan at Sevastopol during the Crimean War and later provided for Captain Scott's Antartic expedition.

In 1760 John Burgess, the son of a country grocer, set up in business in the Strand in London selling salad oils, truffles, olives and many other items to tickle the epicurean palate, all imported from abroad. He soon began to invent many of his own table delicacies but it was his Original and Superior Essence of Anchovies, made from anchovies caught by the busy fleet of Gorgona fishing boats off Leghorn which earned him worldwide repute.

John Burgess & Son were awarded their first Royal Warrant by Queen Victoria and they later held it to George V and George VI. Today they are manufacturers of pastes and creamed horseradish to The Queen, but they also produce a range of other products including mint sauce, stuffed olives, mushroom ketchup, capers, cocktail gherkins and cranberry sauce.

John Burgess products are available from grocers, delicatessens and supermarkets.

The original John Burgess premises in The Strand, established 1760

CARR'S OF CARLISLE
Caldegate
Carlisle
Cumberland CA2 5TG

Biscuit manufacturers to HM The Queen and HM The Queen Mother.

The physical strength of Jonathan Dodgson Carr, founder of Carr's, was legendary. He could pick up three 20-stone sacks of flour and walk the length of his mill and back with them. But as a devout Quaker he would not have approved of one of the earlier uses of his tins of biscuits. In 1879 the British Army stacked up Carr's biscuit tins to form a barricade behind which our brave lads sheltered at the Battle of Rorke's Drift against the Zulus.

Mr Carr was also a great innovator. He developed the first-ever biscuit-cutting machine which was to lead to mass production and automation. Many a child learnt their ABC from Carr's Alphabet biscuits, one of the first products of the machine.

Carr's took the biscuit when they became the first of Britain's biscuit makers to be awarded a Royal Warrant. Their then handmade biscuits were first patronised by Queen Victoria in 1841. Although today the Royal Warrant holders are sworn to discretion, erstwhile warrant holders had no such scruples. One of Carr's advertisements in 1845 boasted, 'The Queen's biscuits manufactured by J. D. Carr, Carlisle, are in general use at the Royal Household and much approved by numerous respectable families.'

Today Carr's is part of the United Biscuits conglomeration of companies. The warrant-holding product is their table water biscuit.

Carr's biscuits are available from grocers, delicatessens and supermarkets.

WM CRAWFORD & SONS LIMITED
12 Hope Street
Edinburgh
Scotland

Biscuit manufacturers to HM The Queen.

Wm Crawford began in a small shop in Leith, near Edinburgh, two years before the Battle of Waterloo, hence their claim to be 'the oldest of biscuit manufacturers'. Very much a family firm, the descendants of the founder, William Crawford, still

work perfecting their biscuits today.

The company always took care of their staff and had ideas often well ahead of their day. A woman welfare supervisor was appointed to look after the factory girls and there was a PT teacher who put them through their paces during the factory's morning break to keep their figures trim after they had nibbled at too many of the biscuits. One Crawford factory had the country's first industrial dental service, another a chiropody service. Archie Crawford, chairman of the company at the beginning of this century, firmly rejected the title of philanthropist. 'How can you expect anyone to do a decent day's work standing on her feet if she has corns?' In the Second World War a fund was set up to help any of the firm's employees whose homes were damaged in bombing raids. A number of men, from both the factory and the management, joined up in the 59th (4T West Lancs) Medium Regiment. So many in fact that it became known as 'The Biscuit Regiment'.

In 1962 Crawford merged with United Biscuits. Today they are most widely known for their Cream Crackers, Biscuits for Cheese and Sweet Marie Biscuits – all of which can be found in the Royal kitchens.

Wm Crawford biscuits are available from grocers, delicatessens and supermarkets.

FINDUS LIMITED
St George's House
Park Lane
Croydon
Surrey CR9 2AA

Suppliers of frozen foods to HM The Queen and HM The Queen Mother.

There was a time when you could count all their products on one hand but now Findus, who hold their warrant for supplying frozen foods to the Royal palaces, can boast more exotic-sounding moussaka, lasagne, cannelloni and a variety of curries.

Findus owe their birth to two Scandinavian chocolate companies who in 1941 acquired a small fruit and vegetable canning factory at Bjuv in southern Sweden. By 1959 Findus International were formed and today, with over 100 lines in production, they have become a lifeline for many a working mum. The Princess of Wales on opening Findus's new factory was overheard to remark on her particular liking for French Bread Pizza.

Their products range in price from 89p to £1.30 for single meals and can be bought almost everywhere from the local supermarket to Harrods.

Findus frozen foods are available from supermarkets, grocers, supermarkets, frozen food centres and department store food halls around the country.

Above:
Early form of transport for Crawford's biscuits, the bullock-drawn cart which took over the final distribution stage in the Orkney Islands

Left:
French bread pizzas on the conveyor belt at the Findus factory in Longbenton

FORTNUM & MASON PLC

See page 236.

KNOWLES & SONS (FRUITERERS) LIMITED
27/33 Exchange Street
Aberdeen AB9 2DJ
Scotland

Purveyors of fruit and vegetables to HM The Queen and fruiterers and green-grocers to HM The Queen Mother.

Knowles were established in 1886 by the Knowles family who, 'in trouble with the tax man', were forced to sell the business in 1947. Today the company are 'secondary wholesalers' buying fruit and vegetables over the telephone from markets, and occasionally farms, around the country, depending on the availability of the produce. Knowles buy bananas 'just off the boat'. The bananas are then transferred to their 'banana department', a small grey Victorian building where they are ripened by heat treatment.

Although Knowles have five competitors in the 60-mile area they supply to, they say it is 'hard work' that makes their business special and means they have a wider range of produce than many of their competitors. Knowles also have two greengrocers' shops in Aberdeen, one in neighbouring Market Street and the other in Union Street. They originally supplied Balmoral and Birkhall, the Royal family's summer holiday homes, via a garden shop they had in Ballater but this closed down over 12 years ago.

Monday–Saturday: 8.30–5.30 (Knowles shop in 6 Market Street, Aberdeen).

HARRODS
Knightsbridge
London SW1X 7XL

(01) 730 1234

Suppliers of provisions and household goods to HM The Queen, suppliers of china, glass and fancy goods to HM The Queen Mother, and outfitters to HRH The Duke of Edinburgh and HRH The Prince of Wales.

Harrods do not believe in false modesty. While most retailers quote their selling space in square feet Harrods will tell you they have over 15 acres. Their motto is 'Omnia Omnibus Ubique' (everything for everyone, everywhere) and their telegraphic address used to be 'Everything London'. The store has an international reputation for being able to supply anything from a pin to an elephant. The latter claim was put to the test in 1975 after a midnight call ordering a baby elephant as a gift for the then Governor of California, Ronald Reagan. Naturally Harrods delivered. Another telephone call from a woman urgently inquiring about a narcissus which had a name beginning with the letter 'O' sent staff frantically searching through catalogues in the florist department to be later told by the satisfied caller that she only wanted to know the name so she could fill in her crossword. Harrods' green and gold shopping bags have been spotted everywhere from the *QE2* to a Hong Kong junk. They have even been seen making the ascent to Mount Everest. Enough people have bought their groceries at their local shop and then carried them home in a Harrods bag for Harrods to realise the name rates highly in the prestige stakes. As a result they have stepped up their own-brand products like their miniature 'Harrods breath freshener' encased in the distinctive green and gold livery.

Harrods invite their customers to 'enter a different world', which is easier said than done with 11 entrances to choose from. More than 30,000 customers pass through their 125 departments every day. But Harrods is much more than just a shop. You can bank there, take out your insurance, borrow books from the largest commercial library in the world and arrange your holiday through them. They will also take care of your final journey from their funeral department. Although Harrods have not yet sent coals to Newcastle, they have

"Good Lord, Wilkins, is it nine o'clock already?"

sent a Persian carpet to Persia, a refrigerator to Finland, sauna bath equipment to the Middle East, six bread rolls to New York and a pound of sausages to a yacht anchored in the Mediterranean. They have also sent a 35-pence handkerchief air freight to Los Angeles at a cost of £17.50.

In 1849, Henry Charles Harrod, a tea merchant, bought a small grocery shop with a turnover of £20 a week. In 1861 he sold the shop to his son Charles Digby as a blunt lesson that nothing of value comes free. The transaction made such an impression on young Charles that he denied his customers credit for his first 20 years of trading. In 1883, just three weeks before Christmas, Harrods burned to the ground in a fire which lasted all night and lit up most of West London. The following day Harrods' customers received a letter from Charles Digby Harrod which said: 'I regret to inform you that in consequence of the above premises being burnt down, your order will be delayed in the execution a day or two.'

A new Harrods was built and when it opened in 1884 it was more like the department store we know today than the modest grocer shop which Charles Digby's father had sold him. Shortly afterwards the first credit accounts were opened and among the few selected for the honour were Lillie Langtry, Oscar Wilde and Ellen Terry. In 1898 Harrods became the first store in London to introduce the 'moving staircase', similar to the escalators today but without steps. When Queen Mary granted Harrods the Royal Warrant in 1913 she was not the only member of Royalty to shop in the store. Queen Alexandra was a regular customer and the Czar of Russia's children also made an expedition to buy sailor suits which were frequently featured in the photographs taken of them during the last years of the Czar's reign.

Today Harrods hold all four Royal Warrants – one to each member of the Royal family who is able to grant them. They supply provisions to The Queen from their food hall where their flamboyant fresh and smoked fish display can be admired daily. Within the food hall – recently redesigned, and opened by Princess Anne in 1983 – there are 500 different cheeses, 130 types of bread and rolls and 163 brands of whisky. During the Christmas period they sell over 100 tons of Christmas puddings and 45,000 mince pies. New staff are always made aware of the fact that 'Buck House', as the Palace is affectionately known within the store, often telephone to place their orders.

One newcomer to the dairy produce department was so impressed by this that when she got a telephone call from the Prince of Wales ordering 18 pounds of cheddar, she ran ashen-faced through the department shouting, 'It's them. It's him,' only to be told calmly that the Prince of Wales was a nearby pub which also placed regular orders.

Other staff have to get used to stepping out of the lift to find Paul Newman standing there or a host of other celebrities who frequent the store. But one member of staff storming into the book buyer's office with a complaint was not quite prepared to find The Queen calmly sitting there. The staff have to be able to cope with shopping sprees like the one by an Eastern diplomat who spent £35,000 in one hour kitting his daughters out for their new school.

Whether you want to buy a tie for £1,000 or just grab a gin and tonic in Harrods' in-store pub, there is usually help at hand. From the commissionaire on door five who is able to conjure up taxis out of thin air, to the attendant who will look after your pekinese while you shop. Even if you don't buy anything Harrods' ground floor with its cross-section of nationalities in Bermuda shorts to yashmaks is one of the better places in London for watching people.

Monday–Friday: 9–5; Wednesday 9–7; Saturday: 9–6. Two mail order catalogues (magazines) a year which are sent to account customers and can be bought at newsagents around the country. Contact Harrods if you would like one. Price £1.50.

HP FOODS LIMITED
Edinburgh House
Abbey Street
Market Harborough
Leicestershire LE16 9BG

Manufacturers of HP sauces to HM The Queen and manufacturers of HP sauces and canned foods to HM The Queen Mother.

The name 'HP' is today synonymous with sauces, but the popular kitchen table garnish might never have been so successful had it not been for a bad debt. In the late 19th century, Mr Edwin Samson Moore and his son, Eddie, owned two vinegar companies in Birmingham. One of their debtors was a Mr F. G. Garton of Nottingham whom Samson and Eddie Moore visited to retrieve some debts. While the

debt was being discussed, a sauce was cooking in the wash-house copper. Samson Moore noticed a basket-cart in the yard which carried a board announcing 'Garton's HP Sauce' together with a picture of the Houses of Parliament. By the time Messrs Moore left Nottingham they had cancelled Mr Garton's debt and paid him £150 for the name and the recipe.

In 1903 the designs depicting the Houses of Parliament were registered. Soon fleets of donkey carts with uniformed salesmen were touring the country selling miniature bottles of HP sauce door-to-door. A few years later a promotion campaign was launched where 10 shillings was offered to any housewife who could produce a bottle of HP sauce on demand. In 1912 the company introduced Daddies Sauce, a cheaper brown sauce. During the First World War vast quantities of both sauces were shipped to France to make the monotonous diet of bully beef more palatable. In 1930 the company acquired Lea & Perrins (see below) which gave them the monopoly as brown sauce manufacturers, and soon afterwards they launched HP Tomato Ketchup. In 1951 the company acquired Norfolk Canneries, fruit and vegetable canners, and with their joint resources they introduced HP Baked Beans in 1954.

Today HP Foods are a member of the food division of the Imperial Group.

HP sauces and canned foods are available from grocers and supermarkets.

LEA & PERRINS LIMITED
PO Box 31
Worcester
Worcestershire WR5 1DT

Purveyors of Worcestershire sauce to HM The Queen.

The recipe for Lea & Perrins Worcestershire sauce was first brought to England in 1835 by Marcus, Lord Sandys, who returned from India after holding the office of Governor of Bengal. On arriving in his native Worcestershire he took the recipe to Mr John Lea and Mr William Perrins who owned a pharmacy in the town of Worcester. Lord Sandys asked the two chemists to make up the sauce for his own private use which they did as well as preparing a quantity for themselves to satisfy their own curiosity. When Mr Lea and Mr Perrins tasted the sauce they found it unpalatable and consigned the jars to the

LEA & PERRINS' SAUCE—The First Introduction.

cellar. Some time later when they came to throw the jars away they tasted the sauce again and found it had matured into 'quite a superb' taste. The reputation of the sauce soon spread and in 1837 Mr Lea and Mr Perrins obtained Lord Sandy's permission to keep the recipe and sell the sauce commercially.

The ingredients which go to make up the sauce come from all over the world. The main ingredient is anchovies, matured in 70-gallon oak casks in a saturated solution of brine for many years, before being mixed with spices. The exact ingredients, proportions and maturing processes are a closely guarded secret to this day and only a handful of people know the recipe.

Lea & Perrins Worcestershire sauce is available from grocers, delicatessens and supermarkets.

McVITIE & PRICE LIMITED
The Edinburgh Biscuit Works
Waxlow Road
Harlesden
London NW10 7NU

Biscuit manufacturers to HM The Queen.

McVities may bake a better biscuit but as far as the Royal family are concerned, they are also a dab hand at baking wedding cakes. Their first sortie in this field was for the wedding of Princess Mary of Teck and the Duke of York (later Queen Mary and King George V). Queen Victoria's confectioner could not manage all the wedding fare on his own so outside help was needed and McVities made one of the cakes which Princess Mary found 'the nicest ... the design is so good'. McVities later made the wedding cake for The Queen Mother's wedding and for The Queen when she married in 1947.

The list of ingredients for The Queen's official wedding cake was provided by Buckingham Palace and the ingredients were a gift from the Girl Guides of Australia. The cake was spectacular. It was of four tiers, nine feet high, weighed 500 pounds and took 10 hours to bake. The top tier was kept and redecorated by McVities for Prince Charles's christening on 15 December 1948 – a fine example of traditional thrift.

McVities' biscuits were also popular with Polar explorers. According to a letter written to McVities by the leader of the 1924 Oxford University Expedition, 'If any expedition in the future revisits the North Eastland it will find many of your tins on these icegirt shores – ginger nut tins, digestive biscuit tins, chocolate biscuit tins – all empty, mute tokens of our appreciation of your biscuits. While no one can say that fancy biscuits are essential to any expedition, their effect on morale is astonish-

The wedding cake made by McVities for Princess Marina and the Duke of Kent in 1934

ing, and your biscuits were a shield and buckler against the fog and the snow and the wind and the cold of North Eastland.' Not an early member of the Ecology Party, but clearly a McVities fan.

Today McVitie & Price are part of the United Biscuits empire and their famous Chocolate Homewheats, Royal Scots, Ginger Nuts and Digestives are appreciated throughout the country.

McVitie & Price biscuits are available from grocers, delicatessens and supermarkets.

PROCTOR & GAMBLE LIMITED
See page 18.

RECKITT & COLMAN LIMITED
See page 18.

J. A. SHARWOOD & COMPANY LIMITED
10 Victoria Road
Willesden
London NW10 6NU

Manufacturers of chutney & purveyors of Indian curry powder to HM The Queen.

It is unlikely that chicken vindaloo or lamb Madras are staples on The Queen's dinner table. But at the coronation in 1953 the guests were treated to a mildly curried dish specially created by the Cordon Bleu School and now known universally as Coronation Chicken or Chicken Elizabeth. It is probably the reliving of this happy experience that brings Sharwood's curry powder most often off the Royal shelves.

Sharwood's Royal Warrant (first granted in 1947) is for chutney as well as curry powder. Their Green Label chutney

is the best-known survivor of a wide range of chutneys and pickles.

Sharwood's chutneys and curry powders are available from grocers, delicatessens and supermarkets.

GEORGE STRACHAN LIMITED
East Balmoral
Crathie
Aberdeenshire
Scotland
(and branches)
Crathie (033 84) 224

General merchants to HM The Queen and HM The Queen Mother.

George Strachan proudly showed me an advertisement Harrods had placed in a national paper which read: 'Glen Deveron and Lawson's 12-year-old Scottish Gold – only available from Harrods and Strachan's of Royal Deeside'. In his main shop in Aboyne, Strachan's of Royal Deeside, which is 15 miles east of Balmoral, Mr Strachan has over 380 different brands of whisky. He also has an enormous collection of whisky miniatures which he sells mail order. Whisky collectors from all over the world visit him in the Aboyne shop.

Mr Strachan's father, formerly a grocer in Aberdeen, established the first of the Strachan grocer shops in 1926. After the war he purchased another shop in Ballater, the closest village to Balmoral and then a shop in Braemar. About 25 years ago Mr Strachan rented the general stores in Crathie just outside the gates of Balmoral from where The Queen is rumoured to have bought her sweets when a young Princess. Today it is a small village grocer's with a post-office section at the back of the store. Its only distinguishing characteristic is the series of large black and white photographs of Prince Charles hanging on the end wall.

Monday–Friday: 8.30–1; 2–5.30; Saturday: 8.30–12.30 (George Strachan, General Merchants at Crathie).

TATE & LYLE PLC
Sugar Quay
Lower Thames Street
London EC3R 6DQ

Sugar refiners to HM The Queen.

Mr Henry Tate and Mr Abram Lyle whose surnames formed one of the most famous marriages in the sugar industry never met

Above:
The Tom-Tom man is a symbol of Indian food. You can find him today on Sharwood's Indian Pickle jars

Left:
The little post office cum grocers is only a few minutes' walk from the gates of Balmoral. The Queen, when young, used to walk there for her sweets

each other. Mr Tate had started his sugar business in Liverpool while Mr Lyle had begun his in Greenock. Even when they both opened refineries in London in the late 19th century, just a mile and a half away from each other, their paths never crossed.

Henry Tate was the seventh son of a Unitarian clergyman who worked as a grocer's apprentice before he set up his Liverpool refinery in 1859 making sugar crystals and lumps. Abram Lyle began his working career as a lawyer's clerk. He was a rabid teetotaller, probably due to his father who had taken to 'strong waters' and lost all his money in middle age. Abram Lyle once told a public meeting he would rather his son was brought home dead than drunk. He later became a shipowner and started in the sugar refining business when he accepted a cargo of sugar from a ship in lieu of a debt. Not knowing what to do with the sugar he turned it into golden syrup and carried on refining sugar from thereon. When it came to choosing a logo for his company he chose a picture of the lion killed by Sampson, surrounded by bees with the quotation 'out of the strong came sweetness', which soon made his tins of syrup a household name.

Even during those early days when Tate and Lyle were trading independently and despite the fact they had not met, there was always a tacit agreement not to poach on each other's speciality. Lyle didn't venture into making sugar cubes and Tate never made syrup. When in the 1890s the Lyles heard the Tates were going into syrup production they bought a part of a sugar cube plant and let it be known in the area they had done so. Nothing more was ever heard of either of their plans. Before the First World War the Tates and the Lyles had been fighting each other so fiercely neither had been facing up to the threat of foreign subsidised sugar. By 1918 they were both in financial trouble and Mr Ernest Tate approached Mr Charles Lyle and his brother, Robert, with plans for a merger. Although the Tate company were bigger than Lyle their profits were smaller. An amalgamation took place in 1921 with the Tates as directors and the Lyles as managing directors.

In those days, sugar was bought from grocers who shovelled it into hand-sewn hessian bags, not necessarily with the greatest of accuracy. Tate & Lyle introduced one- and two-pound paper-wrapped cardboard packets. By 1929 the Liverpool sugar firm of Fairrie had amalgamated with Tate & Lyle and the business continued to prosper. The Second World War brought sugar rationing, but Tate & Lyle survived ready for the massive post-war expansion which followed. The new demand for sugar meant they were able to invest in more plants and machinery and begin exporting. In 1949 Tate & Lyle successfully fought off the threat of nationalisation with their Mr Cube campaign. Their advertising posters showed a caricature of a sugar cube teamed with the slogans: 'Tate not State' and 'Mr Cube says: If they juggle with your sugar they'll juggle with your shopping basket.'

Today the company are still controlled by members of both the Tate and the Lyle families. But the two families have never intermarried. Mr Saxon Tate, one of the directors and also one of England's top jockeys, once said that a marriage between a Lyle and a Tate would be like 'crossing a runner with a stayer. You'd get a slow horse which wouldn't last the course.'

Tate & Lyle sugar products are available from grocers and supermarkets.

Tea and coffee

H. R. HIGGINS (COFFEE MAN) LIMITED
42 South Molton Street
London W1Y 2BD

(01) 629 3913

Coffee merchants to HM The Queen.

It used to take Mr H. R. Higgins, coffee-man and founder of the firm, 60 turns of a hand grinder to produce one pound of ground coffee for his customers. Today, with the advent of automation, his children, Tony and Audrey Higgins, the present directors of the company, are relieved of this arduous task.

Mr Higgins began his training in the coffee trade at the age of 16. One of his duties was to clear away the tasting bowls after the accredited coffee tasters had gone to lunch. Before doing this he and his colleagues would themselves taste and discuss the merits of the various samples. When Mr Higgins started his company in 1942, coffee was his hobby as well as his future business. He had a fine collection of coffee books, prints, antique grinders and brass coffee jars some of which are on display in the little shop today. In the 1940s, coffees were blended and sold under a fictitious brand name to keep their ingredients secret. Mr Higgins travelled around the world seeking coffees of outstanding quality and then marketed them under their own identity.

Today H. R. Higgins sell 26 difference varieties of coffee, from their famous Chagga coffee (produced by the Wa-Chagga people living on the slopes of Mount Kilimanjaro in Tanzania) to Brazil Santos (grown in the Sao Paulo region and favoured by Stirling Moss). H. R. Higgins were awarded their Royal Warrant in 1979.

Monday, Tuesday and Thursday: 8.45–5.30; Wednesday: 8.45–6.30; Friday: 8.45–6. Mail order catalogue available for coffees and Higgins' coffee gift pack – price £6 for four quarter-pound packets of coffee, postage free in the UK.

MELROSES LIMITED
Melrose House
Couper Street
Leith
Edinburgh EH6 6HQ
Scotland

Purveyors of tea and coffee to HM The Queen.

In 1812 a Scottish judge of the Court of Session condemned the habit of tea-drinking on the grounds that its increased popularity diminished the revenue from beer duty. This did not deter Andrew Melrose. In the same year he opened Andrew Melrose & Co., a grocer's shop, in Canongate, then one of the chief business centres of Edinburgh. Although tea was not the sole article offered for sale, it was the one in which Mr Melrose was most interested. He had served his apprenticeship in the tea department of Robert Shepherd, the leading grocer in Scotland.

In the early 1830s when the charter of the East India Company expired and trade with the Eastern ports was opened, Mr Melrose immediately established links with China. The first cargo of tea to arrive legally at any port other than London was from Canton. It was landed at Leith in 1835 labelled 'Andrew Melrose & Co.' Buyers from around the country attended the sale. The races of the legendary tea clippers began, many of the clippers carrying Melrose's tea. Each shipper tried to be the first to deliver his cargo of teas from Canton to Britain on the hazardous 17,000 mile journey. Andrew Melrose had three sons working for him at the time, and the company had opened their fourth shop in George Street, which was their headquarters until 1921. In 1837 they were awarded the Royal Warrant as purveyors of grocery to Queen Victoria at Edinburgh. Melrose have held the Royal appointment ever since.

Andrew Melrose died in 1855 and left the business to two of his sons. Four years later an apprentice called John Macmillan entered the company. By 1863 he had sole responsibility for buying and blending the teas. In 1865 he became a partner and was recognised throughout the country as the greatest authority on Indian teas in Britain. In 1890 pre-packing began. Up to this time wholesale tea merchants had sold their tea in bulk, often unblended, to the grocer who weighed it out for his customers as they required it. Now wholesale tea distributors began to blend and sell their own

named packets to the grocery trade. From then on Melrose marketed their goods in packets labelled 'Melrose's Tea'. When John Macmillan died in 1901, Melrose's teas were already known around the world. Today two of his great-grandchildren are the present directors of the company.

Although Melrose had their own retail outlets for many years, in 1970 they decided to concentrate on their wholesale business. Today from their factory in Leith they supply the grocery and catering trades, and their specially blended teas are exported to some 50 countries around the world.

Melrose's range of teas and coffees are available from delicatessens, grocery shops and the food halls of department stores.

NAIROBI COFFEE & TEA COMPANY LIMITED
Shakespeare Street
Watford
Hertfordshire WD2 5HF

Coffee merchants to HM The Queen and HM The Queen Mother.

When David Driver, Nairobi's buyer and blender, describes the taste of their Viennese coffee as 'a slight dark-roasted, bittersweet tang with a little acidity', you know Nairobi are serious about their products.

Nairobi were founded in 1925 and were granted their first Royal Warrant by George V when they were based in London's Mayfair. Today they have moved to Watford where they not only blend and grind coffee but also package and store it. Nairobi are wholesale suppliers to the catering trade, the grocery and delicatessen retail trades and also suppliers of coffee and coffee-making equipment to offices. The company sell a range of 30 different coffees, 2 instant coffees and 15 teas.

Nairobi coffees and teas are obtainable from grocers and delicatessens. Their coffees are also available from the above address for office use, and for larger orders Nairobi can overprint packs with customers' logos and advertising slogans.

RIDGWAYS
Leon House
High Street
Croydon CR9 3NH

Tea merchants to HM The Queen and tea and coffee merchants to HM The Queen Mother.

Ridgways' answer to PG Tips is their Country House brand. It is packeted in a bright red gingham design with Ridgways' distinctive leaf-shaped logo and the Royal Warrant proudly displayed above. However, it is not their biggest seller. That distinction goes to their Imperial Blend tea which sleepyheads can buy in an extra strong Breakfast Blend. If that doesn't get you going at the beginning of the day, nothing will.

Ridgways buy their tea from around the world and blend it in their factory in Liverpool where three skilled tasters sip hard to ensure Ridgways live up to their motto of 'blenders of fine teas'. A lesser-known product of the company is their coffee which you may well have bought unknowingly as wholeberry coffee beans at your local shop. Ridgways sell eight different types of coffee though none of it is sold direct to the public under their own name.

Ridgways were founded in 1836 when Thomas Ridgway, who had previously been working as a tea merchant in Birmingham, moved to London. But apart from the fact that Ridgways were bought by Tate & Lyle in 1977, further details of their history are somewhat sketchy. Ridgways' Royal connection does, however, date from Queen Victoria who granted them their first Royal Warrant as supplier of teas. Thus Ridgways produced their unique HMB Tea, coined 'Her Majesty's Blend', which claims to have been specially blended for Her Majesty. But even that can't be proved.

Ridgways teas can be found at grocers and supermarkets around the country.

'Conversation Piece at Royal Lodge, Windsor', painted by J. Gunn in 1950

THE SAVOY HOTEL COFFEE DEPARTMENT
The Savoy Hotel
1 Savoy Hill
London WC2R 0EU

(01) 836 1533

Suppliers of coffee to HM The Queen.

The Savoy's Coffee Department was set up in 1937 by the chairman's assistant, Ms Olive Barnett. It was in response to the many requests from the hotel guests who wished to drink Savoy coffee in their own homes.

There is only one Savoy coffee. It is a secret blend of four of the world's finest coffees. Raw green beans are purchased on the coffee market, roasted separately to the temperature required and then delivered to the company's hotels and restaurants or packed for despatch all over the world. Savoy coffee was demanded during the war by General Eisenhower when he was commanding the European forces. Today over 10,000 pounds of coffee are bought by customers throughout the world. Among its demanding drinkers are Mick Jagger, George Segal, Tommy Steele and The Queen who awarded the Savoy Hotel Coffee Department her warrant in 1982.

Savoy coffee can be drunk in the Savoy, Claridges, the Connaught and Hotel Lancaster in Paris. It is also available from the Savoy Hotel gift shop, open Monday–Saturday: 7–10; Sunday: 8–10; or mail order from the above address. It costs £2.15 per pound without postage.

R. TWINING & COMPANY LIMITED
216 The Strand
London WC2R 1AP

(01) 353 3511

Tea and coffee merchants to HM The Queen.

Even if you're lucky enough to be invited to a Royal garden party, you won't be drinking the tea drunk in the Royal drawing rooms, though it may well be tea from Twinings. Twinings have been providing tea to Their Majesties since they were granted their first Royal Warrant by Queen Victoria. Today the Royal family also drink Twining's coffee.

Twinings are the oldest ratepayers in the City of Westminster, having been at their current site since 1706. Such is their reputation that over a third of their customers are tourists, coming to see the 'home of Twinings tea'.

Twinings stock a good selection of coffees but their reputation is for tea. You can find anything from the exotic essence of blackcurrant to the more mundane English Breakfast tea. And, of course, Twining's best-selling Earl Grey (47 pence for 125 grams) which has been described as 'a distinctive blend of China and Darjeeling teas, delicately scented with oil of bergamot'.

Monday–Friday: 9.30–5.

Time Off

Collecting

ALBERT AMOR LIMITED
37 Bury Street
London SW1Y 6AU

(01) 930 2444

Suppliers of fine porcelain to HM The Queen Mother.

Albert Amor deal entirely in 18th-century English porcelain. Their most famous customer, The Queen Mother, has a fine collection of botanically decorated Chelsea plates and dishes from the mid 1750s, some of which were bought from Albert Amor and now are occasionally lent to the Burlington House Fair, of which The Queen Mother is a patron.

Albert Amor, an eminent antiquary, established his business in 1903 at 31 and 32 St James's Street. The shop dealt in a large variety of objects from furniture to enamels, but English porcelain was always a speciality. Mr Amor was credited with several discoveries in this field. In 1920 he recognised the Dudley Vases, a set of seven florid and flamboyant gold anchor Chelsea vases painted with panels of figures after Boucher, at a Christie's sale, even though they had turned up in two separate lots. He bought both lots for a total of £6,500 and sold the vases to Lord Bearsted. In 1921 Albert Amor was granted his first Royal Warrant to Queen Mary as antiquary, but the warrant ceased when he retired five years later.

When Mr Amor retired the company were taken over by Leslie Perkins, who had been a partner since the firm began. Within six months he had received another warrant as fine art dealer to Her Majesty. Like Albert Amor, Mr Perkins also made several notable discoveries, one of which was his proposal that the rare but well-known small 18th-century figures universally called 'The Gardener and His Companion' were made at Worcester – which was then thought not to have made any figures. Tests were carried out and Mr Perkins was proved correct.

In the 1920s Albert Amor flourished, moving to new premises in 1928, but within a few years business had fallen away disastrously. In 1934 the firm were forced to move from St James's Street and to sell a large section of their stock at Christie's in a two-day sale 'entirely without reserve'. Soon afterwards, Mr William Larke, one of the company's partners, threw himself under a train in North London. But Leslie Perkins was undeterred. He opened a new shop on the corner of King Street and Bury Street, until a bomb blast in the area at the beginning of the war forced them on to their present address, a smaller shop in Bury Street. Leslie Perkins died in 1953 and the business was taken over by his son, John, who changed the direction of the shop, concentrating solely on fine early English pottery and porcelain.

Anne George, the current managing director, joined the company in 1956 and took her present position in 1973, on the death of John Perkins. Most of the customers are 'interested collectors' from around the world. Mrs George is against porcelain being treated as an investment, 'you can get more money on the stock market these days'.

Monday–Friday: 9.30–4.30. Albert Amor hold exhibitions once or twice a year and publish an accompanying catalogue. For details of the exhibitions contact the above address. The company will mail items around the world.

BRIDGER & KAY LIMITED
24 Pall Mall
London SW1Y 5LP

(01) 839 2153

Postage stamp dealer to HM The Queen.

George V was an avid stamp collector. After his death the collection was bequeathed to the nation. Sometimes part of the Royal philatelic collection is on view to the public, usually at major international exhibitions, and Bridger & Kay are called on from time to time to advise on or obtain special items for the collection.

Bridger & Kay also keep many of their

Above:
Detail of a 'cross-written' letter comprising one folded sheet of paper and containing over 3,000 words. It was posted in 1839 prior to the introduction of penny postage in the UK. It can be bought from Bridger & Kay

customers' collections up to date. With a very substantial selection of stamps on their premises at any one time there are many items to choose from. In their bare, white-walled room – 'indicative of stamp houses' – Bridger & Kay are able to take care of the valuable property they have in stock. 'Water and fire are big problems. Luckily we've got special safes and a good alarm system.'

Bridger & Kay also own Temple Bar Auctions and are philatelic publishers. They hold two auctions a year of British and Commonwealth stamps, occasionally including European and American stamps as well. The company also sell stamps for clients by private treaty, which means that not only do collections stay intact, but the buyer doesn't pay VAT. For Bridger & Kay's private treaty sales on offer, walk past their window and study the noticeboard. They also sell unusual covers and letters, such as an 1829 cross-written letter, dated from before the introduction of penny postage, written in several directions, one on top of the other on the same piece of paper in order to save weight. The letter contains over 3,000 words on two sides of a sheet of writing paper. Intriguing, but somewhat difficult to read.

Even though the firm were established in 1897, Bridger & Kay's biggest coup was in 1962 when a young nurse came into their Strand office with a set of St Helena 'Tristan Relief' stamps. The stamps had been issued on 12 October 1961 by St Helena to raise money for their sister island Tristan de Cunha. But as the stamps had been issued without the permission of the Crown Agents, after a week they were given instructions for them to be withdrawn. In that week St Helena had only sold 434 sets, so the issue was scarce. As an afterthought, Bridger & Kay asked the nurse if she had any relatives in St Helena. She told them about her uncle. One cable later, Bridger & Kay had purchased some complete mint sheets. And although the sets were only worth £200 in 1962, today they sell for over £2,000 and are catalogued at £4,000. 'Serious stamp collecting is one

Right:
391 Strand, the home of Stanley Gibbons from 1891. Today the building is no longer in existence

of the best investments today,' Mr Leverton, their director, told me.

Monday–Friday: 9.30–4.30. Bridger & Kay publish 'King George VI Commonwealth Postage Stamp Catalogue', now in its 15th edition and 'Commonwealth 5 Reign Postage Stamp Catalogue', now in its 14th edition.

STANLEY GIBBONS LIMITED
399 Strand
London WC2R 0LX
(01) 836 8444

Philatelists to HM The Queen.

Stanley Gibbons Ltd, the oldest stamp dealers in the world, started out in life above a chemist's shop in Plymouth. The founder, Edward Stanley Gibbons, was born in 1840, the youngest son of a pharmaceutical chemist. By the age of 15 he had built up an impressive collection of about 20 stamps, including the 1d Black Swan of Western Australia and the 1d Sydney view. But it was only a hobby when Stanley was called upon to take up his place as an apprentice in 'pills and powders'.

In between prescriptions there was plenty of time to nurture his interest in stamps and before long he was prospering as a stamp dealer from a room above the shop. After his father's death, Stanley concentrated solely on stamp trading. His first

lucky break was when he bought a kitbag of Cape Triangular stamps for £5.00 from two sailors who had won them in a raffle. Today the contents would be worth thousands of pounds, but even then Stanley Gibbons estimated he had made £500 on the deal. Another year he cheekily bought up the complete stock of a provisional stamp post office in Wadi Halfa, Anglo-Egytian Sudan. Understandably, the deal caused questions to be raised in the House of Commons.

Sadly, Stanley Gibbons died just a year before the first Royal Warrant was issued to the company in 1914, by George V, a keen philatelist. Today they not only hold the Royal Warrant to Her Majesty the Queen, but in 1971 they were awarded the Queen's Award to Industry for their export achievements.

'399', as their shop in the Strand is referred to by philatelists, is well known for its gallery of famous collections, and specialises in rare stamps, postal history, historical documents, new issue stamps, banknotes and bonds. But the Gibbons empire has not forgotten its humble beginnings. Although the highest price raised at a Gibbons auction was £70,000 for the 'Miss Rose Blekenburg' cover, material for as little as £10 is still as welcome as it was at the little shop over the chemist. Keep collecting. As they say, 'Philately will get you everywhere.'

Monday–Friday: 9.30–5.30; Saturday: 10–12.30. 'Gibbons Stamp Monthly' is issued every month for under £1.

HALCYON DAYS LIMITED
14 Brook Street
London W1Y 1AA

(01) 629 8811

Suppliers of objets d'art to HM The Queen and HM The Queen Mother.

Halcyon Days sell boxes. Round boxes, oval boxes, square boxes, snuff boxes, patch boxes, musical boxes and clocks in boxes. They are decorated with zodiac signs, Shakespearean themes, flowers, messages, heraldic motifs and works of art. Or they are commissioned. When I visited the shop I saw a series of boxes with a picture of Windsor Castle as viewed from the Thames made for Her Majesty's State visit to Japan in 1975 and several boxes with an illustration of the Royal yacht *Britannia* made one year later for Her Majesty's visit to the USA. Some are commemorative boxes. Halcyon Days plan to celebrate Prince William's birthdays until he is five years old with special miniature boxes, each one slightly larger than the next.

Halcyon Days promise their boxes will be 'the antiques of tomorrow'. But the first time the craft of making 'trinkets and curiosities enamelled on copper' was practised in England was in the 1740s when boxes and bibelots were painted entirely by hand. The craft had been started on the continent when craftsmen would emulate the works of art of leading goldsmiths and miniaturist painters of the day on the boxes.

Although the results were captivating, the process was slow. In the early 1750s transfer-printing was invented. Enamels were still made by craftsmen but the intermediate processes of decorating them could be more swiftly executed by engravers and colourists than by the artist painting his own work on to each box. The snuff boxes, scent bottles, étuis and bonbonnières (which held cachoux to sweeten the breath) became acknowledged as works of art in their own right. The two centres of the new technique were Bilston in South Staffordshire and London's Battersea. At York House in Battersea much of the development of transfer-printing took place and Battersea enamels were usually printed in monochrome. In 1756, three years after it had started, the York House factory closed with serious financial problems. By 1745 French enamellers had settled in South Staffordshire and in Bilston the industry was thriving. But a century later production had virtually ceased. With the

Mr and Mrs Stanley Gibbons

advent of the Industrial Revolution, the craftsmen had been enticed away from the small specialist workshops to work in the new factories of the Midlands.

In 1970 Susan Benjamin decided to revive the art of enamelling and liaised with a small family enamelling firm in Bilston. Today her shop sells Battersea and Bilston enamels from 1740 to 1840 as well as her new enamel boxes, picture frames and sewing accessories. Ms Benjamin also sells other things you will find in her shop. The late-18th-century mahogany chest of drawers on display cost £4,250 and the glass display case filled with her collection of boxes cost £65 – empty, of course.

Monday–Friday: 9.15–5.30; Saturday:
9.30–1.30. Mail order catalogue available.
Halcyon Days will mail boxes around the
world.

S. J. PHILLIPS LIMITED
139 New Bond Street
London W1A 3DL

(01) 629 6261

Antique dealers to HM The Queen Mother.

In 1953 the *Sunday Express* featured the story 'How We Gave The Man Who Never Was a Sweetheart'. The story revealed for the first time that during the war British intelligence had created a 'Man Who Never Was'. The corpse of a 'Major Martin' was planted on a beach in Spain in April 1943 with bogus papers intended to trick the Germans into believing that the Allies were planning an attack on Sardinia, instead of their true target, Sicily. Major Martin carried on him, amongst other things, a set of passionate love-letters from his fictitious fiancée Pamela and an invoice from S. J. Phillips Ltd, for a 'single diamond ring, small diamond shoulders, platinum set' with the engraving 'P.L. from W.M., 14.4.43'. The ring had cost £53. 0s. 6d.

Although they are still an extremely lively firm it will probably be a while before S. J. Phillips hit the headlines again. They did feature briefly in April 1975 when the British Museum bought an 11th-century hunting horn from them for £210,000. But since then they have kept a low profile.

S. J. Phillips opened in 1869 at 113 New Bond Street, but moved down the road to their present location in 1966. The shop is a treasure trove of jewellery, silver, porcelain, snuff boxes and scent bottles. It is

no wonder they say that they have 'some things we really don't want to sell'. They also have some incongruous items, including a video-recorder and an Edward Ardizzone illustration, both of which were exchanged in barter from eager and imaginative customers – the latter from the artist himself. S. J. Phillips are experts in jewellery, mainly from the 18th and early 19th centuries, and silver (both British and Continental). You can find anything from an extending 19th-century silver toasting fork with a leather handle costing £500 to a collection of silver mole spoons – used for lifting the tea leaves out of the tea pot. They also sell christening sets, salt and pepper pots and coffee sets made by contemporary silversmiths.

It was for their superb collection of boxes, both snuff and patch, that S. J. Phillips were granted their first Royal Warrant by Queen Mary, a keen box-collector. In 1962 they were granted their most recent warrant by The Queen Mother.

Monday–Friday: 10–5.

B. A. SEABY LIMITED
Audley House
11 Margaret Street
London W1N 8AT

(01) 580 3677

Numismatists to HM The Queen.

Herbert Seaby became a professional numismatist in 1919, founded B. A. Seaby in the 1930s and later compiled the original *Standard Catalogue of British Coins*. His son, Peter, who joined the company in 1936, is an expert on both early British coins and on the gold coinage of the world. Laurence Brown, another director of the company, is an expert on commemorative medals and European coins, and Frank Purvey, managing director of Seaby Publications, specialises in coin photography and is an expert on English coins. Seabys call themselves the 'intellectuals of the coin and medal market'.

On their two floors Seaby deal in antiquities, from 3rd-century BC red ware Tunisian flasks to 2nd-century AD Roman pottery lamps. They also specialise in commemorative medals and coins. Seaby travel round the world buying and selling coins for their collectors, and they advise both collectors and investors, publishing catalogues and specialised articles containing

the results of their research into the history and classification of coins and medals. Every month Seaby's *Coin and Medal Bulletin* is sent out to over 6,000 collectors in 72 countries – 'including behind the Iron Curtain' – and the coins and medals are sold on a first come, first served basis. 'At 8.30 in the morning on the following day, the phone starts ringing and the telex chattering,' Mr Clayton, a professor of Egyptology and one of Seaby's team of experts, told me. 'We keep ourselves amused by guessing which one of the three or so collectors we think might be interested rings first.'

B. A. Seaby were awarded their Royal Warrant to The Queen in 1980.

Monday–Friday: 9–5. Seaby's monthly 'Coin and Medal Bulletin' is available from the above address. It costs £8.50 for 12 issues.

JOHN SPARKS LIMITED
128 Mount Street
London W1Y 0DE

(01) 499 2265

Antiquaries of Chinese art to HM The Queen Mother.

In 1881 John Sparks, a merchant sea captain, founded a shop called the Japanese Art Gallery just off Manchester Square in London. 'Captain' John had started bringing back Chinese and Japanese objets d'art from his Eastern travels. At the time Japanese art was in fashion, inspired by Whistler, the American artist.

In 1929 the company moved to its present premises in Mount Street. By this stage John Sparks was a familiar figure in the London auction houses, but it was first under the direction of his son, Peter, that Sparks became 'a very smart business' selling fine decorative porcelain. Customers such as Queen Mary, a collector of Chinese objects, especially jade, visited the shop once a week. She awarded them their first Royal Warrant in 1938.

John Sparks still specialise in pre-18th-century fine Chinese and Japanese decorative art. And although they have sold a piece for £200,000 they reassured me that they liked customers to be able to come in and buy something 'at well under £100,000'. They can usually find something for £100. Few of their customers are English. Their Greek and Italian customers come to them to buy jade pieces, the French and Germans for their T'ang items

(dating from the 6th and 7th centuries) and the Scandinavians for their blue and white objects. Much of their stock is held for three to four years before it is sold, but as long as the customer is happy, John Sparks feel the wait has been worthwhile. 'The nice thing is when you can get the objects into a home where they can be appreciated – that's the joy of this business.' John Sparks are clearly hoarders by nature. Their archives still hold Captain John's letters home from school.

Monday–Friday: 9.30–5.

Fishing

C. FARLOW & COMPANY LIMITED
5 Pall Mall
London SW1Y 5NP

(01) 839 2423

Suppliers of fishing tackle and waterproof clothing to HRH The Prince of Wales.

'People used to think of Farlow's as a rather snooty game fishing tackle shop,' said Alastair Baxter, the present managing director. 'But today, customers from all walks of life are pleasantly overwhelmed by the range we offer. We aim to sell anything that any fisherman could want.'

As one of the only two fishing tackle shops in central London, Farlow's continue to cater for their traditional customers. Their ground floor is a fisherman's paradise, filled with over 100 types of reel, half a million flies, a wide selection of fishing and shooting books and an enormous collection of rods – from carbon trout fly rods which start at £35 to impregnated split-cane rods which are hand made. For a royal treat, ask if they've still got any of their Royal Tribute Rod series for sale. Farlow's only made 100 in honour of the wedding of their most famous customer.

On the upper floor they sell the country look. Men and women can kit themselves out for fishing or shooting with everything from waders to hats. In their basement you can find a more miscellaneous collection of items. Farlow's have a good range of shooting accessories, including game bags, cartridge belts and gundog training equipment. See how quickly your dog will learn with their Fox Training Scents for only £3.45. Or explore their sea fishing tackle –

'hooks, lines and sinkers basically'. Why not treat your salmon-fishing friend to a Gye net? At £32.50 it's quite large enough for the one that usually gets away.

Monday–Friday: 9–5; Thursday: 9–6; Saturday: 9–4. No catalogue, but Farlow's will mail worldwide.

HARDY BROS (ALNWICK) LIMITED
61 Pall Mall
London SW1Y 5HZ

(01) 839 5515

Manufacturers of fishing tackle to HRH The Prince of Wales.

Mr Porter of Whitechurch in England broke the world record for non-stop fishing (115 hours) using Hardy equipment; Mr Brandt of Aalborg in Denmark caught a 19 pound salmon on his Hardy Fibalite rod; and Mr Jones of Ballymena in Northern Ireland hooked a 23½ pound Thornback Ray using a 50 pound Hardy Saltwater rod.

Hardy's sell their record-breaking equipment in their shop in London's Pall Mall. Between the rows of equipment there's just enough space to cast a line. Their latest rod is made from 'space age' boron. Trying out their Smuggler rod would cause no problem, it's only 15 inches long – ideal for gentlemen poachers to hide in their pocket. Hardy also sell their famed Marquis reels, designed and made at their factory in Alnwick in Northumberland, and a range of fishing accessories from a hook-sharpening stone for £1.95 to a fish smoker at £21.55, as well as their Hardy tie for true Hardy record-breakers.

Hardy Brothers were founded in 1872 by two brothers, William and John James Hardy, who started their business as gunsmiths but soon became widely known as manufacturers of fishing tackle. They were granted their first Royal Warrant in 1910 by the Prince of Wales, later George V, and the company were also patronised by Queen Mary and the Princess Royal. Prince Charles, a keen salmon and trout fisher, granted them his warrant in 1980. And although you may not see him in Hardy's Pall Mall shop, you could catch the Duchess of Kent there.

Monday–Friday: 9–5. Mail order catalogue available from Hardy Brothers (Alnwick) Ltd, Willowburn, Alnwick, Northumberland NE66 2PG. Hardy tackle can be bought from tackle dealers and sports goods stores in most countries around the world.

Games

WADDINGTONS PLAYING CARD COMPANY LIMITED
See page 235.

Music

JOHN BROADWOOD & SONS LIMITED
6 Northampton Street
London N1 2JB

(01) 226 6841

Pianoforte manufacturers to HM The Queen and pianoforte tuner to HM The Queen Mother.

When King George V and Queen Mary visited the Broadwood factory in 1926 the King immediately ordered a Broadwood for Buckingham Palace and Queen Mary another for Sandringham. Prince Albert was known to have a Broadwood Square upon which he and Queen Victoria would play duets. In 1944 Broadwood were commissioned to tune all the instruments at Windsor Castle, including those used by the then Princess Elizabeth and Princess Margaret, who today still plays rather well.

After The Queen succeeded her father in 1952 Broadwood supplied a piano for the liner *Gothic* in which The Queen and The Duke of Edinburgh made their first overseas tour. Today there is at least one Broadwood in every Royal household including the Royal yacht *Britannia*, which was fitted with a Broadwood when it was first furnished in 1954 – today it houses five. In 1977, to mark the Silver Jubilee, the company made a special grand piano named The 250 with its frame painted silver instead of the usual gold. It was presented as a gift to The Queen and is now kept at Balmoral. They also sent a grand piano to Kensington Palace in 1981 as a wedding present for The Prince and Princess of Wales which The Princess enjoys playing. There is even a miniature Broadwood piano in Queen Mary's Dolls House at Windsor Castle.

The first member of the Broadwood family to make pianos was John, a Scottish cabinetmaker who came to London to seek his fortune. He found work with Burkat Shudi, one of the great harpsichord makers. Mr Shudi had already made several harpsichords for Frederick, Prince of Wales, one of which, constructed in 1740, can be seen in Kew Palace today. Together John Broadwood and Burkat Shudi made the harpsichord played by Mozart when he came to London in 1765.

In due course, and in the classic tradition of that time, John Broadwood married his

George V and Queen Mary touring the Broadwood factory in 1926

master's daughter and inherited the business. The harpsichord business thrived under Mr Broadwood's ownership and he was supplying instruments to Thomas Gainsborough, Sir Joshua Reynolds, Johann Christian Bach as well as the Duchess of Marlborough and the Duchess of Bedford. But John Broadwood was developing a keen interest in the pianoforte, at that time an unreliable instrument. He was intent on improving the instrument and began making scientific experiments and introducing new technology until he perfected a method to make his own models.

In those days every well-educated young lady played the piano, and Broadwood's instruments were much sought after around the world. The company also supplied pianos to Clementi, Haydn, Chopin, Mendelssohn and Elgar. Nelson and Wellington were customers and Broadwood's were awarded their first Royal Warrant as pianoforte manufacturers by George II. When John Broadwood's son, Thomas, who had taken over the business, sent a Broadwood to Beethoven in 1817, the composer wrote back: 'I shall look upon it as an altar upon which I shall place the most beautiful offerings of my spirit to the divine Apollo.'

Broadwood pianofortes are available from specialist music shops and top department stores. For piano tuning contact the above address.

STEINWAY & SONS
Steinway Hall
44 Marylebone Lane
London W1M 6EN

(01) 487 3391

Pianoforte manufacturers to HM The Queen.

'Not many people buy a piano on their first visit to Steinway,' Robert Glazebrook, Steinway's general manager, told me. Perhaps this is because people can't decide between Steinway's 24 finishes or possibly that they need to save for the starting price of £5,500.

The first Steinway piano was built in 1836 by a German cabinetmaker named Heinrich Englehard Steinweg, in the kitchen of his home in Seesen in Germany. In 1850 Herr Steinweg emigrated to America with his five sons, became Henry E. Steinway and three years later started Steinway & Sons in a rented loft in downtown Manhattan. Since Mr Steinway had produced 482 instruments in Germany, the first piano made in New York bore the serial number 483. Today each of Steinway's pianos is still numbered consecutively and the company keep a master book with details of the description of each piano and the date it was manufactured, who it was sold to and who owns it today, and when it was last seen or serviced by a member of Steinway.

The former Steinway Hall in Lower Seymour Street, now Wigmore Street

It was Steinway's son, Henry junior, who first decided to promote piano sales by the endorsements of famous musicians. Rubinstein and Paderewski both toured America under Steinway sponsorship, performing, as did many others, in the newly built Steinway Hall on New York's 14th Street. From 1866, for nearly 25 years, until eclipsed by Carnegie Hall, Steinway was the principal concert auditorium in New York. Great pianists could also avail themselves of a 'piano bank', which put borrowed Steinways at their fingertips in many major cities. Following one such loan, this brief note was penned: 'Sincere thanks for the incomparably beautiful Steinway Grand, which certainly is worthy of a better piano player than, yours gratefully, Richard Wagner.' The service still continues. In Britain, Steinway have 30 pianos and in New York over 100, all under 10 years old, which are regularly hired out. The artist pays only to have the piano moved and tuned. Steinway boast that the 'vast majority of concert pianists use Steinway as their preferred piano'.

By the 1880s, 70 per cent of pianos sold in Europe were Steinways and a branch factory opened in Hamburg in the same year. Many notables of the day had Steinways. In 1890, one of them, Thomas Edison, wrote to Steinway: 'Gents. I have decided to keep your grand piano. For some reason unknown to me it gives better results than any so far tried. Please send bill with lowest price.' At the turn of the cen-

tury custom-made pianos were in fashion. Piano number 100,000 with its elaborate carvings was built in 1903 for the White House, and that year Steinway's Royal customers included the Kings of England, Saxony, Sweden and Norway, Hungary and Italy, the Emperors of Germany, Austria and Russia, and the Queen of Spain. Steinway pianos became known as 'the instrument of the immortals'.

'At Steinway we make a small number of pianos for a limited market,' Mr Glazebrook told me. In their 130 years Steinway (now a subsidiary of CBS Inc.) have manufactured half a million pianos. Today they make 5,000 models a year in their factories in New York and Hamburg. Each piano contains no less than 12,000 parts.

Monday–Friday: 9–5.30; Saturday: 9–4.30. Brochures available. Steinway & Sons will deliver, tune, service and renovate pianos anywhere in the UK. They will deliver pianos anywhere in the world.

J. W. WALKER & SONS LIMITED
Brandon
Suffolk IP27 0NF

Thetford (0842) 810296

Pipe-organ tuners and builders to HM The Queen.

This British organ-building firm was founded in 1828 by Joseph William Walker. They can trace their origins through such famous names as George England and Renatus Harris to the illustrious organ builder Thomas Dallam, whose organ case can still be seen in the Chapel of King's College, Cambridge.

Today the company operate under the chairmanship of the founder's great-grandson, Guy Phipps Walker, from their modern purpose-built factory in a sleepy little village in the heart of Suffolk. The work carried out in the workshops today is based on 400 years of tradition and they still use some of the same materials, such as virgin tin and choice timbers, as used in the 16th century by Dallam.

Walker's modern techniques mean that the organs they produce today can withstand the ravages of central heating and the humidity of the tropics. It is this balance between progress and tradition which they say has earned them their reputation for 'artistry and reliability in international organ building today'.

Walker's range of model organs have

The 'New Motor Van'. New York, 1934

been inspired by orders they have received from Chichester Cathedral, the Royal College of Music in London, St Matthaus Kirche in Berlin and the chapel of Gonville and Caius College at Cambridge University. Their standard English organ – 'the musician's instrument' – occupies pride of place in Walker's mechanical action range. They also make the Box organ which made its first appearance in 1981, the Continuo organ for chamber concertos, a range of Positif organs and the Study organ for the serious student who 'is not willing to compromise his technique on electronic devices'.

Monday–Friday: 9–5. Walker organs are available through J. W. Walker & Sons at the above address. Call them to make an appointment or for their leaflet 'Introduction to Walker Organs'.

WATKINS & WATSON LIMITED
Westminster Road
Wareham
Dorset BH20 4SP

Wareham (092 95) 6311

Organ-blower manufacturers to HM The Queen.

Watkins & Watson were started in 1870 and have held their Royal Warrant successively since they were first granted one by George V. Today their warrant is held to The Queen for supplying fanboxes to the Private Chapel at Windsor and the Queen's Chapel designed by Inigo Jones in 1623–7, situated in Marlborough Road facing St James's Palace. Watkins & Watson also provided the fans which supply air to the pipes in organs in, among others, the Royal Festival Hall, the Royal Albert Hall, Westminster Abbey and the Royal College of Music.

The company call themselves 'designers and manufacturers of air movement equip-

ment, centrifugal fans and blowers, air blast cooling and ventilation systems, pipe-organ blowers and humidifiers'. The small group of manufacturing companies which make up Watkins & Watson are involved in industrial and medical applications for their fans as well as the warrant-holding organ-blowing equipment which only accounts for 10 per cent of their business.

Fitting organ-blowing equipment can be both lengthy and costly. Although some church fans can be provided from the company's standard range, a cathedral or concert hall will require a unique cooling system which can take up to a year to make and cost up to £20,000 – though it should last for at least 50 years.

Monday–Friday: 9–5.30. Watkins & Watson offer product repair and aftersales service.

Photography

KODAK LIMITED
Kodak House
Station Road
Hemel Hempstead
Hertfordshire

Manufacturers of photographic supplies to HM The Queen.

George Eastman, the man who developed the first Kodak camera, set out in 1877 to make the world 'picture conscious'. His object was to simplify photography so that the 'world and his wife could photograph the children with no more difficulty than pressing a button'.

George Eastman had discovered what a cumbersome chore photography was when he had begun planning a holiday in the Caribbean. A friend had suggested he should take along a photographic outfit to record his travels. Mr Eastman discovered that the 'outfit' was really a cartload of equipment. He abandoned his trip and began studying photography at night while working as a bank clerk during the day. Before long he read about a new kind of photographic plate (the dry plate) which had appeared in Europe and England and eliminated most of the paraphernalia needed for photography. By 1879 he had made his own dry plate as well as a machine to manufacture them. A year later he had set up in business in Rochester in America selling dry plates. Nine years later the first Kodak camera was introduced. The name

was chosen by Mr Eastman because he liked the letter 'K' and wanted a word which would begin and end with it.

The first Kodak advertisements used the slogan 'You press the button. We do the rest', which was coined by Mr Eastman. The Kodak name was one of the first to sparkle from the new electric advertising signs at that time in London's Trafalgar Square. The Kodak camera was followed in 1900 by the Brownie, a box camera which George Eastman developed specifically for children. In 1912 Mr Eastman's ambition to have a laboratory devoted exclusively to photographic research was realised when the Kodak Research Laboratories were built at Kodak Park on the outskirts of Rochester. Today the company operate research laboratories around the world.

Kodak photographic supplies are available from photographic retailers, chemists and department stores.

WALLACE HEATON LIMITED
127 New Bond Street
London W1A 1AF

(01) 629 7511

Suppliers of photographic equipment to HM The Queen, HM The Queen Mother, HRH The Duke of Edinburgh and HRH The Prince of Wales.

Most of the Royal family are keen photographers. The Queen is frequently photographed holding her Rollei 35 or her Leica M3 at sporting events and on her foreign tours, and a Wallace Heaton photograph wallet can sometimes be spotted on Her Majesty's desk. Prince Andrew, the most recent member of the Royal family to establish himself as a photographer, had an exhibition of ten of his photographs of views from the windows of Buckingham Palace, Balmoral and Windsor Castle in November 1983 at an elegant gallery in London's Mayfair. His photographs were not for sale.

In the back of the shop in Bond Street, Mr Maxwell, an ex-photographer and today director of Wallace Heaton, welcomes visits from the Royal family or other well-known customers. He calls it a 'quiet oasis in the middle of London' where customers can drop by to discuss their photographic queries.

Since Wallace Heaton were established, over 140 years ago, they have become the place both professional and amateur

The 14-year-old Princess Elizabeth in the music room of Windsor Castle practising the piano

photographers turn to. Many of their customers have been with them for over 50 years – and some of their staff too. Their attitude is, 'If it's the best we've got it', and Wallace Heaton stock the latest equipment in the field of televisions and computers, binoculars and microscopes, darkroom equipment and, of course, anything for the camera. 'We get a lot of very wealthy people who like things that are new and unusual – a bit out of the ordinary,' Mr Maxwell told me. Wallace Heaton were the first in London to sell such novelties as talking calculators.

Until 1972, when Wallace Heaton were bought by Dixons, the company used to publish *The Wallace Heaton Blue Book* – 'the photographer's bible'. It took the staff four months to write and included articles on photography and reviews of photographic equipment available. Although they no longer produce this they still have a camera repair service and a printing service where they will copy old photographs and documents, including confidential ones, and make poster prints (20″×30″) of a colour photograph for £9.95. They also continue their retouching service which The Queen Mother used recently for a photograph on one of her Christmas cards. It was a photograph of The Queen Mother smiling. But she was standing in front of a large crowd of people. It was no problem for Wallace Heaton's retouchers. Before long The Queen Mother was standing alone in front of a cloudy sky, still smiling.

Monday–Friday: 9–6; Saturday: 9–5.
Wallace Heaton can develop and print your photographs in their own darkroom.

No picnic would be complete without a Thermos flask

Picnics

THERMOS LIMITED
Ongar Road
Brentwood
Essex

Manufacturers of vacuum vessels to HM The Queen.

The name of Thermos is today synonymous with the vacuum vessels they manufacture. They have been making containers for keeping hot things hot and cold things cold since the turn of this century.

The method of using a vacuum to store liquids at hot and cold temperatures was devised in 1892 by a Scottish scientist, Sir James Dewar, for the purpose of storing chemicals at a low temperature. His apparatus involved two glass bottles sealed one inside the other with the air pumped out from between the two. Sir James had to go to Germany to find a glass-blowing expert who could make his first glass vacuum bottles. At first they were only used in laboratories, but in 1898 they became available to the public under the name of the Dewar Vessel. They were extremely fragile and broke easily.

Sir James had never patented the idea, preferring to donate it to science, but his German glass-blower, Reinhold Burger, was quick to recognise the marketing potential of such a product and in 1903 patented the idea himself. He changed the outer glass construction to a metal casing and added a drop of mercury between the outer and inner casing which condensed and formed a mirror surface on the glass, giving the flask better insulation. A newspaper competition was run to find a name for the product and the winner was Thermos, derived from the Greek word *therme* ('heat'). In 1907 a group of British businessmen secured the patent rights for the British Empire, South America and a host of other countries. They registered Thermos as a trademark and formed the company Thermos Ltd. The first metal flasks as we know them were introduced to the Edwardian gentlefolk as the 'finest trouble savers ever known'. Early advertisements urged them to use the flasks for 'the bachelor's tea and shaving water' – hopefully in different flasks. But the ultimate advertisement was a poster featuring a St Bernard dog and a Thermos flask with the caption 'Necessary equipment for life-saving'.

The familiar bottle shape has changed little since it was first manufactured. The 1920s brought the art deco flasks of thermolite (an early synthetic used to imitate onyx and alabaster), the Motoring flask – available in colours to 'match the upholstery of the coachwork' – and the classic corrugated model which came with a gold- rather than silver-coloured glass interior and was sold for half a crown. The war brought utility flasks which were standard issue for the Home Guard and bomber pilots. For The Queen's coronation, Thermos supplied the Royal party with vacuum jugs for use in Westminster Abbey and the public with flasks coloured souvenir gold and depicting Royal profiles. In the 1950s plastic was used for the first time instead of metal. Today flasks are a combination of both metal and plastic. The Thermos flask

received its ultimate refinement in the 1970s when the cup was given a handle.

Thermos were awarded their first warrant from George VI in 1946. Today the company hold their warrant to The Queen. Royal Thermos flasks can today occasionally be seen peeping out from inside the picnic bag in the back of the car when the Royal family are attending sporting events.

Thermos vacuum vessels are available from supermarkets, camping equipment stores and department stores.

CROSS PAPERWARE LIMITED
PO Box 3
High Street South
Dunstable
Bedfordshire LU6 3HX

Manufacturers of disposable tableware to HM The Queen.

Cross Paperware produce everything the would-be-party-giver might need. Their colourful range of paper and plastic tableware is varied to suit any occasion from the grandest garden party to the family barbecue – which The Queen has been known to enjoy when staying at Balmoral. And the advantage of their throwaway table settings is that no one gets left with the washing-up afterwards.

The company set up their first factory in North London in 1891 and moved to their present site in Dunstable at the turn of the century. Today they are part of the British Printing and Communication Corporation. Cross Paperware received their Royal Warrant in 1975 and now hold it for all their products which include paper napkins, doilies and cake cases as well as plates and cups. They also produce plastic cutlery, drinking straws and tablecloths and an extra-strong paper dinner set which can conveniently be put in the microwave.

Cross Paperware products are available from stationery stores, supermarkets and department stores.

Reading and writing

BEROL LIMITED
Oldmedow Road
King's Lynn
Norfolk PE30 4JR

Manufacturers of Venus pencils to HM The Queen.

Berol describe their Venus pencils as 'truly top quality, capable of the subtlest expression and control, and made from the finest materials'. Most of us would describe them as hexagonal shaped with a dark green 'crackle' finish and 'Berol Venus' stamped in gold down the side. They are available in a choice of 14 degrees, from 6B (extra soft and black) to 6H (very hard). Their HB (hard and black) pencil is also made with an eraser tip.

Berol pencils are 'graphite pencils'. 'The lead pencil is completely misnamed,' they told me. It is however a clue to the origin of the pencil. The ancient Greeks and Egyptians used lead for writing and ruling guidelines. They developed a thin rod of lead which became known as a lead pencil.

The first deposit of graphite (pure black carbon) was found in Cumbria in 1546. Initially shepherds used the graphite for marking sheep but graphite soon replaced lead for marking and writing. But the only pure graphite ever found was that first deposit in Cumbria and the substance became so popular that armed guards were needed to carry it to London for the use of the English Guild of Pencil Makers who at that time had a world monopoly on the sale of pencils. In 1795 when war had cut France off from both the English and German sources of pencil supply, and from graphite, Napoleon commissioned one of his officers to try to make supplies go further. The officer made a mixture of graphite and clay and fired it in a kiln. He not only produced an excellent writing instrument but had also found a method of grading pencils from hard to soft simply by altering the amounts of clay used.

Today Berol, using the same ingredients, can produce over 59,000 pencils an hour. Their pencils are made in 17 different degrees of hardness. Berol Ltd are a subsidiary company of Berol Corporation in Connecticut in the States. The company also make pens and markers, paints and painting equipment, papers and leisure products.

Berol Venus pencils are available from stationers, art supply stores and department stores.

HATCHARDS LIMITED
187/8 Piccadilly
London W1V 9DA

(01) 439 9921

Booksellers to HM The Queen, HM The Queen Mother, HRH The Duke of Edinburgh and HRH The Prince of Wales.

The only thing wrong with Hatchards is that it doesn't open on Saturday afternoons. Otherwise, in the view of many, it is a bookshop on a grand scale. This certainly seems to be the view of the Royal family. It's the only London booksellers to be granted a Royal Warrant, let alone all four.

Thomas Joy, the managing director for 20 years and Member of the Royal Victorian Order since 1979, is regarded by many as the doyen of British booksellers. Surrounded by photographs of Royalty and one of him being kissed by Twiggy, he told me how to run a successful bookshop: 'First, you must understand books; secondly, you must have staff that understand books and finally, you must stock them.'

When John Hatchard opened his shop in July 1797 at the age of 29, he did so with a capital of £5. On his death, 52 years later, Hatchards' annual turnover was half a million pounds. Hatchards' haven't looked back. They recently extended their premises so they now have 10,000 square feet of selling space, with a stock of everything from 'the book of the day' to a selection of rare books.

Monday–Friday: 9–5.30; Saturday: 9–1. Several mail order catalogues available throughout the year.

The exterior of the shop: 187/8 Piccadilly

Below:
The Queen being introduced by Mr Joy to Philip Ziegler, Salman Rushdie, James Herriot, Gordon Honeycombe and Catherine Gaskin at an Authors of the Year party, 1982

MAGGS BROTHERS LIMITED
50 Berkeley Square
London W1X 6EL

(01) 493 7160

Purveyors of rare books and manuscripts to HM The Queen.

Even though Maggs Bros is often 'overcrowded with millionaires', according to John Maggs, the fourth generation of the family in the business, it is the soft-sell

A book plate dating from 1855 when Uriah Maggs first started trading as a bookseller

technique that these antiquarian booksellers employ. 'One never talks about investment in books. What one does is tell you how lovely the book is.' No other approach would seem fitting in the elegant Georgian house overlooking Berkeley Square.

The large ground floor of the house looks and feels like a library in a private home. Large wooden desks are covered with books and old well-used typewriters, the marble fireplace is decorated with marble inlay patterns, Oriental prints hang from the walls, and glass-fronted bookshelves filled with antique books reach up to the ceiling with wooden library steps placed strategically around the room. With the dimly lit atmosphere all one needs is tea and crumpets and one could spend the rest of one's life delving into Maggs Bros' collection of books.

Every month Maggs send out one of their extensive catalogues to 'the converted' – their previous customers. This feature of the company was started at the turn of the century when specialist catalogues were sent out for featuring the latest books, manuscripts, autograph letters and prints on offer. In catalogue No. 188 issued in 1902 they also had an interesting sideline – coronations seats: 'We still have some seats available to view the Procession. Price on application.'

The company was started in 1853, three years after Uriah Maggs and his father left the village of Midsomer Norton in Somerset to start a new life in the Metropolis. After several failures, Uriah Maggs, who had always been interested in books, decided to take up bookselling and began by selling his own library. He traded first from his home but soon moved to London's

Paddington from where he not only dealt in books but ran a circulation library. In 1938, after a number of moves, the company settled in their present address with the blue plaque above the front door announcing that the house was the former residence of George Canning (Statesman) from 1770 to 1827. In amongst Maggs's collection can be found books from the Great 1611 'He' Bible, for £10,000 to lesser works at £1.00. They also sell autographs from Elizabeth I and Florence Nightingale to Henry VIII and Woodrow Wilson.

Monday–Friday: 9.30–5. Maggs Bros produce 12 or more catalogues a year on specialist subjects, such as 'Continental Miscellany' and 'Autograph Letters and Historical Documents'. Most are free of charge and available from the above address.

JOHN MENZIES PLC
107 Princes Street
Edinburgh EH2 3BA
(and branches)

(031) 226 6214

Booksellers to HM The Queen Mother.

To ignorant Sassenachs the most controversial aspect of John Menzies is how to pronounce the name. The answer is 'MING-ESS', with the stress on the 'MING'. Menzies' own staff are advised to remember this limerick:

There was a young lady called Menzies,
Who asked, 'Do you know what this thenzies?'
Her aunt with a gasp
Replied, 'It's a wasp,
And you're holding the end where the stenzies.'

Prince Charles reading

A Mowbrays staff outing to Day's Lock near Oxford in 1908 to mark the company's 50th anniversary

*Right:
Mowbrays staff despatching parcels of* The Sign *inset in Oxford.* The Sign *was a parish magazine first published by Mowbrays in 1905. The first issue sold over 100,000 copies*

Founded in 1833, the firm have remained in family hands with four generations of John Menzies at the top who have expanded the business from a single shop in Edinburgh, selling books, periodicals and stationery, to a modern nationwide company with about 200 outlets. They also now own two other Royal Warrant holding companies: Frank Smythson (see page 188) and Jones Yarrell, who are the traditional suppliers of newspapers and magazines to the Royal homes, the Royal yacht and the planes of the Queen's Flight.

The advent of the railways and their accompanying station bookstalls furthered the Menzies name. Until the station closed in 1961, the Ballater bookstall at the terminus of the Deeside line served the Royal household at Balmoral. It was the job of the manageress to keep suitable stocks that could entertain the Royal family on their long train trip south.

The heart of John Menzies has remained faithful to Scotland with its headquarters still in central Edinburgh, but the rest of its empire extends throughout the UK flourishing on its legacy of Scottish thrift and acumen.

Monday–Saturday: 9–6; Tuesday: 9.30–6; Thursday: 9–7 (107 Princes Street branch).

A. R. MOWBRAY & COMPANY LIMITED
28 Margaret Street
London W1N 7LB

(01) 580 2812

Suppliers of fine bindings to HM The Queen Mother.

In 1969 Mowbrays were given a new image. The bookshop, until then a place where clergymen had seemed to predominate, became a general bookshop. The Bibles, prayer books and theological titles can still be found in the first-floor gallery of the shop, but the ground floor now caters for the secular public with its selection of cookery, drama and poetry books, new titles and bestsellers. Mowbray also sell bookplates, bookmarks, greetings cards and wrapping paper.

Alfred Richard Mowbray, who founded the company in 1858, was an ardent follower of the Oxford Movement whose purpose was to bring about a Catholic revival in the Church of England. Because of his weak heart he had made plans to move to New Zealand where the climate was better. But when the Reverend Thomas Chamberlain, vicar of St Thomas's in Oxford, suggested that there was a need for a religious bookshop in Oxford, Mr Mowbray decided to stay and start one. The bookshop was opened in Oxford's Cornmarket, for the sale of religious prints, books and cards. In 1867 the company began printing and publishing religious leaflets and tracts including a monthly parish newspaper, *The Gospeller*. Six years later the first Mowbray branch was opened in London but in 1875 Mr Mowbray had a heart attack and died. His widow, Susan, carried on the business, publishing books that she hoped would achieve wider sales than those her husband had published. She succeeded: a communicant's manual, *Helps to Worship*, had by 1972 sold almost three million copies.

The same year A. R. Mowbray were granted their Royal Warrant as suppliers of fine bindings to The Queen Mother. The company still bind books for, mainly, the Church but also anything from a favourite children's book to visitors' books and, for one enthusiast, a complete collection of railway magazines. Book binding may take up to two months. Mowbrays also have a team of calligraphers who will use their skills on book plates, certificates or birthday cards in many different styles of lettering.

Monday–Friday: 9–5.30; Thursday: 9–6.
A. R. Mowbray will deliver round London and mail any book orders within 24 hours to any country in the world. For further information about their fine bindings, contact the above address.

THE PARKER PEN COMPANY LIMITED
PO Box 12
Newhaven
East Sussex BN9 0AZ

Newhaven (0273) 513233

Manufacturers of pens, pencils and inks to HM The Queen.

The surrender of the Argentinian forces on South Georgia was signed by a Parker pen.

Another wrote the agreement to release the American hostages in Iran. Queen Juliana of the Netherlands used a Parker to sign her abdication and since 1962 Her Majesty The Queen has used a Parker pen filled with Parker ink.

Parker say their 'ultimate achievement has been in giving the quality beloved of kings and queens at a price the whole literate world can afford'. Yet in 1983 they introduced the 'ultimate writing instrument', the Premier Collection – a range featuring the world's most precious metals – the most luxurious of which is the handcrafted 18 carat gold fountain pen costing £1,700.

The Parker Pen Company was born almost 100 years ago in the home of an impoverished American schoolteacher in Janesville, Wisconsin. George S. Parker taught at the local school of telegraphy and to supplement his income sold pens for the Holland Foundation Pen Company. Students often brought their broken pens to Mr Parker for him to repair which made him realise how the infant fountain pen could be turned into a reliable writing instrument. He invented the Lucky Curve fountain pen. The pen was 'jointless' – 'no joints to leak, no screw to break and no old-fashioned nozzle'. In 1889 Mr Parker took out his first patent and found he had become a pen manufacturer. The Lucky Curve pen was his company's main product until the 1920s.

In the First World War, Mr Parker designed the Trench pen which provided

A Parker Pen advertisement in 1926

soldiers with a portable ink plant as well as a writing instrument. A 1916 advertisement for the Trench pen read: 'The pen has a little attachment at the end of the fountain opposite the pen point for carrying a supply of ink tablets. Drop a tablet or two into the barrel, fill with water, and the pen is ready to write.' After the war, Parker brought out the high ink capacity Duofold pen, costing $7. Millions were produced. To demonstrate the quality of its products, Parker arranged unique stunts. Pens were dropped from the rim of the Grand Canyon, thrown from aircraft and run over by London buses to prove their durability. In 1933 Parker introduced their Arrow clip design. Mr Parker died in 1937, four years before Parker began manufacturing pens in England.

'A pen is something you write with,' say Parker and they make sure their pens write. Even their ballpen refills are subjected to a 'battery of torture tests'. They are frozen and baked repeatedly to simulate climate changes, vaulted to a 7,000 foot altitude on a pressure chamber and forced to write tens of thousands of figure eights on a test-writing machine to ensure they last.

Parker pens, pencils and ink are available from appointed retailers. The Parker Pen Company also offer an aftersales service and will clean, polish, service or repair your old pen. All Parker writing instruments are guaranteed providing that only genuine Parker refills and inks are used.

FRANK SMYTHSON LIMITED
54 New Bond Street
London W1Y 0DE

(01) 629 8558

Stationers to HM The Queen.

Smythson's consider themselves an authority on the social graces. 'People come here because they know we won't let them do anything wrong,' Thomas Neate, the director of the New Bond Street shop and author of *The Smythson Guide to Social Letter Writing*, told me.

'People come in for the best,' Mr Neste said. In their stationery department, Smythson's still sell their Bond Street Blue paper, formulated by Frank Smythson at the beginning of the century. They also specialise in producing writing paper – they are the only people in London to offer stationery with coloured borders – visiting cards and invitations for the diplomatic corps, which are engraved by their skilled engravers. They have also been known to produce stationery to match the colour of the interior livery of one of the 'top British cars'.

The Smythson Guide to Social Letter Writing recommends having everything printed, from your address at the top of your notepaper to a standard reply on your invitation acceptance cards and your address on the back of your envelopes. All 'in the interest of good style'.

The shop is known as a 'diary publisher's'. Before each New Year the shop stocks over 100 different diaries. They also have a large selection of address books, including one for jet-setters with three sections for London, Paris and New York addresses. Smythson's sell a range of leather items, from polo books and wallets to attaché cases and jewellery boxes. And, of course, a wide choice of pens.

Monday–Friday: 9.15–5.30; Saturday: 9.15–12.30 (except Bank Holiday Saturdays when Smithson's is closed). Brochures are available 'though it helps if customers know our merchandise'. Frank Smythson Ltd will mail worldwide.

TRUSLOVE & HANSON
205 Sloane Street
London SW1X 9LG

(01) 235 2128

Truslove & Hanson are booksellers and Court stationers. They have supplied the Royal household with stationery in the past. Their large shop on two floors, decorated in late 1960s style, carries a wide range of books on all general subjects with particular reference to new titles in fiction, biography, history, current affairs, travel, sports, pastimes and the arts. One of their customers, The Princess of Wales, visited the shop – famed for the individual attention it gives its customers – twice in 1983 and bought a selection of new titles including a biography of Oscar Wilde.

Truslove & Hanson were founded by Mr Truslove and Mr Hanson in 1890 on Oxford Street. In 1872 the Sloane Street branch was opened and, by the time the company were taken over by W. H. Smith, there was another branch in Clifford Street at which Queen Mary and the Princess Royal bought books. By the 1960s the only remaining branch was the Sloane Street shop. Their Court stationery section at the back of the shop still supplies all kinds of printed and engraved stationery, including their Sloane range which comes in eight colours from lime green to plum.

Monday–Friday: 9–5.30; Wednesday: 10–7; Saturday: 10–5. Mail order catalogue available free of charge for books and stationery. Truslove & Hanson mail worldwide.

Relax with the television

DOMESTIC ELECTRIC RENTALS LIMITED
Apex House
Twickenham Road
Feltham
Middlesex TW13 6JQ
(and branches)

Suppliers of television receivers to HM The Queen.

DER, who are one of the major high street television rental shops, have held their Royal Warrant since 1968 although they have been supplying television sets to the Royal household since the late 1950s.

Televisions have progressed rapidly since The Queen's coronation was televised on primitive black and white sets. Today DER's sets range from the portable with an in-built clock radio to the teletext systems which at the flick of an infra-red remote-control switch allow you to view the latest update of the news, the weather forecast and the latest sports results. The company, forever looking ahead, hope soon to offer televisions with built-in burglar alarms to protect the entire house as well as an 'interactive' television which connects to the telephone, allowing you to book your holiday, ask for your bank statement or do the shopping from your television screen.

Domestic Electric Rentals television rentals start from £7.50 per month for a 14 inch colour portable to £50.85 for a 26 inch supersound with teletext and full remote control. Video recorders range from £13.95 monthly to £61.35. Consult the telephone directory for your local supplier.

DYNATRON RADIO LIMITED
Molesey Avenue
West Molesey
Surrey KT8 0RL

Manufacturers of television and radio-gramophones to HM The Queen.

'Every Dynatron audio and colour television cabinet radiates style,' they tell me. Dynatron's televisions and audio products are pieces of furniture, blending traditional craftsmanship with modern technology. Televisions feature finger-touch tuning, cordless remote control and picture tubes

The development of Robert's Radios

which provide hi-brightness daylight viewing. They are housed in cabinets ranging from reproduction Regency to Queen Anne style in mahogany, walnut or a range of teak veneers and many feature an in-built drawer for the video recorder. Their music suites have the appearance of a late Georgian or Regency side-table with pull-out speakers at the side instead of drawers and a mock drawer at the front which provides access to the turntable.

The company were founded in 1927 and since then have installed radio and gramophones in British embassies and consulates around the world. They began making televisions in 1938. Since 1981 Dynatron have been owned by the Roberts Radio Company (see below).

Dynatron televisions and radio-gramophones are available from radio and television outlets, hi-fi shops and department stores.

ROBERTS RADIO COMPANY LIMITED
Molesey Avenue
West Molesey
Surrey KT8 0RL

Radio manufacturers to HM The Queen. Manufacturers and suppliers of radio receivers to HM The Queen Mother.

Roberts' original suitcase-style radios in their leather cases with carrying straps can be spotted in most British films of the 1940s and 50s in scenes of families gathered round the kitchen tables with their Roberts' radios listening to the latest war bulletins or Royal announcements.

When Harry Roberts and Leslie Bidmead formed the Roberts Radio Company in 1932, their aim was to produce hand-made radios which would justify the title of 'the finest of all portables'. During the Second World War they made various radio equipment for the armed services and in 1956 received their first Royal Warrant from The Queen. Today Roberts make a range of radios in teak cabinets as well as their original-style portables with wooden and leather finishes which have been revamped to meet the modern market. Their stereo and radio cassette recorders can be found on street corners blasting out disco sounds for street dance groups.

Roberts radios are available from radio and television stockists, hi-fi shops and department stores.

Riding

BRIDLEWAYS MANUFACTURING LIMITED
Smithbrook Kilns
Rural Craft Centre
Nr Cranleigh
Surrey GU6 8JJ
Cranleigh (0483) 276145

Saddlers and harness makers to HM The Queen.

'Like all crafts, making saddles is an art,' David Boot, the managing director of Bridleways, told me. His saddles are custom-built to the requirements of his clients. Bridleways are one of the few firms still making sidesaddles which are according to Mr Boot, 'becoming popular again with young ladies'. A hand-stitched sidesaddle takes 10 days for the saddler and his apprentice to make, with its 12 stages of construction. An astride saddle is cheaper and simpler to make. There are seven stages which will take about three days to complete as only one man works on each saddle. A sidesaddle starts from £800 and an astride saddle from £300.

Bridleways were started in 1980 by David Boot, who had apprenticed as a saddle and harness maker. The company were awarded their Royal Warrant three years later. They are a small firm, with two apprentices and three craftsmen including Mr Les Coker, who has been making saddles for over 60 years and who made saddles for George VI. Today his saddles are sold to 'famous people and VIPs both in England and abroad'. Bridleways' harnesses are made by the whole group rather than by an individual. A single set of harnesses for gig horses costs from £900 and a team set for four horses starts at £3,500 and takes four weeks to make.

In their shop, Bridleways carry a basic range of riding outfits, including jodhpurs, jackets and boots, and they can have riding habits for sidesaddle enthusiasts specially made.

Monday–Friday: 9–5. To order a saddle or harness visit Bridleways and discuss your requirements.

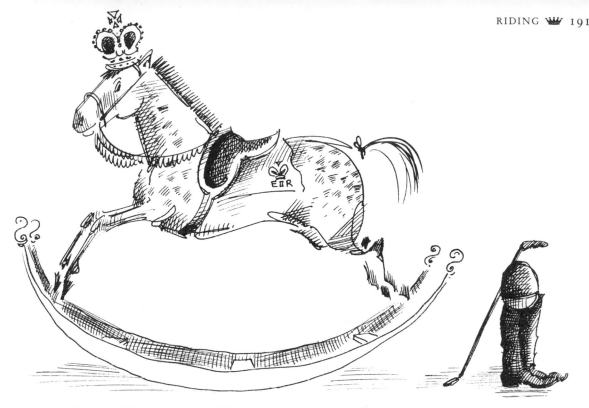

GIBSON SADDLERS LIMITED
Sales
Paddock Lane
Newmarket
Suffolk

Newmarket (0638) 662330

Suppliers of racing colours to HM The Queen and HM The Queen Mother.

The Queen and The Queen Mother first registered their racing colours in 1949 after they had jointly bought the steeplechaser Monaveen. Since then The Queen Mother's colours comprising of a pale blue shirt with buff stripes and pale blue sleeves and a black cap with a gold tassel have been worn by many winning jockeys riding the horses she owns today. The Queen – whose colours are purple with gold braid for the body of the jacket, scarlet for the sleeves and a black velvet cap with a gold fringe – is currently one of the country's most knowledgeable horse breeders. Winston Churchill once confided to his private secretary that he spent his time during his weekly visit to Buckingham Palace talking with The Queen about racing.

The Royal family's racing silks are today made by Gibson Saddlers, a company based in the heart of racing country at Newmarket, regarded by some to have one of the best racecourses in the world. From their shop, which sells everything from saddles to horse bandages and is situated next to a paddock, they put together thousands of permutations of colours for racehorse owners. The task is usually pre-empted by a consultation with Benson & Hedges (see page 138) who keep details to ensure no two people have the same colour combinations. All the silk comes from London, and a racing set, made up by a team of six on site, can cost between £60 and £125 depending on the amount of work and the trimmings chosen.

Monday–Friday: 9–5.30; Saturday: 9–12.

W. & H. GIDDEN LIMITED
15d Clifford Street
London W1X 1RF

(01) 734 2788

Saddlers to HM The Queen.

One of W. & H. Gidden's recent assignments was making harnesses for the mules who were going to carry video equipment for a BBC film crew working in Afghanistan. The harnesses were so successful, the BBC sold them to the tribesmen on leaving.

Giddens are the last firm still making saddles in central London. 'We make them on the old principle of one man to one

Overleaf:
The Queen Mother, then Queen Elizabeth, holding a harness made by Champion & Wilton (today part of W. & H. Gidden) in 1943. She is followed by the two Princesses and King George VI on their bicycles

saddle,' Michael Gidden, the present director, told me. At their workshops in the East End their 20 staff can do 'anything with leather'. 'Our saddles last too long,' Mr Gidden said. The average saddle hand-made by Giddens can survive for up to 40 years. The company produce up to 10 saddles a week which start from £295 each. Giddens are also the sole British importers for Stübben saddles, starting at £390. And the shop will part-exchange your old saddle for a new one. They recently part-exchanged a 1959 saddle, in good condition, for £150. 'When the owner had bought it from us,' Mr Gidden told me, 'the saddle had cost only £44.'

The company started in 1804 in Oxford Street as a leather tanner and curriers and soon began making harnesses and saddles. Today their three-storey corner shop appeals to everyone from the adolescent girl rider to foreign governments and Royal households. 'We're not in an image trade, it's very informal,' Mr Gidden said. Clearly riders enjoy delving around the cheerful shop, poking their heads into the many nooks and crannies and chatting to the young assistants who are all horse-mad and prepared to try to find anything for their customers. When I visited the shop one of them was ringing round for a rich client who wanted to buy six Arab ponies.

Monday –Friday: 9–5.15; Saturday: 10–1. Mail order catalogue available. W. & H. Gidden will mail worldwide.

MATTHEW HARVEY & COMPANY LIMITED
**PO Box 38
Bath Street
Walsall
West Midlands WS1 3BY**

Bitmakers to HM The Queen.

Matthew Harvey & Co. aren't exactly sure which member of the Royal family uses their bits but one of many horseshoes and bits they replated after the Royal wedding in 1981 was presented to them as a memento of the occasion.

Matthew Harvey make stainless-steel, rubber, vulcanite, nickel and nickel-plated riding hardware. Their wide range of bits includes snaffles, bradoons, gag bits, Liverpool and Buxton bits, Weymouths, racking and Sundry bits. They also make spurs and stirrups, curbs and hooks. Over the years, Matthew Harvey say they have probably made just about every variation of a bit and in their pattern room, next to their steel and nickel foundries, they have literally thousands of moulds from which any bit can be manufactured.

The company were started in 1838 to produce saddlery hardware, and in particular bits, spurs and stirrups. Since then buckles, hoof picks, boot pulls and terrets have been added to the range. All the products are manufactured at their Bath Street premises and the company claim to be the only British company left making stainless-steel riding hardware from start to finish.

Matthew Harvey & Co., with their staff of 100, also manufacture commercial vehicle fittings for ambulances and buses and also produce fittings for vintage cars. This part of their business is an offshoot from their carriage fittings, such as rein rails and shaft tips, which they still make.

Matthew Harvey & Co. were awarded their Royal Warrant in 1976.

Matthew Harvey & Co. bits are available from your saddler. If you require a bit not in stock ask your saddler to contact Matthew Harvey. They can make any bit to suit your requirements.

KEITH LUXFORD (SADDLERY) LIMITED
57/59 High Street
Teddington
Middlesex TW11 8HA
(and a branch in Esher, Surrey)

(01) 977 4964

Saddlers, horse clothiers and harness makers to HM The Queen. Saddlers and horse clothiers to HRH The Prince of Wales.

Keith Luxford's blue and white check day-rugs and quarter-sheets cover the horses in the Royal Mews stables. The check material used is angora serge – very rarely seen today – and if more rugs were to be required by the Royal Mews new supplies of cloth would have to be specially woven. Day-rugs are Keith Luxford's speciality – costing approximately £50 each – and Mr Luxford, the managing director, personally cuts each rug himself. Trained in window display when he left school, Mr Luxford is convinced that his flair for colour and design stems from this early training. 'You used to only be able to buy navy, green, fawn and grey rugs. We now sell 10 colours, including royal blue and

purple.' But even with his flamboyant taste, Keith Luxford drew the line when they were asked to make rainbow coloured rugs. 'We had to say no.' Keith Luxford will design and incorporate into his rugs exclusive logos and monograms for the sponsors in the equestrian world.

Mr Luxford is a keen rider and used to own a stables. 'I judge horses and can talk to head coachmen and stud grooms in a practical 'horsey' language they will understand.' He often makes special harnesses for problem horses and he is always on call to 'troubleshoot' at Royal events and processions in case of breakages and urgent repairs.

Mr Luxford carries an enormous selection of saddlery, perhaps more than 200 in stock, including polo, dressage and sidesaddles, most of which are produced in their own workshops.

Monday–Saturday: 9–5.30 (Teddington shop). Keith Luxford Ltd have a mail order catalogue and will mail worldwide.

J. SALTER & SON
23 High Street
Aldershot
Hampshire GU11 1BW

Aldershot (0252) 20692

Manufacturers of polo sticks to HRH The Prince of Wales.

The Royal polo stick maker, Raymond Stanley Turner, began working for J. Salter & Son, sports outfitters, in 1942. 'I started there when I was 14 at the bottom, bottom bottom,' Mr Turner told me. 'Today I am the proprietor and one of the few bosses who still wears an apron.'

Polo players, including Prince Charles, who was introduced to Mr Turner by former customers The Duke of Edinburgh and Lord Mountbatten, come to J. Salter & Son from around the world for their sticks. One of the first invitations Prince Charles, a keen polo player, extended to Lady Diana Spencer was to watch him play polo on a weekend in July 1980. He took her to see him play with his team Les Diables Bleus at Cowdray Park in Sussex, one of the few surviving polo clubs in England.

Mr Turner and an assistant make all the sticks by hand, with each stick taking an hour and a half to make. The cane used for the sticks comes from the Far East and Mr Salter works on it, doing 'as many things to it as a cook might do to a pound of flour'. He still uses natural woodworking glues,

and most of the sticks are made to customers' requirements. 'The characteristics of the person is what's important.' Mr Turner mentally records each of his customer's likes and dislikes. The best sticks are made 'when you've got the right sort of material for the right person at the right time'. He was once asked by Moss Bros if they could stock his sticks, but he refused. It is impossible to supply them in great quantities. A polo stick from J. Salter & Son starts at under £20.

Mr Turner works 12 hours a day, also repairing old sticks and making polo balls as well as running the shop with its staff of 10. 'I work with a clear conscience and I work a full day. If anyone can do any better than that, well, good luck to them.'

Monday–Saturday: 9–5.30. J. Salter & Son have a mail order catalogue and will mail around the world, but don't get upset if not everything mentioned in the catalogue is in stock.

Shooting

The Rigby single-barrel flintlock pistol, 1786

HOLLAND & HOLLAND LIMITED
33 Bruton Street
London W1X 8JS

(01) 499 4411

Rifle makers to HRH The Duke of Edinburgh.

Although most of Holland & Holland's customers shop there for reasons of personal preference, many come out of family loyalty and a familiar request is, 'Make me a gun like my father's.' Luckily Holland & Holland keep full records of all the guns they have ever made.

Holland & Holland's shop opened in London over 150 years ago. Shooting then was almost exclusively a pastime for men, but ironically it was Queen Victoria who gave the company the right to call their best guns 'Royal'. Today Holland & Holland have an international shooting clientele who regard their shop as a handy rendezvous, especially if they're on their way to Northwood, Holland & Holland's shoot-

ing ground in Middlesex where shooting lessons cost £23 an hour plus cartridges and clays.

On their two floors you can buy shooting clothes and accessories, from a pair of green stockings to their handmade cartridge bags which start at just over £20. However, their reputation is for guns. As Jeremy Clowes, one of their directors, put it: 'Some of our customers know about guns; but most customers come to us because we know about guns.'

Holland & Holland have an ever-changing selection of second-hand guns both of their own make and other quality English makes which they will alter to your measurements, taking into account your height, length, fullness of face and length of neck. They will also repair your old gun. But the ultimate extravagance must surely be a pair of Holland & Holland's best shotguns. They'll cost you £25,000, but each gun will have taken over a 1,000 man-hours to make. It's said they're worth the three-year wait. But if you're impatient, Holland & Holland will hire you a gun for your weekends – just remember to book it well in advance.

Monday–Friday: 9–5.15. Mail order listing of Holland & Holland's products available on request.

JAMES PURDEY & SONS LIMITED
Audley House
57/8 South Audley Street
London W1Y 6ED

(01) 499 1801

Gun and cartridge makers to HM The Queen and HRH The Prince of Wales and gunmakers to HRH The Duke of Edinburgh.

'The Royal family of England is one of the many families who for six generations – from Queen Victoria to Prince Charles – have been users of Purdey guns and rifles,' say James Purdey & Sons.

Purdey's Long Room which acts as both the board room and the company's showroom has the air of an opulent men's club. The rectangular table in the middle of the room is covered with a red cloth, the walls are filled with portraits of the Purdey family, photographs, etchings and shooting records. The glass cabinets carry the famous Purdey guns and the vaulted ceiling and leather-covered chairs add to the impression of Victorian splendour. Their guns too are splendid. Each gun is built in their London factory to the personal measurements and sporting requirements of their customers, to ensure the gun is an extension of the shooter's arm. A hammerless ejector game gun starts at £11,000 – without the case. Purdey recommended their guns should annually be stripped down and thoroughly overhauled by their own craftsmen.

The elegant corner shop can also 'outfit the sportsman completely in the English style'. They sell a range of clothing and accessories from shooting seats and gun covers to pigeon clays and game books.

Monday–Friday: 9–5. Mail order catalogue available.

JOHN RIGBY & COMPANY (GUNMAKERS) LIMITED
13 Pall Mall
London SW1Y 5LU

(01) 734 7611

Rifle and cartridge makers to HM The Queen.

The firm has had Royal connections almost as long as it has been established. John Rigby & Co. set up as rifle and gunmakers in 1735 in Dublin and one of their early orders was to provide a pair of pistols for 'the last King of America', as David George Locke Marx, the present owner, rather quaintly called George III. In 1865 John Rigby & Co. opened a London branch and 33 years later closed the Dublin premises when John Rigby junior was appointed superintendent of the Royal Small Arms Factory. The company went on to pioneer the modern high velocity nitro express rifle and in 1897 introduced the first .450 calibre cordite rifle. They were awarded their first Royal Warrant by Queen Victoria. Today they hold one to The Queen for providing the rifles used by Her Majesty during the deer-stalking season at Balmoral.

John Rigby & Co. were bought by Mr Marx in 1969 and today can be found in 'a funny little hole under the road' (a basement in Pall Mall). The 'bread-and-butter' part of the business is in selling accessories, which include handmade canvas and leather rifle and gun cases and reconditioned second-hand weapons. But their forte is their stalking and big game rifles and shotguns, made specially for Rigby by ex-directory London workshops. The

guns can cost £12,000 and take up to two years to make. Their warrant-holding rifles can cost around £2,000, with a .416 Big Game magazine rifle selling for £1,600. Rigby sell their proprietary Rigby .275 HV deer stalking ammunition and .416 big game ammunition, 'ideal for really big game such as elephant, kodiak bear and water buffalo', as well as stocking metal cartridges of most makes and calibres.

Monday–Friday: 9.30–5.30. Mail order catalogue is available with helpful information to American customers regarding import regulations. John Rigby & Co. will also re-stock, re-barrel, re-black and clean any rifle or gun.

Sportswear

HEAD SKI–WEAR, LUI E LEI SPORTSWEAR LIMITED
45 Milton Trading Estate
Nr Abingdon
Oxfordshire OX14 4RU

If you want a head start on the ski slopes this year, why not follow the Royals down the piste in copycat ski suits from Head. They dressed The Princess of Wales for her last skiing holiday in a cerise all-in-one ski suit with quilted shoulders and diagonal pockets for £350. She also bought four more of their designs from Harrods (see page 156) – 'in fashionable purples and plums' just to ring the changes.

But while The Princess of Wales leads the world as a trendsetter, her husband does not appear to be so fashion conscious. 'He has a navy zip-together suit made out of high stretch lycra fabric. You can buy a similar one for £270. It's the perfect suit for the person who is interested in skiing as it allows total body movement,' said Robert Bright, the managing director of Lui e Lei. But he added, 'He seems to have had it for ever.'

Head are an American-owned company but their European operation is controlled from Munich. Clothes are imported by Lui e Lei – their sole distributors in the UK. Head see themselves as the innovators of the sportswear industry. 'We were the first to make zip-together suits, use stretch fabrics and the first to use leather. We treat sportswear as if it were a high fashion business.' They use only the best materials, specially treated leather, silks and cottons. They also charge the best prices, from £150

to £1,500 for a white calf leather suit, waterproofed of course.

Their clothes are worn throughout the world by foreign Royal families as well as film stars and professional skiers, including Irene Epple, one of the top three women skiers in the world. But Head have never moved heavily into the area of sponsorship. 'We sell the finest quality clothing and that is what the customer pays for, not for exorbitant fees to sports personalities.'

Head also make a range of tennis and golf, yachting and leisure wear as well as matching accessories to complete the total look, from sweaters to leg warmers, gloves, hats and bags.

Head clothing is available from 'serious ski shops' and major department stores and sports shops.

LILLYWHITES LIMITED
Piccadilly Circus
London SW1Y 4QF

(01) 930 3181

Outfitters to HM The Queen.

Lillywhites have been making history since the late 1800s. They designed the aviation suit worn by Amy Johnson on her solo flight to Australia. They made the first pair of shorts worn at Wimbledon and they financed the first cricket Test Match.

The firm was founded by James Lillywhite, a keen cricketer, who opened a retail sports shop in London's Haymarket in 1863. It was an opportune moment for such a venture. Increasing affluence and leisure time meant there was more interest in sport. The game of croquet was new to Britain and badminton had only just been invented. People were becoming interested in athletics, and soccer and rugby were popular. By 1925 when they moved to their present site in Piccadilly Circus, Lillywhites were already catering for 34 sports.

In 1940 Lillywhites went to war. They supplied the first paratroop boots and string vests and were contracted to supply clothing for the Admiralty and officers of the women's service. When ski equipment was needed by the 5th Battalion Scots Guards and the 51st Highland Division for a ski corps to assist the Finns on border patrol against the Russians, Lillywhites sent two of their company directors along as technical experts.

The company received their first Royal Warrant as shoemakers to George VI. In

1955 they were granted their Royal Warrant as outfitters to The Queen, and Lillywhites Edinburgh were appointed bowmakers to the Royal Company of Archers, Her Majesty's bodyguard for Scotland. Today Lillywhites design outfits for the Royal Air Force aerobatic team and since 1960 have been making the costumes of the British team for the parade at the Winter Olympics.

Their shop in Piccadilly has trained experts who can give advice to newcomers on any sport. They claim to supply everything for sport and leisure and if you want something which is not in stock, they say they can get it for you. Lillywhites are a member of the Trusthouse Forte Group of Companies and the largest single sports goods retailer in the UK.

Monday, Wednesday and Friday: 9.30–6; Tuesday: 9.45–6; Thursday: 9.30–7; Saturday: 9.30–5.30. Lillywhites mail order catalogue is on sale at the shop, price £1.00, or can be mailed on request.

NORDICA
Via Montebelluna 15/A
31040 Trevignano
Treviso
Italy

The Princess of Wales chose a pair of white Nordica ski boots to complement her ski suit when she went skiing in Lichtenstein with Prince Charles in January 1984. The boots were made to the shell design – a process of laminating plastic over leather for better durability – which was first in-

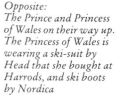

Opposite:
The Prince and Princess of Wales on their way up. The Princess of Wales is wearing a ski-suit by Head that she bought at Harrods, and ski boots by Nordica

troduced to the skiing world by Nordica in 1967. The boots also had buckles – another Nordica innovation earlier in 1962.

Nordica began as a company making leather boots and shoes over 60 years ago in Italy. As the popularity of Alpine skiing increased, the Nordica factory expanded and by the late 1960s they were making over 500,000 pairs of ski boots a year. Today they claim to hold the number one position in world sales. Their boots are worn by Tamara McKinney, winner of both the women's world cup overall and the world cup giant slalom titles. In 1983 the company produced a collection of six boots, including the unisex Trident boot which has a unique forefoot air system allowing air through the front of the boot while still keeping it insulated from the cold. Prices start at £40 to £109 for competition boots.

Nordica Boots are available at sports shops and department stores.

GEORGE SMITH & COMPANY
Bridge Street
Ballater
Aberdeenshire
Scotland
Ballater (0338) 55432

Sporting outfitters to HM The Queen, HM The Queen Mother and HRH The Prince of Wales.

The outside of George Smith's tiny shop on the main street of Ballater is laden with Royal crests. Since the shop was opened by Mr Smith's grandfather in 1870 it has received much Royal attention, being awarded its first warrant by Queen Victoria in 1884, and its most recent by The Prince of Wales 97 years later.

The shop is located only a few miles from Balmoral and caters mainly for tourists, especially those who have arrived ill equipped for their holiday in Deeside. Tourism in the area is seasonal. In the winter the few who arrive come to ski and, even though George Smith's stock is much reduced, they can always buy a warm jumper or jacket from him. In the spring the fishing season starts and with it the influx of tourists who have brought with them the wrong tackle for the local fishing. Mr Smith will sell them the necessary equipment and mend their broken rods. The summer season brings campers to the area who may buy a rucksack or a dog lead, and after the Glorious Twelfth the season

Swaine & Adeney at 185 Piccadilly in 1880

will be open for shooting sticks and cartridge belts.

'I'm open seven days a week, and sometimes 24 hours a day.'

SWAINE ADENEY BRIGG & SONS LTD
185 Piccadilly
London W1V 0HA

(01) 734 4277

Whip and glove makers to HM The Queen, umbrella makers to HM The Queen Mother.

Swaine Adeney's visiting book is filled with comments like 'a great store for a man'. As Robert Adeney, the chairman, put it: 'We have everything the conservative man requires, for work and for play. The City man can buy his umbrellas, his gloves, wallet, shoes and ties here and the country man his picnic baskets, shot guns, saddles and wellington boots.' Yet the Royal Warrants held today are for the female members of the Royal family.

Swaine Adeney Brigg have been trading in Piccadilly since 1750 and have held a Royal Warrant since they were first granted one by George III as whip makers. In his office Robert Adeney proudly displays a photograph of The Duke of Edinburgh with his holly driving whip, A similar one would cost you from £120 – Mr Adeney cut the holly himself.

Monday–Friday: 9–5.30; Saturday: 9–4.30. Mail order catalogue available and Swaine Adeney will mail worldwide. As one of their famous customers, Don Everley said, 'A dream come true.'

Tennis

EN-TOUT-CAS LIMITED
See page 52.

Theatre

KEITH PROWSE & COMPANY LIMITED
Second Floor
Banda House
Cambridge Grove
London W6 0LE
(and branches)

(01) 741 9999

Theatre ticket agents to HM The Queen Mother.

The name Keith Prowse suggests a company started in the 1960s by an ex-ticket-tout, but Keith, Prowse & Co. – as the company was then called – was founded in 1780 by a Mr Keith and a Mr Prowse. Keith Prowse now claim the title of the world's largest theatre ticket agency 'by a long way' according to Mr Burns, their managing director.

Keith Prowse can supply tickets for everything except Glyndebourne. They have over 40 different shops and outlets including one in Harrods and one in the City. Tickets can be ordered and paid for over the phone, providing you have a credit card, and they will be posted to you.

Keith Prowse have held their warrant for many years and have firmly established a place for themselves in London theatre society. They hold between 10 and 25 per cent of the seats at all London theatres daily. They even hold four seats in every major London theatre on every day of the week in case the Royal family want to go to the theatre. Keith Prowse also cater for sporting events. They are the official ticket agents for Royal Ascot, the Derby and the FA Cup Final at Wembley. But tickets for Wimbledon – unless you live abroad – can be slightly more difficult. If you book through Keith Prowse you'll have to pay for lunch in the marquee as well.

Telephone the above number for ticket reservations, or visit your local Keith Prowse agency.

Travel

Luggage

JOHN BARTHOLEMEW & SON LIMITED
12 Duncan Street
Edinburgh EH9 1TA
Scotland
Edinburgh (031) 667 9341
Suppliers of maps to HM The Queen.

Bartholemew's building in Duncan Street has a noble façade. Its Grecian columns and pediment reach up to the Edinburgh skyline, while below in the narrow street it gives the impression of some Athenian temple reconstructed in an overgrown suburb of Piraeus. Through the front door you step on the tessellated floor where the mosaic-style cracks have been multiplied as a memento to the heavy burden of paper stocks which it bore when *The Times Atlas* was being prepared there in 1922. A great globe confronts you ahead, hanging in chains and housed in a classical rotunda; above that runs a fragment of Ciceronian dialogue which translated reads: *'How fortunate is he who, engaged in trivial affairs, can keep in mind the vastness of the whole world.'*

Bartholemew's maps make sure you do keep the vastness of the world in mind even down to the minutest detail. Anyone who has ever used a map for any part of Britain may well have used a Bartholemew half-inch, with its dark blue corners and red lettering above which is the Royal coat of arms. Today a glance round their foyer shows a cartographical parade. There are maps of the world and pocket atlases, a football history map, the clan map of Scotland, a children's map of London and even the wanderings of Bonnie Prince Charlie reproduced on an up-to-date map.

The company was founded by John Bartholemew in the 1820s. He began engraving copper plates for street maps and guide books. John Bartholemew was one of the first to take the mystique out of cartography. In 1840 he was producing atlases for study in the classroom and

students could be found flicking through the pages of maps in the public library as they would a captivating thriller book. But it was John Bartholemew's son, John junior, who took cartography into new fields in 1870 when he introduced layer colouring. He used delicate tints of greens and browns for the plains and foothills, shading to a darker brown for the highlands with a touch of white for the Matterhorn. He extended the system to include the seas. It was easy to see the overall terrain at a glance.

The maps of his father's day had been given artistically coloured outline and boundary lines but the body of the map was traditionally blank except for the lettering. When John Bartholemew junior's maps were put on show at the Paris Exhibition in 1878, cartographers from all over the world were aghast, convinced they would be out of a job the next day because map reading had suddenly become extremely simple. In 1882 John Bartholemew, under the instructions of Robert Louis Stevenson, produced the ever-memorable map of Treasure Island for the frontispiece of the book which finally launched the author on his path of success. By 1888 geography had ceased to be the study of the exclusive academic élite and by the time Edward VII came to the throne in 1901 the Bartholemew atlases were showing the world distribution of malarial regions, the incidence of child mortality and a pictorial survey of flora and fauna through the year.

Bartholemew's received their Royal Warrant to George V, but they lost it in 1962 when their grantee died, and they didn't receive it again until 1974.

On a visit to the premises today you would find a member of staff studying the newspaper all day. Their job is to read every line of *The Times* and make out an index card and reference for any news item which may effect cartography in the near future. Bartholemew's maps, compiled from satellite photographs and computerised information, are constantly changing so that they are always up to date.

Monday–Friday: 8.45–4.45. Bartholemew maps are available from the above address and also from newsagents and booksellers. Mail order catalogue available.

J. & J. CASH LIMITED
Kingfield Road
Coventry
Warwickshire CV1 4DU

Coventry (0203) 555222

Manufacturers of woven name tapes to HM The Queen.

Cash's woven name tapes have been used by 'generations of parents (including the Royal family) for marking their children's clothes'. Their name tapes, now in a choice of five different type styles and four different colours, have been seen in the backs of shirts, on the tops of socks and down the sides of towels of British schoolchildren from when Cash began manufacturing them at the start of this century.

Coventry has been a wool town since the Middle Ages. When the Huguenots later settled there, they brought with them silk weaving skills for which the city then became known. In 1846 two brothers, both silk merchants, John and Joseph Cash, opened a weaving factory in Coventry, using jacquard looms to weave silk ribbons for their fashion-conscious Victorian clientele. At the turn of the century Cash's began to weave labels for manufacturers to identify their own products. Their name tape industry had begun.

Today Cash's create miles of ribbon, millions of individually woven name tapes, bright red personalised luggage straps and silk gifts, from pincushions and perfume sachets to 'love cushions' and spectacle cases, which they export round the world.

J. & J. Cash's woven name tapes are available mail order from the above address.

LINGUAPHONE INSTITUTE
209 Regent Street
London W1R 8AU

(01) 734 7572

Publishers of recorded language courses to HRH The Duke of Edinburgh.

Whether it is Finnish or French, Polish or Portuguese, Spanish or Serbo-Croat, American English or just plain English you want to learn, you could take a lesson from

Opposite: Linguaphone in action

The Duke of Edinburgh and learn it the Linguaphone way. Since 1966 the company has held the Royal Warrant to Prince Philip as publishers of recorded language courses for their 28 different languages offered.

The Linguaphone system was invented in the early 1920s, in the days of the gramophone, by Jacques Roston, who managed the business until his death in 1947. Since then over four million people have learnt a language with the Linguaphone method of 'listening, understanding, then speaking'. The language is mastered by listening to conversations designed to 'unconsciously make you pick up the essentials of grammar and syntax'. Linguaphone also provide books to study with their recorded courses, intended to help you read and write the language you are learning. They claim that 'The average student spending half an hour to an hour a day should work through the complete course in several months.' A course costs £135 and a recently introduced system of learning by video is available for the French language – though you can't study that way on your way to work.

Monday–Friday: 9–5.30. Mail order catalogue available in 101 countries.

MAYFAIR TRUNKS LIMITED
3 Shepherd Street
London W1Y 7LD

(01) 499 2620

Suppliers of luggage to HM The Queen and HM The Queen Mother.

It is hardly surprising to discover that The Queen, as the most travelled monarch in British history, has her own luggage suppliers. In 1978 Mayfair Trunks were awarded their Royal Warrant from The Queen Mother, and a year later they received one from The Queen.

Mayfair Trunks, as the name suggests, used to make their own trunks, but those days are gone. Mr Crawley the owner told me: 'Everything today is mass produced.' To remind him of the good old days, Mr Crawley keeps a small selection of antique crocodile-skin and white leather cases in his office which he lends out to film crews.

Opened in 1912, Mayfair Trunks is one of the oldest shops in Shepherd Street, just off Shepherd Market. The premises itself are on one floor and packed with suitcases and trunks, one nesting inside the other, from floor to ceiling. There are cases for

every taste and every occasion in canvas, vinyl, aluminium and leather – with or without wheels. If you can't make up your mind, Mr Crawley will give you his advice on the most suitable case for you. And, if you like, he will sell you an umbrella, notecase, wallet and the essential luggage-tag too. Mayfair Trunks also still supply some handmade leather briefcases and executive cases which start at £100.

The main breakages in suitcases are in the handles, which they'll repair from £8. As Mayfair Trunks are able to mend most suitcases in about a week, the service they offer is perfect for the fly-in, fly-out business executive. Claridges, the Connaught, the Hilton and the Savoy all send their guests' luggage there to be repaired.

Monday–Friday: 9–5; Saturday: 9–1.

PAPWORTH INDUSTRIES
Papworth Everard
Cambridge
Cambridgeshire CB3 8RG

Travel goods makers to HM The Queen and trunk and cabinetmakers to HM The Queen Mother.

The Papworth Village Settlement was founded in 1916 by Dr (later Sir) Pendrill Varrier Jones. The village was set up as a rehabilitation scheme for TB patients and their families to provide them with a complete work (Papworth Industries) and home environment. The first Royal visitor to the Papworth factories and workshops two years after they opened was Queen Mary. Her Majesty was so impressed by the scheme that she immediately donated

£1,000 which enabled them to buy the Papworth Home Farm with its 200 acre holding. Queen Mary later took to calling on Dr Varrier Jones unannounced, telling him she wanted to look at the place 'as it really is'.

Papworth Travel Goods, the division which now holds Royal Warrants to both The Queen and The Queen Mother, was established shortly after the First World War. Skilled craftsmen were employed by the company to pass on their expertise to the disabled war veterans who were to be employed by the division. The industry was soon at the forefront in the manufacture of hand-crafted leather cases. During the Second World War their skills were redirected to produce Admiralty suitcases and a variety of leather and canvas articles for the armed forces. In the 1950s Papworth were asked to design and produce a

special range of wardrobe trunks and cases for the Royal family. Papworth told me: 'Our luggage is designed and built to last a lifetime', with the result that today they are more likely to repair Royal trunks damaged on foreign trips than resupply the Royal household with luggage.

Papworth still use only the best of top-grain hides for their luggage, but the style of luggage has changed considerably since they first began. It has developed from large and heavy steamer trunks to today's lightweight leather carry-on flight cases. In 1983 The Duke of Edinburgh presented the Design Council's Award to Papworth for their soft luggage designed by the Japanese designer Yuki.

Papworth Village still continues to provide homes and employment for the disabled as well as those who have had heart surgery at Papworth Hospital, now famous for heart transplants. The village, together with its newer sister village Enham in Hampshire, employs a workforce of nearly 1,000 people, of whom over half are disabled.

Papworth luggage ranges from £40 to £250 and is available from luggage retailers and department stores.

Motor cars and mopeds

EDWARDES (CAMBERWELL) LIMITED
221/3/5 Camberwell Road
London SE5 0HG

(01) 703 3676

Suppliers of mopeds to HM The Queen.

Edwardes have been supplying the orderlies at Buckingham Palace with mopeds for nipping in and out of the London traffic on various errands for the past 15 years. They also recently delivered four bicycles up to Sandringham for use by the Royal family over the New Year period.

At their shop in South London, founded in 1908 by the present Mr Edwardes's grandfather, they sell both Raleigh and Hercules bicycles, as well as their own models. At any one time they have over 800 bicycles on show and another 3,000 carefully tucked away in the storeroom. They also sell all the bicycle accessories you could want from fluorescent ankle bands to puncture repair kits. Their most popular moped model – for those who are past bicycles – is the little Honda model at £300.

Edwardes also sell motorbikes for anything up to £4,000.

Monday–Friday: 8.30–5.30. Closed on Thursdays. Edwardes can service mopeds.

FORD MOTOR COMPANY LIMITED
Eagle Way
Brentwood
Essex

Motor vehicle manufacturers to HM The Queen, HM The Queen Mother and HRH The Prince of Wales.

Ford have held a Royal Warrant since 1945 but now they have three to their credit for supplying motor vehicles, mainly cars, to the Royal family. There are a selection of Ford Escorts in the Royal Mews for everyday use. For while the Daimler might be fine for grand occasions even a princess might find it a bit ostentatious just for popping down to the shop. The Princess of Wales has a Ford Escort and Prince Charles a Ford Granada.

The original Ford car was built by Henry Ford in America in 1896 and the first two Model A Fords arrived in England seven years later. By 1924 the now-famous site at Dagenham was producing 500 cars a day. Today that figure has doubled and there are 15 other Ford plants in the UK making a range of models from the small Fiesta at about £3,500 to the luxurious Granada 2.8i Ghia X automatic at £13,000.

With Royalty and VIPs such as the Archbishops of Canterbury and York as well as diplomats on their list, Ford are experts at 'stretching' their cars to make them longer. They just chop one in half and add the extra inches to the middle. Sounds simple? It actually takes 100 men and women between 8–10 weeks to make the 17 foot, seven-seater Windsor.

Ford motor vehicles are available from Ford dealers throughout the world.

JAGUAR CARS LIMITED
Browns Lane
Allesley
Coventry
Warwickshire CV5 9DR

Manufacturers of Daimler and Jaguar cars to HM The Queen Mother.

Prince Charles has recently been flying the

flag for Britain by driving one of the country's most prestigious cars – a luxurious Jaguar Sovereign HE. The dark blue saloon with its light grey interior was delivered direct from Jaguar's Coventry factory to Buckingham Palace in March 1984. The Prince, who also drives a sporty Aston Martin, ordered the new Jaguar in 1983.

Jaguar cars, fondly known as 'big cats', are the 'chosen transport of many of the world's most successful people – individuals who wish to travel swiftly and in style', say Jaguar. Among them are Prime Minister Margaret Thatcher and the miners' leader Arthur Scargill. Britain's police force have Jaguar saloons for high-speed motorway use, and a converted Jaguar once used by a fire fighting team in an attempt to break the world land speed record today holds the record as the world's fastest fire engine.

Prince Charles's patronage of the Jaguar firm has rekindled some Royal links from the past, for the firm also supply Daimler cars which until 1948 – when Prince Philip ordered a Rolls-Royce (see page 209) – had held pride of place as the number one state car in the Royal Mews. Edward VII, when Prince of Wales, bought a Daimler as the first ever Royal car in 1900 – the year of Gottlieb Daimler's death and 30 years after Mr Daimler had invented the Daimler engine. The Royal Daimler was used for the first time on a public occasion in 1904.

The Jaguar company was established as the Swallow Sidecar Company from a small workshop in Blackpool in 1922. The

Above:
An Aston Martin DB6 Mk 2 Volante model as owned by The Prince of Wales

The Jaguar Sovereign HE as purchased by the Prince of Wales in March 1984

founders, William Walmsley and William Lyons, began by producing cigar-shaped motorcycle sidecars. After nine years of experiments the first complete motor car was launched by the company in 1931, known as the SS1. In 1934 SS Cars Ltd was born but during the Second World War when the initials 'SS' were hardly likely to sell anything at all, the name was dropped in favour of Jaguar – which had already been used to describe a series of SS cars. The Daimler company was bought by Jaguar in 1960 and today their luxury limousines and saloons alongside Jaguar's saloons and racing cars run the gamut of British automobile engineering.

Daimler and Jaguar cars are available from appointed Daimler and Jaguar dealers.

LEYLAND VEHICLES LIMITED
Lancaster House
Leyland
Preston PR5 1SN

Manufacturers of commercial vehicles to HM The Queen.

In her bachelor-girl days at Coleherne Court, Lady Diana Spencer found her little red Leyland Mini Metro handy for dodging the press. Today she doesn't have to make such daring escapes but she still owns a Leyland car. The Princess of Wales has a custom-made apple green Mini reported to have been given to her by Prince Charles for her 21st birthday, complete with folding roof and enough space in the back for carrycot and Nanny Barnes.

Leyland hold their warrant for supplying vehicles to The Queen, which in the last 20 years alone has included trucks for the Royal estates as well as a horsebox for Princess Anne based on a Leyland Boxer. They used to supply their agricultural tractors to the Royal estates as well, but these are no longer in production.

The company have been making vehicles since the early 1900s. They are now the world's leading suppliers of double-decker buses and the largest suppliers of public transport, selling in over 140 countries throughout the world. They have their own commercial plants in places as far afield as Madras, Nigeria and Turkey.

Leyland trucks have been used to help build a maternity hospital in Tanzania and build and maintain the most complex motorway systems in Europe. And when Khalfan Human Al Adawy wanted to

move the mountains surrounding Muscat, he bought a Leyland Landtrain – a specially designed truck to operate in almost any type of terrain.

At their head office in Leyland, the town from which they took their name, they are continually researching new designs. Their new purpose-built test track with 3.9 miles of roads, hills and high-speed circuits allows them to test their vehicles to maximum speed.

Leyland vehicles are available through Leyland dealers.

ROLLS-ROYCE MOTORS LIMITED
Pym's Lane
Crewe
Cheshire CW1 3PL

Motor car manufacturers to HM The Queen.

'Whether you call it charisma, mystique, aura or simply presence, a Rolls-Royce is required to show its quality of breeding in its appearance.' Rolls-Royce continue: 'Our cars are designed to stand out in a crowd. To inspire admiration and wonder in all who see them. More like a piece of fine art than a car, really.'

There are five Rolls-Royces in the Royal Mews at Buckingham Palace. The first one was ordered by Prince Philip in 1948, who broke over 40 years of tradition with Daimler, since 1904 the suppliers of state cars. The first Rolls-Royce, the Phantom IV, was delivered to Clarence House, then the residence of Princess Elizabeth and Prince Philip, in 1950. But it wasn't until 1952 that the Rolls was officially upgraded to number one state car. After the coronation it was sent to the coachbuilders Hooper & Co. to be painted Royal claret – a shade of maroon so dark it almost looks black – and to have the number plates removed. Rolls-Royce's later model, the Phantom Landaulette, was bought by The Queen in 1954. Two years later Her Majesty had it (and three Rolls-Royce engineers) shipped to Nigeria for her tour of the country. Two of the other Rolls's in the Royal Mews are Phantom Vs, dating back to the early 1960s. In 1978 the latest addition, the Jubilee Rolls Phantom VI, arrived. It is the 'largest, most stately and most exclusive' model of the Rolls-Royce range, measuring 19 ft 10 in and weighing 2½ tons. Designed by Rolls-Royce es-

pecially for state occasions, it has an electrically operated hood and an elevating rear seat which can be raised four inches for Royal processions. All the state Rolls-Royces are large enough to seat seven passengers comfortably and have plenty of scope for luxury fittings such as a colour television, video recorder, radio telephone and cocktail cabinet. The latter was declined by The Queen in favour of a stereo tape recorder on which she can play her favourite military band music.

'The interiors of a Rolls-Royce should be relaxing and cheerful, to make travelling an enjoyable experience, not a tiresome chore,' say Rolls-Royce. Each of their cars is air-conditioned, the seats are covered with Connolly hide, the facia panels and doors are veneered with Burr walnut and the floors are covered with Wilton carpets (see page 12).

The Rolls-Royce company was started by Frederick Henry Royce, a miller's son, and Charles Stewart Rolls, third son of the Baron of Llangattock. In the late 1800s Mr Royce was working as an electrical and mechanical engineer and Mr Rolls was a motor dealer who was so dismayed by the amount of noise and vibration he was getting from his own car that he designed the Royce 10 hp. Mr Royce and Mr Rolls set up in business together in 1904 to produce 'motor cars of exemplary quality'. In 1911, they introduced the Spirit of Ecstasy mascot – popularly known as the 'flying lady' – after they became dismayed at the variety of mascots from black cats to toy policemen which people were putting on their radiators. Rolls-Royce commissioned a designer, Charles Sykes, to design a mascot which would convey the spirit of the

The solid silver mascot of St George and the Dragon was designed for The Queen by Edward Seago before Her Majesty's Accession

car. He made them 'a little graceful goddess who has selected road travel as her supreme delight'. But the 'flying lady' is always removed from whichever Rolls-Royce The Queen is travelling in and replaced by a solid silver mascot of St George and the Dragon, designed for her by Edward Seago.

The 'personal fingerprint' of a Rolls-Royce is the traditional front grille, jealously guarded throughout the world by patent and copyright restrictions. Each grille is handmade by a team of a dozen craftsmen and although they all look identical, no two grilles are ever the same. A Rolls-Royce limousine takes about nine months to make, and a Landaulette, 'a little longer'. The cars range in price from £55,240 for a Silver Spirit to £83,122 for the Camargue Saloon. That's just for the basic model – one of the most expensive cars in the world. Rolls-Royce run a school of instruction to teach chauffeurs how to handle a Rolls. After all, they say: 'It's not just a car – it's an investment.'

Rolls-Royce cars are available through appointed Rolls-Royce dealers.

VAUXHALL MOTORS LIMITED
PO Box 3
Luton
Bedfordshire LU2 0SY

Luton (0582) 21122

Motor vehicle manufacturers to HM The Queen.

The first motor car to bear the Vauxhall name appeared in 1903. It was produced by a London-based engineering company which had been founded by Alexander Wilson in 1857. But the Vauxhall name dates back to the 13th century. It was derived from an adventurous French mercenary by the name of Fulkes de Brealte of the court of King John. The soldier was hired to do some of the dirtier deeds of the unpopular King. For his many unsavoury services, Fulkes was made Sheriff of Oxford and Hertford and granted the Manor of Luton. He was also an ambitious social climber who married one of the foremost ladies of the time, the widow Margaret de Redvers. Gradually the couple's house on the south bank of the Thames became known as Fulkes Hall, later Fawkes Hall, Foxhall and ultimately Vauxhall. Along his climb up the social ladder Fulkes had been allowed to have his own coat of arms for which he chose the emblem of the Griffin, a

mythical creature – half eagle and half lion. When Alexander Wilson set up his engineering company at the Vauxhall ironworks he decided to take the Griffin as his company badge. The badge is now used on all Vauxhall cars.

At first Mr Wilson's main products were marine engines used in the tugs on the River Thames as well as in donkey pumps, cranes and other engineering lines. In the 1890s the company made their first petrol engine which was used for the Jabberwock river launches. The single cylinder engine was thought to be the basis for the first car engine.

In 1905 the Vauxhall company moved their business to Luton which brought the Griffin back to the town where Fulkes had been granted his manor. Five years later the company produced a C-type sports model – 'the first true sports car from Britain' – called the Prince Henry after the 1910 Prince Henry Trials in Germany, where the car proved to be totally reliable at over 70 mph on the long rugged trial.

During the First World War the Vauxhall factory had built 25 hp staff cars for the British Army but during the Second World War they began making Bedford trucks. Over a quarter of a million were produced during the six years of the war, but the distinctive square-nosed military trucks which streamed off the production lines at that time have since been replaced by more sophisticated flat-faced Bedfords like the pollution-free electric Bedford van kept at the Royal Mews, which Prince Philip uses for short journeys into town. Vauxhall produced their millionth Vauxhall Viva car in 1971, but production of that model ceased in 1979. Today their most popular cars are the Chevette and the Cavalier.

Vauxhall motor vehicles are available from appointed Vauxhall dealers.

Vehicle hire

GODFREY DAVIS EUROPCAR LIMITED chauffeur drive: **Davis House Wilton Road London SW1V 1LA** (and branches)

(01) 834 6701

self-drive:
**Bushey House
High Street
Bushey
Watford WD2 1RE
(and branches)**

(01) 950 5050

Motor vehicle hirers to HM The Queen.

Who would have thought that the Royal family would need to hire a car? One of the more suprising warrant holders is Godfrey Davis Europcar who were awarded their Royal Warrant in 1983. It's taken them 61 years since the company was founded in 1922 by, of course, Mr Godfrey Davis, who offered Talbot Darracqs for hire – with chauffeur if required. Now the company has 260 rental locations in Britain plus, via their membership of the Europcar International system, the ability to offer their customers car rental at over 2,600 offices in 104 countries throughout the world. Thoughtfully, they put a map in each car, so that globetrotters can always find their way back to the nearest Godfrey Davis outlet.

Although during the war car hire was classified as an 'essential service', Godfrey Davis being engaged in providing transport for London's anti-aircraft defences, today car hire is considered a luxury. Prices for hiring a car start from £13.50 per day plus 15p per mile, but for those who prefer driving a Jaguar XJ6 or similar, prices can escalate up to £65 with 45p a mile after the first 50 miles.

You might on the odd occasion need to make use of another Godfrey Davis service – their chauffeur drive cars. These are available in central London, at Heathrow and Gatwick airports and in 20 key cities around the country. A direct transfer from Heathrow to the West End or the City will only set you back £25 if you choose a Granada saloon, though the Rolls costs double. To negotiate the traffic and get you to your appointments on time are a team of experienced and deferential chauffeurs, who are 'almost certainly' members of the Institute of Advanced Motorists, complete with grey uniforms and peaked caps.

Godfrey Davis offer special rates for theatre outings, weddings, Royal garden parties and investitures – you never know when that might be worth knowing.

See telephone directory for your local Godfrey Davis Europcar branch or contact one of the above addresses.

**W. L. SLEIGH LIMITED
99 Shandwick Place
Edinburgh EH2 4SD
Scotland**

Edinburgh (031) 226 3080

Motor vehicle hirers to HM The Queen, HM The Queen Mother and HRH The Prince of Wales.

A Canadian couple liked the chauffeur Mr Sleigh provided for them so much they asked him to give them an eight-week tour of Scotland, which they repeated the following year. 'The Scots are by tradition a warm-hearted and generous people,' Mr Sleigh says. 'Our chauffeurs, all highly trained, take a pride in their local knowledge which they are only too willing to impart to our clients.' His cars, complete with their chauffeurs in smart navy blue uniforms and peaked caps, can be hired for a short trip from the airport to your hotel or for a long tour of the Central Highlands.

One of the most difficult tasks Mr Sleigh has undertaken, since he started his company in 1974, was transporting all the Commonwealth heads of state to a conference at Gleneagles Hotel in South Perthshire. His team of six luxury limousines (Daimlers) and five saloon cars (Ford Granadas) was not large enough, and they had to use coaches. W. L. Sleigh will cater for both business and holiday itineraries, making hotel bookings and providing foreign-speaking guides if necessary. To hire one of their chauffeur-driven luxury limousines costs £95 per day for approximately 100 miles or eight hours' travelling, and the same trip in the saloon car will cost £75 per day. However, to travel in style from Waverley station to Holyroodhouse is only £11.

Mr Sleigh was awarded his Royal Warrant from The Queen in 1973, from the Queen Mother in 1978 and from Prince Charles in 1980.

Monday–Friday: 9–5.30; Saturday: 9.30–11.30. Brochure available.

In Her Majesty's Service

Banking

COUTTS & COMPANY
440 Strand
London WC2R 0QS
(and branches)

(01) 379 6262

Coutts & Co.'s greatest claim to fame is that The Queen and most of the Royal family bank there and have done so for generations. Coutts, now wholly owned by National Westminster Bank, can also boast of being one of the oldest surviving banks in London and the first to open outside the City of London.

John Campbell of Lundie, formerly an apprentice to an Edinburgh goldsmith, left Scotland and in 1692 set up as a goldsmith banker at 'the sign of the Three Crowns in the Strand'. He adopted the sign for his seal, adding his initials to the three crowns.

Coutts' first important customer was the Prince of Wales, later George II, who visited them in 1716 and bought a set of dressing plate including 'a shaving bason', a 'chocolate pott' and a 'shugar pott'. However, this was an isolated incident and it was not until the reign of George III that Coutts & Co. held the Royal accounts. Coutts suppose that the Privy Purse accounts may have been opened with the bank on the advice of John, 3rd Earl of Bute, a tutor of George III, whose parents had banked with Coutts. From then to the present day, every succeeding sovereign has maintained an account with Coutts. When George III opened his account, Thomas Coutts was a partner in the bank. Another partner at the time was Edmund Antrobus, from Congleton in Cheshire, a young bill broker, whose company is still flourishing as stockbrokers under the name of James Capel & Co., with Her Majesty as one of their clients.

That Coutts has an impressive list of customers is hardly surprising. The bank expects a certain amount from their customers that would preclude all but the very wealthy from banking there. 'What we're not is a mass market bank,' say Coutts. 'We want customers who are earning a reasonable salary, say £20,000–£25,000, or have got or are likely to accumulate capital.' And to emphasise the point they provide free banking only if you keep an average of £1,000 in your current account. Coutts may bend their rules if your parents bank with them or you are personally recommended to them by one of their established customers.

Traditions are still maintained. All male members of the permanent staff must wear frock coats and stiff collars and must be clean shaven. There is a ratio of 10 customers to every Coutts clerk and 650 to each bank manager. The bank promises a prompt response to your letters or queries and guarantees that the person who deals with you will remember your name. Customers are given leather covers for their cheque books, and every Coutts statement has itemised cheques. The only tradition Coutts has forsaken is the quill pens that formerly were found on their counters – 'the customers nicked them'.

If you earn over £20,000 a year and would like to open an account with Coutts, contact them at the above address. Brochures available.

Carpet cleaners

JOHN FREDERICK LIMITED
5 The Parade
Holders Hill Road
Mill Hill
London NW7 1LY

(01) 346 2065

Carpet cleaners to The Queen Mother.

Stirling Moss, John Alderton and The Princess of Wales share The Queen Mother's taste when it comes to carpet cleaning.

John Frederick's striking white and royal blue carpet showroom is situated in a modern shopping precinct where the bulk of the rest of their business takes place, selling carpets and making curtains. Mr

Burns recommends that carpets have an annual shampoo or steam clean. His prices start at around £1 a square yard for shampooing and slightly more for steam cleaning.

John Frederick were established in 1928 and received their Royal Warrant in December 1965.

Monday–Friday: 9–5. No mail order catalogue ('We receive most of our work through recommendation').

JET CARPET CLEANERS LIMITED
2/4 High Road
Ickenham
Uxbridge
Middlesex

Ruislip (71) 74985

Carpet cleaners to HM The Queen.

Mr Adams, the founder of Jet Carpet Cleaning, described the company as 'conscientious tradesmen'. Since Jet started in 1971 (they received their Royal Warrant eight years later) their business has expanded greatly. Today they operate within a 30 mile radius of Uxbridge (which includes Windsor Castle), with half of their work domestic and half commercial.

Jet Carpet Cleaning also clean upholstery and will visit your home to give you a quotation. Each of their vans carry 'all methods' of carpet cleaning with them,

from shampoo to steam to dry cleaning, so they can pick the best method to clean each of the carpets in your home, depending on the state of the carpet, the type of carpet and the amount of furniture in the room. Jet Carpet Cleaning recommend your carpets and upholstery should be protected by a spray of Scotchguard – you can buy your own aerosol or ask Jet to do the spraying for you for a minimum cost of £25.

Monday–Friday: 9–1, 2–5; Saturday: 9–1. Jet Carpet Cleaners have a minimum charge of £25 plus VAT for customers in the immediate area and £30 plus VAT for customers further afield, such as in London.

THE PATENT STEAM CARPET CLEANING COMPANY
Furmage Street
London SW18 4DF

(01) 874 4333

Carpet cleaners to HM The Queen.

Are your Aubusson carpets or Persian rugs looking a little the worse for wear? Then you, like the Royal household, need the services of the Patent Steam Carpet Cleaning Company. And if you happen to live with ordinary fitted carpets, don't worry, they will clean those too.

Since 1873 Patent Steam have been cleaning carpets and rugs. Their company actually began the previous year with a

An example of the amount of dust which Patent Steam's process could remove from carpets in the 1890s

failure. The founders of the firm, Sidney Simmonds and Alfred Tullidge, had intended to start a business selling a new type of carpet beating machine to the carpet cleaning trade. Finding no buyers after a year, they gave up and went into carpet beating themselves. As they say, 'If you can't beat 'em, join 'em.'

Patent Steam don't flinch at unusual requests. They have cleaned the carpet in Harold Macmillan's bedroom in Downing Street, a sheepskin-covered Mini for the International Wool Secretariat and a 40 ton carpet in Windsor Castle.

Patent Steam will clean your fitted carpet on site for under £1 a square yard. Their method is intriguing – if slightly worrying. Watch as they pump soapy water over the carpet and then extract the water at very high speed, before the backing of the carpet can get wet. Or let them collect your rugs and clean them at their premises.

Monday–Friday: 9–5. Rugs can be collected anywhere within the London postal district and slightly further afield if required. Price list available upon request.

PILGRIM PAYNE & COMPANY LIMITED
Latimer Place
London W10 6QU

(01) 960 5656

Cleaners of soft furnishings and carpets to HM The Queen.

Mr Sanderson, Pilgrim Payne's managing director, believes the company's expertise lies in their specialisation. Pilgrim Payne only clean and finish soft furnishings, carpets, curtains and upholstery; they won't touch garments. Recently, on being asked to clean a 17th-century tapestry, they consulted the Victoria & Albert Museum's textile conservation department and were advised not to touch that either.

Pilgrim Payne have no standard prices.

Instead they will come to your home, or the Houses of Parliament, or a major hotel, stare at the soiled carpet and shabby upholstery and give a quote for cleaning them. Over 130 years of experience at your doorstep – with no obligation.

Monday–Friday: 8–5.30; Saturday: 8–1. Brochures available.

Cleaners

KLEEN-WAY (BERKSHIRE) COMPANY
8 Brooke Place
Binfield
Bracknell
Berkshire RG12 SJ11

Bracknell (0344) 483804

Chimney sweepers to HM The Queen and HM The Queen Mother.

As is to be expected, the busiest time for chimney sweeps is the Christmas season. Not necessarily in anticipation of Father Christmas's arrival but due to the long, cold winter nights. Between September and February, John Gamble cleans five to seven chimneys a day, charging from £7 a chimney. It's not a job Mr Gamble specially enjoys, so he works fast, taking only an hour per chimney, deriving satisfaction from the clean chimneys he leaves behind him. If Mr Gamble finds a bird's nest in the chimney, that is hard work.

Mr Gamble took over the chimney sweep business in 1977 from his father who had received his warrant 14 years earlier when the Royal household spotted his advertisement in the local paper. Mr Gamble remembers being taken to Windsor Castle to watch his father cleaning the chimneys when he was a little boy. Today he cleans them himself, visiting the castle once a

The inside of the Pilgrim Payne plant

Opposite:
The Chenille Axminster carpet laid on the dais supporting the throne was cleaned in situ by Patent Steam on 24 October 1958 in readiness for the State Opening of Parliament by The Queen

Left:
Patent Steam hand-cleaned the sheepskin-covered Mini used for publicity purposes by the International Wool Secretariat

month. He also cleans the chimneys at the Royal Lodge in Windsor for The Queen Mother. When John Gamble's father was working he used to do 'lower class work', Mr Gamble said. At least today there's one consolation. 'Due to the vogue for real fires, we're now so busy we can pick and choose'. Mr Gamble cleans all the private chimneys himself: 'You can't employ other people – nobody does the job as you would.'

Monday–Friday: 9.30–5.30. Kleen-Way operate only in Bracknell, Ascot and Sunningdale areas.

Edward VIII, The Queen Mother and a host of showbusiness celebrities. And although it may take four men one day to clean the windows at Clarence House, the Mayfair window cleaners are just as happy making the windows of a flat or small house shine. The company were awarded their Royal Warrant in 1959.

Monday–Friday: 8–5. The Mayfair Window Cleaning Company work only in certain areas of London. Telephone them and they will send one of their 10 window cleaners round to your home to give you an estimate before starting work.

MAYFAIR WINDOW CLEANING COMPANY LIMITED
374 Wandsworth Road
London SW8 4TD

(01) 720 6447

Window cleaners to HM The Queen Mother.

The Mayfair Window Cleaning Company have only ever turned down one request. It was when they were asked to clean the windows of an 18th-floor flat with no access to the inside of the flat. The well-known motto 'The customer is always right' in their case means that they often have to risk life and limb cleaning inaccessible and virtually impossible-to-reach windows.

Since the Mayfair Window Cleaning Company started in 1910 they have cleaned windows for The Prince of Wales, later

SECURICOR CLEANING LIMITED
77/83 Vicarage Crescent
London SW11 3JY
(and branches)

(01) 223 2105

Office cleaning contractors to HM The Queen.

The Securicor Group bought Janitorial Services and with it inherited their Royal Warrant 12 years ago. Since then they have made their own contribution to the cleaning business. Every Securicor cleaner employed is subjected to a rigid screening process to ensure that they can be trusted to work in a security sensitive area. It is a similar vetting to the one Securicor have been putting their guards through for years, but never before had it been applied to cleaners.

The Securicor Group was started in 1935

It takes four men one day to clean the windows at Clarence House, The Queen Mother's London residence

by Lord Willingdon and Henry Tiarks who both lived in London's fashionable West End. Inspired by the number of burglaries in their neighbourhood they organised a man to patrol between their two houses when they were away on holiday, and found themselves the envy of the area. The next step was to provide a similar service for others, which they did. They employed 12 elderly gentlemen in uniform to roam the streets of London protecting houses from burglaries. They were described by the Labour MP George Lansbury as symbolising 'the first halting steps down the road to Fascism'.

It was only after the war that Securicor established the company in its present form and began its path to success. Securicor offer a whole gamut of protection services from guarding and patrolling to cash transportation and a worldwide courier service.

Monday–Friday: 9–5 (London branch).
Securicor Cleaning operates for commercial customers around the country.

MESSRS C. PATMAN
1d Arbury Road
Cambridge
Cambridgeshire
Cambridge (0223) 357434
Clock repairer to HM The Queen.

Messrs Patman have been repairing the clocks at Sandringham since they were granted their first Royal Warrant in 1962. The clocks are usually sent down from the estate to the little workshop behind the Patman premises which were opened in 1934. Many of Patman's customers have been coming to the shop since before the war to have their clocks repaired (a general overhaul starts at £5). Patmans do not sell clocks but they do sell and repair watches (from £7.85 for a service). They also sell 'bits and pieces of jewellery'.

Monday–Saturday: 9–1, then 2–5.30.
Closed on Thursday.

Furniture and clock repairers

W. MOIR
41½ Union Street
Aberdeen AB1 1HQ
Scotland

Clock repairer to HM The Queen.

Every July, William Moir packs his bags and takes a fortnight's 'busman's holiday' at Balmoral Castle. His job is to service the 70 clocks which will be needed for the Royal family's summer visit. 'The Royal family are very time conscious,' he told me.

In his workshop high above Aberdeen's main thoroughfare, Mr Moir always has a backlog of clocks and watches to repair. He started repairing clocks over 40 years ago, after an apprenticeship of making clocks – 'I even used to cut wheels.' Today he is so much in demand by his customers that there is always more work to do than there are hours in a day. Mr Moir, who works alone, services all the town clocks in Aberdeen and in his workshop also sells a few watches and straps. Mr Moir charges £6.50 to clean a watch and from £40 to clean and overhaul a grandfather clock. He is prepared to tackle anything except anniversary (400 day) clocks and cuckoo clocks.

Monday–Friday: 8.30–1, then 2–5.30.

ANNA PLOWDEN
190 St Ann's Hill
London SW18

Restorers of fine art objects to HM The Queen.

After studying archaeology at London University, Anna Plowden spent 18 months in Baghdad restoring the Nimrod ivories. On returning to London in 1966, she decided to use her skills commercially. Today, with partner Peter Smith who formerly worked at the British Museum, she runs her business restoring fine art objects. They received their first Royal Warrant from The Queen in 1983.

Anna Plowden is keen to point out the difference between her business and that of an antiques, furniture or picture restorer. 'We restore antiquities and three-dimensional works of art,' she told me. The company will repair the paintwork on organs or tables, but not on pictures; they will mend the inlay work, such as mother-of-pearl, ivory or wood, on chests of drawers – particularly if Oriental. They will also repair the fixtures on furniture, but not reupholster sofas. The firm also specialise in restoring ceramic vases and pots. 'We do works of art that nobody else wants to do. We are not a run-of-the-mill furniture restorers.'

Today Ms Plowden looks after her staff of 25, who include silver and goldsmiths, stone carvers, and master cabinetmakers, and no longer works on any restoration herself. The company's main clients are large auction houses, the National Trust and international museums. They also send staff around the country to work on site on commissions such as the cleaning and restoration of the Birmingham concert organ which is currently in operation. They charge £16 an hour, with a minimum charge of £30. 'We try to discourage the worst of the old brown teapots brigade with our minimum charge.' Most of the work is dealing in small objects which take between two and three weeks to repair, but a lifesize bronze Roman statue could take up to a year. As Ms Plowden says: 'Every object is a different problem. It's also a lot of fun.'

Monday–Friday: 8.30–5.30. Ring Anna Plowden Ltd to make an appointment to visit the workshops. The company will collect and deliver in the London area for £8.

THWAITES & REED LIMITED
Union Road
Croydon
Surrey

(01) 684 0068

Turret clockmakers to HM The Queen.

Thwaites & Reed have been turret clockmakers since 1740 and hold the record as the oldest established clockmakers in the UK. Amongst the many clocks they can call their own in London are the Horse Guards clock in Whitehall and the two clocks at Somerset House. Abroad, their clocks can be seen in Harare (formerly Salisbury) Cathederal, Zimbabwe, and in the Smithsonian Institution at Washington, DC. One of their most recent clocks was made for Fortnum & Mason (see page 236) in 1964 and is the largest clock to be built in this country since Big Ben was constructed in 1861.

Today the demand for large mechanical clocks is almost non-existent. Thwaites & Reed instead use their expertise to make domestic clocks for 'the upper end of the market'. You can buy them in most good jewellers from between £150 and £4,000.

Thwaites & Reed received their Royal Warrant in 1982, though they are now more involved in looking after turret clocks than making new ones. Once a year they visit the clocks at Hampton Court, Kensington Palace, St James's Palace and the Quadrangle at Windsor to carry out whatever repairs are necessary. For the last eight years they have also maintained Big Ben.

Monday–Friday: 8.30–4.30. Call Thwaites & Reed first in case they're all out on an emergency.

Launderers

LILLIMAN & COX LIMITED
34 Bruton Place
London W1X 7AA

(01) 629 4555

Dry cleaners to HM The Queen, HM The Queen Mother and HRH The Prince of Wales.

There has to be something top-drawer about a dry cleaner which differentiates between day dresses and gowns in its ladies' price list.

Lilliman & Cox were founded in 1944 by Sidney Lilliman, a master tailor, and Arthur Cox, a technical expert in the dry-cleaning field. Their aim was to establish a modern dry-cleaning service using the latest machines and solvents. Today their expertise goes hand in hand with their reassuring philosophy that 'your clothes are precious to us too'.

The company specialise in cleaning furs, suede and leather, riding wear (hunting jackets), all types of uniforms, theatrical costumes and 'clothes for the wedding day'. They also dry clean raincoats at a cost of £13 which includes reproofing them. Dry cleaning a chiffon gown costs £21 and sprucing up a headscarf, £4.

The Fortnum & Mason clock took Thwaites & Reed three years to build. Both of the side pavilions have hinged doors which open at every hour and through these appear the four-foot-high figures of Messrs Fortnum & Mason. As the clock begins to chime, the figures move forward, turn towards each other and bow. Once the chimes have ended, they bow again, then turn round and return to their respective pavilions

Monday–Friday: 8.30–5.30. If you live in London, Lilliman & Cox will collect and deliver, and for country dwellers they offer a postal service. Telephone the above number for details, price list is available.

SYCAMORE LAUNDRY & DRY CLEANERS (LEMAN BROTHERS)
4 Old Town
London SW4 0JZ

(01) 622 3333

Launderers and dry cleaners to HM The Queen, HM The Queen Mother and HRH The Duke of Edinburgh. Launderers to HRH The Prince of Wales.

In 1865 Mrs Buckland and her daughter, Eleanor, of Rectory Grove in South London, started taking in washing for the local gentry who lived in the neighbouring large houses. Fifteen years later, Eleanor Buckland married a Mr Leman, a wholesale tobacconist who soon realised the potential of the laundry industry and decided to develop his wife's business instead of his own. He moved Sycamore Laundry to the company's present address in Old Town, a house with a large garden at the back in which the laundry and cleaning works were slowly built.

In 1922 the company introduced dry cleaning, in those days a comparatively recent development. When Mr Leman died in 1926, his sons, Alex and George, took over the business. After the war the company was struggling due to the strains of the war years. Alex and George Leman were also suffering from poor health and both died in the early 1950s. Alex Leman's son-in-law, Tom McBride, a chartered accountant, and George Leman's son, Dennis, continued to run the business. In the early 1970s they were awarded a Royal Warrant from The Queen, The Queen Mother and The Duke of Edinburgh, and their fourth warrant was granted to them by Prince Charles in 1980.

Sycamore Laundry offers not only a laundry and dry-cleaning service but will dye clothes and fabrics. They also have a re-covery service – re-covering eiderdowns and pillows. To clean the inside of a pillow and restuff it with feather and down costs between £3 and £5.

Monday–Friday: 9–1, 2.30–5; Wednesday and Saturday: 9–1. Sycamore Laundry will collect and deliver in central London. Price list available on request.

Miscellaneous

THE ROYAL BRITISH LEGION POPPY FACTORY LIMITED
20 Petersham Road
Richmond
Surrey TW10 6UR

(01) 940 3305

Poppy manufacturers and suppliers to HM The Queen.

The Poppy Factory has been described as a 'truly human war memorial'. It was started after the First World War and owes its origins to the poignant and now famous poem written by Canadian doctor Colonel John McCrae. As he lay in the trenches of Flanders during the second battle of Ypres he was moved by the sight of the bright red poppies which he saw as an eternal mark for the graves of his dead comrades.

In Flanders fields the poppies blow,
Between the crosses, row on row
That mark our place; and in the sky
The larks still bravely singing fly
Scarce heard amid the guns below.

We are the dead. Short days ago
We lived, felt dawn, saw sunset glow,
Loved and were loved, and now we lie
      In Flanders fields.

Take up our quarrel with the foe;
To you from failing hands we throw
The torch; be yours to hold it high,
If ye break faith with us who die
We shall not sleep, though poppies grow
      In Flanders fields.

The poem appeared in *Punch* in 1915 and an American woman, Moina Michael, was so touched by it she took to wearing a poppy as a mark of respect. Later a French colleague of hers conceived the idea of

Major George Howson (centre front) with Factory staff in 'the early days'

manufacturing artificial poppies. In 1921 French poppies were imported by the British Legion, which had been set up by Earl Haig, for their first appeal. The public's generosity resulted in a staggering £106,000, and a ritual was born.

By the second appeal Major George Howson had set up the first British Poppy Factory with a staff of five in London's Old Kent Road. In a letter to his parents at the time he wrote: 'I do not think it can be a great success but it is worth trying.' Today in their present factory in Richmond more than 150 disabled people produce about 45 million poppies a year alongside 250,000 Remembrance crosses and 70,000 wreaths.

The first large wreath was laid on the Cenotaph in Whitehall in 1924 by the Prince of Wales and now eight wreaths are placed there every Remembrance Sunday by members of the Royal family. Each year the Poppy Factory is also responsible for laying out the Field of Remembrance in St Margaret's, Westminster. A standard 17 inch wreath costs £7.50.

Poppies, wreaths and crosses are available from the Poppy Factory, Richmond, or through the Royal British Legion.

Photographers

A. C. COOPER LIMITED
10 Pollen Street
LONDON W1R 9PH

(01) 629 7585

Fine art photographers to HM The Queen.

A. C. COOPER (COLOUR) LIMITED
(address as above)

Fine art colour photographers to HM The Queen.

A. C. Cooper used to operate from the humble address of Rose and Crown Yard until they were bombed out during the war. The company then rose like a phoenix from the ashes to more opulent Bond Street, where they stayed until about 10 years ago when they moved to their present address. Their customers today are mainly auction houses like Bonhams, Christies, Phillips and Sotheby's, as well as art dealers.

Much of their work is for catalogue and book illustrations. A. C. Cooper have also taken the photographs for the catalogues for many of the Royal collections on exhibit at The Queen's Gallery and frequently visit Windsor Castle to photograph the Royal collection. A. C. Cooper also work for the National Trust.

The company were founded in 1918 and received their first Royal Warrant in 1953.

Monday–Friday: 9–5.

TIM GRAHAM
18 Hollycroft Avenue
London NW3 7QL

(01) 435 7693

Tim Graham won the Royal Photographer of the Year title for a photograph he took of Prince Charles and The Princess of Wales on the deck of the Royal yacht *Britannia.* Tim Graham described the scene: 'I was with a lot of other press photographers on the dockside at Gibraltar, waiting for The Prince and Princess of Wales to appear on the deck, when the press officer offered me an alternative. Either I could have a position on the quay, looking up to the rail of the ship, quite close to the couple, or I could get up on the roof of a building some distance away and look down on them. Most of the photographers played safe and opted to stay on the quay but I took the gamble and went up on the roof. I got a full-length shot of Charles and Diana, but because I was looking at them from behind I could see what the photographers on the quay couldn't – that they were holding hands.'

Tim Graham went on his first Royal tour in 1968 photographing Princess Anne when she accompanied The Queen to Austria, and in 1978 he went freelance to concentrate on expanding the library of Royal pictures he had taken over the years. To photograph the Royal family, Tim Graham carries four Nikons around his neck and shoulders. 'One area in which amateurs really slip up when trying to get shots of Royalty is in failing to realise just how long the lenses you use need to be.' It is usually possible to see him at the forefront of any crowd surrounding the Royal family, trying to get the best position.

Tim Graham's photograph of Prince Charles and Lady Diana Spencer taken at Buckingham Palace on the day of their engagement was chosen by the Royal couple as a particular favourite. It was used

for the special Royal engagement postage stamp in 22 Commonwealth countries and also to accompany the Royal Mint commemorative crown. His first official Royal photo session was in 1982 when Mr Graham was invited to Buckingham Palace to photograph Prince Edward for a set of official portraits released to celebrate the Prince's 18th birthday. Tim Graham would rather have chosen a more informal setting, but, he says, 'I was successful in getting the Prince's dog, a labrador called Frances, for inclusion in the outdoor pictures. She's a lovely dog and I thought that besides making the shots more informal she would relax the Prince – and would give us something to talk about during the session.' Prince Charles complimented Mr Graham on the Edward pictures when he was privileged to be the first photographer to take a picture inside Highgrove House – a photograph of Prince Charles to accompany an article in *Woman* magazine. His photographs have been described as among the most relaxed and informal ever taken of the Royal family.

Tim Graham and his wife, Eileen, run a picture library of Mr Graham's photographs. Contact them at the above address for further details.

PETER GRUGEON STUDIO
Yield Hall Lane
Reading
Berkshire

Reading (0734) 51521

Photographers to HM The Queen and HRH The Prince of Wales.

Ms Stockwell, the present holder of the Royal Warrant for the Peter Grugeon Studio, is to this day unsure as to how The Queen came to hear about her former boss, the late Peter Grugeon. Mr Grugeon was one day asked to submit his portfolio to Buckingham Palace with a view to being commissioned to take photographs of the Royal family. The first commission came in 1975 when Mr Grugeon and Ms Stockwell, then his assistant, went to Windsor Castle to take a series of pictures. Some of the shots were informal, while others can today be seen gracing the walls of civic institutions. The photographic team later went to Buckingham Palace for the Jubilee celebrations and in 1978 were granted their Royal Warrant to The Queen. It was followed by another to The Prince of Wales in 1980, the year Peter Grugeon died.

Tim Graham's photographs of the Royal engagement were used on postage stamps in 22 Commonwealth countries

$1·20 ♛ E͆R

Royal Wedding · 29th July 1981
PITCAIRN
ISLANDS

Today the studio are responsible for many of the photographs taken of The Prince of Wales in regimental uniform. Other clients who have followed the Royal family's example are the novelist Barbara Cartland and the Duke and Duchess of Kent.

Monday–Saturday: 9–5.30. All photographic sessions must be booked. Details from the above address.

LICHFIELD STUDIOS
20 Aubrey Walk
London W8 7JG

(01) 727 4468

When Burberrys (see page 70) wanted to show the world the kind of people who wore their products, they were stumped. They were unable to advertise that their customers included Her Majesty The Queen and other members of the Royal family, so their art director decided to use the next best thing: The Queen's cousin, Patrick, the 5th Earl of Lichfield, who having left the Grenadier Guards in 1962 was showing promise in his new career as photographer. 'I remember Patrick saying

at the time that he would have to charge us a stiff fee,' recalls Chris Hudson, Burberry's art director. 'I held my breath and he asked for £135.'

For years Lord Lichfield has taken the photographs for Burberry advertisements, always appearing in them himself, modelling an overcoat or similar Burberry garment, in the presence of an attractive and aristocratic lady. Among the ladies Lord Lichfield used in his photographs were Charlotte Hambro (mother of one of The Princess of Wales's bridesmaids), Lady Carina Frost (David Frost's wife) and his own wife, Lady Leonora Grosvenor, daughter of the late Duke of Westminster, whom Lord Lichfield married in 1975.

By the age of seven Lord Lichfield had 'taken to the camera'. In his five years in the army he immersed himself in the Ilford *Manual of Photography* on off-duty moments. When he left the service he immediately became a photographer, beginning by working as a darkroom technician and soon taking shots in the studio. Lord Lichfield progressed from photographing specimen meat-pies to more interesting subjects including portrait commissions, fashion assignments and advertising photography. Today he travels over 200,000

Patrick Lichfield behind the scenes at the Royal Wedding in 1981. The Princess of Wales is reassuring the youngest bridesmaid, Clementine Hambro, under the watchful eye of her new mother-in-law

The Queen Mother celebrating her 80th birthday with her two daughters. All three are wearing the timeless royal blue satin capelets made especially for the occasion by Hardy Amies. The photograph was taken by Norman Parkinson

miles a year on a variety of assignments. In 1981 Lord Lichfield was chosen to take the official photographs for the Royal wedding. The same year he also published his first two books – *The Most Beautiful Women* and *Lichfield on Photography*.

Lord Lichfield takes portraits on commission. Contact him at the above address.

NORMAN PARKINSON
Tobago
West Indies

Norman Parkinson was sacked from his first job as a society photographer's assistant, but the reference he took with him read: 'It is possible that one day he may take a good photograph; he is a very original man.' The 'good' photographs he has taken since he began 50 years ago include some of the most candid pictures of

the Royal family as well as glamorous shots of the world's superstars.

Norman Parkinson puts himself in the category of 'tradesmen' to the Royal household and although he is one of their favourite photographers he says a picture session with The Queen can still leave him fumbling for words. Like the time he was asked by the Post Office to photograph The Queen and Prince Philip for the Silver Jubilee stamp in 1977. Mr Parkinson finished his 20 minute session with The Duke of Edinburgh and waited 'counting my insistent heartbeats' with his eyes on the door of the White Drawing Room for The Queen to arrive. In the meantime a section of mirrored wall had opened behind him and The Queen had entered carrying a pile of crowns informally placed one on top of the other in an old cardboard box. 'Parks' (as he is affectionately known) was startled by the entrance. He turned to The Queen and nervously said: 'Your Majesty, I would like to introduce . . .' At that point, he recounts, 'I forgot everybody's name

The Royal photographer has shared many intimate moments with the Royal family. He says a weekend at Balmoral 'en famille' is an 'enormous amount of fun'. But as well as his Royal connections, Parks is also regarded, along with Avedon and Penn, as having practically invented fashion photography. He was *Vogue*'s star photographer for over two decades and discovered many of the most celebrated models of the postwar period. Parks has been described as 'wedded to the notion of glamour'. Now in his early 70s, he lives with his wife, Wenda, a former actress, in Tobago in the West Indies.

Norman Parkinson was asked to take the photograph for the 20 pence stamp to commemorate Their Majesties Silver Wedding Anniversary in 1972

including my assistant's and my own.'

Mr Parkinson has taken many of the official Royal birthday photographs, including those of Princess Anne on her 21st birthday and ones of The Queen Mother on many of her birthdays. The most famous of these was for Her Majesty's 80th birthday when Parks thought it 'imperative that this wonderful lady should be photographed with her two daughters'. He proposed the idea and they agreed on a time before lunch one Sunday in June at the Royal Lodge in Windsor. Mr Parkinson 'hazarded a guess that the three ladies would present themselves to my camera in eau-de-nil silk, pink shantung and a polkadot dress'. Parks wanted to take a photograph that would not date. He had three capelets made by Hardy Amies (see page 77) in some royal blue satin that Mr Parkinson had brought back with him from New York. The Queen Mother took to the idea straight away, lifting her string of pearls over the cape and advising The Queen and Princess Margaret where to position their brooches for the best effect. Mr Parkinson recalls: 'I was issuing instructions, trying to get the best picture: "Ma'am, a little this way. Ma'am, come forward two inches. Ma'am, chin up a fraction", when Princess Margaret really put me in my place: "Listen, Parks, it's absolutely no use you Ma'aming us like this, because we haven't the slightest idea who you are referring to. You see, we are all Ma'am".' At which, Mr Parkinson reveals, everyone in the room collapsed with laughter.

LORD SNOWDON
22 Launceston Place
London W8 5RL

(01) 937 1524

One of the first published photographs by Anthony Armstrong Jones was one he took when he was a pupil at Eton. The photograph was of Upper School after the bombing and was criticised by the *Eton Chronicle*, who said: 'This photograph would have been more lively if there had been people in it.'

Heath Robinson, Lord Snowdon imagines, would probably have approved of his room at Eton. 'It was stuffed full of electronic gadgets, flashing lights and wire pulleys. The black-out curtains drew automatically when you opened the door; a system of flashing lights wired to switches under the lino in the passage warned of possible unwanted intruders. When I was ill I made more gadgets. One of them was a walking stick which unscrewed in lots of places and contained a crystal set and torch at the top. While watching games, with an aerial up my sleeve and earthed with the walking stick into the ground, I listened to the Home Service through an earphone attached to my top hat,' he says. As enlargers were expensive during the war, he made one for himself from large tomato soup cans and bits from a scrap-heap.

After Eton, Mr Armstrong Jones went to Jesus College, Cambridge, where he read Natural Sciences for ten days and then changed to architecture. He bought his first camera in 1948 — a secondhand Thornton-Pickard (3½×2½″ single lens reflex) with which he took mainly architectural photographs but some portraits. Three years later Antony Armstrong Jones started his apprenticeship with the photographer Baron for £2.15s.1d per week. At the end of the year his first picture was published in the *Tatler*. He had soon converted an ironmonger's shop in Pimlico into a studio and was becoming a regular contributor to *Sketch* as well as to the *Tatler*. In 1958 Antony Armstrong Jones designed the photographic sets for *Keep Your Hair On*, a show which closed after two weeks. He also designed a collection of ski clothes for women but few people bought them – 'The salesgirls directed everyone's attention to sensible Norwegian sweaters.'

Two months after the release of the official 29th birthday portrait of Princess Margaret taken by Anthony Armstrong Jones, the couple became secretly engaged on a visit to Balmoral. In 1960 they married and Antony Armstrong Jones closed his studio in Pimlico. The next year he was created 1st Earl of Snowdon, Viscount Linley. That year Lord Snowdon also began designing the Aviary for London Zoo and took a job with the Design Council. He was invited to join the *Sunday Times*, mainly to work for their new colour magazine.

In 1969 Lord Snowdon (Constable of Caernarvon Castle since 1963) was in charge of the visual aspects of the investiture of Prince Charles at Caernarvon. Lord Snowdon's marriage to Princess Margaret ended in 1978 but he has continued to take many photographs of the Royal family. One of them was the first photograph to be taken of Prince William with his parents (see page 94).

then sometimes once during their stay. Mr Cassie also tunes pianos for Aberdeen University and the Scottish National Trust. Sadly, Mr Cassie is the last of his family to be a piano tuner. His two sons have opted for engineering.

If you live in or around the Aberdeen area, contact Mr Cassie at the above address.

Printers

LEWIS EAST LIMITED
Midland Envelope Mills
Anstey
Leicester LE7 7DB

Leicester (0533) 362128

Manufacturers of stationery to HM The Queen.

Walter East started a small firm of general stationers at the end of the 19th century selling packets of one pen-holder, one pen nib, 12 sheets of notepaper, six envelopes and a blotter – all for 1d. He sent his teenage son Lewis to London with two heavy suitcases of samples, telling him not to come home to Leicestershire again until he had used up all the samples and got some orders. Lewis was more enterprising than Walter had imagined. He took up selling jewellery, clocks and watches as a sideline and soon after his return home he bought a

Piano tuner

WILLIAM C. CASSIE
35 Leslie Road
Aberdeen
Scotland

Aberdeen (0224) 46594

Pianoforte tuner to HM The Queen.

William Cassie has tuned thousands of pianos since he was 21, in 1930, but although an accomplished violinist, he does not play the piano himself. Today he charges £12 to £15 to tune a piano. For the past 20 years, since he was awarded his Royal Warrant, Mr Cassie has tuned all the pianos at Balmoral – from the Steinway grand (see page 176) to the family uprights. He visits Balmoral annually before the Royal family arrive for the summer and

rusty old envelope-making machine and started his own company – Lewis East.

Lewis East Ltd were granted their first Royal Warrant in 1971. Now they use 500 tons of paper and 20 tons of glue to manufacture 200 million envelopes a year.

Lewis East Ltd deliver direct to their customers 'from multinationals to corner shops – from the Scilly Isles to the Shetland Isles' – sometimes in the back of managing director Frank East's car! They sell to individuals as well, though you have to buy by the box. For orders under £20 a £2 delivery charge is added.

GREENAWAY HARRISON LIMITED
Greenaway House
132 Commercial Street
London E1 6NF
(and branches)

(01) 247 4343

Printers to HM The Queen, HM The Queen Mother and HRH The Duke of Edinburgh.

Greenaway Harrison's longest standing client is the Royal household. The company were awarded their first Royal Warrant by Queen Victoria and have held one ever since. Their work for the Royal family includes the personal Christmas card from Her Majesty which in 1983 was an informal colour photograph of the Royal family on board the Royal yacht. They also were asked by Prince Andrew to print his personal Christmas card.

In the hall of Greenaway Harrison's modern offices and printing plant in London's East End stands an Albion press, an old iron printing press designed by R. W. Cope and used by jobbing printers in the early 19th century – to remind Greenaway Harrison of the days when they were letterpress printers. Daniel Greenaway founded his printing business near the Tower of London in 1853, whereas James Harrison had started his in the middle of the 18th century.

Greenaway Harrison, today owned by Lonrho, specialise mainly in printing annual reports and in financial printing and they work for all the merchant banks. With their highly sophisticated computerised typesetting systems and litho printing presses they specialise in multi-colour work – from brochures to calendars. The company also keep a small number of letterpress machines to carry out operations such as the menus they print for the Royal family to be used on board the Royal yacht *Britannia*. Greenaway Harrison also printed the Order of Service for the Royal wedding in 1981. And they print all the black and white Royal Warrants which are presented to warrant holders when they are awarded their warrant by the Lord Chamberlain.

Monday–Friday: 8–6. Catalogue available on request.

RAPHAEL TUCK & SONS LIMITED
Raphael House
Selbourne Road
Blackpool
Lancashire FY1 3PW

Fine art publishers to HM The Queen.

Raphael Tuck produce Christmas cards for The Queen. They have been honoured with the annual task for every monarch since they received their first Royal Warrant in 1893. The warrant was granted in recognition of Raphael Tuck's successful publication of Queen Victoria's letter to the nation after the death of the Duke of Clarence.

John Harwood, the Royal Warrant holder for Carters Seeds, holding his Royal Warrant to The Queen. The warrant was printed by Greenaway Harrison

In 1866 Raphael Tuck started his printing firm in the City of London specialising in colour lithographs. In 1870 he started producing Christmas cards which became an instant success. The venture won him first prize at an exhibition of Christmas cards in 1879, when one of the judges was Sir John Everett Millais, the Pre-Raphaelite painter. Raphael Tuck's reputation grew and by the early 1920s the company boasted that 'There is scarcely a home throughout the country into which Tuck's cards have not found their way.' They now also produce picture postcards and books.

Raphael Tuck's postcards can be found at newsagents, featuring views of British towns and villages and places of interest. They also record topical events of national and international interest and, not surprisingly, pictures of the Royal family form a very important part of their business. The company's traditional greetings cards include their Anglo-art series as well as their postcards and are all stamped with the company's now famous 'easel and palette' trademark and their inscription, 'The world's art service'. The company is today part of the British Printing and Communication Corporation.

Raphael Tuck's greeting cards and postcards are available from card shops, fine art shops and department stores.

Protection

CHUBB & SONS LOCK AND SAFE COMPANY LIMITED
51 Whitfield Street
London W1P 6AA

(01) 637 2377

Patent lock and safe makers to HM The Queen.

Chubb are rumoured to have first come to the attention of the Royal family when the Prince Regent sat on one of their locks with the key protruding. Since then Chubb have never looked back, though it is probably fair to assume the Prince Regent made a habit of doing so more often. But the incident was obviously soon forgotten for the Prince, when he was later George IV, granted Chubb a special licence (the equivalent of a Royal Warrant) in 1823. The Royal patronage established Chubb as one of the leading locksmiths of the day and in 1828 both the Bank of England and the Duke of Wellington started buying their locks from Chubb. The Duke of Wellington bought four locks and a key for his residence at Apsley House, whose postal address today is No. 1, London. In 1841 Charles Chubb, one of the founders, was appointed lockmaker to Albert, Prince Consort.

Chubb presented this case to Queen Mary to protect the carpet embroidered by Her Majesty when it went from exhibition to exhibition at home and abroad

Charles Chubb and his brother Jeremiah who together started the company had served as apprentices to blacksmiths before they patented their first Detector lock in 1818. Soon afterwards, the brothers opened a factory in Wolverhampton. Although various changes have been made in Chubb's original lock the principle of construction has basically remained unchanged. In 1835 they took out their first patent for a 'burglar-resistant' safe.

By 1896 their reputation as safe makers prompted a letter which read: 'Gentlemen, having a very obstopitals wife I require an iron safe to keep her in. Will you please forward a price for the same.' And in 1904, Charles Rolls of Rolls-Royce (see page 209) said he 'dreamed of having a motor car connected with my name just as Chubb is connected with locks and keys'. But their highest praise came in 1959 from the pen of Herbert Smith, a 'rehabilitated' burglar, known throughout his 35 year career as Yorkshire's Burglar Bill. In a letter to George Chubb, who was then in control of the firm, he confessed that the Chubb mortis deadlock was 'definitely invulnerable to light-fingered gentlemen of my profession – myself included'.

Chubb locks and safes are available from registered Chubb dealers. Details from the above address or consult your telephone directory for your nearest branch.

CHUBB ALARMS LIMITED
42/50 Hersham Road
Walton-on-Thames
Surrey KT12 1RY

Walton-on-Thames (09322) 43851

Installers of intruder alarms to HM The Queen.

After the First World War there was high unemployment and many ex-servicemen began putting some of the techniques they had learnt in the services to criminal use. A steady growth in the number of burglaries aroused public anxiety for the safety of their property. People began making their own crude alarm systems. These consisted of tripwires stretched across the floor just off ground level and fastened to pins which had been hammered into the floor or the skirting board. Piles of tins would be strategically placed next to the wires so they would rattle when the burglar tripped and bells would often be hooked over the doors to ensure a racket. In the 1920s, after a series of robberies in large London stores

culminating in the theft of thousands of pounds of jewellery from Harrods (see page 156), Chubb began to develop a photoelectric burglar alarm. In 1928 they introduced an alarm with an invisible beam which was activated by a body or object cutting through it, and was also light-sensitive.

Chubb Alarms systems vary from the familiar local alarm which offers a complete range of alarm bells designed for use alone or in conjunction with a local police station to the more sophisticated Burgoguard, which can detect attempts by unauthorised people to open a safe, even if they are using keys.

Chubb Alarms will carry out a security survey of your premises without obligation. Details from the above address or consult your telephone directory for your nearest branch.

CHUBB FIRE SECURITY LIMITED
Pyrene House
Sunbury Cross
Sunbury-on-Thames
Middlesex TW16 7AR

Sunbury-on-Thames (76) 85588

Manufacturers of Chubb fire extinguishers to HM The Queen.

Chubb Fire Security is the youngest member of the Chubb Group. It was born in 1967 out of the amalgamation of three major fire security companies, Read & Campbell, Minimax and Pyrene. Between

Queen Victoria and the Prince Consort inspecting the safe Chubb made to protect the Koh-i-noor diamond at the Great Exhibition in 1851. At night a mechanism lowered the jewel into the safe below

The casket made by Chubb to be placed by Queen Victoria under the foundation stone of the Victoria and Albert Museum in South Kensington in 1899

them they had over 80 years' experience in fire fighting as well as a Royal Warrant.

Messrs Read and Campbell were two Scottish engineers who originally built bridges in South America and the first to introduce the CO_2 cartridge to expel water or carbon tetrachloride from a fire extinguisher.

Minimax, the oldest of the companies, had made the first popular hand-held extinguisher, which was sold all over the world from Argentina to China. They had also supplied Edward VII with fire extinguishers for his motor car since 1907.

Pyrene had equipped the liner *Queen Mary* in 1933 and later the passenger liners *Queen Elizabeth*, *Oriana* and *Empress of Britain*. They had also equipped the fire-fighting vehicles during the Second World War.

Chubb hold their warrant to The Queen for the Royal Mews Department. The firm make a range of fire extinguishers for use in industry, the home or the car. They also manufacture other equipment such as their optical detectors which detect smoke by the use of a laser beam.

Chubb fire extinguishers are available from registered Chubb dealers. Consult your telephone directory for your local agent.

RENTOKIL LIMITED
Felcourt
East Grinstead
Sussex RH19 2JY

Pest control and timber preservation services to HM The Queen.

The Pied Pipers of Hamelin on a grand scale: formerly known as the Ratin Co. Ltd, Rentokil have been getting rid of unwanted pests since 1927, and as pests don't stick to protocol it's not surprising they are no strangers to palaces and government departments throughout the world. The Royal Warrant is held for pest control at the palaces and on the Royal estates, the sort of places where a rodent with a good set of teeth could run amok gnawing through electricity cables, animal foodstuffs and kitchen scraps.

There is a popular misconception that Rentokil invented woodworm, but although the company were the first to draw the problem to public attention, their business began with killing rats and mice. It was only later that insecticidal chemicals were developed, the first being a fluid which successfully killed off the death watch beetle from the roof of Westminster Great Hall. Today Rentokil employ nearly 7,000 people worldwide. The traditional cloth-capped rat catcher has been replaced by the graduate biologist, and in 1983 the firm's timber division won the Queen's Award to Industry for technological achievement.

Rentokil pride themselves on killing and controlling pests with speed and safety, but they also supply a variety of other services from damp-proofing to woodworm treatment, and their wide range of products includes carpet cleaner, moth proofer and air fresheners.

24 hour service, Monday–Sunday. Consult your telephone directory for your local branch and ask for a free survey.

Christmas

Better presents

ARMY & NAVY STORES LIMITED See page 38.

CALEYS (COLE BROTHERS) LIMITED See page 40.

THE GENERAL TRADING COMPANY
144 Sloane Street
Sloane Square
London SW1X 9BL

(01) 730 0411

Suppliers of fancy goods to HM The Queen, HM The Queen Mother and HRH The Duke of Edinburgh.

In 1963, the General Trading Company took over two Victorian houses in Sloane Street. Today it occupies four. Their buyers travel to Italy, France, India and Portugal to discover small suppliers whose designs they sell exclusively. Their 12 departments sell everything from Rajasthan antiques in their ethnic ('we don't like the word') corner and Flabby Flesh bath herbs by New Age Creations, to staunchly traditional hunting place mats and electric boot warmers and dryers for £15. But anything as mundane as the necessary plug you'll have to buy elsewhere.

The shop is a visual treat set on three floors with everything to go under the Christmas tree or on the wedding table. The GTC will make an initial gift selection for you – a service that's no doubt been offered to the Royal family since the early 1970s when the GTC received their three Royal Warrants, 50 years after the shop first opened.

At Christmas the GTC feels like the most popular place in London – so shop early. Their bridal service also has a good reputation, presumably aided by the rumours that The Prince and Princess of Wales had their wedding list here.

Monday–Friday: 9–5.30; Saturday: 9–2. Mail order catalogue issued at Christmas free of charge. The General Trading Company mail all round the world and will deliver by van in the London postal area. They also have a café run by warrant-holding Justin de Blank (see page 124) where apparently they serve a'wonderful breakfast'.

HARVEY NICHOLS LIMITED See page 115.

PRESENTS LIMITED
129 Sloane Street
London SW1X 9AT

(01) 730 5457

Presents 'is an ideal shop for those without initiative', said Paul Jones, the shop's owner. The business was originally started 20 years ago in Mayfair by an architect who wanted to sell 'unusual and exotic gifts'. Today the shop has moved to Sloane Street and caters for those who want to buy more explicitly humorous gifts without much effort.

Since Paul Jones took over Presents four years ago, the shop has adopted an American influence with an abundance of Snoopy items, clocks that go backwards, cocktail glasses with built-in straws, teapots with feet, cards and wrapping paper. It's filled with obvious, occasionally witty gifts – often with risqué innuendoes. Surely The Princess of Wales, a frequent visitor to the store, can't be that amused by their 'Prince of Wales' coat hangers at £7.90.

Monday–Saturday: 9.30–6; Wednesday: 9.30–7.

THE TOKEN HOUSE
26 High Street
Windsor
Berkshire SL4 1LH

Windsor (07535) 63263

Suppliers of fancy goods to HM The Queen.

Situated opposite the gates of Windsor Castle, The Token House is ideal for last-minute Christmas shopping or for quickly buying an extra crystal glass for that unexpected guest. On the walls of their corner shop, The Token House have photographs of Queen Mary visiting the shop.

Due to their fascinating past, The Token House is often besieged with visits from clubs. The Windsor sub-aqua club has been to explore their medieval well – still filled with water – in the stockroom, which was unearthed when the floor was renewed, and the H. G. Wells club have been to visit the site on which their hero worked as a draper's apprentice. That was before The Token House, when the shop was called Rodgers & Denyer: Court and general milliners, dress makers and furriers.

Today The Token House is 'a high-class china, glass, porcelain, crystal and fancy goods shop' – though they also sell postcards of the Royal family. With their enormous range of specialised goods both on display and in their stockrooms – where customers are often taken – The Token House claims that 'Nowhere else in Windsor can you get as large a range of merchandise.' They sell items from around the world, though mainly from Europe and have all the expected 'names', such as Meissen, Waterford and Dresden. They also have a few unexpected items for sale, such as baking tins in the shape of diamonds, clubs, spades and hearts.

Monday–Saturday: 9–5.30. Open most Sundays in the tourist season. The Token House produce one mail order catalogue annually and will mail anywhere in the world. They will also deliver locally and, if pushed, to London too.

Cards and wrappings

PAPERCHASE
213 Tottenham Court Road
London W1P 9AF
(and branches)

(01) 580 8496

Although the Tottenham Court Road shop is Paperchase's main branch and by far the most spectacular, it is the more initimate Fulham Road branch that The Princess of Wales visited both before and after her marriage and the one which Royal ladies-in-waiting can sometimes be found in.

Paperchase was started in the 1960s by two Royal College of Art graduates who were the first to sell flat paper and board to professional artists and designers. In 1971, Judith Cash, their then manageress, and Edward Pond bought Paperchase and began to extend the range of papers. They saw 'paper as a commodity in its own right' and Judith Cash feels they were responsible for starting the current paper excitement – the exotic wrapping papers, flamboyant greetings cards, brightly coloured notepads and the interminable pop-up books.

At Paperchase a 10-year-old can find pens and silly erasers, a 70-year-old can find artist's and specialist papers and anyone in between will be satisfied too. 'A lot of our range is useful and all of it is fun.' Paperchase have a constantly changing collection of paper and related items – from Advent calendars to paper flowers – and they still cater superbly for the professional artist.

Monday–Saturday: 9–6; Thursday: 10–7 (Tottenham Court Road branch).

VALENTINES OF DUNDEE LIMITED
PO Box 74
Kinnoull Road
Dundee
Perthshire DD1 9NQ
Scotland

Suppliers of Christmas cards and calendars to HM The Queen Mother.

Valentines of Dundee's greeting cards can be bought from major newsagents. But as Royal Warrant holders to The Queen Mother they are responsible for supplying Her Majesty with cards specially for her own use. The Queen Mother chooses the cards she would like to use from a selection of samples which are sent to Clarence House. The cards she chooses will remain exclusive to her and are never put on sale to the public.

John Valentine set up in business in 1825 as an engraver of wood blocks for linen printing. Five years later he was joined by his son James, a portrait artist. James Valentine became a skilled engraver and designed a series of illustrated envelopes which became the forerunners of the picture postcard. By 1840 he had branched into photography and was printing pictures of well-known scenes and local views. It wasn't until 1897 when the government gave permission to write on the reverse of cards that Valentines became the first company to start producing picture postcards. By 1900 they were established as fine art publishers and in 1927 were publishing cards for birthdays and special occasions.

Today Valentines, as part of Hallmark Cards, are one of Europe's largest publishers of greeting cards.

Valentines of Dundee Christmas cards and calendars are available from newsagents and department stores.

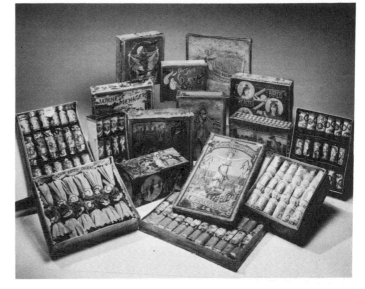

Crackers and games

TOM SMITH & COMPANY LIMITED
Salhouse Road
Norwich
Norfolk NR7 9AS

Norwich (0603) 404904

Suppliers of Christmas crackers to HM The Queen and HM The Queen Mother.

The Christmas cracker – as much a part of the Christmas tradition as turkey, mince pies and Christmas trees – was first invented by Tom Smith, the founder of the company, in 1847. Mr Smith was a Victorian confectioner who during a holiday in France in 1840 became intrigued by the bonbons (sugared almonds sold in twists of paper) which adults would exchange as gifts. He began importing the bonbons to sell in his own shop, improving on the French idea by selling them in brightly coloured papers with 'love mottoes' inside. Tom Smith then tried replacing the almonds with toys and novelties but the idea

A selection of Christmas crackers made by Tom Smith at the turn of the century

was not as successful as he had hoped it would be. It wasn't until one Christmas Day when he kicked a yule log on the fire which cracked and spat sparks that he thought about making a paper bag which opened with a bang and held sweets, novelties and mottoes. By 1847 he had developed the 'snap'.

Tom Smith's Christmas crackers are made all year round by over 200 employees. The company carry over 1,000 different items to place in their crackers, which range from miniatures to crackers over three feet long (for £10.50 each). Their mottoes include the classic banal jokes such as, 'Q. Why are football pitches so wet? A. Because the players dribble', to philosophical statements like, 'The truth is rarely pure, and never simple' (Oscar Wilde). The largest cracker ever made by the company was 18 feet long and contained real people who jumped out and distributed gifts. Crackers used all to be handmade but today demand is so great that all but a few of their giant crackers are made by machine. Tom Smith's also produce indoor fireworks, party novelties, hats, balloons and streamers as well as Christmas trees and baubles.

The company received their first warrant from the Prince of Wales, later Edward VII, and the then Princess of Wales in 1906.

Tom Smith Christmas crackers are available from newsagents, supermarkets and department stores.

WADDINGTONS PLAYING CARD COMPANY LIMITED
40 Wakefield Road
Leeds
Yorkshire LS10 3TP

Manufacturers of playing cards to HM The Queen.

John Waddington started his career in Leeds, printing for the theatre at the beginning of this century. But by 1913 the company was deeply in debt. It was about to be closed when the foreman, Victor Watson, persuaded the directors to let him try to revive the business. At that time there were 23 employees and the company owed £10,000, so the situation was desperate. Victor Watson decided to diversify into playing cards. His son, Norman, later developed new methods of producing playing cards. He also began to perfect the 'surface slip' of a card – an intricate process as it must allow easy shuffling of the cards

yet not too much shine so they don't slip out of your hands.

Waddington's next successful venture was the playing card game Lexicon, which led to an expansion of their games business. The company diversified further, producing folding cartons and cardboard jigsaw puzzles. By now they had acquired a reputation for fine printing and for their knowledge of coating papers and board and of accurate cutting. In 1937 Waddingtons started making waxed paper milk containers, which after the war were used to pack the orange juice sold in the cinemas during sweet rationing. But the pack was never quite perfect. So, 20 years later, Waddingtons developed plastic containers using new thermography plastic technology. This was the beginnings of Plastona (John Waddington) Ltd, who today hold a Royal Warrant to The Queen as manufacturers of disposable plates.

In the 1980s Waddingtons Games Ltd still produce a wide selection of playing cards, from patriotic Union Jack and Scottish Emblem cards to elegant gilt-edged and Royal Gothic cards. They also make a pack of cards with photographs of Buckingham Palace and Windsor Castle on the back.

Waddingtons playing cards are available from toy shops and department stores.

Festive food

CHIVERS & SONS LIMITED
The Orchard Factory
Histon
Cambridge

Purveyors of Christmas puddings to HM The Queen Mother.

Chivers make Christmas puddings especially for The Queen Mother's household. Although they stopped producing puddings commercially about 10 years ago, they still hold the Royal Warrant to The Queen Mother and continue to make 'a small quantity' for Her Majesty each year in their kitchen laboratories.

The Chivers family were Huguenots who fled France in the late 17th century and settled in the Cambridgeshire villages, working in local industry and agriculture. It wasn't until 1873 that the family started to make jam, and a year later they had bought their present site, the Orchard Factory at Histon.

Opposite:
Queen Alexandra enjoying a game of cards with the Duchess of Cumberland, the Empress Dagmar and Christian IX

Although the company was successful it was only seasonal employment for the workforce. In 1885 Stephen Chivers felt 'duty-bound to provide the people with an annual living wage'. He started producing marmalade from Seville oranges and later introduced table jellies, custard powder, lemon curd, coffee essence, mincemeat and Christmas puddings.

In 1907 Chivers made the first jar of Olde English Marmalade which was immediately hailed as 'the aristocrat of the breakfast table'. They were granted their first warrant four years later for preserves by Queen Mary. In 1978 the warrant was changed to 'purveyors of Christmas puddings'.

Today the company is known as Chivers Hartley. They manufacture preserves and desserts under three brand names: Chivers, Hartley and Moorhouse – formerly three separate companies all of whom made Christmas puddings – and are now part of Cadbury Schweppes.

Chivers Hartley products are available at grocers and supermarkets.

FORTNUM & MASON PLC
181 Piccadilly
London W1A 1ER

(01) 734 8040

Grocers and provision merchants to HM The Queen and suppliers of leather and fancy goods to HM The Queen Mother.

Fortnum & Mason has been described as 'the biggest tuckbox in the world'. Little lords and ladies eagerly await their Fortnum & Mason supplies of chocolates, shortbread and fruit cake throughout their years at public school. Later the Piccadilly store provides the discerning dowagers with their very own Aladdin's lamp . . . 'the power to choose gifts beyond the dreams of mortal man'.

Although more than a third of Fortnum's nine million pound annual turnover comes from its other three floors of fashion, toys and gifts, they are all secondary to the food hall, recently refurbished at a cost of one million pounds. The famous emporium with its wooden panelled walls is a happy shopping ground for Royalty from all over the world. Stepping through the door you could be greeted by Mr Arthur Lunn dressed in morning coat and pinstriped trousers, who will patiently guide you around the smoked salmon and esoteric quails' eggs and will point you in the direction of the Beluga caviar. Mr Lunn is now in his late 80s and has been employed by Fortnum's for more than 50 years since his own grocery business folded.

The store say that Mr Lunn 'epitomises everything that we like to think we are', and his 'perfect manner' is displayed at every staff training session. It is not unusual to find Mr Lunn escorting Royalty around the store. Every November the King of Norway strolls into Fortnum's and seeks the assistance of Mr Lunn, who has been looking after him for over 20 years. But Mr Lunn's favourite customer has always been The Queen Mother. Her Majesty has invited him to her staff party at St James's Palace, where he was delighted to find that 'nearly everyone there knew of him'.

The famous store was started in 1707 by William Fortnum, footman in the Royal household of Queen Anne, and his grocer friend, Hugh Mason. The enterprising Mr Fortnum had for a long time a sideline in used candles and sold them at a cut price to the staff at Buckingham Palace. When he realised how well his candle business was doing he persuaded Mr Mason to go into partnership with him. Their first venture is thought to have amounted to no more than a stall in a doorway in Piccadilly selling grocery provisions and, of course, used candles. It progressed to a small shop, which was handed down among the generations of Masons and Fortnums. In the late 1800s one of William Fortnum's descendants, Charles Fortnum, still held an appointment as Groom of the Chamber to Queen Charlotte when he died. No doubt this appointment did no harm to his flourishing business.

Queen Victoria granted Fortnum &

275 birthday candles adorn Fortnum & Mason when the store celebrated its 275th anniversary in 1982

Mason their first Royal Warrant in 1836. One of their commissions for Her Majesty was to send a huge consignment of beef tea to Florence Nightingale in Scutari.

There have been no members of the Fortnum or the Mason family in the business for generations but the fact is not widely publicised by the store. Instead there is still the subtle hint that Mr Fortnum and Mr Mason just might be sitting in a counting house somewhere, quill pens at the ready, dispatching hams, butters and cheeses. In the late 1960s the store hired two men to come in daily, dressed in velvet breeches, braided coats, embroidered waistcoats with lace shirts and powdered faces and wigs to do lively impersonations of Mr Fortnum and Mr Mason. But the charade was discontinued when a tourist fainted after being confronted by 'Mr Fortnum' lighting the way through the store with a candle during a power-cut. She thought she had seen a ghost.

The store was bought more than 30 years ago by Mr Garfield Weston, a Canadian biscuit maker and millionaire, who already owned the Fine Fare chain of supermarkets. Mr Weston had a desire to rise above it all and become 'The Queen's grocer'. As he said at the time, 'Anyone can own a store but there is only one grocer to The Queen.' Today Mr Weston's son, also Garfield, runs the store, but is better known as 'Young Gary' as the staff have taken to calling 57-year-old Mr Weston. His policy is to make the store 'lovable', so customers 'will keep coming back'.

Many people still consider Fortnum's to be the authority on correct form, especially in matters of food and drink. Their advice on making tea is constantly sought and at one time a list was kept of all the major cities in the world together with a list of teas suited to the water in that particular city. The list is no longer in use but Fortnum & Mason will still tell you the best tea to brew from Berlin to Bangkok – provided you let them have a sample of the water.

Fortnum & Mason hampers can be spotted at anywhere from Lord's to Glyndebourne. 'Wherever there is a demand for gracious living in the open air, Fortnum & Mason provide hampers filled with luxuries beyond compare.' Charles Dickens, on spotting 'so many Fortnum & Mason hampers' at the Derby, once wrote: 'If I were on the turf and had a horse to enter for the Derby I would call that horse Fortnum & Mason, convinced with that name he would beat the field . . . Public opinion would bring him in somehow.' Their

Christmas hampers include the Balmoral at £375, which has a selection of soups from asparagus to turtle, as well as pâtés, caviar, brandy and Fortnum's vintage champagne. The less expensive Hever hamper at £15 will just whet your appetite with Christmas pudding, pâté, mustard and a selection of preserves.

The famous Fortnum & Mason restaurant – 'a place where one feels quite at one's stately home' – is today a meeting place for the world, so go early. And their clock above the main entrance with its four feet high figures of Mr Fortnum and Mr Mason which appear on the hour has become a popular landmark. It was erected in retaliation to the one-way traffic system which was introduced in Piccadilly in 1962. The new system distorted the ebb and flow which had passed Fortnum's doors since 1707 and made it impossible for customers to be 'set down at the door' due to the bus lane running in the opposite direction directly in front of the shop. Fortnum & Mason protested, but to no avail. So in 1964 they erected the clock, built by Thwaites & Reed (see page 218), to compensate for Piccadilly losing some of its 'historic panache'.

Fortnum & Mason continue to maintain their old standards. 'There is no way we should be like everyone else,' they say. Next time you are doing your Christmas shopping, remember: 'You don't come to Fortnum & Mason for mere presents; you can buy presents anywhere. At Fortnum & Mason you buy heirlooms.'

Monday–Friday: 9–5.30; Saturday: 9–5. Their annual Christmas catalogue is sent automatically to their account customers and there is a 'token fee' of £1 to non-account customers. Fortnum & Mason will mail worldwide. Like most stores they have a sale twice a year – at Fortnum's it's a 'price reduction'.

EMMETTS STORE
Peasenhall
Saxmundham
Suffolk

Peasenhall (072 879) 250

Curers and suppliers of sweet pickled hams to HM The Queen Mother.

Mr Jerrey, the owner of Emmetts Store, believes The Queen Mother first tasted his sweet pickled hams on the advice of one of her ladies-in-waiting. Her Majesty was so

Queen Victoria, Prince Albert and their family celebrating Christmas at Windsor in 1848

impressed she passed the recommendation on to one of her doctors, now living in retirement in Newbury and a regular customer.

The shop, which was started by Mr Jerrey's grandfather at the turn of the century, has held a Royal Warrant since 1970. Emmetts is a general store, specialising in smoked produce such as their best-known sweet pickled ham, and also selling cider-pickled ham (at £1.95 per pound) and mild cured ham, at £1.25. Mr Jerrey told me that the secret of their produce is patience. The

raw hams have to be left in brine for between 7 and 10 days, pickled for about four weeks and 'smoked in oak' for another five days. But Mr Jerrey is not the best advertisement for his hams: he hates ham. The shop also smokes their own bacon and pork sausages.

Monday–Thursday: 8.30–5.30; Saturday: 8.30–5; Friday: 8.30–6.30. Closed for lunch between 1–2. Emmetts Store runs a mail order service for their smoked produce. Details from the above address.

Index

Abbey Rose Gardens 48
Ackermans Chocolates Ltd 134
Allan & Davidson 25
Allen & Neale (Chemists) Ltd 55
Amies, Hardy Ltd 77
Amor, Albert Ltd 167
Angostura Bitters 137
Aquascutum Ltd 69
Arbeid, Murray Ltd 77
Archibald, James & Sons Ltd 36
Arden, Elizabeth Ltd 60

Army & Navy Stores Ltd 38
Ashley & Blake Ltd 103
Ashley, Laura Ltd 25
Asprey & Co PLC 92

Baker, G. P. & J. Ltd 26
Barrow Hepburn Equipment Ltd 6
Bartholomew, John & Son Ltd 203
Bass Brewing Ltd 138
Baxter, G. G. Ltd 124
Baxter, James & Son 150
Benetton 70
Bellville Sassoon 77

Bennett-Levy, Valerie 7
Benson & Hedges Ltd 138
Berol Ltd 182
Bimbo 119
Black & Edgington PLC 44
Blackall, William 104
Blahnik, Manolo 99
Boyd, John 88
Bradleys (Knightsbridge) Ltd 117
Brannam, C. H. Ltd 36
Bridger & Kay Ltd 167
Bridleways Manufacturing Ltd 190
Brintons Ltd 10
British Nova Works Ltd 13
Broadwood, John & Sons Ltd 175
Bronnley, H. & Co Ltd 61
Brooks, W. & Son (Brook-Jones) Ltd 152
Bryant & May Ltd 40
Budgen Ltd 153
Burberrys Ltd 70
Burgess, John & Son Ltd 154
Burton Group PLC 104
Bury Cooper Whitehead Ltd 10

Cadbury Ltd 135

Caithness Glass PLC 20
Caleys (Cole Brothers) Ltd 40
Callander, R. F. 53
Calman Links (Trading) Ltd 71
Campbell Brothers (Edinburgh) Ltd 130
Campbell, Donald 79
Carlsberg Brewery Ltd 139
Carpets International (UK) Ltd 10
Carr's of Carlisle 154
Carter's Tested Seeds Ltd 48

Cartier Ltd 93
Cash, J. & J. Ltd 204
Cassie, William C. 226
Casson Conder Partnership 27
Champagne J. Bollinger SA 139
Champagne Heidsieck & Co Monopole 143
Champagne Moët & Chandon 146
Charbonnel et Walker Ltd 136
Charles, Caroline 79
Chivers & Sons Ltd 235
Christopher & Co Ltd 140
Chubb Alarms Ltd 229
Chubb & Sons Lock & Safe Co Ltd 228
Chubb Fire Security Ltd 229
Clare House Ltd 27
Cole & Son (Wallpapers) Ltd 28
Collingwood of Conduit Street Ltd 94
Conran, Jasper 79
Cooper, A. C. Ltd 221
Cooper, Frank Ltd 124
Coutts & Co 212
Crawford, D. S. (Catering) Ltd 45
Crawford W. M. & Sons Ltd 154
Crompton Parkinson Ltd 41
Cross Paperware Ltd 182
Cyclax Ltd 62

Daniel, Neville Ltd 58
Davis, Godfrey Europcar Ltd 210
De Blank, Justin (Provisions) Ltd 124
Devlin, Stuart Ltd 195
Dewar, John & Sons Ltd 141
Dewhurst, J. H. Ltd 131
Dobbie & Co Ltd 48

Domestic Electric Rentals Ltd 189
Donald, George & Sons Ltd 28
Donaldson, Andrew Ltd 151
Doulton Fine China Ltd 20
Dragons of Walton Street Ltd 121
Driscoll, Messrs 104
Dunhill, Alfred Ltd 141

Dynatron Radio Ltd 189

Early's of Witney PLC 114
Eastern Counties Leather Co PLC 13
Ede & Ravenscroft 7
Edelstein, Victor 80
Edwardes (Camberwell) Ltd 207
Elegance Maternelle 98
Emmetts Store 237
En-Tout-Cas PLC 52
Express Diary UK Ltd 126

Farman & Son 54
Farlow, C. & Co Ltd 172
Farris, Charles Ltd 29
Findus 155
Firmin & Sons PLC 8
Floris, J. Ltd 62
Ford Motor Company Ltd 207

Fortnum & Mason PLC 236
Fox, Frederick Ltd 89
Francis G. C. 1
Frasers 29
Fratini, Gina Ltd 80
Frederick, John Ltd 212

Garrard & Co Ltd 4
General Trading Co (Mayfair) Ltd 231
Gibbons, Stanley Ltd 168
Gibson Saddlers Ltd 191
Gidden, W. & H. Ltd 191
Glynwed Consumer & Building Products Ltd 41
Goddard, J. & Sons Ltd 14
Goldenlay Eggs (UK) Ltd 126
Goode, Thomas & Co (London) Ltd 21
Graham, Tim 222
Gray, James & Son Ironmongers & Electricians Ltd 15

Great Expectations 98
Greenaway Harrison & Sons Ltd 227
Grima, Andrew Ltd 95
Grugeon, Peter Studio 222

Haggart, P. & J. Ltd 87
Haig, John & Co Ltd 141
Halcyon Days Ltd 169
Hamilton & Inches Ltd 96
Hamleys of Regent Street Ltd 123
Hancocks & Co (Jewellers) Ltd 97
Hardy Brothers (Alnwick) Ltd 173
Harris, D. R. & Co Ltd 55
Harris, L. G. & Co Ltd 30
Harrods Ltd 156

Hartnell, Norman Ltd 81
Harvey, John & Sons Ltd 142
Harvey, Matthew & Co Ltd 193
Harvey, Nichols Ltd 115
Hatchards 183
Hawes & Curtis (Tailors) Ltd 105
Haythornthwaite & Sons Ltd 72
Headlines Hair and Beauty Ltd 56
Head Ski Wear 197
Heal & Son Ltd 112
Heaton, Wallace Ltd 179
Heering, Peter F. A/S 143
Henderson's 72
Henderson, J. & W. Ltd 31
Henlys (Central London) Ltd 2
Higgins, H. R. (Coffee-man) Ltd 162
Hillier Nurseries (Winchester) Ltd 50
Hobbs Ltd 99
Holland & Holland Ltd 196
Hoover PLC 15
HP Foods Ltd 158
Howell, Margaret 82
Hubbard Refrigeration Ltd 42

Inca 73
Ind Coope Ltd 144
IND COOPE LIMITED
IRS Signs Ltd 52

Jaguar Cars Ltd 207
James, Cornelia Ltd 67
Jenners Ltd 31

Jet Carpet Cleaners Ltd 213
Jeyes Group Ltd 16
John, C. (Rare Rugs) Ltd 11
Johns & Pegg Ltd 107
Johnson, Herbert (Bond Street) Ltd 89
Johnson Wax Ltd 16
Justerini & Brooks Ltd 144

K Shoes Ltd 100

Shoemakers Ltd

Keith Prowse & Co Ltd 201
Kent, G. B. & Sons Ltd 57
Kiernan, Kay 59
Kimbolton Fireworks 45
Kinloch Anderson Ltd 107
Kirkness & Gorie 126
Kleen-Way (Berkshire) Co 215
Knight, J. W. (Fisheries) Ltd 151
Knight, Peter Ltd 32
Knowles & Sons (Fruiterers) Ltd 156
Kodak Ltd 179
Krug, Vins, Fins de Champagne SA 145

Launer, S. & Co (London) Ltd 67
Lea & Perrins 158
Leith, G. & Son 127
Lenthéric Ltd 63
Lever Brothers Ltd 17
Lewis East Ltd 226
Leyland Vehicles Ltd 208
Liberty PLC 87
Lichfield Studios 223
Lidstone, Messrs John 131
Lilliman & Cox Ltd 218
Lillywhites Ltd 199
Linguaphone Institute Ltd 204
Lingwood, Richard 2
Lobb, John Ltd 100
Lock, James & Co Ltd 90
Lock, S. Ltd 86
Longmire, Paul Ltd 97
Loss, Joe Ltd 46
Luxford, Keith (Saddlery) Ltd 194

Maggs Bros Ltd 183
Mason, Joseph PLC 3
Mayfair Trunks Ltd 204
Mayfair Window Cleaning Co Ltd 216
Maxwell, Henry & Co Ltd 101
McCallum & Craigie Ltd 116
McVitie & Price Ltd 159
Meenys (Clothes) USA 119
Melroses Ltd 163
Menzies, John PLC 185

Milton, Messrs K. W. 131
Minton Ltd 22
Mirman, Simone 91
Moir, W. 217
Mothercare Ltd 121
Mowbray, A. R. & Co Ltd 186
Moyses Stevens Ltd 36
Murray, J. & D. 55

Nairobi Coffee & Tea Co Ltd 165
Nairn Floors Ltd 12
Neaverson, A. & Sons Ltd 43
Neil, David 83
Newbery, Henry & Co Ltd 33
Night Owls 117
Nordica 199
North, James & Sons Ltd 101

Offord, Gordon J. 3
Oldfield, Bruce 83
Ong, Benny 83

Paperchase 232
Papworth Industries 206
Paragon China Ltd 22
Parker Pen Co Ltd 187
Parkinson, Norman 224
Patent Steam Carpet Cleaning Co 213
Patey, S. (London) Ltd 91
Patman, Messrs C. 217
Paxton & Whitfield Ltd 133
Pears, A. & F. Ltd 63
Penhaligon's Ltd 64
Pilgrim Payne & Co Ltd 215
Phillips, S. J. Ltd 170
Plowden, Anna 217
Pollen, Arabella 84
Poole, Henry & Co (Savile Row) Ltd 108
Presents Ltd 231
Prestat Ltd 137
Pringle of Scotland Ltd 73

Procter & Gamble Ltd 18
Purdey, James & Sons Ltd 196

Quaker Oats Ltd 127

Rawlings, H. D. Ltd 146
Rayne, H. & M. Ltd 102
Reckitt & Colman 18
Redmayne, S. Ltd 109
Reid, Ben & Co Ltd 50
Remploy Ltd 74
Rentokil Ltd 230
Renshaw, John F. & Co Ltd 137
Riche of Hay Hill Ltd 60

Ridgways 165
Rigby, John & Co (Gunmakers) Ltd 197
Rigby & Peller 110
Roberts Radio Co Ltd 190
Rolls-Royce Motors Ltd 209
Rose, L. & Co Ltd 146
Royal Brewery Brentford Ltd 147
Royal British Legion Poppy Factory Ltd 219
Royal Crown Derby Porcelain Co Ltd 23
Rudolf, Z. V. Ltd 92
Ruffell, E. 151
Russell, Gordon Ltd 37

Saccone & Speed Ltd 148
Salter, J. & Son 194
Sandeman, Geo. G. Sons & Co Ltd 148
Sanderson, Arthur & Sons Ltd 33
Savoy Hotel, The PLC 166
Schweppes Ltd 148

Scoles, R. F. & J. 132
Scott-Nichol, John Ltd 111
Scotts Fish Shop 134
Seaby, B. A. Ltd 170
Securicor Cleaning Ltd 216
Sharwood, J. A. & Co Ltd 161

Sheridan, H. M. 133
Ship's Wheel, The 37
Shirras Laing & Co Ltd 41
Simpson (Piccadilly) Ltd 74
Sleepeezee Ltd 113
Sleigh, W. Ltd 211
Slimberland Ltd 114
Smith, George & Co 200
Smith, Tom & Co Ltd 233
Smythson, Frank 188
Snowdon, Lord Anthony 225
Souleiado 69
Sparks, John Ltd 172
Spink & Son Ltd 5
Spode 23
Spratts Patent Ltd 43
Steinway & Sons 176
Stephens Brothers Ltd 109
Stevens & Williams Ltd 24
Stopps, J. & Sons Ltd 128
Strachan, George Ltd 161
Sturtevant Engineering Co Ltd 19
Suttons Seeds Ltd 51
Swaine Adeney Brigg & Sons Ltd 201
Sycamore Laundry & Dry Cleaners 219

Tate & Lyle PLC 161
Tatters 85
Taylor, D. & R. 38
Temple & Crook Ltd 19
Thermos Ltd 180
Thresher & Glenny Ltd 110
Thwaites & Reed Ltd 218
Tissunique Ltd 34
Token House, The 232
Tomlinson & Tomlinson 75
Toms, William S. Ltd 114
Toye, Kenning & Spencer Ltd 5
Truefitt & Hill Ltd 58
Trumper, Geo. F. 58
Truslove & Hanson 189
Tuck, Raphael & Sons Ltd 227
Turnbull & Asser Ltd 110
Twining, R. & Co Ltd 166

Uniroyal Ltd 102

Vacani School of Dancing 120
Valentines of Dundee Ltd 233
Vanvelden, Jan 85
Vauxhall Motors Ltd 210
Veuve Clicquot-Ponsardin 149

Waddingtons Playing Card Co Ltd 235
Walker, J. W. & Sons Ltd 177
Walls Meat Co Ltd 128

Walpole Bros (London) Ltd 116
Warm & Wonderful 76
Warner & Sons 34
Wartski Ltd 97
Watkins & Watson Ltd 177
Weetabix Ltd 129
Whitbread & Co PLC 149
White House, The 119
Whytock & Reid 35
Wiggins, Arnold & Sons Ltd 35
Wildsmith & Co 103
Wilkin & Sons Ltd 129
Wilkinson Sword Ltd 6
Wilson, Andrew & Sons Ltd 47
Wilton Royal Carpet Factory, The Ltd 12
Wood, William & Son Ltd 52
Wood's Pharmacy 56
Worcester Royal Porcelain Co, The 24

Yardley & Co Ltd 65